NEW EXPLORATIONS INTO INTERNATIONAL RELATIONS

STUDIES IN SECURITY
AND INTERNATIONAL AFFAIRS

New Explorations into International Relations

Democracy, Foreign Investment, Terrorism, and Conflict

Seung-Whan Choi

The University of Georgia Press
Athens

© 2016 by the University of Georgia Press
Athens, Georgia 30602
www.ugapress.org
Set in Minion Pro by Graphic Composition, Inc., Bogart, Georgia
Printed and bound by Sheridan Books, Inc.
The paper in this book meets the guidelines for
permanence and durability of the Committee on
Production Guidelines for Book Longevity of the
Council on Library Resources.

Most University of Georgia Press titles are
available from popular e-book vendors.

Printed in the United States of America
20   19   18   17   16   P   5   4   3   2   1

Library of Congress Cataloging-in-Publication Data
Names: Choi, Seung-Whan, author.
Title: New explorations into international relations : democracy, foreign investment, terrorism,
    and conflict / Seung-Whan Choi.
Description: Athens, Georgia : The University of Georgia Press, 2016. | Series: Studies in security
    and international affairs | Includes bibliographical references and index.
Identifiers: LCCN 2015023652| ISBN 9780820349077 (hardcover : alk. paper) | ISBN 9780820349084
    (pbk. : alk. paper) | ISBN 9780820349060 (ebook)
Subjects: LCSH: International relations. |
World politics. | Democracy. | Investments, Foreign. | Terrorism.
Classification: LCC JZ1305.C46 2016 |
DDC 327—dc23
LC record available at http://lccn.loc.gov/2015023652

To Shali Luo, with everlasting love and appreciation

Science is perhaps the only human activity in which errors are systematically criticized and, in time, corrected.

KARL POPPER

The only way that science can make progress is by showing that theories are wrong.

DAVID L. GOODSTEIN

CONTENTS

TABLES AND FIGURES

PREFACE

As political scientists, we purport to explain and predict important events in the contemporary world and to offer policy recommendations regarding those events. Achieving these goals requires empirical research that is thorough and rigorous; however, we are, of course, fallible and unknowingly fail to obtain scientific truth from time to time—there is always room for improvement. As such, replication projects are an efficient means to disseminate and increase scientific knowledge because they build upon the previously established work of fellow scientists. Ideally, we could improve the quality of even the most authoritative studies of political science in an effort to advance scientific progress and provide better policy recommendations while at the same time testing new research ideas with simple but innovative methods. In such vein, this book sets out to gather improved scientific knowledge by testing theories of classic international relations while engaging in original research with new data in the hopes that such a dual approach may lead to scientific breakthroughs in the future and change the political world for the better.

This book can be a valuable resource for future generations of researchers—including advanced undergraduate and graduate students—by shortening the trial and error processes of their own analyses and by providing examples of well-written empirical papers. While future researchers read through each of the replication or original research chapters in this book, I hope that they will learn how to avoid the kinds of obstacles that I encountered myself, as explained below. This book seeks to quickly connect their statistical skills with their political topics, to perform rigorous empirical research, and to engage in replication and original research projects on important political questions. In addition, I hope that the reader will have a better understanding of political science in general and of international relations in particular after being exposed to the diverse and controversial issue areas covered in this book. As a collection of replications and original research on politically important topics, there is no published book comparable where the reader can—in a single volume—grasp the four salient issue areas of the contemporary political world: democracy, foreign investment, terrorism, and conflict.

The writing of this book was a long intellectual journey, involving the resolution of several obstacles. The first was to find a way to apply econometrics and statistical techniques to political questions. I learned my empirical skills from the econometricians and statisticians at the Department of Economics and the Department of Statistics at the University of Missouri-Columbia (MU). Thus, my graduate training provided a wonderful opportunity to acquire highly advanced statistical methods but offered virtually no exposure to quantitative political literature. Furthermore, the fact that the MU Department of Political Science was then dominated by qualitative scholars did not aid me in the struggle to connect my statistics knowledge with traditional political science. At the same time, I was laboring with several theoretically important questions that would later become the centerpiece of my dissertation project. Fortunately, those troubles quickly faded when MU hired Patrick James—my dissertation supervisor—one and a half years before my graduation day. With his caring advice and support, I was able to connect the dots in my dissertation and earn my doctorate within twelve months.

The second obstacle I dealt with was learning how to appropriately conduct rigorous research. Although I felt like I had mastered the state-of-the art theories of econometrics and statistics, textbooks did not teach me how to play with real world data and statistical programming. My earlier data analyses in graduate school were often careless, but I eventually acquired sufficient hands-on experience learning how to begin and end rigorous research on various economic issues. Due to my strong background in econometrics, I was hired by MU's Department of Economics and later by the Missouri State Government's Department of Social Services Research and Evaluation Unit. Working under meticulous economists these several years, I was further instructed on methods of conducting rigorous data analysis, such as identifying the correct estimation methods for different economic problems, performing addition tests for robustness, and double-checking potential errors.

The third obstacle I faced was determining how to train political science graduate students in statistics at the University of Illinois at Chicago (UIC). Although I was hired as an international relations specialist, I was asked to teach two consecutive statistical methods courses. However, because many students expressed an interest in qualitative methods over quantitative ones, they were not all that eager to learn statistical theories and techniques. However, when I started to assign replication projects, and to dramatically reduce my lectures on statistical proofs and properties, I found that they learned better, and more, because they could work on a research topic of replication that they chose themselves. Even many qualitative students developed keen research interests in quantitative fields because they were, through replication projects, exposed to major empirical studies in urban politics, American politics, and international relations.

While doing the research for this book, I have received valuable feedback and help from many people. In particular, by reading through the entire manuscript, Nora Willi has provided me with indispensable research assistance. Special thanks are due to Anahit Gomtsian, Patricia Hajek, and Joshua Pakter who kindly reviewed draft portions of the book. I am especially indebted to David Carment, Constantine P. Danopoulos, Paul F. Diehl, Douglas M. Gibler, Patrick James, John R. Oneal, James A. Piazza, Jeffrey Pickering, Bruce Russett, George Tsebelis, Douglas Van Belle, and John Vasquez, who not only greatly influenced my thinking on the various political and economic issues of this book, but who have also given me very helpful advice on academic life in general. I also owe thanks to Dennis R. Judd, Evan McKenzie, and Dick W. Simpson in the UIC Department of Political Science for providing me with a graduate assistant. Last, but certainly not least, Walter Biggins and Beth Snead at the University of Georgia Press deserve credit for their continued guidance on how best to navigate the jungle of book publication.

Introduction

Gray's Anatomy, a textbook originally written by Henry Gray in 1858, is widely regarded as the most influential work on the subject of human anatomy. This work describes the morphology of the human body and details the process of dissection for the purpose of aiding the scientific study of the structure, position, and interrelation of its various parts. Every accomplished physician, especially surgeons and doctors working in certain diagnostic specialties such as histopathology and radiology, must possess a thorough working knowledge of human anatomy. Just as understanding the process of dissection of the human body is an essential step toward understanding the functions of specific organs and structures in the body, the dissection or interrogation of major findings in empirical political research must be the first step toward an increase in our collective scientific knowledge. Marcus Cicero, the famous Roman political theorist, once said, "by doubting we arrive at the truth." With this aphorism in mind, the eight chapters in part 1 of this book question, or dissect, several influential theories and empirical findings that heretofore have been widely accepted in the discipline of political science in general and in the field of international relations in particular. In addition, because the scientific progress made by remarkable discoveries usually results from finding a new way of thinking about what we have long taken for granted as scientific truth, the five chapters of part 2 explore completely new research ideas and seek to identify undiscovered empirical regularities. The expectation is that this book will point us toward fresh findings and insights in the four salient issue areas of international relations: democracy, foreign direct investment, terrorism, and conflict.

Unlike Marcus Cicero, contemporary political scientists tend to shy away from voicing doubt and raising critical questions. In contrast, researchers from some other fields of social science have done much to improve the rigor of their scientific analyses. For example, in their book *Betrayers of Truth: Fraud and Deceit in the Halls of Science*, Broad and Wade (1983) showed no hesitation in pointing to certain studies in which scientists fudged data or misrepresented results. In 1986, the *American Economic Review* (*AER*)[1] published Dewald, Thursby, and Anderson's NSF-funded article examining the role of replication in empirical economic papers that had been previously accepted by the *Journal of Money, Credit, and Banking* for publication. The main findings of the *AER* article "suggest that inadvertent errors in published empirical articles are a commonplace rather than a rare occurrence" (587–88). In their own reexamination of 1,148 estimated results reported in forty-nine articles in two prestigious psychology journals, Wicherts, Bakker, and Molenaar (2011) found "the reluctance to share data to be associated with weaker evidence . . . and a higher prevalence of apparent errors in the reporting of statistical results." Undoubtedly, publications like these caused some controversy; however, they also significantly contributed to the increased rigor in their respective empirical research traditions (G. King 1995). In particular, their insistence that the replication of research is indispensable to the soundness of all scientific investigation has been adopted as an axiom within their respective scholarly communities.[2]

Unlike empirical research in economics and psychology, political studies have not yet been subjected to this same degree of rigorous scrutiny; more importantly, many of those engaged in political scientific research may be unfamiliar with its presumably rigorous empirical tradition. The growing popularity of empirical political research is based on the belief that any number of political researchers should be able to obtain the same objective empirical evidence. But what would happen if what appears to be objective evidence is, in fact, a statistical artifact or the result of a flawed research design? It would be undesirable, of course, if the replication results were inconsistent with the claims of previous research; therefore, it is necessary to investigate the possible causes of discrepancy, to offer improved estimation methods, and to report new findings. In the attempt to make a meaningful contribution to the scientific advancement of the discipline as a whole, a researcher should consider developing his or her own agenda by engaging in a replication of a previous study. Furthermore, because many potential researchers lack sufficient institutional support and cannot afford the luxury of collecting a costly dataset for each new research project, they should consider an alternative way in which a replication project can offer the opportunity to advance a body of scientific knowledge at minimal cost. This book (1) reanalyzes several authoritative empirical political studies in the attempt to illustrate the ease with which erroneous statistical conclusions may be unknowingly drawn due to a lack of rigorous research traditions and the insufficient scrutiny of previous studies, and (2) demonstrates how one may search for novel ideas at minimal cost by developing new research designs with original data. In so doing, this book offers original findings and insights as well as relevant policy implications regarding the causes and effects of the outbreak of civil war, international conflict, acts of terrorism, democratic governance, and inflows of foreign direct investment.

By demonstrating the way erroneous data analysis can drastically diminish the validity of published empirical studies, this book hopes to give the next generation of scholars the opportunity and encouragement to improve their empirical research so that it can aid scientific progress and, even, revolution.

The accurate analysis of data, using standardized statistical methods, is a critical step in determining the soundness of empirical work and, therefore, in avoiding erroneous inferences and conclusions. For example, ordinary least squares (OLS) regression models make a number of assumptions about independent variables, dependent variables, and the relationships between them; yet, if a researcher ignores or violates the assumptions of this statistical model for some unknown reason, his or her estimated results will be biased and inconsistent, and, thus, the findings will be misleading. For example, it would be incorrect to choose an OLS estimator when the mean of the dependent variable is, perhaps due to the presence of outliers, not a linear combination of the parameters (regression coefficients) and the independent variables. Furthermore, OLS regression models are used under the assumption that each variable on the right-hand side of the equation exerts an independent effect on the dependent variable; accordingly, it would be inappropriate to employ a single OLS equation as opposed to a simultaneous equations model when, due to the presence of reverse causality, that assumption does not hold up. Simply put, accurate statistical analysis is always essential to the soundness of empirical political research, as books and journal articles that lack an empirical foundation are of little use to the advancement of scientific knowledge in the discipline of political science.

Naturally, political scientists will begin an investigation by posing an important research question (e.g., do ethnic and religious antagonisms cause the outbreak of civil war?) that they will treat as the object of their statistical data analysis. They will then develop a theory regarding the question and, based on that theory, will draw certain hypotheses or predictions that can be tested against a set of data that they or someone else has collected. The outcomes of these tests may or may not support the initial theory upon which the hypotheses and predictions were based. Yet, in comparison with empiricists in other disciplines, political scientists appear to be more competent in terms of producing theoretical conjectures/arguments and drawing hypotheses than they are at conducting rigorous empirical analyses. It may be that the relatively late infusion of statistical methods into this discipline is responsible for its emphasis on theory and its weak progress in terms of rigorous data analysis; in extreme cases, there are some political scientists who consider statistical technique an alien language, giving little credit to the interpretation of estimated coefficients and standard errors. An unfortunate trend in political science has allowed researchers who offer persuasive theoretical discussions and speculations, but who conduct less than adequate data analyses, a better chance to publish manuscripts than those researchers whose focus is primarily on the accuracy of their statistical inferences. If we seek, as we well should, the development of political science as a serious discipline, then it is imperative that all researchers be fluent in the language of statistics as well as the language of theory building.

There are those political researchers who believe that a paper should be published on the basis of a strong overall argument or on the strength of the theoretical reasoning behind its empirical modeling. These researchers tend to treat the data analysis component as an afterthought, failing to perform a careful examination of their estimated results, let alone of the validity of their primary data source. On the other hand, when a paper has a somewhat loose theoretical development but a rigorous statistical analysis, its publication is dubious, as some political scientists dismiss estimated coefficients as meaningless. As a result, those book manuscripts and journal papers that are primarily data oriented have a slimmer chance of appearing in the most prestigious scholarly outlets than those oriented toward theory building. While other social scientific disciplines, such as economics and sociology, have been moving toward a more serious consideration of heavily empirical works even with little or no theory, political science maintains its bias against the publication of quantitative studies with a weak theory. Paradoxically, the effect of this bias has been to allow the publication of political science papers with subpar, often flawed, statistical analyses; this is an injustice to the discipline as a whole. It may also indicate that the statistical skills of reviewers — especially at those stages of review where they do not have access to the data and statistical programs — are not sophisticated enough to locate these kinds of empirical flaws, thereby continuing the trend of publication described above.

Once an empirical study is widely circulated and cited, its findings tend to acquire a nearly law-like status, which, once established, is rarely challenged. Furthermore, as replication projects are much less likely to be published than original works, political scientists have less incentive to closely examine the research designs and estimated results of previously published studies. This creates an undesirable research culture that does a disservice to the discipline of political science by dis-incentivizing the interrogation of faulty findings. It is well known that data-driven research progresses scientific knowledge by demonstrating the existence of previously unknown phenomena, by illuminating new relationships between existing phenomena, or by discovering that some widely shared understanding is either incomplete or entirely wrong. In the sixteenth century, for example, scholars such as Galileo Galilei would have been prosecuted had they spoken the scientific truth about heliocentrism versus the well-established theory of geocentrism. Or consider the supersession of Newton's two-hundred-year-old theory of mechanics by Albert Einstein's theory of relativity at the beginning of the twentieth century; it is also worth noting that even though the theory of relativity is now considered to be a cornerstone of modern physics, not all of Einstein's ideas and concepts were eagerly accepted in his time. In general, it appears that contemporary academics have forgotten Karl Popper's (1963, 216) insight in *Conjectures and Refutations: The Growth of*

Scientific Knowledge that "science is . . . perhaps the only [human activity]—in which errors are systematically criticized and, in time, corrected. This is why we can say that, in science, we often learn from our mistakes." It seems, though, that contemporary academic culture views being critical as stepping on the toes of other scholars rather than as an essential part of scientific inquiry. Many political scientists are apprehensive about getting their hands dirty; this attitude impedes the scientific advancement of the discipline.

Of course, political empiricists had their moment in the mid-1990s when replication projects were accepted and encouraged as a legitimate and cost-effective way to publish for academic achievement and career advancement. During this period, a large number of empirical political studies were scrutinized, faulty estimations were discussed publicly, and improved models were suggested. Indeed, Gary King (1995, 445) emphasized that "the most common and scientifically productive method of building on existing research is to replicate an existing finding—to follow the precise path taken by a previous researcher, and then improve on the data or methodology in one way or another." However, the emphasis on replication has faded away or at least drastically diminished since then; qualitative and even quantitative scholars ridicule and marginalize replicated works.[3] Replicated studies are too often rejected for publication on the grounds that they fail to provide stand-alone research, even in cases where they clearly demonstrate a refutation of the major findings from previously published books or journals. This serious and all too common bias against replications deprives researchers of the opportunity to learn from one another's mistakes and help each other proceed to a higher stage of scientific discovery.

As replication projects usually rely on the research design of published studies, they are frequently charged with a lack of stand-alone research. However, it should be noted that while replication projects do use data from previously published works, they usually collect original data with reference to a new and theoretically interesting variable. The charge that replication studies produce no stand-alone research is ironic in the sense that most empirical research already relies on publicly available data sources (perhaps excepting the main variable of contribution). Stand-alone researchers claim to be doing original work, but their data often comes from collections previously published by private and government agencies; furthermore, their estimation methods rarely differ from those of existing studies. While researchers from prestigious institutions are provided with ample material support and are, therefore, more capable of collecting original data, those researchers who are less connected regularly struggle to secure research time and funding. For such researchers, replication is an ideal scientific project with a minimal cost. For example, the availability of the data and research design of John Oneal and Bruce Russett's (2005) democratic peace research program has encouraged the proliferation of work on international conflict. Similarly, Oneal and Russett's statistical model has been widely replicated for years, thus minimizing the possibility of coding errors or faulty model building; ultimately, it has proven to be highly reliable compared to other conflict models.

Replication studies are rarely published in top-tier journals "because this would open up a 'cheap' way for authors to have their work published . . . and every Tom, Dick, and Harriet . . . could potentially seek to replicate some study, just to get published" (Ishiyama 2014, 82). The appropriate response to this criticism would be to question if it is a good idea to publish empirical studies with incorrect or even fabricated data analysis, the findings of which, without rigorous scrutiny, are then allowed to become principles or laws of political research. This practice is as insulting to the scientific community as it is injurious to the accumulation of knowledge. Empirical studies without sound empirical results are like swimming pools without water during hot summer days or fancy sport cars without gasoline during the Fédération Internationale de l'Automobile World Endurance Championship. Those who remain skeptical of the legitimacy of replication projects should ask themselves this question: which of the above approaches—fabrication or replication—is really the cheap way for authors to publish and get promoted? While the former, in fact, makes no scholarly contribution and should—as is commonplace in other disciplines—be swiftly retracted (Tabuchi 2014), the latter contributes to the degree of scientific rigor by pointing out mistakes or questionable methodological choices in published research and also reports new substantive findings on the subject in question.

Perhaps one reason that replication projects are discouraged has to do with the interests of the empiricists themselves. That is, the authors of the original studies may be the loudest voices objecting to replicated pieces that are critical of their published work, as they are unlikely to be comfortable with a project that scrutinizes their statistical models or estimation methods. When a replication study points out a flaw in an empirical model, its originator is likely to resist on the grounds that the replication lacks theoretical innovation. Of course, this is an odd defense considering that the stated goals of such a critique are precisely to demonstrate how the main findings of the published study are unsubstantiated and to suggest an improved or corrected empirical research strategy.

Although the lack of publication opportunities discourages the proliferation of replication projects, some journals do, in fact, require that researchers post their replication data and program files online (see James 2003; Lupia and Elman 2014). This requirement is intended to increase the transparency of empirical research. However, there is a danger that subsequent researchers will use these materials simply to reproduce identical models without performing a careful examination of the estimation methods and measurements; in this case they are prone to repeat mistakes, making the open source policy a moot point.

Although replication projects do continue to appear in some publication outlets, these are highly infrequent. This book argues, therefore, that journal editors and book publishers must provide a greater opportunity for researchers to engage in the critical reexamination of published works. Scholarly exchange requires the ability to constructively criticize and publish improved or corrected versions of original works. This is the only way to increase our discipline's cumulative knowledge and to navigate the path toward scientific discovery, and perhaps even scientific revolution. As Patrick James (2003, 85) correctly points out, "replication is a scientific ideal, but it also turns out to be good for scholars in practical, even career-oriented ways."

The body of this book is twofold. Part 1 consists of eight chapters that scrutinize ten empirical political studies by Bueno de Mesquita et al. (2003), Fearon and Laitin (2003), Gartzke (2007), Hoffman, Shelton, and Cleven (2013), Jensen (2003), Li (2005), Li and Resnick (2003), Piazza (2011), Santifort-Jordan and Sandler (2014), and Savun and Phillips (2009). Most of these ten works represent well-known research programs in political science and have been widely cited over the last decade. Fearon and Laitin's (2003) article is a must-read for anyone who researches civil war; Gartzke's (2007) piece makes one of the most interesting contributions to the international conflict literature; Bueno de Mesquita et al.'s (2003) book is extensively recognized for rigorous formal modeling and a wide range of empirical applications in studies of democracy and public policy; the two articles by Li and Resnick (2003) and Jensen (2003) are pioneering research in the area of foreign direct investment; the four articles by Hoffman, Shelton, and Cleven (2013), Piazza (2011), Santifort-Jordan and Sandler (2014), and Savun and Phillips (2009) employ zero-inflated negative binomial regression, an increasingly popular estimation technique, to the study of terrorist activity; and Li's (2005) piece is one of the most frequently cited studies of terrorism. Each of the eight chapters addresses important statistical and theoretical issues including endogeneity bias, model specification error, fixed effects, theoretical predictability, outliers, and normality of regression residuals. The new statistical analyses in these chapters indicate that the findings and conclusions of the original ten studies are unreliable because the estimated results are likely to be biased and inconsistent. Simply put, these chapters reveal the danger that presents itself when the statistical estimations of empirical studies are insufficiently rigorous.

Part 2 comprises five chapters that aim to locate novel causal factors through the development of original research programs with new datasets in the same research areas as part 1 (i.e., democracy, foreign investment, terrorism, and conflict). Although part 2 includes some discussion on statistical issues, its main purpose is to explore new research ideas. The four research areas may appear to be unconnected at a glance, but each of the five chapters addresses the question of how democracy is related to each of these salient political phenomena. For example, chapter 13 examines the question of whether the foreign policy behavior of the U.S. government—which is considered one of the most democratic regimes worldwide—leads to an increase or decrease in the rate of international terrorism. Because democracy is an essential part of our political lives in the contemporary world, and because it remains a major focus of research and contention in the discipline of political science, understanding why and how it affects or is affected by different political events (such as acts of the U.S. military, international terrorist groups, and multinational corporations) is crucial and should be carefully analyzed. In so doing, each of the five chapters draws some important policy implications, especially concerning the relation of democracy to foreign direct investment and terrorist activity, with some attention also paid to the relation of democracy to civil and international conflict. Accordingly, part 2 is designed to help the reader understand the general patterns and related policy implications of the most controversial political issue areas in the context of democratic governance.

Together, parts 1 and 2 lead the reader to new discoveries and insights regarding four contentious research topics: the causes and effects of civil and international war; growing terrorist threats; democratic governance; and inflows of foreign direct investment. This book intends to benefit students, scholars, and policy makers who are interested in quickly grasping the evolutionary pattern of scientific research on these important political issues, in building their research designs and choosing appropriate statistical techniques, and in identifying their own agendas for the production of cutting-edge research in the above research areas. Most previously published books focus on only one of these research topics. Although these books have their own merits, they fail to provide an overall picture of the various critical issues of the contemporary political world. There are also several edited volumes that may include more than one topic; however, because they are written by several authors, they come from differing perspectives and employ very dissimilar research approaches. In search of scientific knowledge in these four related and crucial research areas, this book offers a single, coherent theme with respect to the interrogation of authoritative empirical studies and in terms of exploring new ideas with original research designs.

Following this introduction, chapter 1 reevaluates Fearon and Laitin's (2003) civil war model. Because Fearon and Laitin's study fails to account for endogeneity problems in their single equation logit model, the estimated results are biased at best and inaccurate at worst. More specifically, the use of an erroneous estimation technique leads Fearon and Laitin to conclude that, contrary to popular belief, democracy, ethnicity, and religion are not causes of civil conflict. However, a reexamination, using a simultaneous equations model to correct for the endogeneity bias, provides evidence that these three variables are indeed important determinants of civil violence. While well-established democracies and religiously diversified countries tend to experience fewer civil wars, ethnically diverse countries are more vulnerable to this type of violence.

Chapter 2 reexamines Gartzke's (2007) capitalist peace model. After replicating Oneal and Russett's (1997, 1999a) democratic peace model, Gartzke's study contends that "capitalism, and not democracy, leads to peace. Additional research is needed to corroborate, extend, and even refute the findings reported here" (180). In response to this open invitation, chapter 2 reevaluates Gartzke's capitalist peace model along with Oneal and Russett's democratic peace model. The chapter finds that while the capitalist peace model suffers from misspecification, observation omission, and sample selection bias, the democratic peace model commits measurement error. After correcting these four errors, chapter 2 demonstrates that capitalism does not mitigate militarized disputes or wars in a consistent manner, but that democracy does.

Chapter 3 reanalyzes Morrow et al.'s (2008) selectorate model, which is an improved version of Bueno de Mesquita et al.'s (2003) selectorate model. Built on fixed-effects models to control for the interaction of geographic region and year, Morrow et al. present evidence for the selectorate theory: "the size of the winning coalition $[(W)]$ is in the theoretically predicted direction and is statistically significant for 28 [(90 percent)] out of 31 different public goods and private benefits" (393). Chapter 3 calls into question the validity of the interaction of fixed-effects models on the grounds that the control for joint fixed effects is unconventional and less efficient. Morrow et al. also overlook country-specific effects and ignore problems with heteroskedasticity and autocorrelation. When more efficient fixed-effects models (i.e., two separate fixed effects of region and year) are implemented along with a correction for the heteroskedastic and serially correlated error term, 23 (74 percent) policy outcomes are no longer explained by W. Moreover, when region, country, and year are controlled for fixed effects along with the correction for heteroskedasticity and autocorrelation, W is either insignificant or in the counterintuitive direction in 27 (87 percent) of the selectorate models.

Arguing that civil liberties better explain public policy outcomes than does the winning coalition (W), chapter 4 evaluates the predictability of Morrow et al.'s (2008) selectorate theory. Morrow et al.'s (2008) selectorate models compare two different features of political institutions: the size of W versus constraints on the chief executive. Their analysis reports that for 25 (81 percent) out of 31 different policy outcomes, W explains more of the variance in these outcomes than do executive constraints. However, after having conceptualized civil liberties as a fundamental and uniquely democratic feature, chapter 4 presents evidence that the inclusion of a variable accounting for the presence or lack of civil liberties contributes to a loss of the robustness, if not the significance, of W in more than 62 percent of the selectorate models. In other words, this chapter finds that countries with high levels of civil liberties are better at providing public goods than are countries with large winning coalitions.

Chapter 5 reevaluates and compares two foreign direct investment models built by Li and Resnick (2003) and Jensen (2003), respectively. It notes that the presence of outliers and influential cases can dramatically change the magnitude of regression coefficients, standard errors, and even coefficient signs (i.e., positive or negative). When researchers fail to account for abnormal observations, the empirical results they report are often misleading. Unfortunately, this fact remains underappreciated in political science generally and in studies of foreign direct investment specifically. Expounding upon the outlier issue, chapter 5 presents a simple simulated example and a replication of two empirical studies that use very similar statistical techniques but come to contradictory conclusions regarding the effect of democracy on FDI inflows. In doing so, the chapter illustrates how outliers can drastically affect the substantive results of regression analysis. With a proper data analysis, this chapter concludes that democratic countries foster more FDI than do authoritarian countries.

Using new data and new diagnostic techniques, chapter 6 further assesses the controversy over the relationship between democracy and FDI inflows: is it positive, negative, mixed, or is there no relationship? Chapter 6 argues that because many existing studies violate the normality assumption in linear models, their estimated results are statistical artifacts, and thus their inferences are misleading. A useful methodological correction is then offered by underscoring the importance of normality tests of regression residuals in case of small or even moderately large samples. The evidence indicates that when the fundamental assumption of normality in the data is upheld, democracies attract more FDI than do autocracies. Therefore, this chapter concludes that developing countries ought to nurture the principle of democratic governance as part of any effort to increase foreign capital for economic growth and development.

Chapter 7 discusses the utility of zero-inflated negative binomial (ZINB) regression, an estimation method that is often used inappropriately in terrorism literature. Because a mismatch between theory and the statistical model is incredibly obvious in four existing studies (i.e., Savun and Phillips 2009; Piazza 2011; Hoffman, Shelton, and Cleven 2013; Santifort-Jordan and Sandler 2014), this chapter makes the point that a reanalysis of published empirical results may not even be required. Existing research supposes that while a large number of countries are immune from terrorism because of their unique political and economic environments, only a small number of countries are exposed to terrorist attacks. Existing research then employs ZINB regression to test this theory. However, ZINB regression is designed exclusively for a cross-sectional dataset and thus not suitable for the cross-sectional, time-series dataset used by those existing studies, in which the presence of excessive zero counts of terrorism is related to individual *observations* with zero terrorist incidents and not to individual *countries*, as theorized. Because the erroneous statistical model has been employed in the four studies listed above, their reported estimates are likely to be biased, and the findings, then, are merely statistical artifacts.

The question of whether democratic institutions attract transnational terrorist activity is a controversial topic in the area of terrorism. Though the rule of law is an essential institutional pillar of any mature democracy, its direct effect on transnational terrorism remains unexplored. Chapter 8 presents a causal mechanism in which the democratic rule of law—conceived as the coexistence of an effective and impartial judicial system in combination with a recognition on the part of the citizens of the law as legitimate—is considered to decrease the opportunity and willingness for ordinary citizens to engage in political violence, thereby preventing democracies from experiencing transnational terrorism. Built off of Li's (2005) cross-sectional, time-series data analysis of 100 countries from 1984 to 1997, this chapter finds that, ceteris paribus, maintaining a high-quality rule of law considerably reduces the number of transnational terrorist incidents while other widely publicized democratic features (such as the political participation and government constraints variables that are reported in Li's work) are statistically insignificant.

The next five chapters switch gears, now seeking general patterns of political phenomena based on original research designs. The five chapters that make up part 2 of this book use original data collection to investigate new ideas related to democracy, foreign investment, terrorism, and conflict; however, the theme that remains common throughout these four issue areas relates to the causes and effects of democratic governance. Chapter 9 addresses the recurring question of why domestic political opposition precipitates a civil war in some (authoritarian) countries but not in others. Drawing on the literature concerning civil-military relations, this chapter argues that because leaders with prior military experience have a greater tendency to repress their citizenry by means of indiscriminate violence, they are likely to enrage opposition sympathizers who in turn are more likely to join dissident organizations in the effort to avenge their grievances; the end result of this process is often civil war. Three historical case studies and a two-stage statistical analysis provide evidence that a country whose top executive has a military background is more likely to indiscriminately repress popular uprisings and, consequently, more vulnerable to the eruption of civil violence. This finding implies that in its attempt to reduce the proliferation of civil war, the United States should help foreign countries to institutionalize civilian control over the military; this is a key feature of democratic political systems.

The choice of a military manpower system is an important security issue, but the topic has not been spotlighted by students of international relations and foreign policy. To broaden the scope of investigation into military manpower systems, chapter 10 combines domestic and international factors from both political and economic categories. A multinomial logit model is tested on an original dataset of military manpower systems spanning over a century; the unit of analysis is the interstate dyad-year. The empirical results show that higher levels of military personnel and expenditure, as well as a general satisfaction with the status quo, are associated with the presence of conscripted forces, while democracy and joint memberships in international organizations are linked to the use of a volunteer military system.

Chapter 11 again turns to Morrow et al.'s (2008) selectorate theory and empirical model in order to examine a controversial issue: do democracies suffer a higher or lower level of terrorist attacks than nondemocracies? Following Morrow et al.'s theoretical arguments, both the size of the winning coalition (W) and the institutional constraints on the chief executive are hypothesized to reduce the number of terrorist attacks. For hypothesis testing, a new dataset is created for 158 countries during the period from 1970 to 2000. The basic results show that W is negatively associated with terrorism, while executive constraints are positively related. However, when regional differences, country, and year fixed effects are accounted for, the dampening effect of W disappears while the counterintuitive effect of executive constraints remains the same. Therefore, this chapter concludes that democratic countries with these two institutional features are generally less successful in their efforts to deter terrorist activity.

Chapter 12 looks at what makes democratic countries attractive to multinational corporations. The existing literature points to domestic audience costs—that is, the costs of upsetting a domestic audience as a result of inconsistent policies. Because they are subject to electoral sanction from those citizens who may be discontented with arbitrary policy changes, democratic leaders are likely to make credible and consistent investment commitments to foreign investors, irrespective of domestic political and economic conditions; the thinking goes, therefore, that democracies are more likely to attract foreign direct investment (FDI) than are nondemocracies. However, the literature seems largely unaware of the potential for domestic audience benefits—that is, the possibility that a democratic leader may use a national economic crisis to his or her electoral advantage by scapegoating foreign firms (i.e., reneging on investment deals and expropriating output or capital); this move would ultimately discourage inflows of FDI. Built on a cross-sectional, time-series data analysis for 70 developing countries during the period from 1980 to 1995, this study finds that democratic developing countries in economic crises are associated with decreased inflows of FDI.

When the United States intervenes militarily into the affairs of another state—whether it is a matter of furthering particular interests or of increasing its global influence—it may produce unintended negative consequences. Chapter 13 examines the impact of U.S. military intervention on the emergence of terrorist activity. It is argued that U.S. military action inadvertently increases the number of terrorist incidents by undermining the domestic security apparatus in the target state and by providing targets for terrorist groups. A cross-national, time-series data analysis of 166 countries during the period from 1970 to 2005 shows that the effect of U.S. military intervention is detrimental to its stated objectives, as it often incites greater terrorist activity. This finding implies that the United States, arguably the most powerful democratic hegemon, ought to be cautious of the use of military force as a foreign policy tool, as it may further provoke terrorist activity abroad.

Chapter 14 summarizes the present findings and suggests directions for future researchers. It appears that empirical political research is not immune from errors of negligence, confirming the necessity of replication for continued scientific progress. This implies that more political science journals and presses, including the *American Political Science Review*, *International Organization*, and Cambridge University Press, ought to require authors to submit their statistical programs along with their empirical manuscripts. This requirement would increase the transparency of empirical research as well as encourage the dissemination and accumulation of scientific knowledge. The next generation of scholars and graduate students can use the existing empirical research and replication materials by training themselves to ascertain novel statistical patterns of important political phenomena. However, making replication materials publicly available is only the first step, as we wait for top-tier journals and book publishers to make "permanent" space for replication studies. In the process of clarifying its argument, this book also provides new empirical findings and relevant policy recommendations in four salient issue areas of international relations: democratic political institutions, foreign direct investment, terrorist events, and conflict.

PART I

Double Take

CHAPTER 1

Democracy, Ethnicity, Religion, and Civil War

Endogeneity Bias

> Great scientific discoveries have been made by men seeking to verify
> quite erroneous theories about the nature of things.
> ALDOUS HUXLEY, "Wordsworth in the Tropics"

Although most existing empirical studies acknowledge that some of the variables included in civil war models are endogenous, they nevertheless rely on a single equation logit analysis that assumes the exogeneity of all independent variables.[1] However, there is much literature to show how such a reliance leads to the reporting of biased estimates (Miguel, Satyanath, and Sergenti 2004; Bueno de Mesquita 2005; Sobek 2010; see also James, Solberg, and Wolfson 1999; DeRouen 2000; DeRouen and Sobek 2004; McLean and Whang 2010; Thies 2010; Whang 2010). This study, then, offers a methodological improvement to the existing statistical models by focusing on the most widely cited and replicated civil war model, namely, that built by Fearon and Laitin (2003); in the process, this study challenges the main findings of their civil war research.

Before the publication of Fearon and Laitin's (2003) work, it was widely accepted by scholars, policy makers, and journalists that countries with more ethnically or religiously diverse populations have a greater risk for civil war, especially in the presence of political discrimination (e.g., Gellner 1983; Huntington 1996). At first glance, Fearon and Laitin's (2003, 75) single equation logit analysis of 161 countries from 1945 to 1999 appears to have successfully refuted this commonly held belief; their findings indicate that when per capita income and population are considered alongside other conflict-related factors, the main causes of civil war are other than democracy (used as a proxy for broadly held grievances/discriminations in their study), ethnic difference, or religious difference. Compelling as they are, these results may be spurious due to the fact that the single equation logit analysis overlooks the endogeneity of civil violence in relation to each of the three factors. For example, countries burdened by political grievances are likely to experience higher levels of civil violence; correspondingly, a higher level of civil violence will result in additional political grievances. Therefore, the predictor and the outcome variables are codependent, implying that causality runs in both directions. A single equation logit model fails to capture the nuance of this two-way causal relationship.

Rigorous statistical analysis assumes that each variable on the right-hand side of a single equation exerts an independent effect on the dependent variable; it also assumes that these variables are not correlated with the error term, which means that the outcome variable is not supposed to affect any of the predictors. However, when an endogenous variable is placed on the right-hand side of an equation (e.g., the democracy variable in Fearon and Laitin's single equation of civil war), it becomes correlated with the error term, thereby violating a fundamental assumption of statistical analysis and subjecting the findings to endogeneity bias. By distorting estimated results, endogeneity bias makes it impossible for researchers to accurately conduct significance tests and draw correct statistical inferences. A simultaneous equations model in which two equations of endogenous variables are jointly estimated for robust results is typically recommended as a remedial measure (see James, Solberg, and Wolfson 1999; DeRouen 2000; Greene 2003; DeRouen and Sobek 2004; McLean and Whang 2010; Whang 2010).

Civil war researchers tend to ignore the potential effects of endogeneity bias in their empirical analyses for two reasons. First, due to the dichotomous nature of one of the endogenous variables—the onset of civil war—a standard simultaneous equations estimator designed for two continuous endogenous variables does not apply. Second, the identification of valid instrumental variables is a challenging task in simultaneous equations modeling. Rather than deal directly with these problems, existing studies of civil war either ignore them or rely on ad hoc remedies such as the practice of taking lags of right-hand-side variables and using observations at five-year intervals. As a result, the estimated results are biased at best and totally inaccurate at worst (Bueno de Mesquita 2005; Hegre and Sambanis 2006; Sobek 2010; Whang 2010).

This study reexamines Fearon and Laitin's civil war model in an attempt to offer a methodological improvement—one that takes into consideration the endogenous relationship between the onset of civil war and democracy, ethnicity, or religion. This study postulates that democracy, ethnic fragmentation, or religious division is affected by internal political conflict and that the onset of internal political conflict is likewise affected by each of these three factors. To test the hypothesis, this study draws on Keshk's (2003) two-stage probit least squares model,[2] which provides the necessary methodological correction to Fearon and Laitin's single equation logit analysis; that is, the Keshk estimator is designed to solve the endogeneity problem even in cases where one endogenous variable is continuous and the other dichotomous. After applying Keshk's simultaneous equations model, this study uncovers evidence that, all other things being equal, well-established democracies and religiously diverse countries experience more civil wars, while ethnic diversity indicates that a country is less likely to encounter this type of violence. These new findings indicate that Fearon and Laitin's results are the statistical artifacts of a biased single equation estimation. This study suggests that to better understand the roles played by democracy, ethnicity, and religion in the onset of civil war, future research must formally address endogeneity bias in the effort to ensure accurate statistical inferences and make appropriate policy recommendations.

BUILDING A TWO-STAGE SIMULTANEOUS EQUATIONS MODEL OF CIVIL WAR

The first subsection briefly provides a rationale for the existence of two-way causality between civil war and grievances, thus serving as theoretical justification for this methodological innovation. The second subsection outlines the process necessary to test the two-way causality with a two-stage simultaneous equations model. Finally, the third subsection addresses four potential concerns that arise with simultaneous equations modeling.

Why Two-Way Causality?

Fearon and Laitin's (2003) study finds no evidence that large cultural divisions or broadly held grievances are associated with higher risks of civil war; these findings are based on their introduction of control variables such as per capita income and population into a single equation logit analysis. However, they do note that "intense grievances are produced by civil war—indeed, this is often a central objective of rebel strategy" (88; emphasis in the original).[3] This statement implies the existence of a two-way causal relationship between civil war and democracy (i.e., a proxy for grievances) in the sense that while countries that do not foster democratic governance tend to be more prone to civil war, civil war also negatively impacts the process of democratic governance in those countries by exacerbating the grievances held by minority groups that are not upwardly mobile.

This study attempts to conceptualize a reciprocal relationship between civil war and democratic grievances. Noting that Fearon and Laitin's study has already modeled a causal relationship that moves from grievances to civil war, the new model pays closer attention to the opposite causal relationship wherein civil war may contribute to further grievances. The outbreak of civil war usually results in a great number of military and civilian casualties, as well as enormous costs in property damage; civil wars often devastate national economies, leaving factories and bridges destroyed, livestock and natural resources pillaged, and the machinery of manufacture damaged beyond repair; following such economic devastation, we expect to see a proliferation of private and public grievances for which citizens demand compensation. Furthermore, because participants of civil violence value the exigencies of war over civil liberties, political rights, and the rule of law, the outbreak of civil war may severely curtail the effectiveness of democratic channels of conflict resolution, in which case the growing numbers of grievances find limited opportunity for redress through institutional outlets (Hurwitz 2008; Choi 2010b).

The attenuation of democratic governance emboldens dominant groups to protect their vested interests, potentially limiting or depriving ethnic, religious, and ideological minority groups' rights. Moreover, the death or displacement of a large number of ethnic or religious minority group members may drastically change the demographic composition of the nation in question. As a result, new political and social grievances or tensions related to issues of property, employment, wealth, and political power may be engendered within conflict-prone countries (Huntington 1996; Fox 2004; Bueno de Mesquita 2005). This line of reasoning is consistent with Kalyvas's (2007, 430) observation that "the [civil] war itself aggregates all kinds of cleavages from the most ideological to the most local." This theoretical rationale undoubtedly warrants examination of the effect of the onset of civil war on grievances, which is a missing causal direction in Fearon and Laitin's single equation logit analysis. In other words, the codependence of the outcome variable and each predictor warrants the examination undertaken by this study of the possibility for a two-way causal relationship between the onset of civil war and each of the three causal factors identified in Fearon and Laitin's study.

How to Test the Two-Way Causality?

By replicating Fearon and Laitin's (2003, 84) results from Models 1 and 2 in Table 1.1,[4] this study explores the empirical implications of two-way causality with respect to political democracy and then applies the same method, in sequence, to ethnicity and religion. It is important to note that the analysis in this study is conducted under the implicit assumption that only one of the three variables of interest (i.e., democracy, ethnicity, and religion) is endogenous to the onset of civil war in each of the simultaneous equations models that is presented below, an assumption that is made due to the limitations of existing statistical software.[5] This issue will require further examination and will be revisited at the end of the empirical results section.

For simultaneous equations modeling, this study turns to the two-stage probit least squares method that was developed by Keshk (2003) and has been applied in several existing studies (e.g., Keshk, Pollins, and Reuveny 2004; Hegre,

Oneal, and Russett 2010; Thies 2010; Whang 2010). At the first stage, this study assumes democracy to be a function of the onset of civil war, per capita income, national material capabilities, and Islam. Because there is no formal model that predicts key determinants of democracy on theoretical grounds, the choice of these variables was made after reviewing existing empirical studies that, as a whole, find a causal connection between democracy and each of the four factors listed above; of the four, national material capabilities and Islam are included as instrumental variables.

In a system of M simultaneous equations, any one equation is identified if the number of exogenous variables excluded from that equation is greater than or equal to the total number of endogenous variables in that equation less one. Gujarati (2003, 753) stresses that "the order condition is usually sufficient to ensure identifiability." By the order condition, the democracy equation (and the civil war onset equation) is identified. The validity tests for the two instrumental variables are addressed in the empirical results section. Because finding valid instrumental variables is a difficult undertaking, and because the purpose of this study is not to explain as much variance in democracy as possible but to account for endogeneity, other control factors that might be included are not included in this research project.[6] The inclusion of variables such as standard of living and education would mean that the empirical results reported below are not comparable to Fearon and Laitin's study, due to shorter data points and a smaller sample size.[7]

The dependent variable, democracy, at the first stage is obtained from the original data collection of Fearon and Laitin. Their study uses the Polity IV data to measure the level of democratic governance (see Marshall and Jaggers 2007). Polity provides an eleven-point additive score for both democracies and autocracies (each score ranging from 0 to 10). Subtracting the autocracy score from the democracy score gives an overall polity score that ranges from full democracy (+10) to full autocracy (−10).[8]

As noted, this study expects to find that the onset of civil war is causally related to a deterioration in the quality of democracy and to an intensification of public and private grievances.[9] It is easy to imagine how civil violence would be detrimental to democratic political systems. This is because civil conflict drastically weakens a government's ability to protect the political rights and civil liberties of its citizenry, and because the challenges posed by active minority groups may disrupt democratic election processes and socioeconomic safety nets. For example, civil wars waged in the name of national security may end up breaking down the democratic tradition of the rule of law, thereby rendering the public less likely to seek resolution of political and economic grievances through fair and impartial justice systems (Hurwitz 2008; Choi 2010b). As a result, civil wars exacerbate, rather than alleviate, grievances. For this analysis, the onset of civil war variable is coded as 1 when a civil war occurs and as 0 otherwise; the relevant data are derived from Fearon and Laitin's study.

It is well known that increased economic development is likely to improve the quality of democratic political systems. For example, based on a panel data set of over a hundred countries from 1960 to 1995, Barro (1999) finds that the propensity for a country to adopt democratic governance rises along with its per capita gross domestic product (GDP). Other research shows that poverty is the most important predictor in explaining the development of democracy (Londregan and Poole 1996; see also Geddes 1999). Pursuing the same line of reasoning, this study includes per capita income as a determinant of democracy. The per capita income variable is once again collected from Fearon and Laitin's data set. Furthermore, it has been argued that when countries possess abundant material capabilities, such as iron and steel production, they are more likely to democratize (Huntington 1991; Diamond 1999; Przeworski et al. 2000). To account for such a tendency, this study includes the Composite Index of National Capability score collected from the Correlates of War's national material capabilities data set (Singer, Bremer, and Stuckey 1972). Consulting several existing studies led to the inclusion of Islam also at the first stage of the simultaneous estimation. Huntington (1991) and Fish (2002) argue that countries whose population is predominantly Muslim are less likely to become democratic because their cultural beliefs and values are not compatible with liberal democracy. After examining the existence of democratic practices in six Islamic countries (Algeria, Egypt, Iran, Malaysia, Pakistan, and Sudan), Esposito and Voll (1996) conclude that these countries do not embrace the Western manifestation of democracy. Midlarsky's (1998) work offers additional empirical evidence that Islam is negatively associated with liberal democracy. The Islam variable measures the percentage of Muslims in each country and is gathered from the Fearon and Laitin data set.

The second stage of simultaneous equations modeling includes the same variables that appear in Fearon and Laitin's (2003, 84) single equation logit Model 1. The dependent variable is the onset of civil war, and the independent variables are democracy, ethnicity, religion, prior war, per capita income, population size, mountainous terrain, noncontiguity, new state, and political instability. A brief explanation of these variables follows. Democracy is expected to be associated with lower risks of the onset of civil war insofar as it tends to discourage discrimination and repression along cultural or other lines (as noted, the Polity IV data collection is the source of the democracy variable). Ethnic or religious tensions are also commonly believed to be instigators of civil war. The ethnicity variable is operationalized using data from *Atlas Narodov Mira* (1964), which reports the probability that two randomly drawn individuals in a country will be from different ethno-linguistic groups; the religious variable is measured primarily in consultation with the CIA Factbook (2008).

Prior war is a variable accounting for the possible impact in relation to any distinct civil wars that were ongoing in the previous year; prior war is coded as 1 if a civil war was ongoing in the previous year and as 0 otherwise. Then per capita income is introduced to measure the financial and bureaucratic aspects of state capacity. The assumption is that countries with fragile financial, military, and political institutions are more likely to experience civil wars due to weak local policing and corrupt counterinsurgency practices. This variable is collected from Penn World Table and World Bank data and is measured in thousands of 1985 U.S. dollars; these measures are lagged one year to ensure that they affect the likelihood of the onset of civil war rather than the other way around. Population size must also be controlled because civil wars are more likely to occur in populous countries; this is a lagged term of the log transformed data on the total population in thousands, which is gathered from World Bank figures. Finally, it has been argued that countries with mountainous terrain have a higher risk of the onset of civil war than do other countries because they provide natural sanctuaries—caverns and forested hills—for rebels; this is a logged term of an estimated percentage of mountainous terrain according to the coding of geographer A. J. Gerard.

Civil war is more likely to occur when potential rebels reside in a territorial base that is separated from the country's center by water or distance (e.g., Angola from Portugal). This variable is coded dichotomously: 1 for noncontiguous countries and 0 otherwise. Oil-exporting countries offer a greater incentive for rebels to compete for state power because state power means control over the oil supply; using World Bank data, this variable is also dichotomous and is coded as 1 if at least one-third of a country's export revenues come from fossil fuels and as 0 otherwise. New states are also expected to be associated with higher risks of the onset of civil war within the first two years of independence; the reason is, of course, that such countries no longer have the protection of the military umbrella of their former imperial powers. Relatedly, political instability at the center is an indication of a country's weak and disorganized institutional structure, making a separatist or center-seeking rebellion more likely; this is operationalized as a dummy variable indicating whether a country has had a three-or-greater score change on the Polity IV regime index in any of the three years prior to the country-year in question.

What Are the Potential Concerns of Simultaneous Equations Modeling?

This study discusses four potential critiques regarding simultaneous equations modeling. First, one may contend that because ethnic and religious diversity are macro-structural variables that do not vary over time within each country, they are unlikely to be endogenous to the onset of civil war. A civil war in Sri Lanka, for instance, may not create more Tamils or other new ethnic groups. More importantly, while internal conflict may change the salience of ethnic identity, the measure of ethnic fractionalization used in Fearon and Laitin's study fails to capture the pattern (i.e., it does not properly capture the underlying concepts of interest). In other words, both the ethnic and the religious fractionalization measures used in Fearon and Laitin's study have a static construction despite evidence that civil war often does actually affect ethnic and religious configurations.

The contention that civil conflict does not cause changes in these measures would be a valid point if the present study relied only on time-series data for a single country (e.g., Sri Lanka or India), whose level of ethnic and religious diversity does not vary over time. This empirical analysis is not, however, a single-country study. As in Fearon and Laitin's data analysis, this study takes full advantage of cross-sectional, time-series data, allowing for the detection of a general pattern between the outcome variable and predictors even in situations where the former does not change within a single country but instead varies across countries (see Greene 2003; Gujarati 2003; Wooldridge 2009). Because ethnic and religious diversity does indeed vary across countries, the first stage of the simultaneous equations model predicts the average changes of ethnicity and religion in relation to the onset of civil war. The level of ethnic and religious diversity across countries reflects the outcome of internal political conflict over years (e.g., displacement across countries); as such, it is assumed that simultaneous equations models with cross-sectional, time-series data sufficiently capture the endogenous dynamics. Interestingly, the same logic applies to Fearon and Laitin's work, which could not have obtained the estimated coefficients for ethnicity and religion if their civil war models had relied only on time-series data instead of cross-sectional, time-series data. In their single equation model, ethnicity and religion are on the right-hand side and have no variation; therefore they would have been correlated with the constant term and would have failed to produce an estimation. Of course, by taking advantage of cross-sectional, time-series data, Fearon and Laitin were able to circumvent this potential collinearity problem in their own empirical analysis.

To further address the concern over the static nature of ethnicity data, it will be useful to collect time-varying measures of ethnic groups and their political relevance to replace Fearon and Laitin's ethnic fractionalization variable. For this task, this study later turns to Wimmer, Cederman, and Min's (2009) Ethnic Power Relations data set, which provides time-varying ethnicity-related variables.[10] After testing endogeneity bias against Fearon and Laitin's model, this new data set allows us to perform an additional test for robustness, which reveals that when the endogeneity bias is corrected, ethnicity is, in fact, positively correlated with the outbreak of civil war. Note that Posner's (2004) Politically

Relevant Ethnic Groups (PREG) is not used for this study because PREG values are constructed only for African and Asian countries; in addition, the data are not yet available to the public.

One might also argue that because some studies report ethnic polarization—as opposed to diversity—as the key factor in explaining the relationship between a local culture and the onset of civil war (e.g., Montalvo and Reynal-Querol 2005), this study should examine the effect of ethnic polarization rather than diversity. This contention would be compelling if this study failed to find evidence of ethnic diversity as an important cause of civil war. More importantly though, such a contention misperceives the point of this study, which is not a reexamination of the debate between ethnic fractionalization and polarization, but a critique of the methodology employed in Fearon and Laitin's original civil war model. Nevertheless, as a check for robustness, this study tests the effect of ethnic polarization in the next section.

A survey of the empirical results reported in the next section reveals that the value of the pseudo R^2 in Fearon and Laitin's original single equation model is similar to that in our own simultaneous equations models. Rather than be suspicious of the lack of increase in explained variation within the simultaneous equations models, one should note that the similarity of pseudo R^2 values is related to the fact that our models are not designed to explain variation but to address endogeneity bias. In addition, one should also keep in mind that there are some technical difficulties that arise with the attempt to compare the goodness of fit test in Keshk's (2003) simultaneous equations model with that of Fearon and Laitin's original single equation model; because the former is not designed to provide necessary post-estimation statistics, this study is unable to conduct nonnested modeling tests (e.g., the Vuong and Clarke tests).

EMPIRICAL FINDINGS

Table 1.1 shows statistical results using Fearon and Laitin's single equation logit model as well as Keshk's simultaneous equations model.[11] To save space, the subsequent discussion is limited to the theoretically interesting variables that appear at the second stage of the simultaneous equations modeling (which, again, is the main focus of this study); the results of the other controls are discussed only minimally. Model 1 successfully replicates Fearon and Laitin's (2003, 84) single equation logit Model 1 because we see that the significance level for each coefficient and its sign are exactly the same.[12] As reported in Fearon and Laitin's study, the onset of civil war is closely associated with per capita income and population, but not with democracy, ethnicity, or religion.[13]

Model 2 takes into account the endogeneity of democracy and the onset of civil war by including national capabilities and Islam as instrumental variables.

TABLE 1.1   Simultaneous Analysis of Civil War Onset and Democracy

Variable	Replicated Model 1	Democracy Model 2	Democracy Model 3	X-POLITY Model 4
Democracy				
Civil war onset		−3.891*** (0.710)	1.368*** (0.369)	0.820*** (0.204)
National capabilities		17.923** (7.563)	3.158 (3.942)	9.720*** (2.777)
Islam		−0.062*** (0.005)	−0.071*** (0.003)	−0.040*** (0.002)
Per capita income			0.744*** (0.054)	0.393*** (0.034)
Constant		−8.150*** (1.592)	1.957** (0.763)	10.355*** (0.439)
F-statistic		555.74	530.15	471.43
Prob > *F*-statistic		0.001	0.001	0.001
R^2		0.212	0.255	0.242
Civil War Onset				
Democracy	0.028 (0.017)	−0.037* (0.022)	−0.037* (0.022)	−0.079* (0.044)
Ethnicity	0.229 (0.386)	0.080 (0.162)	0.080 (0.162)	0.032 (0.176)
Religion	0.323 (0.526)	0.140 (0.212)	0.140 (0.212)	0.211 (0.234)
Prior war	−0.919** (0.316)	−0.324** (0.131)	−0.324** (0.131)	−0.539*** (0.163)
Per capita income	−0.328*** (0.071)	−0.087** (0.030)	−0.087** (0.030)	−0.099** (0.033)
log(population)	0.255*** (0.075)	0.094** (0.033)	0.094** (0.033)	0.131*** (0.036)
log(% mountainous)	0.206** (0.087)	0.081* (0.035)	0.081* (0.035)	0.065* (0.039)
Noncontiguous state	0.354 (0.287)	0.361* (0.162)	0.361* (0.162)	0.543*** (0.174)
Oil exporter	0.823** (0.289)	0.105 (0.167)	0.105 (0.167)	0.119 (0.179)
New state	1.646*** (0.463)	0.829*** (0.229)	0.829*** (0.229)	1.013*** (0.243)
Instability	0.607** (0.236)	0.318*** (0.103)	0.318*** (0.103)	0.275** (0.115)
Constant	−6.656*** (0.749)	−3.259*** (0.314)	−3.259*** (0.314)	−2.913*** (0.434)
Pseudo R^2	0.092	0.092	0.092	0.110
Observations	6,214	6,214	6,214	5,913

Note: Standard errors are in parentheses.

*p < .05, **p < .01, ***p < .001

After conducting an empirical test for the presence of such a relationship, this study finds evidence that the error terms are correlated, indicating that democracy is indeed endogenous to the onset of civil war. This study also tests for the validity of its instrumental variables in order to check (1) whether the instruments are uncorrelated with the error term (i.e., instrument exogeneity)[14] and (2) whether the instruments are irrelevant or weak (i.e., instrument relevance);[15] these are two essential conditions for the validity of the instrumental variables. The test results show that national capabilities and Islam are indeed valid instrumental variables in both of these senses.

The top part of Model 2 reports the estimated coefficients and their standard errors from the democracy equation at the first stage, while the bottom part displays the estimates from the onset of civil war equation at the second stage. Given that several studies underscore the importance of checking for instrument relevance (e.g., Staiger and Stock 1997; Stock 2002), this study briefly discusses whether national capabilities and Islam are relevant instruments. Instrumental relevance (strength of instruments) is typically assessed in terms of the F-statistic in relation to a null hypothesis that posits that the coefficients of the variables used as instruments are all zero in the first-stage regression. The smaller the F-statistic, the weaker the instrument(s); the rule of thumb is that an F-statistic of less than 10 indicates possibly weak instruments.[16] Since Model 2 shows an F-statistic of 555.74, it is reasonable to argue that national capabilities and Islam are not weak instruments.

Unlike the replicated results in Model 1, which are obtained with Fearon and Laitin's single equation logit regression, the bottom part of Model 2 reveals that when endogeneity bias is taken into account, democracy becomes significant at the 0.05 level with a negative sign (see the shaded cell). This result indicates that as the quality of democratic governance improves, the risk of the onset of civil war decreases, a finding that corroborates several previous studies arguing that democratic institutions discourage social discrimination along the lines of cultural difference, which otherwise are a root cause of rebellion (e.g., Gurr 2000; Elbadawi and Sambanis 2002; Hegre 2002; Reynal-Querol 2002).

Because statistical significance does not necessarily ensure a meaningful finding in a practical sense, the substantive effects of the variables should also be reported for empirical verification. Not surprisingly, the substantive analysis supports the main argument of this study that democracy has an ameliorating effect on the likelihood of civil war. The risk that any country will experience internal conflict decreases by 14 percent when the level of democracy increases by one standard deviation, and by 26 percent when democracy increases by two standard deviations. It is worth noting that given the high human and financial costs associated with civil war, even a small change in the predicted probability of political violence should not be dismissed. Indeed, reducing the annual probability of a civil war by 14 or 26 percent is hardly trivial when one recognizes that a single incidence of civil war could easily cost millions of dollars in damages, not to mention an inestimable amount in human life. This substantive analysis is based on Model 2 due to the fact that the democracy variable in Model 1 fails to achieve statistical significance, so calculating its substantive effects is meaningless.

Model 3 extends Model 2 by adding per capita income at stage one. Lest one assert that per capita income is a weak instrument when used at the first stage due to the fact that it is one of the most robust predictors of the onset of civil war in Hegre and Sambanis's (2006) study, this study notes that this is based on a misperception of simultaneous equations modeling. That is, because per capita income appears at both the first and second stages of the modeling process, it is treated not as an instrumental but as an exogenous variable in the simultaneous equations; of the variables appearing in stage one, national capabilities and Islam are instrumental, but per capita income is not.

When per capita income is included at stage one in Model 3, the onset of civil war variable remains significant, as in Model 2, but in the counterintuitive direction. In fact, the inclusion of per capita income causes the coefficient for the onset of civil war to point in the opposition direction, while national capabilities become insignificant. This change occurs because per capita income is the most powerful predictor of democracy; we see that its correlation with democracy (0.38) is much higher than that with the onset of civil war (−0.01) and national capabilities (0.10). Alternatively, one may argue that when confronted with civil violence, ruling elites are more willing to accommodate the grievances of minority groups than they otherwise would be, which effectively enhances the overall quality of democratic governance. In fact, several previous studies provide evidence of a positive correlation between civil violence and institution building in East Africa and Southeast Asia (e.g., Weinstein 2005; Slater 2010). Ironically, these findings validate the claim of Chilean dictator Augusto Pinochet that "sometimes democracy must be bathed in blood." Consistent with the empirical results of Model 2, the bottom part of Model 3 shows that democracy contributes to a reduction in the likelihood of the onset of civil war.

Vreeland's (2008) study shows that a Polity composite democracy score is problematic for studies of the relationship between democracy and civil war insofar as certain components of the composite score refer to the already existing presence of political violence and civil war. For this reason, the empirical results in Models 2 and 3 (which are based on a composite democracy score) may appear to be unreliable. To account for such a concern, this study uses Vreeland's X-POLITY variable in place of Fearon and Laitin's democracy variable in Model 3 of Table 1.1;[17] X-POLITY is significant at the 0.05 level with a negative sign (see the shaded cell). This result confirms the hypothesis that democracy has a dampening effect on the onset of civil war when accounting for endogeneity bias.[18]

It is worth noting that Fearon and Laitin's insurgency variables, such as per capita income and population, still matter as predictors of the onset of civil war even when the two-stage models are used for estimation. Perhaps this finding implies that both the grievance and insurgency arguments about the onset of civil war are correct. In light of these results, future research should consider the possibility of building a unified theory of the onset of civil war.

Table 1.2 displays simultaneous analyses of the onset of civil war with respect to ethnicity and religion.[19] Models 1 through 10 are once again built upon the replicated Model 1 in Table 1.1, after having replaced democracy with ethnicity or religion. More specifically, Model 1 in Table 1.2 is designed to test the reciprocal relationship between ethnicity and the onset of civil war. As discussed above, this model assumes that civil war will aggravate existing ethnic antagonisms, and that the onset of civil war may itself be the result of ethnic fractionalization, an assumption that is consistent with Kalyvas' (2008, 1046) argument that "[ethnic] identity is partly endogenous to the war." In order to estimate the predicted values of ethnicity at stage one, this analysis uses the same predictors as Model 3 in Table 1.1.[20] The ethnicity variable emerges as a contributing factor to the onset of civil violence (see the ethnicity variable in the shaded cell). As many journalists, policy makers, politicians, and academics have observed, ethnically diverse countries are at a greater risk for the onset of civil war (e.g., Moynihan 1993; Huntington 1996). These findings also agree with those of a few existing studies that highlight the contributory role played by ethnic diversity in the risk of civil war (e.g., Sambanis 2001; Wimmer and Min 2006; Wimmer, Cederman, and Min 2009).[21]

In order to make comparable the ethnicity equation of Model 1 in Table 1.2 and the democracy equation of Model 3 in Table 1.1, the former includes national capabilities as one of its four predictors; note, however, that Model 2 in Table 1.2 replaces national capabilities with legislative veto players. Some existing studies have presented a theoretical expectation regarding the effect of legislative veto players on ethnic diversity, arguing that when due to constituent pressure more legislative veto players are opposed to the advancement of the rights of ethnic minorities, it is unlikely that ethnic diversity will be promoted publicly (Tsebelis 1999, 2002). In addition, the empirical correlation between legislative veto players and ethnicity (-0.183) is stronger than that between national capabilities and ethnicity (-0.023). For these reasons, the present study performs a robustness test by introducing legislative veto players—in place of national capabilities—as an instrumental variable in the ethnicity equation. The present study employs Henisz's (2000) data collection on veto players wherein he measures the level of institutional constraint produced by the three key veto players in each country's policy-making process: (a) the executive, (b) the lower legislative chamber, and (c) the upper legislative chamber.[22] The Henisz measure captures the political

TABLE 1.2 Simultaneous Analysis of Civil War Onset, Ethnicity, N*, Polarization, Exclusion, and Religion

	Ethnic Fractionalization		Ethnic Exclusion		N*		Ethnic Polarization		Ethnic Fraction	Religion
Variable	Model 1	Model 2	Model 3	Model 4	Model 5	Model 6	Model 7	Model 8	Model 9	Model 10
Ethnic Fractionalization, N*, Polarization, Minorities, or Religion										
Civil war onset	0.034** (0.013)	0.006 (0.011)		0.597*** (0.107)		−0.045*** (0.012)		−0.016 (0.010)	0.176*** (0.029)	−0.084*** (0.016)
National capabilities	0.246* (0.138)									0.965*** (0.180)
Legislative veto players	−0.072*** (0.017)			−0.817*** (0.190)		−0.131*** (0.024)		−0.076*** (0.016)	−0.140** (0.053)	
Islam	0.001*** (0.000)	0.001*** (0.000)		0.002** (0.001)		0.002*** (0.000)		0.001*** (0.000)	0.001** (0.000)	−0.001*** (0.000)
Per capita income	−0.013*** (0.002)	−0.015*** (0.001)		0.012 (0.020)		0.004* (0.002)		−0.004** (0.001)	0.006 (0.006)	−0.008** (0.003)
Constant	0.495*** (0.027)	0.452*** (0.023)		3.273*** (0.219)		−0.094*** (0.025)		0.500*** (0.020)	0.814*** (0.058)	0.203*** (0.033)
F-statistic	141.39	139.88		112.53		242.16		30.32	228.44	67.92
Prob > F-statistic	0.001	0.001		0.001		0.001		0.001	0.001	0.001
R²	0.084	0.085		0.073		0.235		0.023	0.150	0.042
Civil War Onset										
Ethnic fractionalization	2.670* (1.273)	3.255** (1.335)					−0.011 (0.446)	−2.006 (2.821)	2.938** (1.268)	0.615* (0.307)
Ethnic polarization							1.074* (0.601)	5.546 (7.292)	−0.941 (0.651)	
Religious fractionalization	−1.057* (0.621)	−1.411* (0.654)	0.224 (0.523)	−1.209* (0.718)			0.519 (0.578)	0.419 (0.421)	−1.143* (0.631)	−1.670* (0.920)

	(1)	(2)	(3)	(4)	(5)	(6)	(7)	(8)	(9)	(10)
N*				1.480*	0.676	1.639*				
				(0.739)	(0.689)	(0.895)				
Ethnic exclusion			0.218**							
			(0.076)							
Democracy	0.013*	0.012	0.025	0.040*	0.060**	0.030**	0.025	0.002	0.014	0.008
	(0.008)	(0.008)	(0.018)	(0.019)	(0.025)	(0.011)	(0.019)	(0.010)	(0.009)	(0.007)
Prior war	-0.594***	-0.686***	-1.053***	-1.421**	-1.000**	-0.454*	-0.920**	-0.698	-0.481***	-0.358**
	(0.171)	(0.188)	(0.326)	(0.550)	(0.424)	(0.182)	(0.334)	(0.495)	(0.150)	(0.131)
Per capita income	-0.074*	-0.066*	-0.322***	-0.064	-0.312***	-0.133***	-0.398***	-0.179**	-0.082*	-0.107***
	(0.038)	(0.038)	(0.072)	(0.044)	(0.084)	(0.033)	(0.089)	(0.063)	(0.040)	(0.030)
log(population)	0.069*	0.072*	0.249***	-0.109	0.369***	0.187***	0.254***	0.215	0.036	0.095**
	(0.037)	(0.037)	(0.079)	(0.117)	(0.108)	(0.053)	(0.078)	(0.158)	(0.047)	(0.033)
log(% mountainous)	0.111**	0.124***	0.166*	-0.194	0.308*	0.090	0.209*	-0.076	0.151***	0.052
	(0.037)	(0.039)	(0.092)	(0.145)	(0.145)	(0.059)	(0.099)	(0.236)	(0.050)	(0.039)
Noncontiguous state	0.215	0.362**	0.689*	0.900**	0.287	0.141	0.671*	0.902	0.248*	0.171
	(0.132)	(0.153)	(0.317)	(0.387)	(0.370)	(0.169)	(0.326)	(0.938)	(0.143)	(0.128)
Oil exporter	0.107	0.063	0.655*	-0.555	1.342***	0.431*	0.679*	0.315*	0.096	0.158
	(0.170)	(0.175)	(0.296)	(0.471)	(0.382)	(0.192)	(0.329)	(0.166)	(0.162)	(0.154)
New state	0.542*	0.636*	1.956***	0.713*	2.619***	1.241***	1.525***	0.728*	0.656*	0.808***
	(0.255)	(0.281)	(0.516)	(0.396)	(0.511)	(0.268)	(0.579)	(0.336)	(0.308)	(0.229)
Instability	0.244**	0.273**	0.668**	0.238*	0.404	0.136	0.531*	0.238*	0.196*	0.247**
	(0.104)	(0.109)	(0.245)	(0.135)	(0.365)	(0.162)	(0.266)	(0.125)	(0.119)	(0.102)
Constant	-3.623***	-3.818***	-6.888***	-2.866***	-8.016***	-4.032***	-7.084***	-5.921	-3.060***	-2.631***
	(0.384)	(0.417)	(0.801)	(0.426)	(1.220)	(0.555)	(0.887)	(3.640)	(0.404)	(0.414)
Pseudo R^2	0.095	0.099	0.103	0.099	0.164	0.167	0.106	0.099	0.109	0.093
Observations	6,214	6,002	5,697	5,697	3,160	3,160	5,175	5,175	5,175	6,214

Note: Standard errors are in parentheses.

$*p < .05$, $**p < .01$, $***p < .001$

constraints imposed by the lower and upper legislative chambers on the executive, regardless of the specific policy issues; it is a continuous measure on a scale of 0 (least constrained) to 1 (most constrained).[23] Model 2 replicates the results of Model 1, after replacing national capabilities with legislative veto players.[24] The legislative veto players variable is significant and in the theoretically hypothesized direction. A look at the estimates of the onset of civil war equation at the second stage of simultaneous equations modeling reveals that the significance of the ethnicity variable increases to the 0.01 level, indicating that civil war is more likely to occur as ethnic fragmentation increases.

As noted, Fearon and Laitin's ethnic fractionalization variable is static; it is a one-time "snapshot" of a country rather than a dynamic measure. It is, therefore, not adequate for an empirical evaluation of the hypothesis that a change in ethnic tensions will reduce the likelihood of civil war onset. Furthermore, a similar difficulty is encountered when testing the opposite causal hypothesis— that a civil war will affect a country's ethnic tensions. Because civil violence may strengthen ethnic attachments in a theoretical sense, we would expect an endogenous variable to display dynamism and change within a time series; unfortunately, the empirical measures fail to reflect this expected change. As noted earlier, the cross-sectional nature of the ethnicity-related measures do allow for empirical estimation; however, it does not adequately address the issue of endogeneity bias. It is therefore important to show evidence that within a single country, ethnicity may aggravate the risk of civil war and that civil war may likewise proliferate or aggravate existing ethnic divisions.

To address this concern directly, Wimmer, Cederman, and Min's (2009) time-varying ethnic exclusion variable is used in this analysis; this variable is borrowed from the Ethnic Power Relations data set and measures the ethnopolitically relevant share of the excluded population within the total population. Political relevance, for the purposes of this study, indicates that an ethnic group is capable of achieving a minimal level of political mobilization or, on the other hand, that its members are being subjected to intentional political discrimination on the basis of their particular ethnic backgrounds. Political exclusion, then, occurs when members of a particular ethnic group are being excluded from service or representation in the executive branch of government. The executive branch refers to the political executive, including presidential and governmental cabinet positions and executive offices, as well as the top ranks of the national militaries and bureaucracies. To correct the positive skew of the data, this study uses logged transformation. This is consistent with the assumption that an increase in the proportion of the excluded population is associated with an increase in the likelihood of civil war at lower levels of exclusion more than at higher levels.

Model 3 displays replicated results obtained after Fearon and Laitin's ethnic fractionalization variable is replaced with Wimmer, Cederman, and Min's

(2009) ethnic exclusion variable. The ethnic exclusion variable is statistically significant at the 0.01 level, which is consistent with the results reported in Wimmer, Cederman, and Min's (2009) study. Model 4 is constructed to account for the reciprocal relationship between ethnic exclusion and civil war. As it does in Models 1 and 2, the ethnic exclusion variable again achieves significance. The robustness tests in Models 3 and 4 confirm that civil war and ethnicity are endogenous and that the latter is a cause of the former.

A recent dialogue between Cederman and Girardin (2007) and Fearon, Kasara, and Laitin (2007) contributes further to a scientific understanding of ethnicity as a possible cause of civil war. Cederman and Girardin's study replicates Fearon and Laitin's (2003) single equation logit models after replacing the original ethnicity variable with N^*—an index of ethno-nationalist exclusion in Eurasian and North African countries. Cederman and Girardin (2007) find evidence that countries whose leaders are from an ethnic minority are exposed to a higher risk of internal political conflict than those whose leaders are from an ethnic majority. In response, Fearon, Kasara, and Laitin's (2007) study shows that when N^* is properly reanalyzed for measurement error, "it is neither statistically significant nor substantively strong" (187). Of course, one conspicuous weakness of the research is its exclusive reliance on a standard single equation logit model that fails to account for the fact that ethnicity and civil violence are codependent.

Model 5 replicates Fearon, Kasara, and Laitin's (2007, 189) Model 6 after adjusting for the availability of data on legislative veto players; the results are used for the simultaneous equations in Model 6.[25] The replicated results agree with those of Fearon, Kasara, and Laitin's single equation logit analysis (i.e., N^* is statistically insignificant).[26] However, as the shaded cell in Model 6 shows, when it is treated as endogenous to civil war onset, N^* becomes significant. What is important to note is that after the endogeneity problem has been properly addressed, ethnicity emerges as a good predictor of internal political conflict.

Montalvo and Reynal-Querol's (2005) study reports evidence that ethnic polarization—as opposed to fractionalization—is related to the outbreak of civil war; however, Schneider and Wiesehomeier's (2010) replication study refutes these findings. Schneider and Wiesehomeier demonstrate that "ethnically polarized countries do not face a substantially higher risk of violent conflict" (1). By incorporating Montalvo and Reynal-Querol's measure of ethnic polarization into Fearon and Laitin's civil war model, the present study contributes to this debate. Importantly, though, Montalvo and Reynal-Querol's data include 138 countries, while Fearon and Laitin's data consist of 161 countries; therefore, when the two data sets are merged, 18 out of the 138 countries in Montalvo and Reynal-Querol's sample are dropped because they do not appear in Fearon and Laitin's sample.[27] As a result, this study uses only 120 out of Fearon and Laitin's 161 sample countries, reducing the total number of observations for empirical tests from 6,214 to 5,175.

Model 7 presents the replicated results of Fearon and Laitin's Model 1 in Table 1.1, after having added Montalvo and Reynal-Querol's ethnic polarization variable. Because the ethnic polarization variable is statistically significant with a positive sign and the ethnic fractionalization variable is not,[28] ethnically polarized countries do appear to be more vulnerable to the onset of civil war than their counterparts. This finding is in line with Montalvo and Reynal-Querol's conclusion. However, when reverse causality is considered in Model 8 (i.e., the reciprocity between ethnic polarization and the onset of civil war), the damaging effect of ethnic polarization disappears. This second finding is consistent with Schneider and Wiesehomeier's (2010) study, which concludes that ethnic polarization is, in fact, not a main determinant of civil war. Model 9 replicates Model 8 with respect to the simultaneous relationship between ethnic fractionalization and the onset of civil war and, not surprisingly, finds that ethnic fractionalization once more emerges as a contributing factor to the increased risk of the onset of civil war.

Model 10 focuses on the two-way causal relationship that may exist between religion and the onset of civil war.[29] We should remember that Fearon and Laitin's (2003) "null" findings are counterintuitive insofar as it is commonly believed that religious diversity will increase a country's risk for civil war (see also Gellner 1983; Huntington 1996). The empirical results of the present study also show a contrary picture to that commonly perceived regarding the role of religion. When endogeneity bias is correctly factored into a simultaneous equations model, the religion variable does become significant, but its sign is in the counterintuitive direction (see the religion variable in the shaded cell).[30] This finding should not be surprising in light of James' (2010) observation that monotheistic societies are more vulnerable to religious wars than are polytheistic societies due to the fact that the latter tend to be more flexible in terms of dogma and so generally allow for a certain amount of latitude within their belief systems. From this point of view, it is not difficult to see that countries become more acceptable and tolerant in regard to personal and political differences when they are exposed to more diversified religious beliefs. If a diversity of religious beliefs is embraced as a basis for consolation, peace, and love, then its pacifying effect on civil violence would be no surprise. Zaidise, Canetti-Nisim, and Pedahzur (2007) provide evidence that religious people are less supportive of political violence than are nonreligious people, and that this is particularly true among Israeli Jews and Muslims. Several other studies also argue that religion acts as a force for peace, including Gopin's (2000) historical study of religious people who served as peace makers across a number of cultures; this perspective posits that religion can play a critical role in the construction of a global community of nonviolence (see also Weigel 1991; Abu-Nimer 2001).

Table 1.3 displays results placing an emphasis on "ethnic war" as a subset of civil war. As Sambanis notes in his 2001 study, ethnic wars have an important implication; that is, they arise largely from political grievances or from discrimination against minority groups, rather than from a lack of economic opportunity. If this argument is correct, it provides additional support for the results of the democracy, ethnicity, and religion variables in Table 1.3. Model 1 displays the replicated results of Fearon and Laitin's (2003, 84) single equation logit Model 2. The results are consistent with what their study reports: while democracy and ethnicity have no bearing on the onset of ethnic war, religion has a positive association.

When Model 2 treats democracy and the onset of ethnic war as endogenous, the democracy coefficient is significant at the 0.01 level, while the effect of per capita income is greatly reduced. This result echoes those of previous studies (e.g., Gurr 2000; Sambanis 2001) insofar as it finds that well-established democracies are better able to provide ethnic minorities with peaceful channels for conflict resolution, thus significantly diminishing the risk for ethnic warfare. Model 3 accounts for the endogeneity problem between ethnic diversity and ethnic war. The ethnicity variable is again significant at the 0.001 level and in the hypothesized direction, while both per capita income and population lose their significance. Model 4 replaces Fearon and Laitin's ethnic fractionalization variable with Wimmer, Cederman, and Min's (2009) ethnic exclusion variable in order to account for the change in ethnic composition that takes place within the time-series data. The results in Model 4 are similar to those in Model 3; that is, ethnicity matters. Furthermore, the results in Model 5 are consistent with those in Model 10 in Table 1.2, both indicating that religious diversity exerts a dampening effect on the likelihood of ethnic warfare.

One may wonder why the population variable becomes insignificant in Models 3 through 5 of Table 1.3. Population size is considered to be one of the most powerful predictors of the onset of civil war, although it is an almost trivial predictor if one assumes that high fatality definitions of civil war (such as that employed in Fearon and Laitin's study) are much more easily satisfied in states with a high population. The present study speculates that ethnicity and religion outperform population due to the fact that the outcome variable is the onset of ethnic warfare "due predominantly to political grievance rather than [to] lack of economic opportunity" (Sambanis 2001, 259). In a statistical sense, then, population explains much less of the variance in ethnic war than does either ethnicity or religion.

Remember that the analysis above is conducted under the implicit assumption that only one of the three variables (i.e., democracy, ethnicity, and religion) is endogenous to the onset of ethnic war in each of the simultaneous equations found in Models 2, 3, 4, and 5 in Table 1.3. This assumption is made because

TABLE 1.3   Simultaneous Analysis of Ethnic War Onset

Variable	Replicated Model 1	Democracy Model 2	Ethnicity Model 3	Exclusion Model 4	Religion Model 5
Democracy, Ethnicity, Ethnic Exclusion, or Religion					
Ethnic war onset		2.170***	0.283***	0.503***	0.075***
		(0.456)	(0.049)	(0.110)	(0.017)
National capabilities		6.758	0.396	3.828	0.148
		(6.384)	(0.731)	(2.542)	(0.228)
Islam		−0.072***	−0.000	0.003**	−0.001***
		(0.004)	(0.000)	(0.001)	(0.000)
Per capita income		0.670***	0.015	−0.003	0.014***
		(0.088)	(0.011)	(0.023)	(0.003)
Constant		4.266***	1.131***	3.306***	0.553***
		(1.033)	(0.107)	(0.251)	(0.038)
F-statistic		329.64	254.25	64.76	90.89
$Prob > F$-statistic		0.001	0.001	0.001	0.001
R^2		0.206	0.166	0.053	0.067
Ethnic War Onset					
Democracy	0.032	−0.094**	0.024*	0.039*	0.010
	(0.023)	(0.031)	(0.011)	(0.021)	(0.009)
Ethnicity	0.292	−0.114	6.069***		1.403**
	(0.612)	(0.251)	(1.874)		(0.472)
Ethnic exclusion				1.308*	
				(0.630)	
Religion	1.602*	0.916**	−2.335**	−0.519	−3.088**
	(0.755)	(0.312)	(0.967)	(0.597)	(1.185)
Prior war	−0.855*	−0.195	−0.446**	−1.084**	−0.276*
	(0.395)	(0.160)	(0.172)	(0.416)	(0.161)
Per capita income	−0.372***	−0.073*	−0.015	−0.109**	−0.080*
	(0.100)	(0.038)	(0.050)	(0.045)	(0.040)
log (population)	0.373***	0.158***	−0.075	−0.055	0.058
	(0.112)	(0.048)	(0.084)	(0.116)	(0.055)
log (% mountainous)	0.093	0.006	0.138**	−0.244*	−0.030
	(0.110)	(0.044)	(0.054)	(0.140)	(0.048)
Noncontiguous state	0.462	0.638**	0.201	0.700**	0.444*
	(0.411)	(0.225)	(0.187)	(0.296)	(0.203)
Oil exporter	0.743*	−0.174	0.033	−0.310	−0.042
	(0.372)	(0.209)	(0.186)	(0.341)	(0.186)
New state	1.606**	0.982***	0.365	0.782*	0.814**
	(0.571)	(0.283)	(0.328)	(0.409)	(0.277)
Instability	0.359	0.251*	0.185	0.227	0.151
	(0.317)	(0.138)	(0.145)	(0.166)	(0.134)

TABLE 1.3   continued

Variable	Replicated Model 1	Democracy Model 2	Ethnicity Model 3	Exclusion Model 4	Religion Model 5
Constant	−8.288*** (1.109)	−4.191*** (0.476)	−3.942*** (0.475)	−3.613*** (0.554)	−2.200*** (0.654)
Pseudo R^2	0.107	0.116	0.121	0.119	0.105
Observations	5,104	5,104	5,104	4,628	5,104

Note: Standard errors are in parentheses.

$^*p < .05$, $^{**}p < .01$, $^{***}p < .001$

Keshk's (2003) simultaneous equations model cannot compute more than one endogenous relationship at a time. To be more specific, Keshk's Stata syntax for the simultaneous equations model allows researchers to include only one endogenous variable in each parenthesis in the command line, making it impossible to accommodate three endogenous relationships at once. Existing studies such as Keshk, Pollins, and Reuveny (2004), Hegre, Oneal, and Russett (2010), Thies (2010), and Whang (2010) make the same assumption when they employ Keshk's (2003) estimator. Future research should attempt to expand Keshk's work and explore the possibilities for accommodating additional relationships. In the meantime, when only one of the three variables of interest is included in each simultaneous equations model, only one endogenous relationship is measured at a time. By keeping the democracy variables, for instance, while dropping both ethnicity and religion from the previous specification of the simultaneous equations of Model 2, the results will show solely the effect of democracy. Models 1, 3, 5, and 7 in Table 1.4 show the replicated results of the reduced, single equation logit models, results that are similar to the original findings of Fearon and Laitin's (2003, 84) Model 2 of Table 1.1. While religion reaches statistical significance, democracy and Fearon and Laitin's ethnic fractionalization fail to do so. After Models 2, 4, 6, and 8 account for the endogeneity problem, democracy, ethnicity, and religion all prove to be causal factors in the onset of ethnic war. Democracy and religion are likely to decrease the risk of ethnic war, whereas ethnic diversity is likely to increase it.[31] These results further confirm those from the full models reported in Table 1.3.

CONCLUSION

Upon reporting that it is not grievances but insurgency conditions that matter, Fearon and Laitin's study has become one of the most influential civil war studies. In fact, Blattman and Miguel (2009, 31) note that Fearon and Laitin's civil

TABLE 1.4. Simultaneous Analysis of Ethnic War Onset: Robustness Tests

	Replicated	Demo	Replicated	Ethnicity	Replicated	Exclusion	Replicated	Religion
Variable	Model 1	Model 2	Model 3	Model 4	Model 5	Model 6	Model 7	Model 8
Democracy, Ethnicity, Ethnic Exclusion, or Religion								
Ethnic war onset		3.646***		0.090***		0.354***		−0.046**
		(0.811)		(0.023)		(0.113)		(0.015)
National capabilities		3.824		0.538*		5.086*		0.512**
		(10.778)		(0.290)		(2.414)		(0.175)
Islam		−0.076***		0.000*		0.004***		−0.001***
		(0.006)		(0.000)		(0.001)		(0.000)
Per capita income		0.876***		−0.005		−0.017		0.000
		(0.155)		(0.004)		(0.020)		(0.002)
Constant		7.313***		0.676***		2.921***		0.281***
		(1.814)		(0.052)		(0.256)		(0.035)
F-statistic		342.98		93.28		55.54		83.29
Prob > F-statistic		0.001		0.001		0.001		0.001
R^2		0.212		0.068		0.046		0.061
Ethnic War Onset								
Democracy	0.028	−0.060*						
	(0.022)	(0.027)						
Ethnicity			0.791	8.156*				
			(0.564)	(3.871)				
Ethnic exclusion					0.306**	0.904*		
					(0.107)	(0.495)		
Religion							1.699**	−3.205**
							(0.681)	(1.312)

Prior war	−0.892*	−0.254	−0.849*	−0.630**	−1.015**	−0.889**	−0.798*	−0.216
	(0.398)	(0.158)	(0.393)	(0.237)	(0.419)	(0.351)	(0.388)	(0.164)
Per capita income	−0.410***	−0.096**	−0.327***	0.008	−0.371***	−0.109**	−0.349***	−0.105**
	(0.101)	(0.038)	(0.099)	(0.075)	(0.101)	(0.046)	(0.091)	(0.036)
log (population)	0.384***	0.148***	0.361***	−0.106	0.428***	0.025	0.399***	0.106*
	(0.109)	(0.045)	(0.114)	(0.130)	(0.120)	(0.089)	(0.109)	(0.049)
log (% mountainous)	0.035	0.003	0.051	0.292*	−0.035	−0.152	0.075	−0.084
	(0.104)	(0.041)	(0.106)	(0.140)	(0.115)	(0.101)	(0.108)	(0.057)
Noncontiguous state	0.500	0.517**	0.522	−0.049	1.070**	0.680**	0.577	0.558**
	(0.419)	(0.215)	(0.418)	(0.239)	(0.461)	(0.283)	(0.405)	(0.218)
Oil exporter	0.652*	−0.090	0.487	0.072	0.244	−0.248	0.644*	−0.062
	(0.363)	(0.201)	(0.356)	(0.183)	(0.389)	(0.309)	(0.357)	(0.188)
New state	1.695**	0.908***	1.761***	0.068	1.994**	0.828**	1.732***	0.960***
	(0.572)	(0.272)	(0.564)	(0.489)	(0.676)	(0.354)	(0.563)	(0.287)
Instability	0.369	0.229*	0.446	0.288*	0.454	0.263*	0.426	0.149
	(0.314)	(0.134)	(0.311)	(0.163)	(0.334)	(0.154)	(0.311)	(0.132)
Constant	−7.389***	−3.640***	−7.827***	−5.833***	−8.595***	−3.937***	−8.502***	−1.783*
	(1.047)	(0.420)	(1.056)	(1.217)	(1.209)	(0.522)	(1.116)	(0.804)
Pseudo R^2	0.096	0.098	0.097	0.099	0.116	0.104	0.103	0.099
Observations	5,104	5,104	5,104	5,104	4,628	4,628	5,104	5,104

Note: Standard errors are in parentheses.

*$p < .05$, **$p < .01$, ***$p < .001$

war model has "[become] the standard formation for most cross-country work that followed." The salience of Fearon and Laitin's work is due to their remarkably consistent empirical findings that there appears to be no causal relationship between the onset of civil war and democracy, ethnicity, or religion; interestingly, their conclusion squarely contradicts the widespread public perception of the major causes of internal political conflict.

Although there has been a series of critiques aimed at the Fearon and Laitin study, no previous study has challenged their method of estimation itself by pointing out that the "null" findings can be attributed to the use of an erroneous estimator: a single equation logit regression. Fearon and Laitin's single equation logit analysis fails to take into consideration the possibility of endogeneity bias between ethnic grievances and the onset of civil war. In fact, Fearon's (2003, 199) study emphatically points out that "it cannot be assumed, without argument, that ethnic distinctions are wholly exogenous to other political, economic, and social variables of interest . . . many examples, such as Somalia, show that political violence can lead or force people to identify more strongly along ethnic lines that formerly were less salient,"[32] yet Fearon and Latin (2003) ignore the endogeneity issue nonetheless. The present study fills that gap by demonstrating that their "null" findings are merely the statistical artifacts of a biased single equation estimation that overlooks the fact that the onset of internal war and these three factors are reciprocally determined.[33]

After correcting for endogeneity bias with a two-stage simultaneous equations model (which is an appropriate econometric estimator for continuous and dichotomous endogenous variables), democracy and religion are correlated with peace in respect to intrastate violence; ethnic tensions, on the other hand, appear to be a catalyst for civil war. It is also important to note that in terms of significance levels, the empirical evidence for democracy, ethnicity, and religion is more compelling in relation to ethnic warfare estimation than it is to civil warfare estimation. The significance of per capita income and population in the ethnic war models in Tables 1.3 and 1.4 is dramatically weakened or even disappears, while democracy, ethnicity, and religion emerge as the main contributing factors. In fact, these findings corroborate Sambanis' (2001) early study demonstrating that ethnic wars have more relevant policy implications than do civil wars because ethnic wars are primarily caused by the political grievances raised by minority groups rather than they are by poor economic conditions.

The findings of this study suggest that future research should seek to account for the endogeneity problem with a formal method capable of explaining and understanding the role of political grievances with respect to the onset of civil wars (Vasquez 1997, 1998). In other words, this study has added weight to the argument that endogeneity matters insofar as its discovery reveals additional layers of the effect had by political grievances on the outbreak of civil war. Given the fact that internal political conflict imposes tremendous suffering upon entire populations and destabilizes regional and international communities (Brown 1996), a solid understanding of the root causes of civil war is crucial so that academics and politicians can offer policy recommendations that avoid exacerbating already-devastating situations. That is, although increasing per capita income may reduce the likelihood of civil war, as prescribed in Fearon and Laitin's study, it does not allow us to directly tackle the political grievances of minority groups, which, it turns out, often harbor the generative tensions of civil warfare. The simultaneous analysis done in this study implies that by properly dealing with the grievances of their ethnic minorities, countries can lower their risk for the onset of civil war.

CHAPTER 2

Capitalist Peace, Democratic Peace, and International War

Model Specification Errors

> Absent justification, statistical critiques of robust empirical associations
> should change as little as possible from standard analyses. . . . Other-
> wise, it is hard to know what novel aspect of the specification accounts
> for the different results.
>
> ALLAN DAFOE, JOHN R. ONEAL, AND BRUCE RUSSETT,
> "The Democratic Peace"

Since the collapse of the Soviet Union, myriad research questions of what causes liberal peace have been explored (e.g., Gibler 2007; Choi 2010a, 2010c, 2013). In particular, Russett and Oneal's (2001) study on the democratic peace has emerged as one of the most influential research programs in the area of international conflict, crisis, and war. However, several recent studies have taken a new direction by attempting to distinguish which liberal peace argument has more explanatory power. For example, Gartzke's (2007) study on the capitalist peace, built off Oneal and Russett's (1997) democratic peace model, represents one of these new groundbreaking studies. It reports that "economic development, free markets, and similar interstate interests all anticipate a lessening of militarized disputes or wars. This capitalist peace also accounts for the effect commonly attributed to regime type in standard statistical tests of the democratic peace" (166). Gartzke concludes with an intriguing statement that "the statistical models I develop, and the findings that I present, can be altered, possibly in ways that again show that democracy matters" (182). In response to this open invitation, this study reevaluates Gartzke's capitalist peace model along with Oneal and Russett's democratic peace model.[1]

A reexamination of these two models on the liberal peace leads to some interesting developments. This study identifies that the capitalist peace model suffers from model misspecification, observation omission, and sample selection bias, while the democratic peace model commits measurement error. Two data sets are fitted to compare the relative importance of capitalism and democracy: all dyads and politically relevant dyads. After correcting those four problems, this study uncovers that whereas capitalism does not emerge as a cause mitigating militarized disputes or wars in a consistent manner, democracy does.

THE CAPITALIST PEACE MODEL: THREE ERRORS

Based on a sample of all dyad years from 1950 to 1992, Gartzke's (2007) work addresses the question of whether capitalism exerts a pacifying effect on the onset of international conflict.[2] It proposes that the absence of militarized disputes between democracies is largely explained by the fact that since democracies tend to espouse capitalism, the likelihood of disputes is greatly reduced. More specifically, economic development, globalization of capital, and similar state policy interests are hypothesized to lead dyads to be less likely to experience a dispute. For empirical testing, the capitalist peace model is built on a replication of the democratic peace model of Oneal and Russett (Oneal and Russett 1997, 278, Model 1, Table 2; see Gartzke 2007, 176n47), which "allows for ready comparison of results and diminishes the danger that [his] findings result from idiosyncrasies in coding or model specification" (173). The model consists of a lower score of democracy, a higher score of democracy, capitalist variables, and several control variables.[3]

Model Specification Error: Peace Years

Taking note of Beck, Katz, and Tucker's (1998) methodological suggestion, Gartzke's capitalist peace model includes three temporal spline variables (i.e., spline1, spline2, and spline3) to control for time dependence. However, a peace year variable that measures the number of peace years since the last conflict and that serves as the base variable to create those three spline variables is left out. Since logit splines require that all four variables be included together, the exclusion of a peace year variable makes the estimates of the capitalist peace model untenable. Because Gartzke's study does not control for the complete spline function for the years of peace, it obtains inconsistent parameter estimates and incorrect standard errors.[4] Dafoe (2011, 256–57) provides a detailed discussion on how the omission of a peace year variable leads to an estimate of the hazard rate with a poor fit to Gartzke's data as well as causes Oneal and Russett's democracy variable to be weaker than it should be. Thus, the capitalist model is misleading because its estimation suffers from omitted variable bias. These omissions explain why the effect of democracy does not hold up in the capitalist peace model, rather than the capitalist variables winning over the democracy variable in competition. As demonstrated in the next section, when the model specification error is properly corrected, democracy reemerges as a pacifying factor in a consistent manner, whether a crisis is related to a militarized dispute or a war.

Observation Omission: Regional Dummies

When statistical software drops some observations upon the execution of a model, it issues warning notes. Generally, researchers investigate whether those drops are a justifiable procedure in order to obtain unbiased and consistent estimates. If researchers overlook critical error messages about observation drops and report coefficients and standard errors as they are, their findings may be misleading or, even worse, erroneous. The next section illustrates how ignoring warning notes about observation drops can stymie one's analysis. In particular, this relates to Gartzke's study, which does not analyze the implications of warning notes regarding dropped observations that are caused by the inclusion of regional dummy variables.

Sample Selection Bias: All Dyads versus Politically Relevant Dyads

Sample selection bias is caused by the selection of a particular sample instead of conducting a census of the population. Gartzke's study examines the capitalism-conflict connection with a focus on all dyads but not on politically relevant dyads. However, the use of all possible dyads is open to two criticisms. The first is theoretical; for example, there is no reason to expect a militarized dispute between Malaysia and Uganda. The second is methodological, as the inclusion of all possible dyads makes the nonzero militarized dispute event extremely rare. Politically relevant dyads that either share a border or include at least one major power are considered more conflict prone than any other type of dyad because they are exposed to more opportunities to interact, increasing the likelihood of conflict. For this reason, students of conflict have emphasized the importance of politically relevant dyads over all dyads (e.g., Russett and Oneal 2001; Lemke and Reed 2001). The next section demonstrates that when the capitalist peace model is fitted with politically relevant dyads, capitalist variables become less robust and in some cases insignificant.

THE DEMOCRATIC PEACE MODEL: ONE ERROR

Oneal and Russett (1997, 1999a) put forward a theoretical argument that democratic leaders in both states in a dyad are restrained from engaging in a dispute due to institutions and practices of democratic governance. The nature of democratic governance in both states invites various political participants such as legislators, bureaucrats, interest groups, and the public into the foreign policy decision-making process. Their participation in the democratic process inevitably slows down the onset of military violence.

Measurement Error: Democracy (Low) and Democracy (High)

Oneal and Russett's (1997, 273, 283) theoretical discussion on democracy leads to two hypotheses: (1) "the likelihood of dyadic conflicts is primarily determined by the less constrained of the two states in a dyad" (i.e., weak link assumption; see Dixon 1994) and (2) "increasing the political distance separating the pair makes the dyad more prone to conflict." Thus, the democratic peace hypotheses can be straightforwardly modeled as follows: international conflict = β_1 + β_2Democracy(Low) + β_3PoliticalDistance + β_{4+k}OtherControls + ε_1 (Equation 1). In this equation, Democracy(Low) is operationalized as the lower score between the two democracy scores in a given dyad, while PoliticalDistance is operationalized as the difference between the higher and lower democracy scores in a dyad.[5]

However, in Oneal and Russett's (1997, 281; see Equation 5) study, the two hypotheses are tested in a *strange* fashion: international conflict = β_1 + β_2Democracy(Low) + β_3Democracy(High) + β_{4+k}OtherControls + ε_2 (Equation 2). Whereas Democracy(Low) is the same as what appeared in the first equation, Democracy(High) is not a direct measure of the PoliticalDistance hypothesis but a summation of Democracy(Low) + PoliticalDistance. This model specification leads to a *biased* estimate of Democracy(Low). From an econometric point of view, Oneal and Russett's democratic peace model is equivalent to: international conflict = β_1 + β_2Democracy(Low) + β_3(Democracy(Low) + PoliticalDistance + β_{4+k}OtherControls + ε_2 (Equation 3). When rearranged, the model becomes: international conflict = β_1 + (β_2 + β_3)Democracy(Low) + β_3PoliticalDistance + β_{4+k}OtherControls + ε_2 (Equation 4) (Tsebelis and Choi 2009).

In sum, as indicated in Equation 4, the measurement error caused by the inclusion of the higher democracy score instead of a direct measure of political distance nullifies the purpose of introducing the weak link assumption that is the basis of Oneal and Russett's original prediction on Democracy(Low).[6]

REEXAMINING THE CAPITALIST AND DEMOCRATIC PEACE MODELS

This study replicates Gartzke's Model 5 in Table 1 (2007, 177) and Model 7 in Table 2 (181).[7] Model 5 is representative of Gartzke's capitalist model. It includes all democracy and capitalist variables along with several control variables as causes that mitigate all militarized interstate disputes (MIDs). Note that the substantive effect analysis shown in Figure 1 (179) in Gartzke's study is based on Model 5. Model 7 predicts determinants of wars. Gartzke's study appears to rely on militarized dispute data due to their greater frequency and war data to further test the essence of the democratic peace theory.

Table 2.1 shows the reestimated results of Gartzke's capitalist peace Model 5. For each of the two dependent variables (i.e., militarized disputes and wars), three models are fitted. The first model is a replication of Gartzke's model. The second model corrects the omitted variable bias by adding a peace year variable to the first model. Lastly, the third model remedies the measurement error by replacing Democracy(High) with PoliticalDistance. Model 1 successfully replicates Gartzke's Model 5 in which the dependent variable is all militarized interstate disputes (MIDs). Because Gartzke's study omits a peace year variable, Democracy(Low) is shown to be insignificant. In other words, since his study fails to control for temporal dependence correctly due to the omission of the peace year variable, the correlation between democracy and peace becomes weaker. The omitted variable bias contributes to a failure of correctly tracing out the path of temporal dependence, generating an imprecise estimate of the hazard rate. As a result, the coefficient of Democracy(Low) becomes smaller, and its standard error becomes larger, leading to the insignificance of the test results.

When Beck, Katz, and Tucker's (1998) spline function of the years of peace (i.e., peace years, spline1, spline2, and spline3) are correctly specified in Model 2, Democracy(Low) becomes significant at the 0.01 level, indicating that democracy reduces the likelihood of militarized disputes. However, since Model 2 still suffers from the previously identified measurement error, Model 3 corrects this by introducing PoliticalDistance instead of Democracy(High). Again, the pacifying effect of democracy persists at the same level of significance. Across Models 1 to 3, the three capitalist indicators for market integration (i.e., Fin. Open.[Low]), the interaction between economic development and contiguity (i.e., GDPPC * Contig.),[8] and interests (i.e., INTERESTS) also appear to show significance in the hypothesized direction.

With two minor modifications, Model 4 replicates Gartzke's Model 7, where the dependent variable is wars. The wars variable is recognized as the deadliest form of conflict. Interestingly, among the three capitalist variables, the INTERESTS variable is excluded from Gartzke's Model 7. The rationale for this decision is that the variable "is not statistically significant. . . . This makes sense as fatal conflicts and wars disproportionately involve resource competition (Senese 2005; Vasquez 1993), rather than the policy disputes captured by the interest variable" (Gartzke 2007, 180). However, this study puts the variable back into the model not only because it is one of the three capitalist peace variables, but also because it may influence leaders' war behavior under the correct model specification. In addition, this study excludes the six regional dummies from Gartzke's Model 7 to correct for the observation drop error. Gartzke's Stata do-file reveals that 4,881 observations for Europe and 1,434 observations for South America were dropped out of estimation due to no variation in the observations of the dependent variable, which undoubtedly caused the estimated coefficients to be biased. To avoid dropping these observations, this study excludes all the

TABLE 2.1 Logit Regression of Liberal Variables on International Conflict

Variable	All MIDs			All Wars		
	Replicated	Peace Years	Demo Diff	Replicated	Peace Years	Demo Diff
	Model 1	Model 2	Model 3	Model 4	Model 5	Model 6
Democracy (Low)	−0.0171	−0.0282**	−0.0370**	−0.0951*	−0.1076*	−0.0894*
	(0.0119)	(0.0107)	(0.0143)	(0.0477)	(0.0490)	(0.0482)
Democracy (High)	−0.0022	−0.0088		0.0378	0.0182	
	(0.0125)	(0.0110)		(0.0332)	(0.0328)	
Political Distance			−0.0088			0.0182
			(0.0110)			(0.0328)
Trade Dep. (Low)	−5.4023	4.8571	4.8571	−99.2129	−50.0391	−50.0391
	(9.0358)	(6.4173)	(6.4173)	(165.7359)	(131.6930)	(131.6930)
Fin. Open. (Low)	−0.2468***	−0.2051***	−0.2051***	−0.6612***	−0.5238***	−0.5238***
	(0.0581)	(0.0502)	(0.0502)	(0.1745)	(0.1589)	(0.1589)
GDPPC (Low)	0.0002***	0.0002***	0.0002***	0.0004***	0.0004***	0.0004***
	(0.0000)	(0.0000)	(0.0000)	(0.0001)	(0.0001)	(0.0001)
GDPPC * Contig.	−0.0003***	−0.0003***	−0.0003***	−0.00027	−0.0004*	−0.0004*
	(0.0000)	(0.0000)	(0.0000)	(0.00022)	(0.0002)	(0.0002)
INTERESTS	−0.9824***	−1.0254***	−1.0254***	1.5095*	0.5298	0.5298
	(0.2005)	(0.1634)	(0.1634)	(0.8497)	(0.7911)	(0.7911)
Contiguity	3.7404***	3.4783***	3.4783***	4.7966***	4.8116***	4.8116***
	(0.2734)	(0.2592)	(0.2592)	(0.9239)	(0.8175)	(0.8175)
Distance	−0.4164***	−0.3789***	−0.3789***	−0.6173***	−0.4718**	−0.4718**
	(0.0853)	(0.0896)	(0.0896)	(0.1948)	(0.1789)	(0.1789)
Major Power	1.4035***	1.3824***	1.3824***	1.4143	1.0447	1.0447
	(0.2733)	(0.2320)	(0.2320)	(1.1347)	(1.1006)	(1.1006)
Alliance	−0.0073	0.1530	0.1530	−1.2558**	−0.7385	−0.7385
	(0.2334)	(0.1905)	(0.1905)	(0.5311)	(0.5351)	(0.5351)
Capability Ratio	−0.1506**	−0.0953*	−0.0953*	−0.9019***	−0.8194***	−0.8194***
	(0.0555)	(0.0498)	(0.0498)	(0.1936)	(0.2179)	(0.2179)
Peace Years		−0.6366***	−0.6366***		−0.9601***	−0.9601***
		(0.0525)	(0.0525)		(0.2549)	(0.2549)
Spline1	0.0047***	−0.0070***	−0.0070***	0.0038**	−0.0125***	−0.0125***
	(0.0006)	(0.0009)	(0.0009)	(0.0016)	(0.0038)	(0.0038)
Spline2	−0.0044***	0.0049***	0.0049***	−0.0029	0.0094***	0.0094***
	(0.0007)	(0.0008)	(0.0008)	(0.0018)	(0.0028)	(0.0028)
Spline3	0.0016***	−0.0015***	−0.0015***	0.0007	−0.0032**	−0.0032**
	(0.0004)	(0.0003)	(0.0003)	(0.0009)	(0.0011)	(0.0011)
CONSTANT	−1.0878	−0.2776***	−0.2776	−3.2875*	−2.2022	−2.2022
	(0.7615)	(0.7956)	(0.7956)	(1.4587)	(1.3754)	(1.3754)
N	166,140	166,140	166,140	166,140	166,140	166,140
Log-likelihood	−2078.058	−1912.658	−1912.658	−187.2447	−165.875	−165.875
Chi²	1607.35***	1971.50***	1971.50***	289.85***	643.44***	643.44***

Note: Numbers in parentheses are robust standard errors adjusted for clustering on dyads.

*$p<0.05$; **$p<0.01$; ***$p<0.001$, one-tailed tests

regional dummies from the Gartzke model.[9] By both including the INTERESTS variable and excluding the regional dummies, this study makes the results from the subsequent war models more comparable to those from the previous militarized dispute Models (1 through 3) where the INTEREST variable was present and the regional dummies were absent. Put differently, with these two minor changes, this study is allowed to employ the same number of total observations (i.e., 166,140), regardless of the nature of the dependent variable, while enhancing the comparability between the statistical models.

Model 4 in Table 2.1 is a replication of Gartzke's Model 7 with the aforementioned two modifications. Unlike Gartzke's estimates reported in Model 7, the Democracy(Low) variable passes the standard significance test. More critically, the GDPPC * Contig. variable turns out to be insignificant,[10] and the INTERESTS variable is supported but in the wrong direction. Of course, one should be cautious in placing too much faith in these results due to the omitted variable of peace years. Model 5 reports the results upon the correction of the omitted variable bias in Model 4 by including a peace year variable. It reveals that democracy undoubtedly matters. While Fin. Open.(Low) and GDPPC * Contig. appear to show a constraining effect, INTERESTS has no bearing on the onset of wars. According to Model 6, which corrects the biased coefficient and standard error of Democracy(Low) by including PoliticalDistance instead of Democracy(High), the significance of Democracy(Low) continues to survive in competition with the three forces of capitalism.

In an effort to eschew sample selection bias, the sample of all dyads is confined to politically relevant dyads. These dyads are considered to be the most dangerous dyads in conflict studies because they have more opportunities and capabilities to interact. Again, Gartzke's study overlooks an analysis of politically relevant dyads whereas this study explores their implications as part of testing the robustness of the previous findings, which may be subject to sample selection bias. Table 2.2 displays the results. Both Models 1 and 2 are corrected for all four of the previously discussed errors. Models 1 and 2 reveal the independent explanatory power of the Democracy(Low) variable in predicting the onset of conflict, irrespective of dispute type. Among the capitalist variables, the Fin. Open.(Low) variable produces a pacifying effect across all models whereas the INTERESTS variable fails to achieve this effect across the same models.

It should be noted that, as Zelner (2009) points out, the sign of the coefficient on the interaction term, GDPPC * Contig., does not necessarily correspond to the hypothesized direction, and the standard error of this coefficient is not directly useful for the statistical significance test. These difficulties of interpreting interaction terms require special caution. For this reason, this study turns to the graphical method developed by King, Tomz, and Wittenberg (2000) and extended by Zelner (2009). The interaction effect between GDPPD(Low) and Contiguity is shown in Figure 2.1.[11] While the first two graphs are drawn against

TABLE 2.2   Logit Regression of Liberal Variables on International Conflict: Politically Relevant Dyads

	MIDs	Wars
	Democratic Difference	Democratic Difference
Variable	Model 1	Model 2
Democracy (Low)	−0.0210*	−0.0889*
	(0.0124)	(0.0497)
Political Distance	0.0053	0.0206
	(0.0109)	(0.0343)
Trade Dep. (Low)	1.6748	−36.2768
	(5.1949)	(100.2275)
Fin. Open. (Low)	−0.1459***	−0.5944***
	(0.0470)	(0.1747)
GDPPC (Low)	0.0001***	0.0005***
	(0.0000)	(0.0001)
GDPPC * Contig.	−0.0001*	−0.0005**
	(0.0001)	(0.0002)
INTERESTS	−0.6558***	0.9602
	(0.1580)	(0.8184)
Contiguity	1.0979***	−10.4748
	(0.3270)	(not estimated)
Distance	−0.1511***	−0.4485**
	(0.0493)	(0.1845)
Major Power	−0.4026	−13.0496
	(0.2632)	(not estimated)
Alliance	0.0156	−0.9986*
	(0.1835)	(0.5169)
Capability Ratio	−0.1168**	−0.7525***
	(0.0473)	(0.2190)
Peace Years	−0.6010***	−0.8493***
	(0.0509)	(0.2376)
Spline1	−0.0066***	−0.0108**
	(0.0009)	(0.0036)
Spline2	0.0047***	0.0082**
	(0.0008)	(0.0029)
Spline3	−0.0015***	−0.0028**
	(0.0004)	(0.0012)
CONSTANT	0.3751	12.6813
	(0.5271)	(not estimated)
N	14,750	14,750
Log-likelihood	−1397.337	−123.645
Chi²	1004.33***	not estimated

Note: Numbers in parentheses are robust standard errors adjusted for clustering on dyads.

*p<0.05; **p<0.01; ***p<0.001, one-tailed tests

FIGURE 2.1 An Interaction Effect between GDPPC (Low) and Contiguity:
Politically Relevant Dyads

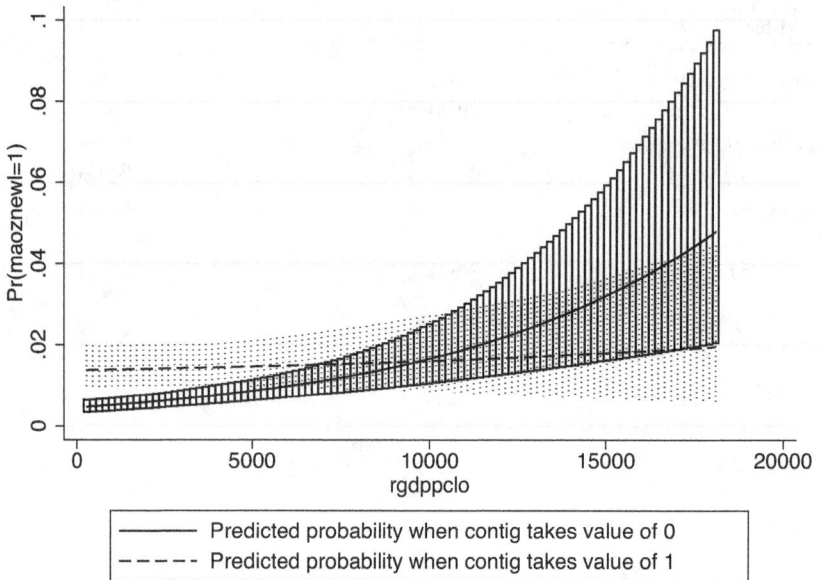

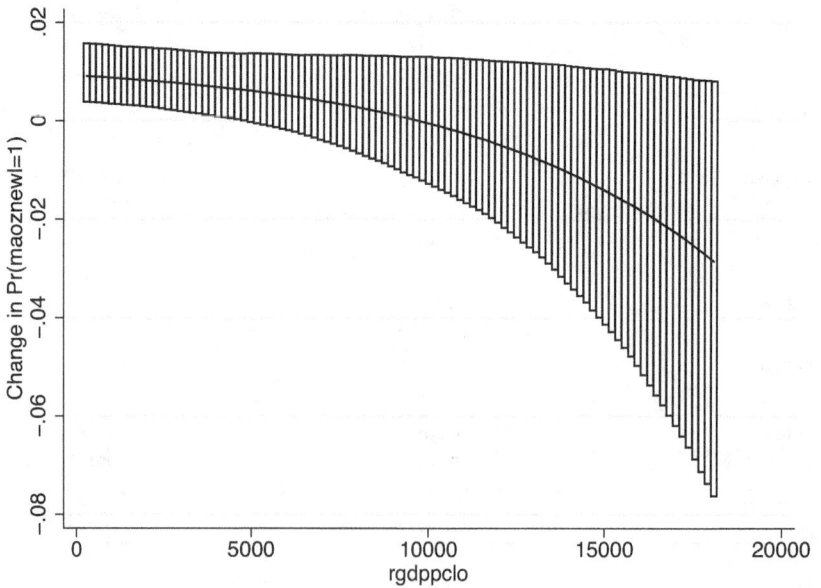

Model 1 MIDs

FIGURE 2.1   continued

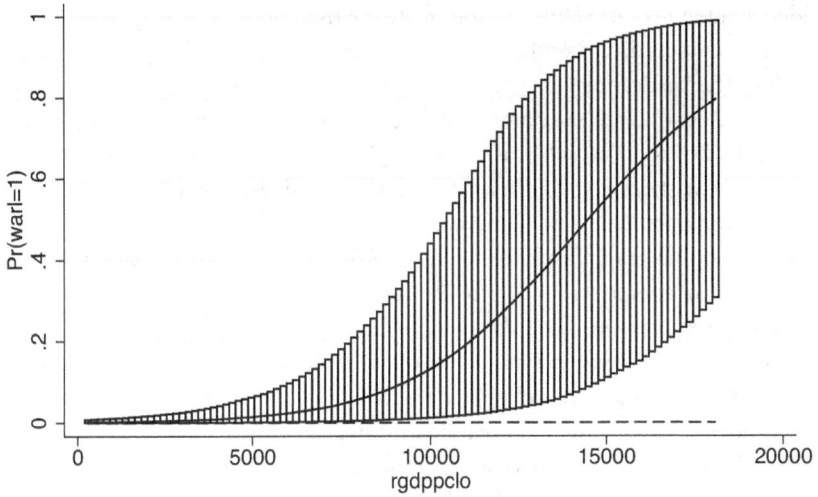

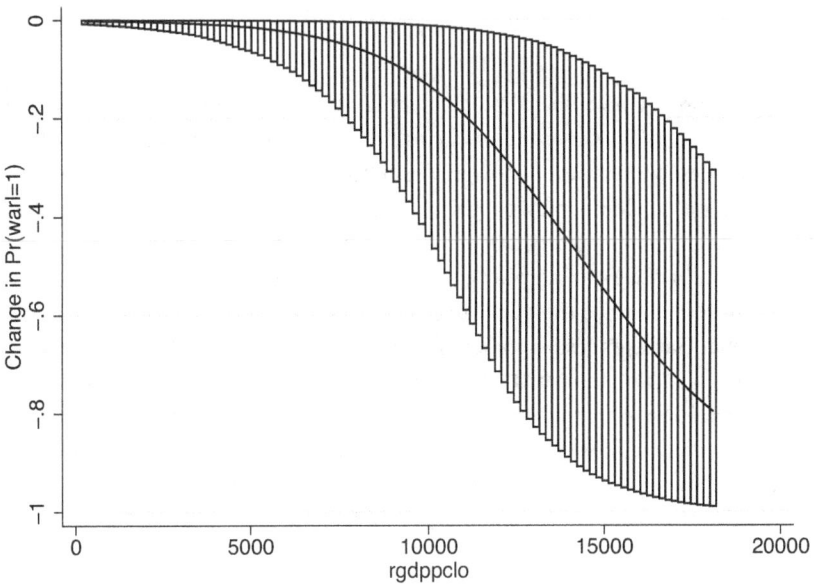

Model 2 Wars

politically relevant MIDs, the second two graphs are drawn against politically relevant wars. The graphs on top portray the predicted probabilities and confidence intervals for GDPPC * Contig., while the bottom two graphs show the difference in predicted probabilities associated with a unit change in contiguity (i.e., the vertical distance between contiguity and noncontiguity in the top graphs). According to the dotted predicted line in the first top graph, it appears that the likelihood of politically relevant MIDs increases, though it is small, when dyadic states enjoy high levels of economic development and are neighboring countries. This is not consistent with Gartzke's hypothesis. Furthermore, the first bottom graph displays that most of the 95 percent confidence intervals include zero, effectively rendering the coefficient on GDPPC * Contig. as statistically meaningless. According to the second two graphs, there is no interaction effect between economic development and contiguity. The dotted line represents the predicted probability when Contiguity takes the value of 1, but the probability line does not move either downward or upward, indicating that GDPPC * Contig has no causal effect on wars. In sum, this robustness test confirms that the liberal peace is hardly a product of capital, economic development, and interests, although capital markets alone appear to have some pacifying effect on politically relevant militarized disputes or wars.

CONCLUSION

The question of which liberal peace matters more has become a salient issue in the scientific study of international conflict during the last two decades. Studies of the democratic peace show evidence that in explaining the prevalence of interstate peace, democracy outperforms all other factors. However, Gartzke's (2007) recent study reports that the capitalist variables of capital markets, the interaction between economic development and contiguity, and shared interstate interests remove the pacifying effect of democracy. This study demonstrates that Gartzke's results indicating that capitalism causes democracy to become insignificant are statistical artifacts of biased estimations due to model misspecification, observation omission, and sample selection bias. When these errors are properly corrected, democracy retains its explanatory power in relation with interstate conflict. It appears that democracy dies hard in the midst of the challenging forces of the three capitalist factors.

Logit Regression of Liberal Variables on Militarized
Interstate Disputes: Replications

Variable	Model 1	Model 2	Model 3	Model 4
Democracy (Low)	−0.0641***	−0.0103	−0.0152	−0.0107
	(0.0139)	(0.0137)	(0.0140)	(0.0128)
Democracy (High)	0.0356***	0.0077	0.0074	0.0080
	(0.0100)	(0.0122)	(0.0120)	(0.0122)
Trade Dep. (Low)	−37.8343**	−16.9177*	−24.3312*	−5.2063
	(15.8743)	(10.0734)	(14.0447)	(8.4729)
Fin. Open. (Low)		−0.1877***	−0.2116***	−0.2143***
		(0.0529)	(0.0604)	(0.0588)
GDPPC (Low)			0.0001*	0.0002***
			(0.0000)	(0.0000)
GDPPC * Contig.				−0.0003***
				(0.0000)
INTERESTS				
Contiguity	2.0028***	2.7595***	2.7581***	3.4285***
	(0.2112)	(0.3022)	(0.3060)	(0.3063)
Distance	−0.6108***	−0.4742***	−0.4643***	−0.4327***
	(0.0835)	(0.0972)	(0.0967)	(0.0928)
Major Power	2.5152***	2.0301***	1.9481***	1.9734***
	(0.2567)	(0.3738)	(0.3680)	(0.3557)
Alliance	−0.4299*	−0.2381	−0.2342	−0.2172
	(0.2030)	(0.2404)	(0.2356)	(0.2318)
Capability Ratio	−0.3040***	−0.1286*	−0.1273*	−0.1295*
	(0.0548)	(0.0598)	(0.0596)	(0.0578)
Africa	0.4437	0.1726	0.2841	0.1780
	(0.3202)	(0.3626)	(0.3633)	(0.3644)
Asia	1.3172***	0.7064*	0.7720*	0.6314*
	(0.2462)	(0.3609)	(0.3577)	(0.3644)
Europe	−0.9231***	−0.9167*	−0.9871*	−0.8978*
	(0.2948)	(0.5070)	(0.5044)	(0.4635)
Middle East	1.3296***	1.0086***	0.8818**	0.9785***
	(0.2668)	(0.3140)	(0.3198)	(0.3088)
North America	0.1425	0.7021	0.7250	0.7517
	(0.3379)	(0.4746)	(0.4748)	(0.4771)
South America	1.3191**	0.8872*	0.8315*	0.8811*
	(0.4395)	(0.4024)	(0.4009)	(0.3937)
Peace Years				
Spline1	0.0051***	0.0045***	0.0044***	0.0044***
	(0.0005)	(0.0006)	(0.0006)	(0.0006)
Spline2	−0.0049***	−0.0041***	−0.0040***	−0.0041***
	(0.0006)	(0.0007)	(0.0007)	(0.0007)

continued

Variable	Model 1	Model 2	Model 3	Model 4
Spline3	0.0029***	0.0015***	0.0015***	0.0015***
	(0.0003)	(0.0004)	(0.0004)	(0.0004)
CONSTANT	−0.4677	−1.1358	−1.2880	−1.8606*
	(0.7076)	(0.8399)	(0.8302)	(0.8089)
N	282,287	174,548	171,509	171,509
Log-likelihood	−5120.999	−2170.270	−2146.564	−2121.190
Chi²	1868.46***	1717.58***	1719.86***	1698.78***

Note: Numbers in parentheses are robust standard errors adjusted for clustering on dyads.

*$p<0.05$; **$p<0.01$; ***$p<0.001$, one-tailed tests

APPENDIX TABLE 2.2   When Peace Years Are Included

Variable	Model 1	Model 2	Model 3	Model 4
Democracy (Low)	−0.0747***	−0.0236*	−0.0275*	−0.0226*
	(0.0136)	(0.0125)	(0.0127)	(0.0116)
Democracy (High)	0.0331***	0.0019	0.0017	0.0022
	(0.0095)	(0.0106)	(0.0105)	(0.0107)
Trade Dep. (Low)	−25.3397*	−8.3074	−13.0888	4.5299
	(12.4518)	(9.1031)	(12.7440)	(6.3126)
Fin. Open. (Low)		−0.1772***	−0.1971***	−0.2008***
		(0.0489)	(0.0547)	(0.0524)
GDPPC (Low)			0.0001*	0.0002***
			(0.0000)	(0.0000)
GDPPC * Contig.				−0.0003***
				(0.0000)
INTERESTS				
Contiguity	1.8932***	2.5555***	2.5562***	3.2307***
	(0.1988)	(0.2818)	(0.2858)	(0.2822)
Distance	−0.5448***	−0.4246***	−0.4179***	−0.3895***
	(0.0799)	(0.0997)	(0.0994)	(0.0960)
Major Power	2.5086***	2.1088***	2.0183***	2.0389***
	(0.2405)	(0.3263)	(0.3203)	(0.3053)
Alliance	−0.1320	−0.1106	−0.1171	−0.1073
	(0.1879)	(0.2058)	(0.2020)	(0.1971)
Capability Ratio	−0.2793***	−0.0857	−0.0830	−0.0882*
	(0.0504)	(0.0540)	(0.0540)	(0.0512)
Africa	0.4353	0.2790	0.3740	0.2824
	(0.2914)	(0.3190)	(0.3221)	(0.3228)
Asia	1.2510***	0.6365*	0.6908*	0.5730*
	(0.2464)	(0.3023)	(0.3015)	(0.3070)

Variable	Model 1	Model 2	Model 3	Model 4
Europe	−0.8344**	−1.0642*	−1.1318*	−1.0556**
	(0.2816)	(0.4905)	(0.4886)	(0.4401)
Middle East	1.2672***	0.8523**	0.7351**	0.8452**
	(0.2373)	(0.2892)	(0.2945)	(0.2867)
North America	0.1115	0.6796	0.6804	0.7565*
	(0.3214)	(0.4198)	(0.4310)	(0.4258)
South America	1.1679**	0.8194*	0.7633*	0.8358**
	(0.4047)	(0.3552)	(0.3554)	(0.3531)
Peace Years	−0.6509***	−0.6249***	−0.6224***	−0.6144***
	(0.0409)	(0.0549)	(0.0545)	(0.0536)
Spline1	−0.0079***	−0.0068***	−0.0068***	−0.0067***
	(0.0007)	(0.0009)	(0.0009)	(0.0009)
Spline2	0.0058***	0.0048***	0.0048***	0.0047***
	(0.0006)	(0.0007)	(0.0007)	(0.0007)
Spline3	−0.0019***	−0.0015***	−0.0015***	−0.0015***
	(0.0003)	(0.0003)	(0.0003)	(0.0003)
CONSTANT	−0.0503	−0.4121	−0.5412	−1.1108
	(0.6664)	(0.8594)	(0.8519)	(0.8371)
N	282,287	174,548	171,509	171,509
Log-likelihood	−4716.397	−2012.004	−1990.117	−1967.084
Chi²	2509.64***	2323.39***	2280.29***	2295.69***

Note: Numbers in parentheses are robust standard errors adjusted for clustering on dyads.

$*p<0.05$; $**p<0.01$; $***p<0.001$, one-tailed tests

CHAPTER 3

A Reanalysis of the Selectorate Model

Fixed Effects, Heteroskedasticity, and Autocorrelation

> Essentially, all models are wrong, but some are useful.
> GEORGE E. P. BOX AND NORMAN R. DRAPER, *Empirical Model-Building and Response Surfaces*

Drawing on existing methods of econometrics (e.g., Green, Kim, and Yoon 2001; Wooldridge 2002; Greene 2003; Acemoglu et al. 2005, 2008; Brambor, Clark, and Golder 2006; Bai 2009), this study examines the validity of the selectorate model and its results, as well as suggests corrections to its overall research design. The selectorate model is based on Bueno de Mesquita, Smith, and Siverson's (2003) selectorate theory.[1] Relying on the assumption that the ultimate goal of an elected official is to remain in office, the selectorate theory stipulates that the size of the minimum winning coalition (W) that selects the leader provides an independent predictive power that helps to explain a wide range of public policy outcomes. In order to empirically test their hypothesis, Bueno de Mesquita et al. build a selectorate model that includes both W and the residuals of democracy (which control for other aspects of democracy) as predictors.[2] Their cross-sectional, time-series data analysis appears to lend support to the selectorate theory by finding that the provision of public goods such as the promotion of civil liberties, education, health care, and national security is likely to increase as W increases; likewise the provision of private goods such as the high premium for black market exchange, corruption, and construction grants is likely to decrease as W increases.

Clarke and Stone (2008) were the first to question the validity of Bueno de Mesquita, et al.'s selectorate models. Their claim is that Bueno de Mesquita et al.'s findings are subject to omitted variable bias. Their data analysis demonstrates that Bueno de Mesquita et al. are misled by biased estimates stemming from the inclusion of the residuals of the democracy variable (as opposed to its original term) on the right-hand side of the selectorate model. The residualized democracy variable exaggerates the significance level of the W variable by increasing the magnitude of the estimated coefficient and decreasing its standard error. After replacing the residuals of democracy with its original term in an effort to correct the biased estimation, Clark and Stone find that W lacks significance in about half of the public policy areas tested.

In response, Morrow, Bueno de Mesquita, Siverson, and Smith (2008) refute Clarke and Stone's inclusion of both W and the original term of democracy in the same selectorate model on the grounds that "all but one element in the estimation of W is also used by Polity to estimate Democracy" (394). For this reason, Morrow et al. offer an alternative model specification that emphasizes the importance of controlling for aspects of democracy other than W in testing their theoretical arguments. (A democracy may, for instance, invest more than will an autocracy for reasons other than those provided by the selectorate theory.) To control for aspects not explained by the selectorate theory, they introduce institutional constraints on the chief executive (a key component of the composite Polity democracy score) into their alternative model.[3] Accordingly, this alternative selectorate model assumes a public policy outcome to be a function of W and executive constraints. Morrow et al.'s results show that for 25 (81 percent) out of the 31 different public goods and private benefits, W explains more of the variance in policy outcomes than does the executive constraints variable. They also show that W "is in the theoretically predicted direction and is statistically significant for 28 [(90 percent) public policy areas]" (393).

Although Morrow et al.'s study modifies the original selectorate model in response to Clarke and Stone's criticisms, some inherent estimation problems remain. It is well known that cross-sectional, time-series models will produce biased and inefficient estimates if they fail to control for unobserved individual heterogeneity. In order to avoid running into this type of bias, Morrow et al.'s modified selectorate model appears to include an interaction term of geographic region and year as a control for the presumed spatiotemporal dependence in the data (to use their language, "in particular parts of the world in particular years") (Bueno de Mesquita et al. 2003, 136). However, their interaction fixed-effects model is erroneous insofar as it fails to include all constitutive terms in the model specification (Brambor, Clark, and Golder 2006; Bai 2009), ignores the unique characteristics of each country (Green, Kim, and Yoon 2001; Bai 2009), and overlooks estimation problems related to heteroskedasticity and autocorrelation (Wooldridge 2002; Greene 2003). Consequently, their interaction fixed-effects model is not as efficient as it should be, rendering their findings untenable. As shown in this study, when more efficient fixed-effects models (i.e., two-way fixed effects of region and year) are implemented along with a correction for the heteroskedastic and serially correlated error term, 23 (74 percent) of the policy outcomes are no longer explained by W. After having accounted for heteroskedasticity and autocorrelation, the estimate of the two-way fixed effects of country and year reveal that W is either insignificant or in the counterintuitive direction in 28 (90 percent) of the public policy areas. When region, country, and year are controlled for fixed effects along with a correction for heteroskedasticity and autocorrelation, W is either insignificant or in the counterintuitive direction in 27 (87 percent) of the selectorate models.

FIXED EFFECTS, HETEROSKEDASTICITY, AND AUTOCORRELATION

As noted above, Morrow et al.'s selectorate model controls for fixed effects by focusing on the interaction effect between geographic region and year. In *The Logic of Political Survival*, they note that "to alleviate the problem that our results might be the consequence of spurious temporal or spatial effects, in every cross-sectional, time-series analysis we include the interaction of geographic region and year as a set of fixed-effect dummy variables . . . each analysis includes a variable for Europe in 1950, Europe in 1951, North America in 1950, North America in 1951, and so on" (136). Unfortunately, the inclusion of the interaction between region and year is insufficient to control for the fixed effect due to the omission of its constitutive terms in their model specification. Furthermore, because the fixed-effects selectorate model neglects the time-invariant effect of the country and fails to take into account heteroskedasticity and autocorrelation, its coefficients and standard errors are biased, causing significance tests to be unreliable.

Fixed effects, in general, explore the relationship between independent and dependent variables within a unit (country, region, person, company, etc.). Each unit has its own individual characteristics that may or may not influence the independent variables (e.g., being a male or female might influence one's opinion on a certain issue). When implementing fixed effects, researchers operate under the assumption that they are controlling for something within an individual unit that may impact or bias the predictor or outcome variables. Fixed effects remove the effect of time-invariant characteristics from the predictor variables so that researchers can have a more precise assessment of the predictors' net effect (Wooldridge 2002; Greene 2003). This was the rationale behind the selectorate model with fixed effects. The researchers claimed that the presence of a set of fixed-effect dummy variables "makes our tests especially demanding, since we have removed any temporal and spatial factors that might be the actual explanation for shifts in the values of our dependent variables" (Bueno de Mesquita et al. 2003, 137).[4]

However, the claim becomes questionable when Morrow et al.'s selectorate model with fixed effects is closely scrutinized. This study notices that without adequate explanations, the fixed-effects selectorate model deviates from a standard fixed-effects model. A standard econometric model that takes into account two-way fixed effects of region and year is generally written in this form:

$$PublicPolicyOutcome_{irt} = \alpha + \beta_1 W_{irt} + \beta_2 ExecutiveConstraints_{irt} + v_r + \mu_t + \varepsilon_{irt} \text{ [Equation 1].}$$

In this equation, $PublicPolicyOutcome_{irt}$ is predicted by W_{irt} and Executive-Constraints$_{irt}$ while controlling for the two-way fixed effects of region and year.[5] In the notation $PublicPolicyOutcome_{irt}$, i denotes the country, r denotes the region, and t denotes the time period. The v_r's refer to a full set of regional dummies capturing any time-invariant characteristics that may be correlated with W or the level of executive constraints.[6] The fact that v_r has no t subscript indicates that it remains constant over time. The μ_t's refer to a full set of time effects reflecting common trends in the level of $PublicPolicyOutcome_{irt}$ that may be associated with W or the level of executive constraints. The fact that μ_t has neither i nor r as subscripts indicates that it is stable across countries or regions. The error term ε_{irt} captures all other omitted factors that may affect PublicPolicyOutcome$_{irt}$, with $E(\varepsilon_{irt})=0$ for all i, r, and t. Standard pooled ordinary least squares (OLS) regression may be used to estimate Equation 1 if the space and time dimensions of the pooled data can be ignored. However, when the true model is given by Equation 1 and the v_r's or the μ_t's are correlated with W or executive constraints, then standard pooled OLS estimators become biased and inconsistent. Even though ε_{irt} is assumed to be uncorrelated with the predictors, we know that standard pooled OLS estimators will also become biased and inconsistent if either v_r or μ_t is correlated with any of the predictors (see Wooldridge 2002; Greene 2003; Acemoglu et al. 2008).

As indicated above, Morrow et al. assume that the region-specific effects vary across years; accordingly, their selectorate model is built to control for the interaction of region and year instead of estimating separately the region-specific and the year-specific effects. In other words, the selectorate model deviates from the standard fixed-effects model by including only an interaction term between region and year and not its constitutive terms. It is written in the following form:

$$PublicPolicyOutcome_{irt} = \alpha + \beta_1 W_{irt} + \beta_2 ExecutiveConstraints_{irt} + v_r{}^*\mu_t + \varepsilon_{irt} \text{ [Equation 2].}$$

In this equation, $v_r{}^*\mu_t$ is an interaction term between v_r and μ_t.[7] Compared to Equation 1, this model specification does not consider the region effects, v_r, and the year effects, μ_t, separately. Bueno de Mesquita et al. (2003, 136, 137) provide no rationale for including the interaction term without its two constitutive terms but simply assert, "we generally do not discuss the fixed effects in the text, because they are strictly statistical corrections of no substantive interest regarding the tests of our theory. Their presence, however, makes our tests especially demanding, since we have removed any temporal and spatial factors that might be the actual explanation for shifts in the values of our dependent variables." However, this is an erroneous assertion because the interaction term of region and year fails to effectively "[remove] any temporal and spatial factors that might be the actual explanation for shifts in the values of our dependent variables."

Readers are not informed why it is that the interaction fixed-effects model in Equation 2 excludes all constituents of the interaction term, a choice that is contrary to common practice, which requires us to include all constitutive terms in a model specification for interaction models (Brambor, Clark, and Golder 2006; Bai 2009). When researchers omit constitutive terms, their results are biased and, therefore, their inferences and conclusions are inaccurate. The estimates reported by Morrow et al., then, are biased because their interaction fixed-effects model fails to include all constitutive terms (i.e., region and year) and so does not in fact "[remove] any temporal and spatial factors that might be the actual explanation for shifts in the values of [their] dependent variables."

The inefficiency of Morrow et al.'s interaction fixed-effects model can be attributed to the fact that it imposes restrictions on factors and factor loadings. Bai's (2009) study discusses these restrictions and offers econometric proofs of the disadvantages associated with the unwarranted use of interaction fixed-effects models; in order to save space, this study does not deal with those details. Instead, following Bai's recommendation, this study turns to the Hausman test statistic in order to evaluate which specification (Equation 1 or Equation 2) provides a more precise estimation for the data. Hausman's specification test compares an estimator I (which is supposed to remain consistent) with an estimator II (which is efficient under the assumption being tested); the null hypothesis conveys that the estimator II is indeed an efficient (and consistent) estimator of the true parameters (Hausman 1978). When the Hausman test is conducted against Morrow et al.'s selectorate data, the standard fixed-effects model in Equation 1 turns out to be a better choice than the specification in Equation 2.

It is also important to note that the standard fixed-effects model in Equation 1 is based on the assumption that the error term follows classical assumptions— that is, $\varepsilon_{irt} \sim N(0, \sigma^2)$. However, because the i index refers to cross-sectional observations and the t index refers to time series observations, the classical assumption for ε_{irt} is unlikely to hold. In other words, the cross-sectional, time-series data analysis of fixed effects is likely to report biased estimates due to the fact that the error term is heteroskedastic or serially correlated. When the error variance is heteroskedastic (for example, when the variance depends on the value of one or more of the independent variables), the estimated standard errors will be spurious, causing significance tests to be unreliable. In addition, when there is autocorrelation over time, the estimated standard errors from OLS regression are biased in a way that is not remedied with an increase in sample size (Wooldridge 2002; Greene 2003). For these reasons, researchers should consider a likelihood-ratio test for heteroskedasticity and a Wooldridge test for autocorrelation prior to the running of regression models. (The null hypothesis of the former test is no heteroskedasticity; that of the latter is no first-order correlation [Wooldridge 2002; Drukker 2003].) The results of these tests show that the null hypotheses are rejected, indicating that the selectorate model calls for correction of both panel heteroskedasticity and temporally correlated errors.

To demonstrate the importance of employing standard fixed effects along with a correction for heteroskedasticity and autocorrelation, this study replicates Morrow et al.'s (2008, 397–99) 31 selectorate models; these results appear in the first column in Table 3.1.[8] In order to remain consistent with Morrow et al.'s research, and for the sake of simplicity, this study's discussion focuses on *W* and executive constraints. *W* is a normalized ordinal measure ranging from 0 to 1 (i.e., 0, 0.25, 0.50, 0.75, and 1). The executive constraints variable is also a normalized measure; its smallest value is 0, and its greatest is 1. Having obtained the same results as Morrow et al., the replication is a success. These results are reported in columns 1a and 1b in Table 3.1. *W* shows significance in 28 out of 31 (90 percent) of the selectorate models. Columns 2a and 2b present the results obtained after controlling for standard fixed effects and after correcting for heteroskedasticity and autocorrelation in the selectorate models. A total of 23 (74 percent) of the policy outcomes are no longer explained by *W*. It should also be noted that the correction for heteroskedasticity and autocorrelation yields robust standard errors, a factor that Morrow et al. neglected to implement in their model estimation. Using robust standard errors has become common practice in empirical studies. Because they are typically larger than nonrobust standard errors, this practice raises the bar for significance tests and thus should be viewed as an effort to draw more accurate inferences and conclusions.

The standard fixed-effects model removes the effect of time-invariant characteristics related to region and year but not to country.[9] In existing empirical studies, country fixed effects are more commonly controlled for than are region fixed effects due to the fact that the unit of analysis for pooled data is more often country-year rather than region-year. In this sense, it is crucial to consider that the political system of a particular country (rather than region) could, for example, have some effect on trade or GDP. Because Morrow et al.'s data format is also cross-national, time series, the major source of potential bias in the selectorate model is the likelihood that something within the country (as opposed to the region) will impact *W* or executive constraints. Of course, if Morrow et al.'s data were constructed in cross-regional, time-series format, controlling for the regional characteristic would make more sense. It appears that by using the interaction fixed effects of region and year for the cross-national, time-series

TABLE 3.1   Reanalysis of the Selectorate Model

Dependent Variable	Region-Year Interaction Replicated		Region and Year Robust SEs†		Country and Year Robust SEs		Region, Country, and Year Robust SEs		Region-Year Interaction and Country Robust SEs	
	W	Exe Con	W	Exe Con	W	Exe Con	W	Exe Con	W	Exe Con
	1a	1b	2a	2b	3a	3b	4a	4b	5a	5b
Log Income	2.21*** (0.11)	0.32*** (0.08)	2.14* (1.05)	0.31 (0.38)	0.12 (0.10)	-0.13 (0.10)	0.13 (0.16)	-0.13 (0.06)	0.01 (0.03)	-0.08*** (0.02)
% Investment	4.44*** (0.93)	-3.48*** (0.64)	4.12 (2.89)	-3.24 (0.58)	-0.71 (2.48)	-1.33 (1.76)	-0.75 (2.19)	-1.33 (0.97)	-0.19 (0.93)	-1.39* (0.72)
% Save	7.46*** (1.49)	-2.97*** (1.03)	7.80 (5.07)	-2.89 (3.53)	2.49 (2.38)	-4.28* (2.50)	2.26 (2.64)	-4.27* (2.12)	2.31* (1.33)	-4.26*** (0.10)
Consumption	-6.70** (2.34)	-1.96 (1.63)	-6.65 (7.50)	-1.77 (3.70)	1.24 (3.00)	-0.61 (2.57)	1.24 (3.07)	-0.61 (2.17)	2.02 (1.53)	-1.77 (1.20)
Expenditures Reported	0.69** (0.24)	1.49*** (0.17)	0.76** (0.26)	1.83*** (0.18)	0.56 (0.48)	0.63 (0.41)	0.56 (0.48)	0.63 (0.41)	0.30 (0.46)	0.27 (0.35)
Expenditures	-1.32 (2.09)	3.67** (1.42)	-0.85 (4.89)	3.30 (1.97)	-2.42 (5.21)	-0.06 (4.34)	-3.08 (2.90)	0.04 (1.33)	-4.26* (2.36)	0.77 (1.153)
Kleptocracy	-4.57* (2.66)	-0.56 (1.71)	-3.99 (4.68)	-0.99 (2.20)	-2.33 (4.73)	-0.61 (4.95)	-2.33 (2.68)	-0.61 (1.70)	-1.84 (1.66)	-0.51 (1.81)
Civil Liberties	0.98*** (0.11)	3.17*** (0.08)	0.92* (0.39)	3.17*** (0.37)	0.46 (0.35)	2.28*** (0.29)	0.54* (0.21)	2.25*** (0.36)	0.60*** (0.12)	2.30*** (0.11)
Political Rights	2.15*** (0.10)	3.43*** (0.08)	2.10** (0.50)	3.42*** (0.35)	2.04*** (0.36)	0.66*** (0.32)	2.13** (0.45)	2.63*** (0.44)	2.11*** (0.18)	2.73*** (0.13)
Tax Revenue Reported	2.51*** (0.27)	0.90*** (0.21)	2.06*** (0.27)	0.96*** (0.21)	-1.53* (0.67)	-0.25 (0.69)	-1.53* (0.67)	-0.25 (0.69)	-2.09*** (0.60)	0.37 (0.55)
Per Capita Income Reported	2.01*** (0.23)	1.37*** (0.19)	1.82*** (0.23)	1.43*** (0.18)	-2.18** (0.94)	1.04 (1.18)	-2.18** (0.94)	1.04 (1.18)	-2.86*** (0.74)	4.42 (0.60)

	(1)	(2)	(3)	(4)	(5)	(6)	(7)	(8)	(9)	(10)
War (Interstate or Civil)	-0.65*** (0.18)	-0.07 (0.15)	**-0.22** (**0.17**)	-0.09 (0.13)	**-1.08*** (0.24)**	-0.11 (0.17)	**-1.08*** (0.24)**	-0.11 (0.17)	-0.83*** (0.23)	-0.03 (0.19)
Education Expenditures	1.15*** (0.17)	0.80*** (0.13)	**1.07** (**0.70**)	0.74 (0.45)	**-0.62*** (0.32)**	0.31 (0.35)	**-0.60*** (0.22)**	0.30 (0.20)	**-0.72*** (0.11)**	0.55*** (0.09)
Average Years of Education	1.77*** (0.22)	1.59*** (0.17)	**1.67** (**1.29**)	1.61* (0.52)	**0.19** (**0.20**)	0.01 (0.16)	**0.19** (**0.11**)	0.01 (0.13)	0.22*** (0.06)	-0.03 (0.06)
Illiteracy Rate	-11.23*** (1.94)	-6.02*** (1.50)	**-10.18** (**6.34**)	-4.95 (6.13)	**0.66** (**1.45**)	2.56* (1.40)	**0.63** (**0.86**)	2.57* (0.86)	**-0.21** (**0.29**)	0.06 (0.28)
Female Secondary Education	-3.53*** (1.07)	-0.35 (0.86)	**-3.42** (**2.59**)	-0.65 (1.22)	**-0.82** (**1.78**)	0.55 (1.37)	**-1.17** (**1.90**)	0.73 (1.76)	**-1.33** (**1.11**)	-0.17 (0.69)
Life Expectance	8.42*** (0.76)	2.47*** (0.58)	**8.86** (**4.62**)	1.99 (2.24)	**1.53** (**1.07**)	-0.63 (0.87)	**1.30** (**0.73**)	-0.48 (0.61)	0.68* (0.34)	0.05 (0.28)
Death Rate	-3.21*** (0.41)	0.16 (0.31)	**-3.20** (**2.45**)	0.28 (1.72)	**0.24** (**0.83**)	0.21 (0.62)	**0.48** (**1.20**)	0.08 (0.59)	**-0.19** (**0.28**)	-0.26 (0.21)
Infant Mortality	-36.67*** (3.39)	-8.20*** (2.53)	**-37.36** (**29.14**)	-7.57 (16.00)	**-2.79** (**6.17**)	-5.20 (4.54)	**-0.19** (**4.09**)	-6.60* (2.91)	**-1.02** (**1.78**)	-9.39*** (1.47)
Health Expenditures	1.56*** (0.43)	0.79** (0.33)	**1.50** (**1.52**)	0.79 (0.92)	**-0.29** (**0.47**)	0.62 (0.46)	**-0.29** (**0.26**)	0.62 (0.33)	**-0.11** (**0.28**)	0.56* (0.28)
Doctors per 1,000 People	0.47*** (0.14)	-0.14 (0.10)	**0.45** (**0.26**)	-0.10 (0.25)	**0.17** (**0.11**)	0.06 (0.11)	**0.18** (**0.21**)	0.05 (0.07)	**0.02** (**0.07**)	0.01 (0.05)
Hospital Beds per 1,000 People	2.94*** (0.64)	0.36 (0.47)	**2.65** (**1.96**)	0.24 (1.03)	**-0.21** (**0.25**)	0.52 (0.32)	**-0.26** (**0.19**)	0.54 (0.38)	**-0.17** (**0.22**)	0.68** (0.24)
Rate of Low Birth Weight	-6.85*** (1.93)	2.06 (1.45)	**-7.40** (**5.87**)	2.11 (3.47)	**-2.88*** (1.35)**	0.42 (1.14)	**-3.05** (0.79)**	0.50 (0.71)	**-2.64** (**1.60**)	0.31 (1.22)
Immunization Rate of One-Year-Olds for Measles	13.37*** (2.72)	-5.46** (2.05)	**12.95** (**7.17**)	-4.95 (4.36)	**1.01** (**8.11**)	-2.47 (5.66)	**1.76** (**4.07**)	-2.72 (7.89)	**0.82** (**3.53**)	-3.22 (3.16)
Immunization Rate of One-Year-Olds for DPT	22.16*** (2.67)	-4.97** (2.00)	**22.59** (**6.26**)	-4.99 (4.02)	**3.96** (**7.78**)	-3.50 (5.25)	**4.84** (**6.35**)	-3.77 (6.01)	**2.05** (**3.09**)	-3.23 (2.16)

continued

TABLE 3.1 continued

Dependent Variable	Region-Year Interaction Replicated		Region and Year Robust SEs†		Country and Year Robust SEs		Region, Country, and Year Robust SEs		Region-Year Interaction and Country Robust SEs	
	W	Exe Con	W	Exe Con	W	Exe Con	W	Exe Con	W	Exe Con
	1a	1b	2a	2b	3a	3b	4a	4b	5a	5b
Access to Safe Drinking Water	17.05*** (5.57)	5.83 (4.32)	16.15 (15.19)	6.29 (9.81)	-1.76 (4.31)	3.73 (3.71)	-2.54 (2.56)	4.18 (3.34)	-1.75 (3.38)	3.52 (2.20)
Gov't Expenditures on Social Security	0.69 (0.72)	1.41** (0.56)	0.46 (1.29)	1.49 (1.09)	-0.15 (0.74)	0.64 (0.77)	-0.15 (0.48)	0.64 (0.49)	-0.45 (0.39)	0.49 (0.30)
Openness to Trade	19.74*** (3.77)	-0.74 (2.92)	20.36 (19.92)	-2.47 (13.46)	-1.45 (3.21)	-0.11 (3.39)	-1.65 (2.54)	-0.09 (3.83)	-2.90 (1.77)	0.20 (1.85)
Black Market Exchange Premium	-0.20** (0.08)	-0.09 (0.06)	-0.26 (0.26)	-0.03 (0.12)	-0.29 (0.35)	0.34 (0.30)	-0.31 (0.17)	0.35* (0.14)	-0.18 (0.12)	0.26** (0.09)
Corruption Index	6.47*** (0.82)	-0.24 (0.57)	6.27* (3.10)	-0.34 (1.75)	0.08 (0.90)	0.53 (0.56)	0.08 (0.80)	0.53 (0.46)	0.03 (0.91)	0.68 (0.61)
Construction Expenditures	-7.37 (5.82)	-0.65 (4.10)	-7.16 (15.69)	-0.71 (9.29)	-5.53 (6.81)	-2.38 (5.91)	-5.53 (9.90)	-2.38 (5.71)	-4.87* (2.53)	-5.41* (2.43)

Note: Robust standard errors, corrected for heteroskedasticity and autocorrelation.

***$p < .001$, **$p < .01$, *$p < .05$, one-tailed tests

data, Morrow et al. fail to effectively remove the time-invariant characteristic of the country. Given the structure of Morrow et al.'s pooled data collected across country and year, it is, for the time being, necessary to control for the country-specific effect. In doing so, this study can better verify the robustness of the selectorate model's empirical findings.[10] Columns 3a and 3b show two-way fixed effects of country and year along with a correction for heteroskedasticity and autocorrelation. W is either insignificant or in the counterintuitive direction in 28 out of 31 (90 percent) of the selectorate models.

The results presented so far have been based on either two-way fixed effects of region and year (i.e., Models 2a and 2b) or two-way fixed effects of country and year (i.e., Models 3a and 3b). The former do not consider country-specific effects because they ignore the uniqueness of each country, while the latter fail to control for the specific characteristics of the region to which any individual country belongs. Models 4a and 4b in Table 3.1 are built to remedy the potential weaknesses of each of the two-way fixed-effects models by incorporating three-way fixed effects of region, country, and year.[11] As shown in Models 4a and 4b, when region, country, and year are controlled for fixed effects along with a correction for heteroskedasticity and autocorrelation, W is either insignificant or in the counterintuitive direction in 27 (87 percent) selectorate models. Interestingly, when country fixed effects are incorporated into the interaction fixed-effects estimations of Morrow et al.'s selectorate models, W is either insignificant or in the counterintuitive direction in 24 (77 percent) of the models. Models 5a and 5b in Table 3.1 report the results.

One might argue that the inclusion of fixed effects controlled for country, year, and region removes all institutional variation from the available sample. However, such a criticism contradicts the rationale behind Bueno de Mesquita et al.'s selectorate model building where they first implemented the interaction fixed effects (disregarding the fact that it was not correctly specified and thus failed to remove the consequences of spurious temporal or spatial effects). Indeed, all of Bueno de Mesquita et al.'s statistical models (with a single exception) take into account the interaction fixed effects; but once again, in Bueno de Mesquita et al.'s (2003, 137) own words, the presence of a set of region and year dummies "makes [their] tests especially demanding, since [they] have removed any temporal and spatial factors that might be the actual explanation for shifts in the values of [their] dependent variables." By accounting for time-invariant characteristics such as country, year, and region, this study has corrected the misspecification of the interaction fixed-effects model of Bueno de Mesquita et al. and has been able to assess the W variable's net effect more accurately than ever before.

CONCLUSION

The relationship between democratic institutions and public policy outcomes has emerged as an important research area in the study of political science. Bueno de Mesquita et al.'s *The Logic of Political Survival* attempts to provide theoretical and empirical direction for this research. The present study, however, shows that there are inherent flaws in the research design of the selectorate model and that those flaws negatively affect the validity of its estimated results. It finds, first, that the selectorate model relies on a less than adequate fixed-effects estimator that focuses on an interaction term of region and year in which all constitutive terms are omitted. Second, it fails to remove the effect of time-invariant characteristics such as country. Finally, it suffers from heteroskedasticity and autocorrelation problems. When these issues are properly addressed, the results (as shown in column 4a) indicate a causal effect of W in only 4 (13 percent) of the public policy areas (i.e., civil liberties, political rights, interstate or civil war, and rate of low birth weight). These results shed serious doubt on the empirical applicability of the selectorate model and, due to the lack of empirical evidence, run counter to the claim that the selectorate theory "is surprisingly broad in its implications" (Bueno de Mesquita et al. 2003, xi). In fact, the empirical results reported in Table 3.1 seem to indicate the opposite insofar as the only statistical model to garner empirical support in a consistent manner was that of political rights.

CHAPTER 4

Examining the Predictability of the Selectorate Theory

Which Aspect of Democracy Explains Better, the Winning Coalition or Civil Liberties?

If the facts don't fit the theory, change the facts.
ALBERT EINSTEIN

Understanding the different effects of democratic regimes remains an important issue for academics and policy makers alike (see Gowa 1999; Bernhard, Broz, and Clark 2002; Broz 2002; Choi and James 2007; Gibler 2007, 2008; Svolik 2008; Hayes 2012). For example, the recent debate between Bueno de Mesquita et al. (2003), Clarke and Stone (2008), and Morrow et al. (2008) has contributed to the advancement of our scientific knowledge regarding the variety of public policy outcomes produced by features of democratic political systems. At the heart of this debate is the question of whether the effect produced by the size of the minimum winning coalition (W) is stronger than the effects produced by other democratic institutions. By regressing a wide range of public policy outcome variables on W and the residuals of democracy, Bueno de Mesquita et al.'s original study presents evidence that W outperforms the residualized democracy variable, which was introduced to avoid the criticism that the democracy variable overlaps conceptually with W.

However, Clarke and Stone's study calls into question the findings of Bueno de Mesquita et al. by demonstrating that democracy, in fact, outweighs W, rather than the other way around. Clarke and Stone's study econometrically demonstrates that Bueno de Mesquita et al.'s estimations are biased and inconsistent due to their having used the residualized democracy variable in place of the original. In response to Clarke and Stone's methodological critique, Morrow et al.'s study questions the validity of including both W and the democracy variable in the same selectorate model "[on the grounds that] all but one element in the estimation of W is also used by Polity to estimate Democracy" (394). For this reason, Morrow et al.'s study offers a "refined" selectorate model, emphasizing the importance of controlling for aspects of democracy that are not captured by the *W* variable. Morrow et al.'s refined selectorate model relies on an alternative set of econometrics by replacing the democracy variable with constraints on the chief executive. The executive constraints variable is collected from the Polity data set. Morrow et al.'s study reports that for 25 (81 percent) out of the 31 different public goods and private benefits, *W* explains more of the variance than does the executive constraints measure.

Morrow et al.'s findings that *W* outperforms executive constraints might be convincing if the study had offered a theoretical explanation of how executive constraints differ from *W* regarding the provision of public goods. More importantly, it should be noted that the executive constraints variable is not capable of capturing those democratic characteristics that are not part of the selectorate theory. For example, its data construction is such that it assigns the highest level of executive constraint to many autocracies as well as democracies (e.g., Egypt scores 7—the highest level of executive constraints—although its political system is generally considered to be autocratic). Because Morrow et al.'s empirical models employ a measure of executive constraint that cannot properly differentiate between democracies and autocracies, their inferences and conclusions are erroneous.

Furthermore, the refined selectorate model fails to incorporate civil liberties as a determining factor. Because leaders who promote and respect civil liberties are democratic and not autocratic, civil liberties are a more precise measure of the exclusive features of democratic governments.[1] This study argues that a civil liberties variable, as measured by Freedom House's civil liberties index, has important advantages over the use of executive constraints as a measure of democracy that does not overlap with *W*. When the civil liberties variable is incorporated as a remedy for the erroneous selectorate model specification, more than 62 percent of Morrow et al.'s analysis loses statistical support. Specifically, the effect of *W* fades in 9 out of the 29 selectorate models; furthermore, the size of the coefficient of *W* is smaller than that of civil liberties in 9 out of the remaining 20 models. It is also important to note that this study lends support to the claims of Clarke and Stone by finding that the provision of one core public good (i.e., Interstate or Civil War) and two private goods (i.e., Black Market Exchange-Rate Premium and Construction Expenditures) have no relation to coalition size.

The subsequent argument is presented in five sections. Drawing on the concept of time inconsistency (Kydland and Prescott 1977; Bernhard, Broz, and Clark 2002; Broz 2002), the first section identifies the weaknesses of the selectorate theory in terms of its capacity to predict policy outcomes. After having conceptualized civil liberties as an essential and exclusive feature of democratic regimes, section two presents a causal explanation of how it is that countries with high levels of civil liberties are likely to be better at providing public goods than are countries that simply have large winning coalitions. The third section is a discussion of how to test the civil liberties hypothesis, while the fourth presents the empirical results and a discussion of their implications. Finally, section five summarizes the key findings and contributions of the present study.

THE SELECTORATE THEORY'S STRENGTH
IS ALSO ITS WEAKNESS

To summarize, Bueno de Mesquita et al.'s (2003) selectorate theory stipulates that in order to maintain power, political leaders must always satisfy the winning coalition. The winning coalition, in democratic countries, is the number of people whose support is needed for a leader to be reelected. The theory provides a systematic account of the relationship between the minimum winning coalition and the universality of government spending and presents a detailed formal mathematical model supported by logical proofs; it claims a broad applicability across political systems as well as the capacity to explain a large number of public policy outcomes.

The rationale behind Bueno de Mesquita et al.'s claim in *The Logic of Political Survival* is that "[political leaders] spend the revenue raised in a manner designed to help keep incumbents in office, particularly by sustaining support among members of their winning coalition" (8). This logic assumes that leaders attempt to maximize the welfare of their winning coalition in a consistent manner; accordingly, large winning coalitions produce successful public policies. However, such an assumption ignores the political reality that leaders often have incentives to change public policies in an effort to appease their winning coalition and bolster their chances for reelection. As Freeman (2002, 901) points out, "the motivations of elected officials are such that they consistently 'distort' what would otherwise be 'optimal [public] policy,' thereby creating unnecessary, harmful levels of inflation, reduced output, etc." In a similar vein, Lizzeri and Persico (2001) maintain that politicians may sometimes choose not to provide socially desirable public goods because the benefit of such goods is not as easily targeted to the winning coalition as are the benefits of pork-barrel spending.

Put formally, elected officials often find it politically advantageous to deviate from a stated policy stance, therefore leading to an inadequate provision of public goods. Milton Friedman (1968), a recipient of the Nobel Prize in Economics, warned us long ago of this kind of political opportunism and, accordingly, suggested the introduction of a constitutional rule requiring constant economic growth as a way to avoid the hazardous public effects of self-interested politicians. As the constitution is incredibly difficult to change, Friedman proposed to provide a sort of insurance against political opportunism. Of course, there are a very few countries whose public policy decisions avoid the taint of political self-interest, even with a constitutional guarantee. As in the United States, the Bank of Korea and the Bank of Japan relinquish independent authority over monetary policy to elected officials who meddle with it primarily for political advantage (Chung 2000). Similarly, in his *Financial Times* article, Stephen King (2013) also observes that "whether they like it or not, central bankers are being dragged into the political fray.... Central bankers are making decisions that are more political than economic." In this sense, we can see that the assumption of the selectorate theory fails to realistically account for the effects of political opportunism, thereby ignoring the problem of time inconsistency.

Flynn E. Kydland and Edward C. Prescott (1977) were awarded the Nobel Prize in Economics on October 11, 2004, for their development of the concept of time inconsistency. Time inconsistency refers to a situation where a decision maker's preferences change over time in such a way that what is preferred at one time is inconsistent with what is preferred at another time. In democratic countries, elected leaders are easily tempted, for the sake of political survival, to depart from ideal strategies aiming to safeguard or improve national well-being (e.g., fiscal soundness). Instead, politicians are likely to increase public expenditure over the short term in the effort to accommodate the demands of their winning coalition, thus ensuring their reelection, but to introduce an entirely different policy post-election even while feigning a follow-through on their original positions. For example, it may be ideal in the long run for a national economy to maintain low inflation policies, but politicians may nonetheless encourage high inflation rates in order to achieve economic expansion and increased employment in the short term; such conditions, they assume, will boost their chances of reelection. Of course, the "true state of the world" will be revealed long after these leaders are out of office (Bernhard, Broz, and Clark 2002; Broz 2002; Mersch 2006). Overall, the desire of politicians to redistribute real income to their pre-election winning coalitions creates a time inconsistency problem; that is, it would be wrong to assume that their behavior will remain consistent over time.

More specifically, the desire to remain in office subjects democratic leaders to electoral pressures that encourage them to use monetary policy as a tool to generate temporary economic growth and expansion in employment in the period leading up to an election. From this point of view, it is uncommon that a politician facing an upcoming election will consider the long-term trade-offs between employment and inflation or the overall health of the national economy; thus, time inconsistency is a clear factor. Not surprisingly, self-interested politicians will feign ignorance of the fact that only unanticipated inflation leads to lower unemployment insofar as it depresses real wages. For example, the South Korean government is notorious for artificially lowering the rate of inflation before national elections; but upon the swearing in of the newest batch of officials, monetary policies quickly revert while the government as a whole rhetorically affirms the independence of the Bank of Korea (Chung 2000). Government partisanship is another factor likely to affect the choice of monetary commitments. Because a left-wing government's winning coalition is the working class, it tends to emphasize public policies claiming to increase employment and wealth redistribution; a right-wing government, on the other hand, must satisfy business and middle-class interests by controlling the rate of inflation (Bernhard, Broz, and Clark 2002). When changes in government partisanship occur, the direction of public policy shifts dramatically; this causes policy decision making to be rather inefficient. Consequently, the problem of time inconsistency is likely to distort the provision of public goods in democratic countries, often resulting in high deficits and, therefore, an increase in future taxes.[2]

Morrow et al. (2008, 394) predict that "large winning coalitions induce leaders to shift public policy away from private benefits and toward the provision of public goods." However, when the time inconsistency problem is taken into account, it becomes clear that the predictive power of the selectorate theory weakens. The need for democratic leaders to secure the loyalty of their winning coalition is the very root of the time inconsistency problem. The pervasiveness of political opportunism and the effects of partisanship indicate that democratic leaders do not necessarily work harder to provide socially desirable public goods, as they move away from the private benefits of pork-barrel spending. In other words, there is a possibility that when democratic leaders provide public goods in a consistent manner, they do so because of some third factor that does not conform to the logic stipulated in Bueno de Mesquita's selectorate theory. The next section suggests civil liberties as an important third factor and discusses how it is that countries with high levels of civil liberties provide public goods more consistently than do countries with large winning coalitions.

DEMOCRACY, CIVIL LIBERTIES, AND POLICY OUTCOMES

Despite the fact that what exactly constitutes democracy is contested and controversial, scholars typically categorize democracies in terms of electoral versus liberal (see Munck 2009). Electoral democracy refers to the existence of free and fair elections, while liberal democracy goes beyond free elections to refer to governments that sanctify majority rule and the consent of the governed, and promote a respect for civil liberties and political rights. As the Economist Intelligence Unit (2008, 16) puts it, "all modern definitions, except the most minimalist, also consider civil liberties to be a vital component of what is often called 'liberal democracy.'" In the same vein, Skaaning (2008, 36) aptly points out that "Robert A. Dahl (1971, 3) [also] incorporates freedom of speech and press as well as freedom of association and assembly in his polyarchy criteria."

In their construction of the Polity data set, Marshall and Jaggers (2007, 13) conceptualize democracy in terms of three essential and interdependent features:

> [First] is the presence of institutions and procedures through which citizens can express effective preferences about alternative policies and leaders. Second is the existence of institutionalized constraints on the exercise of power by the executive. Third is the guarantee of civil liberties to all citizens in their daily lives and in acts of political participation.

The first concept associated with democratic institutions and procedures has provided the basis for the construction of four of the five subcomponents of the Polity composite index: competitiveness of executive recruitment, openness of executive recruitment, regulation of participation, and level of competitiveness in elections. The second concept associated with democracy provides the basis for constraints on the chief executive, which is the last subcomponent of the Polity composite index. Unfortunately, the third basic feature of democracy— civil liberties—has not yet been developed as an individual component of the Polity composite index due to the shortage of data coverage associated with it. In Diamond's (1999, 9) words, Polity acknowledges civil liberties as a major component of democracy but, because of the paucity of data, does not incorporate them. As is discussed below, the collection of existing civil liberties data started in the early 1970s and so does not reach as far back as the Polity data, which begin in the year 1800. Interestingly, while Bueno de Mesquita et al. (2003) consider coalition size to be conceptually related to democracy,[3] they also refer to civil liberties as a key contributory feature of definitions of democracy. They point out that democratic "characteristics include, among others, an independent judiciary, free press, *civil liberties*, legal constraints on leaders, norms of conduct, and reliance on law" (73, emphasis added). In *Measuring Democracy*, Munck (2009, 128–29) conceptualizes democracy as a system of governance that highly respects standard political rights associated with the election of representatives as well as with civil liberties. Such political rights include the following: universal and equal voting rights, the right to run for office, the right to free and fair elections, and the right to regular elections. The civil liberties discussed above include the following: the opportunity for citizens to participate in the political process, which means the right to a free press and to information, as well as to the freedoms of association, assembly, expression, and movement. In sum, it is reasonable to argue that, conceptually, democracy is closely related to the presence of civil liberties in that a high degree of democratic governance manifests as a political respect for the freedoms of thought, speech, and assembly (Bollen 1986, 1990).

This study argues that civil liberties are a compelling causal factor in the explanation of successful public policy outcomes insofar as they increase the transparency of the political process, thereby improving the public's ability to monitor and criticize the government with respect to its policy commitments. This argument is borrowed from the insights of economic studies on the functioning of governments versus competitive markets (Brautigam 1992; Isham, Kaufmann, and Pritchett 1997) as well as from a political scientific understanding of political system transparency (Broz 2002). In competitive markets, shareholders and consumers provide incentives to the managers of private corporate firms to try to maximize profits. If a manager's job performance is substandard, shareholders will punish the firm by switching to alternative investments. Likewise, consumers can marginalize firms by purchasing products and goods from alternative companies. However, shareholders and consumers do not apply similar pressure to public officials through these channels of choice. Instead, they encourage the government to perform better by advocating for transparency, accountability, openness, predictability, and the rule of law. As Hirshman (1970) puts it, efficacy is promoted in competitive markets through the exercise of citizen choice, while governments are principally disciplined through the exercise of citizen voice—that is, by the freedom of citizens to monitor the actions of their elected officials for incidences of opportunism as well as the liberty to vote out of office those politicians who have been deemed unsatisfactory for whatever reason.

The concept of "citizen voice" is different from the selectorate theory. While the former treats a population as an active "policy demander" whose interest is its own well-being, the latter focuses primarily on winning coalitions as instruments employed by politicians seeking reelection who, essentially, function as "policy suppliers."[4] As noted above, the predictability of the selectorate theory is not as strong as it could be due to its singular focus on the policy supply side and its ignorance of the realities of political opportunism and partisanship. This theoretical simplification of a complex reality undoubtedly leaves out a—if not the—crucial political element: the time inconsistency problem, which, we posit, often leads to poor public policy making. This study turns the selectorate theory on its head by drawing attention to how it is more often the policy activism of a citizenry, rather than the political maneuvering of a body of politicians, that leads to healthy policy outcomes. This study argues that the empowerment of citizen voice makes it more difficult for a government to betray public interest by espousing one policy and effecting another; in doing so, it helps to significantly resolve the time inconsistency problem.

It is commonly accepted that high levels of civil liberties (including freedom of individual expression, dissent, and criticism, a pluralistic and free media, and the ability of groups to organize) increase the transparency of the political process. If political decision making were transparent, governments would find it difficult to avoid the costs of political opportunism by concealing their actions from the public; this, again, reduces the problem of time inconsistency. When democratic citizens enjoy high levels of civil liberties, they can more effectively voice policy preferences and monitor for incidences of opportunism; thus they are more likely to be active participants in the public decision-making processes. Therefore, citizen voice goads the efficacy of political leaders with respect to the provision of public policies (Broz 2002; Choi and James 2007). For instance, countries with high levels of civil liberties are the most likely to enhance the availability and quality of general health care due to the fact that their citizens have the opportunity to more vigorously pressure public officials to improve the physical and mental health of the population; that is, what will matter to these politicians is not only the support of their winning coalition but also the support of the public as a whole. More importantly, because civil liberties enhance the transparency of the political process, they allow an attentive public to act as government watchdogs, to obtain information on government reneging, and to hold it accountable; once again, these activities reduce the problem of time inconsistency. Consequently, we would expect to see a higher level of civil liberties associated with substantial increases in health care expenditure.

There are several empirical studies showing the potential link between respect for civil liberties and good governance. For example, Isham, Kaufmann, and Pritchett (1997) report evidence that, all other things being equal, countries with the strongest civil liberties have government projects with an economic rate of return that is between 8 and 22 percent higher than those countries with the weakest civil liberties. In a similar vein, Harms and Ursprung (2002) report that countries that respect civil and political freedoms are likely to attract a higher level of foreign direct investment. Drèze and Sen (1989) provide evidence that countries with a high quality of civil liberties, and in particular those with a strong free press, are the same as those that have never experienced a major famine. Broz (2002) finds evidence that civil liberties are associated with a decrease in political opportunism with respect to central bank independence and control of inflation. With these conclusions in mind, this study hypothesizes that as the quality of civil liberties improves, greater efficacy in government action will follow, and thus the provision of public policies should increase.

HOW TO TEST THE HYPOTHESIS OF CIVIL LIBERTIES

The civil liberties hypothesis is tested using a standard statistical model of democracy studies. In particular, Morrow et al.'s (2008) refined selectorate model is the frame of reference for this examination of the effect of civil liberties on policy outcomes. The selectorate model is built to assess the independent effect of W while controlling for other aspects of democracy. More specifically, Morrow et al.'s study examines the effect of W while controlling for the democratic effects of division of power (and other constraints) on executive power through the Polity subcomponent XCONST. In other words, the introduction of executive constraints is meant to assuage the criticism that the significance of W is an artifact of omitted variable bias. Thus, W and the omitted variable are incidentally correlated and/or W is simply a proxy for the true omitted variable.

For the purposes of Morrow et al.'s study, the choice of the subcomponent of the Polity composite index could be theoretically justifiable insofar as XCONST is intended to capture the checks and balances between the executive and other decision makers in democratic societies. However, when it comes to the operationalization of the Polity subcomponent, Marshall and Jaggers (2007) take note of the decision-making restrictions imposed by any accountability group, whether democratic or autocratic. While the term typically refers to legislatures in Western democracies, such accountability groups may also include "the ruling party in a one-party state; councils of nobles or powerful advisors in monarchies; [or] the military in coup-prone polities" (23).

For example, if any accountability group or groups have effective authority equivalent to or greater than the executive in most areas of political activity, a country receives 7 points on a scale of 1 (least constrained) to 7 (most constrained). This coding procedure mistakenly allows a country with a high score on executive constraints to be considered a democracy by default, even if it is, in fact, an autocracy in which the executive is checked by some powerful nonpolitical group. For example, Egypt shows a high level of executive constraint but is considered an autocratic state. Egypt scores 7 on the Polity subcomponent of executive constraints, while its Polity composite score is 1 on a scale of 10 (most autocratic) to 10 (most democratic). From the standpoint of empirical analysis, then, it is difficult to support Morrow et al.'s claim that the individual constraint component of the Polity composite index is associated with the diffusion of power under a democracy. Executive constraints are not, in fact, a sufficient indicator of a unique subfeature of democracy because they refer to a type of political constraint that may be found in any type of polity.

In fact, Morrow et al.'s original data set shows that 29 percent of the total observations (those that score the three highest levels with respect to executive constraints) can be identified as nondemocracies.[5] The substantial percentage of nondemocracies in the data set poses a significant challenge to the treatment of the Polity individual component of executive constraints, XCONST, as an accurate and unique indicator of democracy. Although including both W and XCONST in the same selectorate model allows for Morrow et al. to assess the separate effect of each of the two variables, it does not achieve the intended objective because XCONST cannot be considered a feature unique to democratic regimes. That is, although Morrow et al. may be correct in justifying the theoretical necessity of controlling for other aspects of democracy in the refined selectorate model, their chosen measure, executive constraints, is inadequate for empirical verification. Other scholars have been equally critical of the use of XCONST as a measure of democratic political constraints. For example, Glaeser et al. (2004, 277) point out that "a closer look at how [XCONST] is constructed immediately reveals that it is an outcome measure, which reflects not the [executive] constraints, but what happened in the last election. When countries have inconsistent electoral experiences, their scores fluctuate wildly. For example . . . Argentina fluctuates between the worst scores under generals, and the best ones after elections, even when the elected leaders undermine the legislature and courts."

While the problematic construction of XCONST nullifies its capacity to act as a control for a unique feature of democracy, civil liberties offer a more reliable control variable. Civil liberties are a unique feature of democratic regimes because democratic regimes are the only ones that promote and respect civil liberties (see Dahl 1971; Bollen 1986, 1990; Bueno de Mesquita et al. 2003; Skaaning 2008; Munck 2009). The underlying assumption of democratic rule is that an increase in the quality of civil liberties will equate to an increase in the common good, therefore contributing to the stability of the regime itself. Of course, evaluating the quality of civil liberties across countries and time is a challenging task. Fortunately, Freedom House (2009) has compiled a measure of the quality of civil liberties that is considered to be the best data set currently available in terms of both scope and quality (Keech 2009, 9). On both theoretical and empirical grounds, Freedom House's civil liberties variable is an accurate measure of different aspects of democracy and can serve to remedy Morrow et al.'s erroneous selectorate model specification. As discussed above, civil liberties represent a unique feature of democratic regimes. Accordingly, the civil liberties variable meets Morrow et al.'s theoretical requirement that "any test of selectorate theory against a measure of democracy must parse out elements of democracy that lie outside that theory from those within it" (394). A measure of civil liberties has no connection with Polity because it is not part of the Polity data collection, thus eliminating the concern that it may be empirically (though not theoretically) correlated with the size of the winning coalition. Morrow et al.'s study operationalizes the key concept of the winning coalition size based on three of the Polity subcomponents (i.e., competitiveness of executive recruitment, openness of executive recruitment, and competitiveness of political competition) as well as an indicator of the nature of the regime (which comes from Arthur Banks 2010).

Unlike the size of the winning coalition, Freedom House's civil liberties measure taps into democratic qualities such as the freedoms of expression and belief, associational and organizational rights, the rule of law, and personal autonomy. Freedom House assesses the degree of an individual's freedom to develop views, institutions, and personal autonomy apart from the state on a seven-point scale, with low scores indicating a high degree of freedom and high scores indicating a low degree of freedom. The conceptual and empirical distinctions included in Freedom House's civil liberties variable helps to facilitate Morrow et al.'s original theoretical objective, which aims at "[weeding] out the effects of the size of the winning coalition on the provision of public goods and private benefits from other features of political systems commonly associated with democracy" (395).

REPLICATION AND REASSESSING THE
REFINED SELECTORATE MODEL

This section replicates Morrow et al.'s (2008, 397–99) 29 selectorate models, which appear in the first column in Table 4.1, and then introduces the civil liberties variable as a competing feature of democracy outside of the selectorate theory.[6] It should be noted that Morrow et al. originally reported 31 models in total, but the replication of this study is limited to 29 models because the two remaining models are related to the civil liberties variable. One of those models considers the quality of civil liberties as the dependent variable; it is considered to be a public good provided by political leaders who are accountable to a large winning coalition, but not by those accountable to a small one. The other excluded model employs political rights as the dependent variable. Given the fact that the political rights variable captures the capacity of individuals to participate freely and effectively in the selection of political leaders and policy makers (Freedom House 2009), it may overlap with the concepts of winning coalition size and civil liberties. Therefore, it is not included in our own empirical tests. This study indeed finds that both W and civil liberties positively affect the provision of political rights, although the coefficient size of the former is much smaller than that of the latter.

Some may find it of interest to understand how Bueno de Mesquita et al. (2003) justify the use of civil liberties as one of their dependent variables. As discussed, Bueno de Mesquita et al. refer to civil liberties as one of the essential characteristics of democratic institutions, arguing that democratic "characteristics include, among others, an independent judiciary, free press, *civil liberties*, legal constraints on leaders, norms of conduct, and reliance on law" (73, emphasis added). Nonetheless, the decision of Bueno de Mesquita et al. to use civil liberties as a public good provided by leaders is supported with the following claim: "rather than defining coalition size, as we will show, many of the features that contribute to definition of democracy are themselves expected, endogenous policy consequences that follow from having a large winning coalition and a large selectorate" (73). If this claim is correct, legal constraints on leaders, which are conceived of as another key democratic feature by Bueno de Mesquita et al., could also be treated as a policy outcome. In other words, whereas executive constraints would serve as a dependent variable in the original selectorate model, it serves as an independent variable in the presence of W in the "refined" selectorate model put forward by Morrow et al. (2008). However, they do not tell us what warrants the move of the presumed outcome variable of executive constraints to the right-hand side of the equations.

Perhaps it is worth thinking about Morrow et al.'s intent in the context of Judea Pearl's (2000) causality graph approach. Suppose that the dependent variable of interest is Y. Morrow et al. would argue that W causes executive constraints and Y. However, Morrow et al.'s refined selectorate model indicates that executive constraints cause Y, without disputing the fact that W affects executive constraints. In this framework, the claim made by Morrow et al. is precarious without our being able to identify a causal path. Unfortunately, the present study encounters a similar difficulty when testing both civil liberties and W in the same selectorate model; therefore it must be left for future research.

This study now turns to a discussion of its main predictors. W is a normalized ordinal measure ranging from 0 to 1 (i.e., 0, 0.25, 0.50, 0.75, and 1). The seven-point executive constraints variable is also normalized such that its smallest value is 0 and its greatest is 1. For easy interpretation, the civil liberties variable is rerecorded as 7 for the highest level of civil liberties and 1 for the lowest one. Next, by dividing the sum of the score minus 1 by 6, the score is transformed into an ordinal scale of 0 to 1; this conversion facilitates a comparison between the effect of civil liberties and the effects of W and executive constraints. The comparison of effect sizes of W, executive constraints, and civil liberties follows the same approach as that of Morrow et al., who directly compare the magnitude of estimated coefficients after normalization. To assuage the concern that the sizes of these two coefficients are not comparable because they are not on the same scale, this study also analyzes the substantive effects of each variable to determine their relative importance. Finally, because the theoretical expectations are directional, a one-tailed significance test at the 0.05, 0.01, and 0.001 levels is employed.

When set in competition with civil liberties, the effect of W is washed out in 9 (31 percent) out of the 29 selectorate models: Expenditure Reported, Expenditure, Kleptocracy, War (Interstate or Civil), Female Secondary Education, Health Expenditures, Government Expenditures on Social Security, Black Market Exchange-Rate Premium, and Construction Expenditures. The magnitude of the coefficient of W is weaker than that of civil liberties in 9 (45 percent) out of the remaining 20 models where both W and civil liberties show statistical significance: Log Income, Tax Revenue Reported, Per Capita Income Reported,

Education Expenditures, Life Expectance, Hospital Beds per 1,000 People, Immunization Rate of One-Year-Olds for DPT, Access to Safe Drinking Water, and Corruption Index. A more detailed discussion follows.

Table 4.1 shows the nine insignificant selectorate models; to save space, only three theoretically interesting variables are reported in the table, whereas measures of fit such as the R-squared and log-likelihood are not included. Model 1 in each tabulation, which is categorized by each public policy outcome, shows a successful replication of Morrow et al.'s original findings. Model 2 expands Model 1 by including the civil liberties variable. Because civil liberties are, as noted, conceptually and empirically distinguishable from both W and executive constraints, it cannot be claimed that these variables suffer from multicollinearity. As shown, the W variable fails to exert an independent effect on the provision of public goods and private benefits in all nine tabulations, while the civil liberties variable fails in only two cases of public goods (i.e., Expenditure and Construction Expenditures). In general, the significance of W disappears in the presence of the civil liberties variable. The fourth tabulation, more specifically, indicates that the likelihood of War (Interstate or Civil), which is one of the most important public welfare enhancements (see Bueno de Mesquita et al. 2003, 179–86), turns out to be unrelated to coalition size. In addition, the reassessment of the provision of two major private goods—Black Market Exchange-Rate Premium in the eighth tabulation and Construction Expenditures in the ninth—creates additional doubts about the validity of the predictions made by the selectorate model (Bueno de Mesquita et al., 200–207). This study finds that there are no close empirical connections between coalition size and the outcomes for the two private goods; therefore it is difficult to argue that large coalitions discourage the production of private goods by a government.

Although there is no conceptual or empirical overlap between executive constraints and civil liberties, one might still insist that the inclusion of the former inflates the coefficient of the latter and deflates that of W. To address this concern, the executive constraints variable in Model 2 is dropped; the results are shown in Model 3 in Table 4.1. While the coefficient of W becomes statistically significant in only two re-estimated models (see the first and eighth tabulations), the coefficient of civil liberties remains statistically significant in 7 out of 9 areas of public policies. Even in the two models where both W and civil liberties are associated with Expenditure Reported or Black Market Exchange-Rate Premium, after the executive constraints variable is dropped, the coefficient size of W is much smaller than that of civil liberties (0.37 versus 2.62 and 0.15 versus 0.37, respectively).

In their personal note online,[7] Morrow et al. (2008) explain why Clarke and Stone (2008) find no general relationship between W and policy outcomes in

TABLE 4.1   Reanalysis of the Selectorate Model and Democracy

(1) Expenditure Reported

	Model 1	Model 2	Model 3	Model 4
W	0.69** (0.24)	0.25 (0.26)	0.37* (0.19)	0.76*** (0.18)
Executive constraints	1.49*** (0.17)	0.06 (0.20)		
Civil liberties		2.69*** (0.20)	2.62*** (0.17)	2.18*** (0.14)

(2) Expenditure

	Model 1	Model 2	Model 3	Model 4
W	-1.32 (2.09)	-1.51 (2.24)	1.17 (1.80)	1.72 (1.67)
Executive constraints	3.67** (1.42)	2.81* (1.64)		
Civil liberties		1.35 (1.90)	2.28 (1.63)	1.72 (1.50)

(3) Kleptocracy

	Model 1	Model 2	Model 3	Model 4
W	-4.57* (2.66)	-1.32 (2.89)	0.53 (2.37)	-0.19 (2.17)
Executive constraints	-0.56 (1.71)	2.56 (1.97)		
Civil liberties		-9.71*** (2.54)	-8.30*** (2.20)	-8.22*** (1.99)

(4) War (Interstate or Civil)

	Model 1	Model 2	Model 3	Model 4
W	-0.65* (0.18)	0.31 (0.61)	-0.02 (0.38)	-0.18 (0.37)
Executive constraints	-0.07 (0.15)	0.59 (0.53)		
Civil liberties		-2.96*** (0.60)	-2.98*** (0.52)	-2.11*** (0.40)

(5) Female Secondary Education

	Model 1	Model 2	Model 3	Model 4
W	-3.53*** (1.07)	-1.32 (1.16)	-1.17 (0.90)	-1.43* (0.84)

(6) Health Expenditures

	Model 1	Model 2	Model 3	Model 4
W	1.56*** (0.43)	0.65 (0.43)	0.31 (0.34)	1.28*** (0.34)

Executive constraints	−0.35	1.03			Executive constraints	0.79**	−0.49		
	(0.86)	(1.03)				(0.33)	(0.36)		
Civil liberties		−4.13***	−3.51***	−3.44***	Civil liberties		2.94***	2.69***	1.36***
		(0.99)	(0.84)	(0.78)			(0.37)	(0.32)	(0.31)

	(7) Government Expenditures on Social Security					(8) Black Market Exchange-Rate Premium			
	Model 1	Model 2	Model 3	Model 4		Model 1	Model 2	Model 3	Model 4
W	0.69	−0.11	−0.33	1.01*	*W*	−0.20**	−0.15	−0.15*	−0.17*
	(0.72)	(0.73)	(0.59)	(0.56)		(0.08)	(0.11)	(0.08)	(0.08)
Executive constraints	1.41**	−1.04			Executive constraints	−0.09	0.03		
	(0.56)	(0.68)				(0.06)	(0.09)		
Civil liberties		5.21***	4.18***	2.01***	Civil liberties		−0.43***	−0.37***	−0.33***
		(0.84)	(0.67)	(0.63)			(0.12)	(0.10)	(0.09)

	(9) Construction Expenditures			
	Model 1	Model 2	Model 3	Model 4
W	−7.37	0.49	−0.32	−3.13
	(5.85)	(6.50)	(4.98)	(4.61)
Executive constraints	−0.65	3.94		
	(4.10)	(5.10)		
Civil liberties		−2.63	0.01	5.01

Note: Numbers in parentheses are standard errors.

*p<0.05; **p<0.01; ***p<0.001, one-tailed tests.

the presence of Polity Democracy. They contend that in any model the measure with "more differentiation in its scale" will tend to soak up most of the variance and appear statistically significant; they believe that this is why in Clarke and Stone's (2008) analysis Democracy, which is on a twenty-one-point scale, has a bigger effect than W, which is on a five-point scale. One might raise a similar concern regarding the W and civil liberties variables.[8] This study deals with such a concern by rescaling the civil liberties variable from seven points to five points, recategorizing the last four highest categories into two (i.e., categories 4 and 5 together and categories 6 and 7 together),[9] and then converting it to an ordinal scale of 0 to 1. Such a rescaling makes the civil liberties variable equivalent to W, as both are now on a five-point scale (i.e., 0, 0.25, 0.5, 0.75, and 1). Model 4 in Table 4.1 shows the results with the rescaled civil liberties variable; they do not substantially deviate from those in Model 3. In general, civil liberties performs better than W, indicating that the effect of civil liberties on policy outcomes is not likely to be a statistical artifact.

Moving on to the remaining twenty models, this study finds that both W and civil liberties achieve statistical significance in the presence of executive constraints. Table 4.2 provides a summary comparison of the two theoretically interesting variables, W and civil liberties. As shown in the first tabulation, there are nine cases where the civil liberties coefficient is larger than that of the winning coalition size, meaning that the presence of a high quality of civil liberties may have a more substantial influence on the provision of public goods in a democracy than would the presence of large winning coalitions. Note that in the cases of Tax Revenue Reported and Per Capita Income Reported, which are identified as two of the core public goods by Bueno de Mesquita et al. (2003, 179–86), the effect of W is much weaker than that of civil liberties. In the second tabulation, there are only eleven cases whose estimated results are consistent with the theoretical predictions of Morrow et al.'s study; the significant effect of W on the outcome of public goods is confined only to those eleven areas of public policy, indicating limited empirical support for the selectorate theory. Overall, the results of this reanalysis warrant an adjustment to Morrow et al.'s claim that "the size of the winning coalition predicts the provision of public goods and private benefits more strongly than other elements of democracy" (399).

Again, the comparison of the sizes of the estimated coefficient of W and civil liberties follows the same approach as that adopted by Morrow et al. However, the comparison method may not be entirely convincing, as the variables are not on the same scale; thus an alternative method is needed to compare the substantive effects of each variable. To calculate a baseline probability for each public policy outcome against which to make comparisons, this study sets all the variables at their means except for the dichotomous variables (which are set at 0). It then adjusts the variables of greatest interest, one at a time, to discern

TABLE 4.2   Comparison of the Coefficient Sizes of W and Civil Liberties

(1) 9 Cases: The Effect of Civil Liberties Is Greater Than That of W

	Log Income	Tax Revenue Reported	Per Capita Income Reported	Education Expenditures	Life Expectancy	Hospital Beds per 1,000 People	Immunization for Measles	Safe Drinking Water
W	1.67*** ⇨	2.09*** ⇨	1.08*** ⇨	1.00*** ⇨	6.35*** ⇨	1.78* ⇨	11.88*** ⇨	13.25* ⇨
Civil liberties	2.30***	4.05***	3.66***	1.35***	8.12***	2.28***	12.30***	28.30***

	Corruption Index
W	4.66*** ⇨
Civil liberties	5.92***

(2) 11 Cases: The Effect of W Is Greater Than That of Civil Liberties

	% Investment	% Save	Consumption	Average Years of Education	Illiteracy Rate	Death Rate	Infant Mortality Rate	Doctors
W	5.19*** ⇦	7.71*** ⇦	-6.93** ⇦	1.50*** ⇦	-10.38*** ⇦	-3.17*** ⇦	-28.93*** ⇦	0.53** ⇦
Civil liberties	-1.97*	2.76*	0.97	1.25***	-8.16***	-1.03**	-28.07	-0.24

	Low Birth Weight	Immunization for DPT	Open to Trade
W	-5.87** ⇦	20.43*** ⇦	33.63*** ⇦
Civil liberties	-4.63**	13.73***	25.60***

*p<0.05; **p<0.01; ***p<0.001, one-tailed tests.

the change in the predicted probability of each policy outcome. Table 4.3 reports the substantive effects of the same twenty variables reported in Table 4.2. The substantive analysis is largely consistent with what is reported in Table 4.2, with the exception of the case of infant mortality rate in the second tabulation. We see that empirical support for the selectorate theory again vanishes with the inclusion of civil liberties.

This study discusses two possible concerns regarding the empirical analysis reported thus far. The first concern would be that civil liberties, like executive constraints, could be an aspect of both democratic and autocratic regimes. The argument made against the use of executive constraints as a control variable capable of capturing an exclusive feature of democratic regimes was the fact that 29 percent of the total observations in the selectorate data set exhibit high levels of executive constraints but low levels of democracy. In contrast, only 0.5 percent of the total observations in the selectorate data set indicate high levels of civil liberties but low levels of democracy.[10] This statistic strongly suggests that civil liberties are an exclusive feature of democratic regimes. Simply put, no civil liberties mean no democracy.

The second concern is that since W may be correlated with civil liberties in an empirical sense, an estimation of the independent effect of each of these two variables may be problematic. Morrow et al.'s selectorate data set shows a correlation of 0.87 between W and executive constraints and a correlation of 0.76 between W and civil liberties. Scholars suspect a severe multicollinearity problem if the correlation exceeds 0.80 (see Belsley, Kuh, and Welsch 1980; Greene 2003; Gujarati 2003). Accordingly, the use of executive constraints as a competitor with W, as is the case in Morrow et al.'s refined selectorate model, is much more likely than is the inclusion of civil liberties to complicate estimation. More importantly, because Bueno de Mesquita et al. (2003, xi) argue that all political leaders are constrained by "the winning coalition—the subgroup of the selectorate who maintain incumbents in office and in exchange receive special privileges," W may have some conceptual overlap with executive constraints when the winning coalition is also considered to be one of the accountability groups.

It is also important to note that the rationale for introducing civil liberties into the selectorate model is to account for potential omitted variable bias. Although this study acknowledges that a trade-off exists between omitted variable bias and the inefficiency caused by potential multicollinearity, Morrow et al.'s refined selectorate model nonetheless needs to be re-refined because civil liberties are an essential feature of democracy not included in the original selectorate theory, but executive constraints are not. In addition, it should be reemphasized that the correlation between civil liberties and W is lower than that between executive constraints and W.

TABLE 4.3 Examination of the Coefficient Sizes of W and Civil Liberties

(1) 9 Cases: The Effect of Civil Liberties Is Greater Than That of W

	Log Income	Tax Revenue Reported	Per Capita Income Reported	Education Expenditures	Life Expectancy	Hospital Beds per 1,000 People	Immunization for DPT	Safe Drinking Water
W	26% ⇨	23% ⇨	12% ⇨	32% ⇨	11% ⇨	50% ⇨	19.6% ⇨	23% ⇨
Civil liberties	**36%**	**53%**	**52%**	**44%**	**14%**	**66%**	**19.9%**	**54%**

	Corruption Index
W	311% ⇨
Civil liberties	**543%**

(2) 10 Cases: The Effect of W Is Greater Than That of Civil Liberties

	% Investment	% Save	Consumption	Average Years of Education	Illiteracy Rate	Death Rate	Infant Mortality Rate	Doctors
W	**28%** ⇦	**60%** ⇦	**-9%** ⇦	**34%** ⇦	**-25%** ⇦	**-25%** ⇦	**-42%** ⇦	**50%** ⇦
Civil liberties	-9%	17%	1%	27%	-21%	-9%	-43%	-16%

	Open to Trade	Immunization for DPT	Low Birth Weight
W	**71%** ⇦	**36%** ⇦	**-43%** ⇦
Civil liberties	48%	22%	-37%

CONCLUSION

In exploring the empirical link between democracy and public policy, Clarke and Stone (2008) have engaged in a constructive dialogue with Morrow et al. (2008). While the former have offered a methodological solution to the short-coming of the original selectorate model, the latter have refined the model in response to the critique. While they reject Clarke and Stone's econometrics (which reintroduced the original measure of democracy in the selectorate model), Morrow et al. attempt to better illustrate the substantive point (made in *The Logic of Political Survival*) concerning aspects of democracy that are unaccounted for by *W*. However, Morrow et al.'s empirical analysis is imprecise insofar as it mistakenly assumes executive constraints to be a feature unique to democratic regimes. The executive constraints variable is not, in fact, an appropriate control because, by virtue of its construction, it also allows for authoritarian forms of executive constraint to be categorized the same as democratic forms. Thus, Morrow et al.'s study incorrectly specifies the selectorate model in the sense that a not-really-relevant variable of democracy, executive constraints, is included.

In addition to its discussion of the empirical modeling, this study has been critical of the selectorate theory for its ignorance of the time inconsistency problem; that is, the selectorate theory fails to take into account the fact that politicians in a democracy do not necessarily work harder than other leaders to provide socially desirable public goods in a consistent manner (Kydland and Prescott 1977; Bernhard, Broz, and Clark 2002; Broz 2002). Therefore, this study introduces to the selectorate model a civil liberties variable as a competing third factor capable of capturing an essential and unique feature of democracy. The empirical analysis reveals that in the presence of civil liberties the winning co-alition size variable becomes insignificant in 9 out of the 29 selectorate models. Additionally, 9 of the remaining 20 models reveal that the magnitude of the co-efficient of the civil liberties variable is much greater than that of the winning coalition size. The selectorate theory fails to withstand empirical scrutiny in light of the fact that *W* outperforms civil liberties in only 11 (38) percent out of 29 cases. Indeed, when the civil liberties variable is controlled for, the effect of *W* disappears or is much weaker in a wide range of public policies. The findings of this study, then, do not provide support for Bueno de Mesquita et al.'s claim that the selectorate theory "is surprisingly broad in its implications" (Bueno de Mesquita et al. 2003, xi).

This study makes two important contributions to the advancement of our scientific knowledge in reference to the connection between democracy and public policy. First, it contributes to the democracy literature by conceptualiz-ing civil liberties as an exclusive feature of democratic regimes. It puts forward a novel causal explanation of how it is that countries with high levels of civil liberties may put serious effort into guaranteeing desirable policy outcomes. This explanation underscores the power of individual voters as active policy demanders or government watchdogs, an approach quite different from that of the selectorate theory, which focuses solely on the behavior of politicians as policy suppliers. This study argues that because countries with high levels of civil liberties suffer less from the time inconsistency problem than countries with large winning coalitions, the policy outcomes of the former should be better than those of the latter. The empirical analysis supports the argument that civil liberties are indeed a compelling causal factor in the explanation of the provision of public goods across countries and time. In other words, this study goes beyond the selectorate theory to offer us a better understanding of democratic policies, by conceptualizing civil liberties as the foundation for citizen voice, which, in turn, counters the parochial interests of power-seeking politicians. Second, this study argues that Morrow et al.'s study incorrectly specifies its empirical model by including the inappropriate measure of executive constraints from the Polity data set. Since Polity evaluates executive constraints by considering any and all accountability groups that have effective authority equivalent to or greater than the executive, many autocracies also score high on executive constraint when their executive power is defined by a single party or a military junta. In this context, Morrow et al.'s claim that executive constraints measure the diffusion of power under democracy is inaccurate, and therefore their finding that W outperforms democracy as a predictor of various public and private goods is less convincing.

CHAPTER 5

Democracy, Foreign Direct Investment, and Outliers

All statistics have outliers.

NENIA CAMPBELL, *Terrorscape*

The detection and correction of outliers and influential cases that violate the normal independent, identically distributed (i.i.d.) assumption about residual errors is one of the most crucial statistical diagnostics that must be performed for ordinary least squares (OLS) regression models. In the face of a heavy-tailed (outlier-prone) error distribution, a regression prediction line tends to track outlying observations, fitting them at the expense of the rest of the sample data in an attempt to minimize the sum of squared errors. The estimated results in such a case will likely lead to incorrect inferences (see Belsley, Kuh, and Welsch 1980; Gujarati 2003; Agresti and Finlay 1997; Hamilton 2004; J. Hoffmann 2004; Kohler and Kreuter 2005). Though the OLS regression model has a long history and is considered the standard way to fit prediction equations to political data, the political science literature has yet to properly address the hazards accompanying the neglect of a proper diagnostic analysis of outliers. This implies that many empirical findings reported by political scientists are, potentially, statistical artifacts. In particular, students of foreign direct investment (FDI) seem to have been largely unaware of the outlier problem despite the fact that their data are typically not normally i.i.d.

Using a simple simulated data set, I demonstrate below how sensitive the substantive results of regression analysis are to the effects of outliers and influential cases. I then revisit two widely cited studies on the effect of regime type on FDI inflows (i.e., Li and Resnick 2003 and Jensen 2003) to further indicate the importance of outlier analysis in the discipline of political science; I argue that accounting for outliers can help to reconcile the otherwise contradictory findings in these two studies. Additionally, I provide evidence that the improper operationalization of the FDI inflows variable causes a serious outlier problem. If FDI inflows are measured in raw dollar amounts, they are highly sensitive to the outlier problem due to a violation of the normal i.i.d. assumption; however, if FDI inflows are measured as a percentage of total GDP, the impact of outliers and influential cases is drastically reduced. Once the FDI data are corrected for the potential outlier problem, I find that democratic countries attract more FDI than do authoritarian ones, and not the other way around.[1]

THE EFFECT OF OUTLIERS ON REGRESSION ANALYSIS: SIMULATION

Outliers may be produced by coding mistakes, measurement errors, or extreme values within collected data. While the first two kinds of outliers are easily corrected once identified, the last requires more careful attention. This is not to say that all outliers are detrimental to OLS regression analysis, but those that fall extremely far from the rest of the data will dramatically influence or alter estimated regression results. Bollen and Jackman (1985, 511–12) point out that "an outlier observation can only be called influential when its deletion from the analysis causes a pronounced change in one or more of the estimated parameters." That is, an influential outlier is one that is capable of pulling the regression line toward itself in a significant way, thus distorting the slope (see Gujarati 2003). Therefore, in pursuit of more meaningful data analysis, outlier diagnostics must differentiate between simple and influential outliers.

Although influential outliers may have unusual values on the dependent variable (i.e., Y outliers) or an unusual combination of values on the independent variables (i.e., X outliers or leverage), I focus specifically on the empirical implications of Y outliers in instances where their presence or absence drastically changes the obtained values of the estimated regression coefficients. To demonstrate this point, I show how certain Y outliers will pull a regression line "off" of the position to which it would otherwise be fitted if the outliers were not included in the data set. Specifically, I show how Y outliers can cause the sign of the coefficient of the independent variable to change (i.e., from a positive to a negative sign).

For the sake of illustration, I generated a data set of 30 observations using the Stata data-generating process.[2] I created a random independent variable of X and an error term of e_1, with a standard normal distribution (i.e., a variable with a mean of 0 and a standard deviation of 1). Next, I created a dependent variable of Y_1 from the equation $Y_1 = 10 + 3.5*X + e_1$. This is an ideal data set by definition insofar as its errors are normal i.i.d. and outliers are not present. Table 5.1 presents summary statistics. Y_1 and X present an ideal regression problem: Y_1 is linearly related with X, and errors come from the normal distribution. Standard OLS regression produces the following prediction equation:

$$\hat{Y}_1 = 9.80 + 3.48\hat{X}$$
$$(0.18) \quad (0.19)^3$$

TABLE 5.1   Descriptive Statistics without Outliers

Variable	Observations	Mean	Standard deviation	Minimum	Maximum
X	30	−0.0452	0.9157	−1.7005	1.6234
e1	30	−0.2002	0.9411	−1.7875	1.9533
Y1	30	9.6415	3.3207	3.2633	16.5067

TABLE 5.2   Descriptive Statistics with Outliers

Variable	Observations	Mean	Standard deviation	Minimum	Maximum
X	30	−0.0452	0.9157	−1.7005	1.6234
e2	30	2.0853	6.8218	−1.7875	23.8900
Y2	30	11.9270	5.5586	5.3061	28.4793

Because the variable X is statistically significant at the 0.001 level, there exists a positive relationship between X and Y_1. The R^2 shows that 92 percent of the total variation in Y_1 is explained by X. These ideal results are now compared with those from an outlier data set.

To construct such a comparison, I change the error value in the ideal data set in observation 8 from 1.27 to 23.89; in observation 12 from 0.78 to 20.98; and in observation 29 from 0.55 to 21.09. I then create another dependent variable of Y_2 from the equation $Y_2 = 10 + 3.5*X + e_2$ where X values are not changed. Thus, we have a second data set where Y_2 is identical to Y_1, but where three Y outliers are the result of the extreme error of observations 8, 12, and 29. Due to the introduction of these three new error values, the mean, 2.0853, of e_2 is much higher than the mean, 0.2002, of e_1 in the ideal data set. Table 5.2 presents a summary of the statistics. The inclusion of outliers has made each statistic in the shaded cells in Table 5.2 larger than its affiliate in Table 5.1. Standard OLS regression with the outlier data set estimates the intercept and slope as follows:

$$\hat{Y} = 11.89 - 0.91\hat{X}$$
$$(1.02) \quad (1.13)$$

In the presence of the three Y outliers, the coefficient of the variable X no longer significantly differs from zero, and the relationship between X and Y_2 becomes negative; the outliers have raised the intercept (from 9.80 to 11.89) and lowered the slope radically (from 3.48 to 0.91); the standard errors are about six times greater than those in the previous prediction equation. In this case, only 2 per-

FIGURE 5.1   OLS Regression Lines

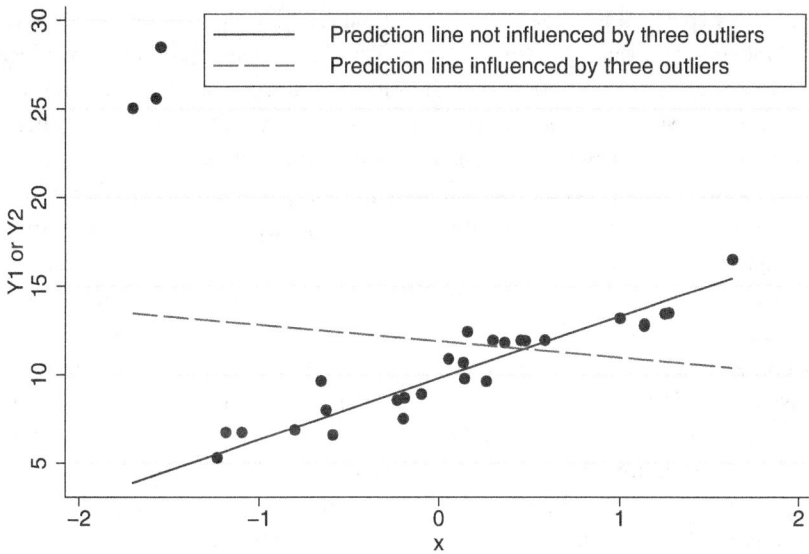

cent of the variation is explained by the X variable, meaning that its explanatory power is much weaker here than in the ideal data set.

Figure 5.1 provides a visual analysis, depicting two regression prediction lines on a simple scatter plot. The solid line predicted from the ideal data set shows a positive relationship between X and Y_1 (i.e., $\hat{Y}_1 = 9.80 + 3.48\hat{X}$), while the long dashed line, resulting from the drastic influence of the three Y outliers in the top left corner, indicates a negative relationship between X and Y_2 (i.e., $\hat{Y}_2 = 11.89 + 0.91\hat{X}$). We can see that the influential Y outliers have dramatically changed the direction of the presumed relationship between dependent and independent variables, thereby producing biased estimates. Figure 5.1 highlights the perils of neglecting Y outlier problems for OLS regression analysis. In a case of extreme Y outliers, the relationship between independent and dependent variables may even be reversed (as shown in Figure 5.1), making statistical inference imprecise and meaningless (see Belsey, Kuh, and Welsch 1980; Agresti and Finlay 1997; Hamilton 2004).

WHY OUTLIERS MATTER FOR STUDENTS OF POLITICAL SCIENCE (AND ESPECIALLY FDI)

Students of political science conduct empirical tests based on causal hypotheses inferred from intuition, conventional wisdom, or theoretical reasoning: "each hypothesis specifies a posited relationship between variables that creates observable implications" (King, Keohane, and Verba 1994, 99). Because hypotheses frequently specify a positive or negative causal relationship between dependent and independent variables, the neglect of Y outlier problems and the reporting of those coefficients that merely corroborate the causal direction of the relevant hypothesis are likely to lead to incorrect inferences that will compromise otherwise scientifically valuable findings. Unlike other serious statistical issues such as multiplicative interaction terms and temporal dependence, this outlier problem continues to go unaddressed in political science research. Furthermore, compared to the problem of multiplicative interaction, the outlier problem is difficult to identify from the empirical result tables that appear in published political studies. For example, looking down the list of the variables in each result table, it is easy to raise a red flag if we see an improper use of multiplicative interaction terms (e.g., if it is missing one of its constitutive terms) (see Braumoeller 2004). However, without obtaining the replication data from the authors and running the proper diagnostic tests of outliers, we will not be able to tell whether empirical findings are distorted by outlying observations. With no method for the quick detection of outliers in published articles and books for which the data are not publicly available, we cannot accurately assess their deviant effects on the estimated results.

Fortunately, in order to illustrate these consequences, I was able to obtain replication data directly from the authors of two articles published in the major international relations journal, *International Organization*, in 2003.[4] Although both articles are recognized for their extension of ongoing debates about democratic institutions to the area of FDI, their contradictory findings about the democracy-FDI link have remained an empirical puzzle. In the first of the two articles, Li and Resnick's study, which questions whether democratic institutions lead to inflows of FDI, sets an extraordinary example in several ways: not only do they identify two causal explanations of democracy, but also their empirical analysis of 53 developing countries during the period from 1982 to 1995 strongly supports their democracy-related hypotheses. Li and Resnick's study reports that while property rights protection is positively related to FDI, democratic constraints on monopolistic behaviors of foreign investors are negatively associated with FDI (Li and Resnick 2003). In a subsequent issue of the journal, then, Jensen's study synthesizes some well-known democracy-related arguments (such as veto players and audience costs) and predicts that democratic institutions encourage more FDI inflows; he finds that the empirical analysis of 114 countries from 1970 to 1997 confirms the positive effect of democratic governance on FDI (Jensen 2003).

Below, I provide an explanation for this empirical puzzle and conclude that Li and Resnick's findings are misleading due to the fact that their regression analysis fails to account for the outlying countries attracting considerably more FDI than average-size countries. More specifically, by revisiting Model 1 as it appeared in Table 1 of Li and Resnick's (2003, 195) study, and Model 13 as it appeared in Table 5 of Jensen's (2003, 606) study, I examine how outlier problems affect the substantive results of each. Both models employ OLS regression because the nature of the dependent variable, FDI inflows, is continuous. I choose Li and Resnick's OLS regression method (i.e., panel-corrected standard errors, or PCSEs with AR[1] correction) in order to compare their empirical findings with Jensen's.[5] This choice is based partly on the fact that Li and Resnick's Model 1 is their main model while Jensen's Model 13 is not;[6] furthermore, although Jensen's Model 13 was presented as part of his sensitivity analysis, its sample consists of developing countries, which corresponds to Li and Resnick's developing countries sample.

Table 5.3 reports my replicated results. The replication of Li and Resnick's model was a success, while that of Jensen's model produced slightly different results, due to the difference in statistical technique. Applying the same significance levels (i.e., *p < 0.10; **p < 0.05; ***p < 0.01) as the two original studies, the replicated results in columns 2 and 3 agree with their original findings with respect to the effects of democratic institutions, which is, of course, the main theoretical and empirical interest of political scientists. As hypothesized, Li and Resnick's model predicts the positive effect of PROPERTY RIGHTS PROTECTION and the negative effect of LEVEL OF DEMOCRACY on FDI inflows; Jensen's model likewise predicts the positive effect of DEMOCRACY. Because the property rights protection variable is not directly related to the outlier problems that affect estimated results, my reexamination focuses mainly on the two models' seemingly contradictory findings: the negative sign of LEVEL OF DEMOCRACY in column 2 and the positive sign of DEMOCRACY in column 3. It is worth noting that despite the fact that Li and Resnick's democracy hypothesis is in opposition to Jensen's, both are measured in the Polity database (on Polity, see Gurr, Jaggers, and Moore 1991). To be precise, Jensen's DEMOCRACY is measured in Polity III, while Li and Resnick's LEVEL OF DEMOCRACY is measured in Polity IV; there is little substantive difference, however, between Polity III and IV.

With reference to these replications, I explain below how to detect outliers with two instrumental diagnostics: a partial regression plot and DFBETAs. I then introduce two possible approaches to control for outliers: the creation of dummy variables and the use of robust regression estimation. Another possible remedy would be the dropping of some outliers from the sample; the deletion of outlying cases one by one allows a researcher to observe the presence of a pronounced change in one or more of the estimated coefficients (see Bollen and Jackman 1985). I do not discuss such an approach here because it has a

TABLE 5.3   The Effect of Democratic Institutions on Inflows of FDI:
Replications

Model 1 of Li and Resnick's Study		Model 13 of Jensen's Study	
PROPERTY RIGHTS PROTECTION	0.0522*** (0.0165)	0.3989*** (0.0782)	LAGGED FDI
LEVEL OF DEMOCRACY	−0.0878*** (0.0254)	0.0165 (0.0407)	MARKET SIZE
REGIME DURABILITY	0.0229*** (0.0091)	0.0771 (0.0778)	DEVELOPMENT LEVEL
POLITICAL INSTABILITY	−0.0172 (0.0191)	0.0285*** (0.0085)	GROWTH
LABOR COST CHANGE	−0.0007 (0.0024)	0.0120*** (0.0024)	TRADE
ECONOMIC SIZE	1.0299*** (0.2855)	0.0061 (0.0115)	BUDGET DEFICIT
ECONOMIC DEVELOPMENT	−0.0973 (0.2836)	−0.0174* (0.0108)	GOVERNMENT CONSUMPTION
ECONOMIC GROWTH	0.0227** (0.0125)	0.0225*** (0.0064)	DEMOCRACY
EXCHANGE-RATE VOLATILITY	−0.0001** (0.0000)		
CAPITAL FLOW RESTRICTIONS	−0.0854** (0.0454)		
WORLD FDI INFLOWS	0.0036*** (0.0009)		
Constant	−25.3194*** (5.5303)	−1.0453 (0.9918)	Constant
Observations	483	1,223	Observations
R-squared	0.21	0.39	R-squared

Note: OLS estimates and standard errors in parentheses are based on panel-corrected standard errors (PCSE)

***$p < .01$, **$p < .05$, *$p < .10$

FIGURE 5.2   Partial Regression Plot: Li and Resnick's Model

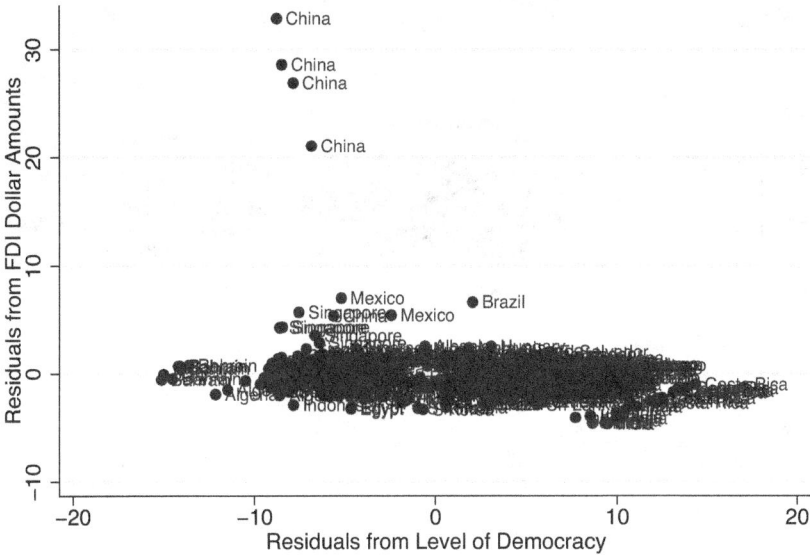

critical flaw; that is, in the discipline of political science, how many published works based on forty or even sixty countries would show the same results if we omitted five of the most extreme outliers? Furthermore, the results of such an approach are similar to those obtained with dummies and robust regression, which are discussed below.

A partial regression plot allows us to visually detect outliers by plotting residuals of variables. It presents a clearer graphic presentation of outliers than does a simple scatter plot. It also enables the detection of other possible violations of OLS assumptions such as curvilinear relationships (Bollen and Jackman 1985, 514).[7] While controlling for other variables, a partial regression plot detects multivariate outliers that are not normal errors and that have the potential to influence multiple regression estimates (see Easterly 2003; J. Hoffmann 2004).

Figure 5.2 displays the partial regression plot for the unexplained portion of FDI inflows against the unexplained portion of LEVEL OF DEMOCRACY in Li and Resnick's analysis. The heavy concentration of points near zero (which is the mean of the residuals) indicates that most observations are unlikely to be outliers. Yet, four observations in the top left corner are identifiable outliers far from the mean of the residuals.[8] The figure shows that these four observations from China, a nondemocratic state that attracts a huge amount of FDI inflows, could be responsible for the negative estimated coefficient for LEVEL OF DEMOCRACY replicated above. The observation years for each outlier are identi-

FIGURE 5.3   Partial Regression Plot: Jensen's Model

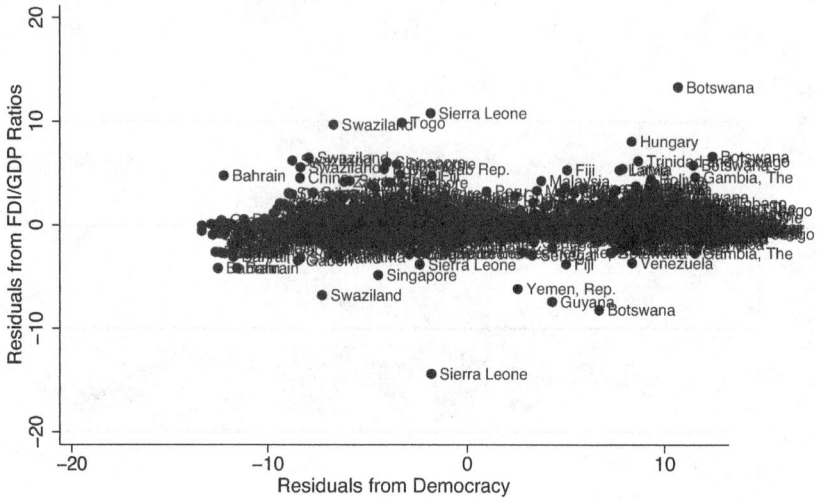

fied as 1995, 1994, 1993, and 1992; given that the study period spans from 1982 to 1995, only the most recent FDI performance of China (i.e., from 1992 to 1995) could be responsible for the negative relationship.[9]

Figure 5.3 shows the partial regression plot for the unexplained portion of FDI inflows against the unexplained portion of DEMOCRACY in Jensen's analysis. Inspection of this figure suggests that there are two apparent outliers (i.e., Botswana and Sierra Leone) in the top right corner and the bottom middle area that could be responsible for the positive relationship between democracy and FDI. We can identify the year 1978 for the outlying observation of democratic Botswana and the year 1985 for nondemocratic Sierra Leone (the entire period of study ranges from 1970 to 1997).

It should be noted that although Figures 5.2 and 5.3 show some large residuals, they are not particularly unusual in terms of their independent variable values. In other words, the two studies under empirical scrutiny are not subject to X outlier problems, but to Y outlier problems. The diagonal elements of the hat matrix also reveal no high leverage, meaning that their X values (or their combination of X values) are not abnormal (see Hoaglin and Welsch 1978). For example, the democracy variable, the main independent variable, is free from the outlier problem.

To further scrutinize the results, I used DFBETAs case statistics that purport to differentiate between simple and influential outliers. DFBETAs are widely used to measure changes either in each regression coefficient independently or in all of the regression coefficients that result when one observation is deleted.

Since the focus of this study is on the relationship between democracy and FDI inflows, DFBETAs are obtained for the coefficient of the two studies' respective democracy variables. Using the threshold of $|DFBETA| > 2/\sqrt{n}$, I identify influential cases that drastically change the coefficient of each democracy variable (i.e., LEVEL OF DEMOCRACY in Li and Resnick's model and DEMOCRACY in Jensen's model) (see Hoaglin and Welsch 1978; Bollen and Jackman 1985). China, from Li and Resnick's model, turns out to have been the most influential observations for the years 1995, 1994, 1993, and 1992; this agrees with our visual analysis of the partial regression plot. Likewise, from Jensen's model, Botswana in 1978 appears to have been the most influential case.[10]

We must then determine how to control for the effects of the farthest outlying and most influential observations of China and Botswana. In other words, we want to understand how much these outliers affect each model's estimated coefficients. Table 5.4 displays the results that we get after having plugged the China and Botswana dummies into the models. The China dummy examines the impact of the four relevant influential outliers (i.e., 1992 to 1995), while the Botswana dummy measures the effect of the one relevant influential outlier (i.e., 1978). The coefficient of the China dummy is statistically significant at the 0.01 level; thus, the outlying observations from authoritarian China lead to an increasing amount of FDI inflows. The inclusion of the China dummy radically alters the magnitude of the coefficient and standard errors for LEVEL OF DEMOCRACY, decreasing each by about a half (i.e., from 0.0878 to 0.0444 and from 0.0254 to 0.0139). This indicates that the negative sign of the democracy variable is drastically influenced by the four Y outliers that represent the recent explosive FDI inflows to nondemocratic China. The R^2 of 66 percent is much larger than the R^2 of 21 percent in the originally replicated model in column 2 in Table 5.3. Similarly, the coefficient of the Botswana dummy in column 3 shows statistical significance at the 0.01 level; thus, the democratic Botswana outlier appears to attract more foreign capital.[11] The presence of the Botswana dummy slightly decreases the magnitude of the DEMOCRACY coefficient, but standard errors shift very little. This indicates that the positive sign of the democracy variable is only marginally affected by the one Y outlier represented by the democratic country of Botswana. The R^2 of 41 percent is a bit larger than the R^2 of 39 percent in the replicated model in column 3 in Table 5.3.

Another way to remedy a model in the presence of influential outliers is to use robust regression estimation. Unlike OLS regression, robust regression resists the pull of Y outliers, giving it better-than-OLS efficiency in the face of nonnormal, heavy-tailed error distribution. Robust regression is an iteratively reweighted least squares procedure that calculates weights for each observation using a Huber function that reduces the weight of observations having larger errors and then bi-weights them from the absolute value of errors; this causes

TABLE 5.4   The Effect of Democratic Institutions on Inflows of FDI: China and Botswana Dummies

Model 1 of Li and Resnick's Study		Model 13 of Jensen's Study	
PROPERTY RIGHTS PROTECTION	0.0197* (0.0147)	0.3773*** (0.0744)	LAGGED FDI
LEVEL OF DEMOCRACY	−0.0444*** (0.0139)	0.0294 (0.0393)	MARKET SIZE
REGIME DURABILITY	0.0102** (0.0053)	0.0820 (0.0767)	DEVELOPMENT LEVEL
POLITICAL INSTABILITY	−0.0056 (0.0081)	0.0238*** (0.0080)	GROWTH
LABOR COST CHANGE	−0.0003 (0.0019)	0.0125*** (0.0024)	TRADE
ECONOMIC SIZE	0.7086*** (0.1983)	0.0055 (0.0106)	BUDGET DEFICIT
ECONOMIC DEVELOPMENT	0.2292 (0.1899)	−0.0191** (0.0101)	GOVERNMENT CONSUMPTION
ECONOMIC GROWTH	0.0070 (0.0072)	0.0205*** (0.0065)	DEMOCRACY
EXCHANGE-RATE VOLATILITY	−0.0001** (0.0000)		
CAPITAL FLOW RESTRICTIONS	−0.1180*** (0.0394)		
WORLD FDI INFLOWS	0.0022** (0.0012)		
China Dummy	22.5413*** (3.7517)	11.6968*** (2.9046)	Botswana Dummy
Constant	−18.8365*** (4.2965)	−1.3539 (0.9270)	Constant
Observations	483	1,223	Observations
R-squared	0.66	0.41	R-squared

Note: OLS estimates and standard errors in parentheses are based on panel-corrected standard errors (PCSE) with AR (1) correction.

***$p < .01$, **$p < .05$, *$p < .10$

weighted least squares regression to drop the change in weights below 0.01.[12] In doing so, it reduces the influence of outliers and influential observations.

Table 5.5 shows the robust regression results.[13] Most intriguing is that the sign of LEVEL OF DEMOCRACY of Li and Resnick's model switches from negative to positive, while that of DEMOCRACY in Jensen's model remains the same. Indeed, democratic institutions have a positive effect on inflows of FDI once Y outlier problems are minimized. It appears that Li and Resnick's original analysis was considerably skewed by outlying and influential Y observations, especially the four China outliers, while Jensen's original analysis was not drastically affected by the presence of Y outliers, even the single case of Botswana.

It should be noted that the results in Table 5.4, obtained from the model with the observation-specific dummies, and those in Table 5.5, from the robust estimates, are not the same. Table 5.4 exposes the effects of the most outlying and influential observations on inflows of FDI by adding the China dummy to Model 1 of Li and Resnick's study and by adding the Botswana dummy to Model 13 of Jensen's study. The results of Table 5.5, on the other hand, are from models that take into account all possible influential cases in their respective robust regression estimates (see Hamilton 2004; J. Hoffmann 2004). Robust regression does not drop China (and the other possibly influential cases), but down-weights it due to the size of its errors. In this way, China has less total influence on the regression line (i.e., the directional sign of the democracy variable), but robust regression estimates still take into account the country's significant role in the FDI economic world.

We now look more precisely at why Li and Resnick's analysis produced misleading results while Jensen's did not. As noted at the outset, the inconsistent empirical findings of these two original studies can be attributed to their respective differences in operationalization of the dependent variable, inflows of FDI. While Li and Resnick measured FDI net inflows in billions of current U.S. dollars (i.e., FDI dollar amounts), Jensen used annual net FDI inflows as a percentage of total GDP (i.e., FDI/GDP ratios).[14] It appears that Jensen's FDI/GDP ratios produced a positive sign for his democracy variable, whereas Li and Resnick's FDI dollar amounts lead to a negative sign for their democracy variable. Unlike the operationalization of FDI dollar amounts, that of FDI/GDP ratios takes into account the different economic size of each country, thereby minimizing the impact of potential outlying observations.[15] Jensen's choice of the FDI/GDP measure leads to the positive sign because it is less likely to violate the outlier assumption than is Li and Resnick's FDI dollar measure. In other words, Li and Resnick's operationalization of the dependent variable inadvertently produces influencing outliers, while Jensen's does not.[16]

In fact, it should be noted that Jensen and McGillivray (2005, 314) recently argued that "[the FDI/GDP ratio] is the best available measure of a country's

TABLE 5.5   The Effect of Democratic Institutions on Inflows of FDI: Robust Regression

Model 1 of Li and Resnick's Study		Model 13 of Jensen's Study	
PROPERTY RIGHTS PROTECTION	0.0039**	0.8001***	LAGGED FDI
	(0.0018)	(0.0078)	
LEVEL OF DEMOCRACY	0.0029**	0.0112	MARKET SIZE
	(0.0016)	(0.0115)	
REGIME DURABILITY	0.0003	0.0222	DEVELOPMENT LEVEL
	(0.0006)	(0.0220)	
POLITICAL INSTABILITY	−0.0078***	0.0062***	GROWTH
	(0.0019)	(0.0025)	
LABOR COST CHANGE	0.0006	0.0013***	TRADE
	(0.0006)	(0.0004)	
ECONOMIC SIZE	0.1262***	0.0045**	BUDGET DEFICIT
	(0.0076)	(0.0023)	
ECONOMIC DEVELOPMENT	0.0348**	−0.0015	GOVERNMENT CONSUMPTION
	(0.0171)	(0.0027)	
ECONOMIC GROWTH	−0.0000	0.0082***	DEMOCRACY
	(0.0021)	(0.0021)	
EXCHANGE-RATE VOLATILITY	0.0000*		
	(0.0000)		
CAPITAL FLOW RESTRICTIONS	−0.0070		
	(0.0059)		
WORLD FDI INFLOWS	0.0001		
	(0.0001)		
Constant	−3.2084***	−0.4252**	Constant
	(0.1871)	(0.2333)	
Observations	483	1,223	Observations

Note: ***$p < .01$, **$p < .05$, *$p < .10$

success in attracting FDI inflows." The FDI/GDP ratio as a dependent variable of FDI is also a standard choice for World Bank economists because it accounts for variation in the economic size of each country (Aykut, Kalsi, and Ratha 2003; see also Ahlquist 2006; Blanton and Blanton 2007). In a theoretical sense, the FDI/GDP measure is the correct choice because students of FDI are interested in investigating whether average democratic or nondemocratic countries induce FDI. That is, their research focus is to find the average of all possible sample countries in each regime type group rather than of one particular country. If the behavior of a particular political regime does not conform to that of the rest of the group (i.e., if China erratically deviates from the general behavioral pattern of nondemocracies), it should have a smaller role in determining the cause of

TABLE 5.6   Li and Resnick's Model 1: Measuring the Dependent Variable in Jensen's FDI/GDP Ratios

Variable	OLS Regression	Robust Regression
PROPERTY RIGHTS PROTECTION	0.0554***	−0.0002
	(0.0221)	(0.0076)
LEVEL OF DEMOCRACY	0.0158	0.0349***
	(0.0188)	(0.0070)
REGIME DURABILITY	0.0125**	0.0150
	(0.0070)	(0.0025)
POLITICAL INSTABILITY	−0.0000	−0.0156**
	(0.0067)	(0.0080)
LABOR COST CHANGE	0.0004	0.0045**
	(0.0028)	(0.0025)
ECONOMIC SIZE	−0.1313*	−0.0249
	(0.0987)	(0.0322)
ECONOMIC DEVELOPMENT	0.6294***	0.3098***
	(0.2383)	(0.0727)
ECONOMIC GROWTH	0.0048	0.0112*
	(0.0132)	(0.0087)
EXCHANGE-RATE VOLATILITY	−0.0001***	−0.0000**
	(0.0000)	(0.0000)
CAPITAL FLOW RESTRICTIONS	−0.1031**	0.0208
	(0.0604)	(0.0251)
WORLD FDI INFLOWS	0.0010	0.0016***
	(0.0011)	(0.0006)
Constant	−1.9011	−1.5759**
	(2.3886)	(0.7943)
Observations	483	483

Note: ***$p < .01$, **$p < .05$, *$p < .10$

change in the dependent variable. In a statistical sense, when our data include some heterogeneous units, "the size or scale effect must be taken into account so as not to mix apples with oranges" (Gujarati 2003, 28).[17]

Table 5.6 shows the results obtained after the dependent variable of Li and Resnick's FDI dollar amounts is replaced with that of Jensen's FDI/GDP ratios in an effort to minimize the detrimental effect of outliers. As expected, the coefficient of the democracy variable in the second column under the OLS regression turns out to be positive, although not statistically significant. However, the coefficient of the democracy variable in the last column under the robust regression shows a positive sign with the 0.01 significance level. These results once again confirm that democratic institutions are positively associated with FDI flows.

CONCLUSION

In this study, I highlight the significance of outlier problems for OLS regression analysis. Unfortunately, students of political science in general, and of FDI in particular, have yet to successfully account for the influence of such observations in their empirical studies. With a simulated exercise, I demonstrate that the failure to properly deal with Y outliers will produce misleading results, the consequences of which may, potentially, be as devastating as an incorrect sign (e.g., a negative rather than a positive sign). By revisiting two well-known studies (i.e., Jensen 2003 and Li and Resnick 2003), I provide evidence that after correcting for the effect of outlying observations, the relationship between democracy and FDI inflows is a positive one. This finding is consistent with Jensen, but in contrast to Li and Resnick. From here we can observe that democratic countries indeed attract more FDI than do authoritarian ones. It is imperative, then, that FDI researchers pay attention to outlying countries, especially those with substantial influence, because the failure to do so may produce misleading results and thus compromise the scientific progress of studies of FDI. A requirement that researchers report the results of robust regression estimation in a brief note may help to prevent future political studies from producing statistical artifacts due to outliers. Just as the coefficient of determination, R^2, provides a reader with crucial information about the proportion of variability in a data set that is accounted for by a statistical model, robust regression results would be instrumental to the evaluation of the effect of potential outlier problems.

Li and Resnick's Model without PROPERTY RIGHTS
PROTECTION

Variable	Replicated	China Dummy	Robust Regression
PROPERTY RIGHTS PROTECTION			
LEVEL OF DEMOCRACY	−0.0881***	−0.0436***	0.0026**
	(0.0263)	(0.0141)	(0.0015)
REGIME DURABILITY	0.0264***	0.0113**	0.0008*
	(0.0091)	(0.0052)	(0.0005)
POLITICAL INSTABILITY	−0.0221	−0.0067	−0.0075***
	(0.0196)	(0.0084)	(0.0018)
LABOR COST CHANGE	−0.0006	−0.0003	0.0006
	(0.0024)	(0.0019)	(0.0006)
ECONOMIC SIZE	1.0827***	0.7259***	0.1197***
	(0.2830)	(0.1958)	(0.0069)
ECONOMIC DEVELOPMENT	0.0717	0.2963**	0.0433***
	(0.2476)	(0.1749)	(0.0154)
ECONOMIC GROWTH	0.0252**	0.0075	−0.0001
	(0.0131)	(0.0073)	(0.0019)
EXCHANGE-RATE VOLATILITY	−0.0001**	−0.0001**	0.0000**
	(0.0000)	(0.0000)	(0.0000)
CAPITAL FLOW RESTRICTIONS	−0.1111***	−0.1276***	−0.0059
	(0.0424)	(0.0389)	(0.0055)
WORLD FDI INFLOWS	0.0048***	0.0026**	0.0002**
	(0.0010)	(0.0011)	(0.0001)
China Dummy		22.6889***	
		(3.7322)	
Constant	−26.6424***	−19.2902***	−3.0580***
	(5.5293)	(4.2157)	(0.1710)
Observations	483	483	483
R-squared	0.21	0.66	

Note: ***$p < .01$, **$p < .05$, *$p < .10$

CHAPTER 6

Explaining the Foreign Direct Investment-Democracy Controversy

Normality of Regression Residuals

[Normality] is required in general for inference making . . . extreme departures of the distribution of Y from normality yield spurious results.
DAVID G. KLEINBAUM, LAWRENCE L. KUPPER, KEITH E. MULLER, AND AZHAR NIZAM, *Applied Regression Analysis and Multivariable Methods*

The foreign direct investment (FDI) Stat Interactive Database of the United Nations Conference on Trade and Development (UNCTD) (2008) reports that in the 1980s, global net flows of FDI amounted to approximately $950 billion. During the 1990s, however, this figure soared up to an astonishing $4,148 billion, which was a 336 percent increase from the decade prior. From 2000 to 2005, this trend continued, eventually growing to a total of $4,812 billion. Accordingly, the effort to understand how multinational corporations determine where to invest their growing capital is an increasingly important research topic in the area of international or comparative political economy. In particular, many in academic and policy circles have attempted to theorize the possibility that democratic institutions provide more favorable investment environments for FDI than does any other regime type.

While theoretically rich, the empirical literature has raised more questions than providing answers for scholars and policy makers in that it demonstrates an inconsistent relationship between democracy and FDI inflows (i.e., positive, negative, mixed, or no relationship). For example, Ahlquist (2006) presents a pooled data analysis demonstrating that democracies attract more net FDI inflows (measured as a percentage of GDP) than do autocracies (see also Feng 2001; Harms and Ursprung 2002; Jensen 2003; Jakobsen and de Soysa 2006; Busse and Hefeker 2007; Choi and Samy 2008). On the other hand, Li and Resnick (2003) suggest that democratic institutions have a negative effect on net FDI inflows (recorded in dollars) and but that there is a positive relationship between property rights protection and FDI (see also Busse 2004). However, in contrast to both of these positions, Blanton and Blanton's (2007) study reveals that there is, in fact, no evidence of a systematic relationship between democratic governance and foreign investment (see also Oneal 1994; Yang 2007; Büthe and Milner 2008).

It is necessary to note that the studies identified above employ alternative measures of FDI as their respective dependent variables and that their samples cover different countries and time periods. Consequently, scholars and policy makers have found it difficult to determine whether the discrepancy in findings has been due to these factors, or whether it is simply the case that most empirical results are not robust. Because the studies do not employ an identical measure of FDI in relation to democracy, for example, they fall victim to a type of internal incoherence and therefore do not offer any guidance for comparison. Choi's (2009) recent study is an exception to this blind spot insofar as it begins with a recognition of these disparate empirical results and so applies outlier diagnostics before replicating Li and Resnick's (2003) seminal work. It concludes that by relying on FDI net inflows in dollar amounts, Li and Resnick essentially ignore the problem of influential outliers in the data, causing the distortion of their estimated results and leading them to erroneously conclude that democracy is negatively associated with FDI.[1]

Though Choi's research sheds light on the democracy-FDI controversy by suggesting the implementation of outlier diagnostics, it would be even more compelling if accompanied by formal normality tests on regression residuals (Shapiro and Francia 1972; Kleinbaum et al. 1998; Lumley et al. 2002; Gujarati 2003; Kutner, Nachtsheim, and Neter 2004; Hamilton 2009). Choi's study neglects to point out the fact that formal normality tests on regression residuals are a more critical step in statistical analysis than is running outlier diagnostics. Normality tests check whether the normality assumption of a linear regression model has been satisfied and confirms, then, whether the desirable follow-on properties of the estimator can be used in a meaningful way; when this assumption has been violated, the consequences can be disastrous, leading researchers to draw unreliable inferences from their estimated results.[2] *Remember that although the dependent variable of a linear regression model need not necessarily follow a normal distribution, the error terms always should.* Because residuals obtained after model fitting approximate the actual unobserved errors, researchers should assess the normality of the residuals in order to assure the validity of the model specification as well as the statistical tests that follow. Since existing studies of FDI (and most in the discipline of political science more generally) overlook normality tests of regression residuals, it is difficult to evaluate the validity of their findings. In this case, the fact that the results of the empirical tests mentioned above have turned out to be mixed and ambiguous comes as no surprise.

One could argue that violations of normality per se are not a serious concern; in larger samples, for instance, inference relies on the Central Limit Theorem rather than on assumptions about residual normality. Although this assertion may be true in most statistical analysis, it does not hold up in the case of foreign direct investment research whose sample size is relatively small. There is no rule regarding the appropriate size for a sample in order to safely apply the large sample theory; it is likely that different sorts of data require different sample sizes (Lumley et al. 2002). Simply put, the large sample theory properties do not necessarily imply finite sample behavior of statistical estimators, thereby giving misleading results for small samples (Ullah 1990). Moreover, Kleinbaum et al. (1998, 117) mention the potential for producing spurious results in the presence of extreme data distributions; in their words, "extreme departures of the distribution of Y from normality yield spurious results." The currently available FDI data do not appear to be "reasonably large enough" to ignore the assumption of normality. For example, my FDI data collection for 123 countries for the years 1970–2007 yields 3,452 observations in total. My analysis indicates that 3,452 is not a large enough number of observations from which to draw reliable inferences on the relationship between democracy and foreign capital activity using the large sample theory. In other words, if the Central Limit Theorem were relevant for this study, the seven different regression models discussed later (each with a different measure of FDI) would all yield similar or consistent inferences and conclusions. Therefore, I argue that due to the extreme data distributions of foreign capital as well as the finite sample size, FDI researchers ought to consider checking the normality of regression residuals in the effort to avoid drawing erroneous inferences and conclusions.

I make five contributions to the FDI literature. First, I present a critique of the research methods employed in the existing literature by demonstrating how a violation of the normality assumption in linear models may produce inconsistent results and incorrect inferences. Second, I underline the importance of univariate normality analysis by introducing the Shapiro-Francia normality test (Shapiro and Francia 1972; Royston 1983; Park 2008). Third, I examine seven different measures of FDI—including two new measures of my own—and discuss the strengths and weaknesses of those measures from an empirical standpoint. Fourth, unlike the mixed findings of existing studies, my empirical analysis shows a consistently positive association between democracy and FDI inflows. My analysis employs the same model specification and estimation methods for all seven versions of FDI measure as dependent variable, thereby enhancing the comparability of the results obtained from all subsequent statistical models. As a robustness check on the positive relationship between democracy and FDI, I perform four sets of multivariate analysis for each of four different estimators: Prais-Winsten multivariate regression (i.e., panel-corrected standard errors

[PCSEs] with AR[1] correction), country fixed effects, Arellano and Bond generalized method of moments (GMM) estimator, and robust regression. Fifth, I collect a comprehensive FDI data set containing 123 developing countries during the period from 1970 to 2007. By collecting the data myself, I am able to examine the most up-to-date phenomena of foreign investment—something that previous studies of FDI were unable to do.

My normality analysis indicates that a linear regression model with

$$\log\left(\left(\frac{\text{FDI}}{\text{POP}}\right)+\sqrt{\left(\frac{\text{FDI}}{\text{POP}}\right)^{2}+1}\right), \log\left(\left(\frac{\text{FDI}}{\text{GDP}}\right)+\sqrt{\left(\frac{\text{FDI}}{\text{GDP}}\right)^{2}+1}\right),$$
$$\text{or } \log(\text{FDI}+\sqrt{\text{FDI}^{2}+1})$$

as its dependent variable is much less susceptible to a violation of the normality assumption than one that draws on net FDI inflows in dollars, FDI/GDP, log (FDI + a minimum), or FDI/population—the four FDI measures most often used in the literature. This suggests that the first three measures should be preferable to students of FDI insofar as the residuals of the respective regression model deviate from a normal distribution far less than do those of the four other models. My multivariate regression analyses reveal that while democracy has no bearing on the last four of the seven FDI measures, it is positively associated with the first three measures. These findings are not surprising given the fact that dissimilar operationalizations of FDI are likely to exert dissimilar influences on the distribution of regression residuals, in some cases generating an extremely nonnormal distribution that will, again, result in biased estimates and incorrect inferences. The multivariate regression results highlight the importance of running a normality check during the early stages of a research project and, as suspected, also reveal that different measures of FDI will lead to dissimilar inferences regarding the relationship between democracy and FDI. Ultimately, I find that when the normality assumption of the model is satisfied, democratic countries appear to attract more FDI than do autocratic countries. The implication is that if developing countries are seeking foreign capital to contribute to their economic growth and development, they should strive to establish and maintain high levels of democratic governance.

ECONOMETRIC MODEL BUILDING

Because the main purpose of this study is a critique of the research methods employed in the existing FDI literature, my own theoretical argument regarding the democracy-FDI connection is minimal. This study does not delve into a theoretical discussion of which aspects of democracy may or may not generate increased FDI, nor does it attempt to determine through which channels democracy may induce more FDI. The democracy-FDI controversy to which I point in the literature has not resulted from a lack of causal explanations or from incomplete theoretical argumentation, but from the use of erroneous measures of FDI for empirical analysis. This study, accordingly, attempts to address the methodological flaws prevalent in the existing FDI literature.

The Benign Effect of Democracy?

I expect that democracies are more likely than autocracies to attract FDI because they offer consistent and credible investment policies. Because democratic leaders' policy decisions are more constrained than their autocratic counterparts, they tend to engage less in expropriation and more in property rights protection. In addition, the "stickiness" of democratic institutions makes reversals of foreign investment policies more difficult and, therefore, less likely. Democratic features such as these help to create an attractive business environment and to reduce political risks for foreign firms wishing to fully use their capital, technology, marketing, and management skills in the pursuit of maximizing profit margins. Moreover, democratic leaders are increasingly cognizant that they may be held electorally accountable to commitments associated with friendly market policies, and that consistent policies serve to increase the confidence of foreign investors. The implication is that because democratic citizens can impose costly electoral sanctions on leaders who make arbitrary economic policy decisions, democracies are more likely than other regimes to consistently generate high levels of policy credibility for foreign investors. That is, in order to avoid electoral backlash, democratic leaders strive to lower investment risks for multinational corporations in a consistent manner; consequently, their economies are more likely to enjoy consistent flows of foreign capital (see Jensen 2003; Ahlquist 2006; Busse and Hefeker 2007; Choi and Samy 2008).

Because all existing empirical studies of FDI include a Polity democracy index, I operationalize democracy using the Polity data set.[3] Polity is built to capture the overall quality of democratic institutions (see Marshall and Jaggers 2007). It provides an eleven-point additive score for both democracies and autocracies, ranging from 0 to 10. If we subtract the autocracy score from the democracy score, we have an overall Polity score ranging from full democracy (+10) to full autocracy (−10). Democracy and autocracy are thus presumed to be opposite poles on a single continuum.[4]

How to Build an Econometric Model of FDI

I begin by collecting a sample of 123 developing countries from the four-decade period between 1970 and 2007. My focus on developing countries should assuage any concern that the presence of highly industrialized democracies (considered prime magnets for foreign investment) necessitates the finding of a positive, statistical connection between democracy and FDI inflows. Relying on the World Bank's *World Development Indicators 2010*, I create seven different measures of FDI as the dependent variable: net FDI inflows in dollars, net FDI inflows divided by GDP, log (net FDI inflows + a minimum positive integer), net FDI inflows divided by total population,

$$\log\left(\left(\frac{FDI}{POP}\right) + \sqrt{\left(\frac{FDI}{POP}\right)^2 + 1}\right), \log\left(\left(\frac{FDI}{GDP}\right) + \sqrt{\left(\frac{FDI}{GDP}\right)^2 + 1}\right),$$

$$\text{and } \log\left(FDI + \sqrt{FDI^2 + 1}\right).$$

I take the first two measures directly from the World Bank source; I construct the next five by transforming the first measure.

It should be noted that while the first five measures have been used in various existing studies of FDI, the last two are original transformations of the dependent variable that, I suggest, will allow for the regression residuals to follow more closely a normal distribution. Net FDI inflows in dollars appear in Chan and Mason (1992), Oneal (1994), Li and Resnick (2003), and Yang (2007); FDI/GDP is used in Jensen (2003), Ahlquist (2006), Blanton and Blanton (2007), and Büthe and Milner (2008); log (FDI + a minimum) is employed in Jakobsen and de Soysa (2006) and Li (2009); FDI/population is used in Harms and Ursprung (2002); log of FDI/population is applied in Busse (2004); and

$$\log\left(\left(\frac{FDI}{POP}\right) + \sqrt{\left(\frac{FDI}{POP}\right)^2 + 1}\right)$$

is used in Busse and Hefeker (2007). Each of these existing studies relies on only one of these FDI measures; not surprisingly, their estimated results are inconsistent and incompatible with one another. Thus, the literature falls short of offering a systematic comparison with respect to the causal determinants of these contrasting results, let alone of providing a conclusive answer to questions about the democracy-FDI connection.

I discuss each of the seven measures in order. The first measure, net FDI inflows in dollars, is the level of FDI net inflows into a country each year, measured in current U.S. dollars.[5] FDI net inflows can be positive, zero, or negative in cases of divestment. Some studies contend that the amount of FDI net inflows is the best measure to use if a researcher's goal is to explain the level of FDI inflows as opposed to, say, the gross amount of FDI entering a country or the amount of FDI relative to a country's population (e.g., Li and Resnick 2003; Li 2009). However, I argue that the use of net FDI inflows in dollars is suspect for two reasons: it fails to account for the relative economic size of each country, and the data do not assume a normal distribution.[6] Due to the first reason, net FDI inflows divided by GDP or total population is preferred to net FDI inflows in dollars in the political economy literature (Busse 2004; Choi and Samy 2008). For instance, Jensen (2003, 597) argues for FDI/GDP because it "is the best measure to examine a country's ability to attract FDI."[7] Because of the second reason, some studies assert that the logarithm of net FDI inflows serves as an alternative measure to net FDI inflows in dollars (e.g., Li 2009). However, taking a log of net FDI inflows is mathematically undesirable because a considerable number of observations in the data are zero or negative and so, after the log transformation, are treated as missing data points. To circumvent this complication in the application of logarithms, the fourth measure (i.e., log [FDI + a minimum]) adds a minimum positive integer, which is just large enough to turn all nonpositive into positive values before log-transforming them.[8] It must be noted, though, that the choice of a minimum constant value can affect the significance levels of the computed coefficients for the logged variables (Santos Silva and Tenreyro 2006).

The fifth measure,

$$\log\left(\left(\frac{FDI}{POP}\right)+\sqrt{\left(\frac{FDI}{POP}\right)^2+1}\right),$$

uses the inverse hyperbolic sine function, $\sinh^{-1}(x)$, as a logarithm (see Busse and Hefeker 2007, 404–5). Because FDI data are recorded in dollars, this transformation gives the slow log-like growth for large values. At the same time, this measure has at least three advantages over a simple logarithm transformation: it does not require FDI net inflows to be positive, it maintains the sign of the original numerical values, and it accounts for country size. Although this measure controls for country size by dividing FDI by total population, it continues to ignore economy size. It fails to account for the fact that the most populated countries are not necessarily the most highly industrialized economies; that is, there are countries with a large population and a relatively low GDP (e.g., China and India). With this in mind, the sixth measure,

$$\log\left(\left(\frac{FDI}{GDP}\right)+\sqrt{\left(\frac{FDI}{GDP}\right)^2+1}\right),$$

is preferable because GDP is a common measure used to account for the relative size of an economy. The purpose of the last measure,

$$\log\left(FDI+\sqrt{FDI^2+1}\right)$$

—which does not consider the effect of economic or country size but does avoid using a minimum positive integer for logarithmic transformation—is to compare its usefulness relative to the other six measures.

Although existing studies have explored a multitude of covariates of FDI, I confine my analysis to five control variables: economic growth, economic development, regime durability, terrorism, and post–Cold War.[9] I have chosen these five particular variables because they are widely used in the literature and because the objective of this study is not to explain as much variance of FDI as possible, but to illustrate and compare the effects of the different FDI measures. I include the first control variable, economic growth, in order to account for the incentive of foreign investors to take advantage of fast-growing market opportunities; it is expected to be positively associated with FDI (Schneider and Frey 1985; Busse 2004; Jakobsen and de Soysa 2006). Economic growth is measured as the annual percentage growth rate of GDP, collected from the World Bank's *World Development Indicators 2009*. The second control variable, economic development, captures the fact that advanced economies tend to attract the most foreign investment due to their higher consumer purchasing power (Jensen 2003; Li and Resnick 2003; Blanton and Blanton 2007; Büthe and Milner 2008). I adopt GDP per capita in a logarithmic form, a conventional measure of economic development, and my data are obtained from the *World Development Indicators 2009*.

The third variable is regime durability. While frequent regime changes may disturb the business activities of multinational corporations, stable political regimes create a secure, and therefore favorable, investment environment (Li and Resnick 2003; Ahlquist 2006; Jakobsen and de Soysa 2006). The regime durability variable records the number of years that a country has gone without experiencing a regime change, with regime change measured as a three-point shift in a country's Polity score for a given year. Data for this variable are garnered from Marshall and Jaggers (2007). The fourth variable, terrorism, captures political instability specifically caused by terrorism, which is supposed to increase the business risks for foreign investors (Enders, Sachsida, and Sandler 2006; Abadie and Gardeazabal 2008; Mancuso, Dirienzo, and Das 2010; Powers and Choi 2012).[10] Terrorism is recorded as the total number of domestic and transnational terrorist events occurring within a country in a given year. These data are retrieved from the Global Terrorism Database (GTD) Explorer, a Web-based interactive visual exploratory tool containing more than eighty thousand cases and dealing with systematic data on all types of terrorist incidents (Lee 2008). The final variable, post–Cold War, is included to highlight the fact that certain changing characteristics of the international system are relevant when studying the movements of FDI. Specifically, a post–Cold War dummy is created in order to reflect the increased investment opportunities that have emerged since the end of the Cold War (as noted at the outset of this study and in the work by Biglaiser and DeRouen [2007]). It is coded as 1 from 1990 forward and as 0 otherwise, and it is expected to have a positive effect on FDI inflows.[11]

Because the dependent variable is continuous, I employ a Prais-Winsten regression (i.e., panel-corrected standard errors, PCSEs, with AR[1] correction), as recommended by Beck and Katz (1995). The choice of this estimation method reflects my desire not only to maintain consistency with previous studies of FDI but also to alleviate the concern that my results are not comparable to those reported in previous studies due to the use of a different estimator. In a recent study, Li (2009) advocates the use of PCSEs to address the problems of heteroskedasticity and serial correlation that are commonly found in pooled panel data. To check the robustness of the main findings reported below, I also implement a fixed-effects regression model that takes into consideration the unique characteristics of each country (Green, Kim, and Yoon 2001). All independent variables are lagged one year to ensure that they cause changes in the dependent variable rather than the other way around.

Both the Prais-Winsten and country fixed-effects regressions assume that all independent variables are exogenous. However, as Busse and Hefeker (2007) point out, it is likely that FDI also exerts a positive impact on economic growth and economic development.[12] To allow for the possibility of endogeneity, I employ the linear dynamic panel-data estimation proposed by Arellano and Bond (1991). Linear dynamic panel-data models include p lags of the dependent variable as covariates and contain unobserved panel-level effects that are fixed or random. By construction, the unobserved panel-level effects are correlated with the lagged dependent variables, causing standard estimators to be inconsistent. Arellano and Bond derive a consistent GMM estimator for the parameters of this model.

Because scholars have expressed varying concerns about each of the three statistical techniques (i.e., Prais-Winsten, fixed-effect, and dynamic panel-data regressions), I do not speculate on which estimation technique is the most appropriate. In fact, as reported below, the estimated results do not change significantly across the different statistical models despite the fact that each estimator has its own strengths and weaknesses. The primary motivation for the introduction of these three techniques is to test the robustness of my empirical findings. While it is not my objective to claim the superiority of one technique over the others, I do indicate which measure of the dependent variable is the most suited to the empirical analysis of FDI after conducting normality tests of regression residuals.

EMPIRICAL FINDINGS

This section begins with a discussion of the univariate normality analysis, presents the findings of tests for heteroskedasticity and autocorrelation, and concludes with the multivariate regression results.[13]

Univariate Normality Analysis of Regression Residuals

Before discussing normality tests of regression residuals, I conduct normality tests on each of the seven FDI measures as a preliminary analysis, which, to some extent, provides a clue to understanding the regression results presented in the next section. It is important to note that for linear regression models, the normality test should be applied to the residuals rather than to the raw scores of a variable, as the latter is not a necessary condition for statistical inferences. Testing for normality of observations is a common procedure in other disciplines such as statistics, psychology, and economics. For example, Hamilton (2009, 141) emphasizes that "many statistical procedures work best when applied to variables that follow normal distribution." For this reason, there is a sizable literature documenting the significance of univariate analysis of normality and a good number of types of normality testing have been proposed (e.g., Shapiro and Francia 1972; D'Agostino, Belanger, and D'Agostino, Jr. 1990; Royston 1983, 1991a, 1991b; Seier 2002; Yazici and Yolacan 2007; Park 2008; Hamilton 2009).

Although simple scatter plots can be used to detect a violation of the normality assumption for each of the seven different FDI measures, they may fail to provide precise information when a pattern is not discernible to the naked eye. As a result, I employ the Shapiro-Francia W' test to detect the presence of non-normality (see Shapiro and Francia 1972; Royston 1991b; Stata Press 2007; Park 2008). Of all the formal normality tests, the Shapiro-Francia W' test allows us to rely on a built-in command provided by a standard statistical software package (i.e., "sfrancia" in Stata) and to perform normality tests on a sample size of more than 2,000 observations (as 3,452 observations are used for my empirical analysis, this is a necessary component of an appropriate normality test). The Shapiro-Francia W' test is an approximate test that modifies the Shapiro-Wilk W (Shapiro and Wilk 1965). The Shapiro-Wilk W is the ratio of the best estimator of the variance to the usual corrected sum of squares estimator of the variance. It is constructed by considering the regression of ordered sample values on corresponding expected normal order statistics, which, for a sample from a normally distributed population, is linear (Royston 1982). The formula is $W = (y, a_1 x_{(1)})^2 / y(x_1 - \bar{x})^2$ where $a' = (a_1, a_2, \ldots, a_n) = m'V^{-1}[m'V^{-1}V^{-1}m]^{-1/2}$, $m' = (m_1, m_2, \ldots, m_n)$ is the vector of expected values of standard normal order statistics, V is the n by n covariance matrix, $x' = (x_1, x_2, \ldots, x_n)$ is a random sample, and $x_{(1)} < x_{(2)} < \ldots < x_{(n)}$. The W statistic is positive and less than or equal to one; closeness to one indicates normality. Since the W statistic requires that the sample size is greater than or equal to 7 and less than or equal to 2,000, Shapiro and Francia (1972) and Royston (1983) extended the test by developing a transformation of the null distribution of W to approximate normality throughout a

TABLE 6.1   Univariate Normality Analysis of Observations: Shapiro-Francia Test

	Observations	W'	V'	Z	Prob > Z
FDI	3,452	0.209	948.953	6.416	0.00001
FDI/GDP	3,452	0.266	881.511	6.400	0.00001
log (FDI + minimum)	3,452	0.142	1030.147	6.434	0.00001
FDI/POP	3,452	0.252	897.262	6.404	0.00001
$\log\left(\left(\frac{FDI}{POP}\right)+\sqrt{\left(\frac{FDI}{POP}\right)^2+1}\right)$	3,452	0.984	19.305	4.582	0.00001
$\log\left(\left(\frac{FDI}{GDP}\right)+\sqrt{\left(\frac{FDI}{GDP}\right)^2+1}\right)$	3,452	0.970	35.474	5.059	0.00001
$\log\left(FDI+\sqrt{FDI^2+1}\right)$	3,452	0.631	443.254	6.226	0.00001

range from 5 to 5,000. For this reason, the Shapiro-Francia W' statistic uses b$'$ = (b$_1$, b$_2$, . . . , b$_n$) = m$'$(m$'$m)$^{-1/2}$ instead of a$'$.

Table 6.1 shows the results of Shapiro-Francia normality tests on each of the seven FDI measures. The easiest way to interpret the test results is to check the values of W' and V'. While small values of W' lead us to reject the assumption of normality, closeness to 1 gives us a cause to accept it. V''s median value is 1 for samples from normal populations. A large value of V' indicates nonnormality. According to these two statistics, it appears that the

$$\log\left(\left(\frac{FDI}{POP}\right)+\sqrt{\left(\frac{FDI}{POP}\right)^2+1}\right)$$

measure is the closest to a normal distribution among the different transformations, with a W' value of 0.984 and a V' value of 19.305. The

$$\log\left(\left(\frac{FDI}{GDP}\right)+\sqrt{\left(\frac{FDI}{GDP}\right)^2+1}\right),$$

and

$$\log\left(FDI+\sqrt{FDI^2+1}\right)$$

measures are the second and third best in terms of normality: their W' values are 0.970 and 0.631, respectively, and their V' values are 35.474 and 443.254, respectively. The other four measures appear to deviate far from a normal distribution, with W' values no larger than 0.266 and V' values greater than 881.511.

After having fitted a linear regression model that includes the six independent variables specified above, and that employs each of the seven FDI measures, in turn, as the dependent variable, I apply the Shapiro-Francia W' test to

TABLE 6.2   Univariate Normality Analysis of Regression Residuals:
Shapiro-Francia Test

	Observations	W'	V'	Z	Prob > Z
FDI	3,452	0.315	822.175	6.384	0.00001
FDI/GDP	3,452	0.266	881.511	6.400	0.00001
log (FDI + minimum)	3,452	0.161	1007.014	6.429	0.00001
FDI/POP	3,452	0.404	715.128	6.351	0.00001
$\log\left(\left(\frac{FDI}{POP}\right)+\sqrt{\left(\frac{FDI}{POP}\right)^2+1}\right)$	3,452	0.871	155.404	5.864	0.00001
$\log\left(\left(\frac{FDI}{GDP}\right)+\sqrt{\left(\frac{FDI}{GDP}\right)^2+1}\right)$	3,452	0.972	33.065	5.009	0.00001
$\log\left(FDI+\sqrt{FDI^2+1}\right)$	3,452	0.633	440.908	6.225	0.00001

the regression residuals. The results—reported in Table 6.2—remain similar to
those presented in Table 6.1. According to the W' and V' statistics, the residuals
from a linear regression model with the

$$\log\left(\left(\frac{FDI}{GDP}\right)+\sqrt{\left(\frac{FDI}{GDP}\right)^2+1}\right)$$

measure as the outcome variable appear to be the closest to a normal distribution. The residuals obtained from models employing the

$$\log\left(\left(\frac{FDI}{POP}\right)+\sqrt{\left(\frac{FDI}{POP}\right)^2+1}\right)$$

and

$$\log\left(FDI + \sqrt{FDI^2+1}\right)$$

measures are the second and third best in terms of normality. The regression
residuals corresponding to the other four measures do not follow a normal distribution.

Based on the normality analysis, it is fair to argue that

$$\log\left(\left(\frac{FDI}{POP}\right)+\sqrt{\left(\frac{FDI}{POP}\right)^2+1}\right), \log\left(\left(\frac{FDI}{GDP}\right)+\sqrt{\left(\frac{FDI}{GDP}\right)^2+1}\right),$$
$$\text{and } \log\left(FDI + \sqrt{FDI^2+1}\right)$$

are less susceptible to a violation of the normality assumption than are FDI,
FDI/GDP, log (FDI + a minimum), and FDI/population. In particular, the normality tests on regression residuals unambiguously suggest that the last three

TABLE 6.3   Heteroskedasticity and Autocorrelation in the Seven Regression Models

	Dependent Variable	Likelihood-Ratio Test for Heteroskedasticity H_0: No Heteroskedasticity	Wooldridge Test for Autocorrelation H_0: No First-Order Autocorrelation
Model 1	FDI	LR chi2(122)=18322.37 Prob > chi2 =0.0001	$F(1, 121)$ =26.686 Prob > F =0.0001
Model 2	FDI/GDP	LR chi2(122)=9100.86 Prob > chi2 =0.0001	$F(1, 121)$ =10.704 Prob > F =0.0014
Model 3	log (FDI + minimum)	LR chi2(122)=17407.32 Prob > chi2 =0.0001	$F(1, 121)$ =24.926 Prob > F =0.0001
Model 4	FDI/POP	LR chi2(122)=15098.86 Prob > chi2 =0.0001	$F(1, 121)$ =10.257 Prob > F =0.0017
Model 5	$\log\left(\left(\frac{FDI}{POP}\right)+\sqrt{\left(\frac{FDI}{POP}\right)^2+1}\right)$	LR chi2(122)=2205.36 Prob > chi2 =0.0001	$F(1, 121)$ =13.961 Prob > F =0.0003
Model 6	$\log\left(\left(\frac{FDI}{GDP}\right)+\sqrt{\left(\frac{FDI}{GDP}\right)^2+1}\right)$	LR chi2(122)=1350.41 Prob > chi2 =0.0001	$F(1, 121)$ =41.558 Prob > F =0.0001
Model 7	$\log\left(FDI+\sqrt{FDI^2+1}\right)$	LR chi2(122)=2932.90 Prob > chi2 =0.0001	$F(1, 121)$ =14.895 Prob > F =0.0002

measures are preferable to the others in an examination of the democracy-FDI connection. As the regression models using the last three FDI measures tend to have more normally distributed residuals, the researcher can have greater confidence in the validity of his or her estimation results.

Multivariate Regression Analysis

Since my multivariate regression analysis is based on cross-sectional, time-series data, I also conduct a likelihood-ratio test for heteroskedasticity and the Wooldridge test for autocorrelation. The null hypothesis of the former test is no heteroskedasticity, and that of the latter is no first-order correlation (Wooldridge 2002; Drukker 2003). The results in Table 6.3 lead us to reject both null hypotheses under each of the seven models and thus require correction for both panel heteroskedasticity and temporally correlated errors.[14] In this context, the choice of a Prais-Winsten regression—PCSEs with AR(1)—is appropriate for addressing these issues.[15]

Table 6.4 shows the multivariate regression results from the Prais-Winsten regression.[16] Based on the coefficient of determination, R^2, which takes on a value of 0.95 for Model 3, one might conclude that the use of log (FDI + mini-

TABLE 6.4 The Effect of Democracy on Inflows of FDI: Prais-Winsten Regression

Variable	FDI	FDI/GDP	Log(FDI+mini)	FDI/POP	$\log\left(\left(\frac{FDI}{GDP}\right)+\sqrt{\left(\frac{FDI}{GDP}\right)^2+1}\right)$	$\log\left(\left(\frac{FDI}{POP}\right)+\sqrt{\left(\frac{FDI}{POP}\right)^2+1}\right)$	$\log\left(FDI+\sqrt{FDI^2+1}\right)$
	Model 1	Model 2	Model 3	Model 4	Model 5	Model 6	Model 7
DEMOCRACY	3.48E+05	0.022	0.003	0.275	0.050***	0.016***	0.156***
	(9.88E+06)	(0.054)	(0.003)	(1.092)	(0.011)	(0.005)	(0.037)
ECONOMIC GROWTH	2.22E-06	0.097**	0.001	0.407	0.014***	0.008**	0.076***
	(3.81E+06)	(0.048)	(0.001)	(0.363)	(0.006)	(0.004)	(0.024)
ECONOMIC DEVELOPMENT	1.06E+09***	0.278	0.028	101.616***	0.846***	0.128***	0.617***
	(2.00E+08)	(0.291)	(0.037)	(20.900)	(0.085)	(0.037)	(0.243)
REGIME DURABILITY	1.39E+07***	0.028	-0.002	0.525*	-0.002	0.001	-0.010
	(5.88E+06)	(0.035)	(0.002)	(0.351)	(0.005)	(0.003)	(0.014)
TERRORISM	4.18E+05	-0.003***	0.000	-0.059**	-0.002***	-0.001***	-0.001
	(8.20E+05)	(0.001)	(0.000)	(0.034)	(0.001)	(0.000)	(0.003)
POST–COLD WAR	4.14E+08	1.805***	0.017	23.562	0.710***	0.425***	2.302***
	(3.47E+08)	(0.520)	(0.035)	(20.310)	(0.166)	(0.099)	(0.462)
Constant	-6.19E+09***	-0.613	22.703***	-610.572***	-3.384***	-0.002	10.881***
	(1.22E+09)	(1.973)	(0.242)	(122.632)	(0.546)	(0.257)	(1.632)
Observations	3.452	3.452	3.452	3.452	3.452	3.452	3.452
R^2	0.02	0.01	0.95	0.03	0.11	0.04	0.04

Note: Prais-Winsten estimates and standard errors in parentheses are based on panel-corrected standard errors (PCSEs) with AR(1) correction.

$***p < .01, **p < .05, *p < .10$

mum) allows the predicted regression line to best approximate the real data points. However, I note that this excessively high R^2 is due to the extremely small variance of log (FDI + minimum) and should not be attributed to the explanatory power of the independent variables. When I regress log (FDI + minimum) on each of the six independent variables separately, I also obtain an R^2 around 0.95 for each test. I find that the standard deviation of log (FDI + minimum) (i.e., 0.457) is very small compared to its mean (i.e., 22.885).[17] The lack of variation in the log (FDI + minimum) measure makes it an undesirable choice for the dependent variable and calls the regression results into question.

The multivariate regression analyses show that DEMOCRACY is not a significant predictor of FDI in the first four models despite the fact that its coefficient takes on a positive sign. However, in the last three models (i.e., Models 5 through 7), which use the FDI measures singled out by the normality tests in the previous section, it is positively and significantly associated with FDI. This illuminates the importance of the normality assumption in establishing a causal relationship between democracy and FDI. A correct characterization of the effect of democracy on foreign capital hinges on whether the regression residuals are normally distributed. Specifically, the transformation of the FDI net value with an inverse hyperbolic sine function as logarithms assures a normal distribution of residuals in a linear regression model, which is conducive to the identification of a causal relationship between democratic institutions and the behavior of foreign investors. This finding should not be surprising given the fact that multivariate regression models are expected to provide reliable statistical inferences on the variable(s) of interest only when the data satisfy underlying model assumptions such as normality of residuals.[18]

Even though the difference between the true value of the parameter and the null hypothesized value remains small, small p-values may occur with an increase of sample size. Put differently, if total observations are large enough, there is a possibility that statistical significance does not necessarily indicate a statistically meaningful or important finding in any practical sense (see Gujarati 2003). With this in mind, the substantive effect for the democracy variable requires closer examination. Table 6.5 reports the substantive effects for the democracy variable that achieved statistical significance in Models 5 through 7 in Table 6.4. Table 6.5 shows evidence that, as compared with a typical country, a more democratic country is likely to attract more FDI. For example, according to Model 6, as shown in the shaded column, a change of one standard deviation of democracy increases the inflows of FDI by 15 percent, two standard deviations by 31 percent, and three standard deviations by 46 percent. A similar pattern for democracy is reported in the rest of the substantive effects analysis.

TABLE 6.5   Substantive Effects of FDI Inflows

	Model 5	Model 6	Model 7
Democracy increased by one standard deviation	15%	12%	7%
Democracy increased by two standard deviations	31%	25%	14%
Democracy increased by three standard deviations	46%	37%	22%

Note: The baseline values are as follows: mean for continuous variables and 0 for post–Cold War.

As I examine the control variables in Table 6.4, I find that countries capable of maintaining a high level of economic growth or development are more likely to attract foreign capital. Countries that experience frequent terrorist incidents may be viewed as unfavorable investment destinations for multinational corporations. Consistent with the economic trend discussed at the outset of this study, investment opportunities have increased in the post–Cold War era. As it is statistically significant and in the hypothesized direction in only two out of the seven models, regime durability appears to have a small impact on multinational investment decisions. I speculate that the weak effect of regime durability may be explained by the behavior of foreign investors who are less concerned with a regime change than economic development or growth.

Although the Prais-Winsten regression model is the standard estimation method for pooled panel data in existing studies (Li 2009), its default is not set to capture country-specific effects. Depending on unique socioeconomic and political conditions that may not necessarily be observable, some countries are bound to do better than others in attracting foreign investors (Green, Kim, and Yoon 2001). To accommodate such an expectation, I conduct an analysis of fixed effects in Table 6.6 by adding country dummies to the Prais-Winsten regression models in Table 6.4.[19] As far as the effect of democracy is concerned, the results are consistent with those reported in Table 6.4: democratic institutions do not contribute to the activities of multinational corporations according to the first four models, but they are positively associated with inflows of FDI based on the last three models.

Table 6.7 presents the results from dynamic panel-data estimations.[20] As noted, I have implemented the Arellano and Bond GMM estimator to allow for the possibility that Prais-Winsten regression and country fixed-effects estimates may be biased due to an endogenous relationship between economic growth and economic development. To be specific, the Arellano and Bond estimator includes the lagged dependent variable as a predictor; differencing each variable removes the country-specific effects, and the differenced equation is then estimated by instrumental variables. Also, by taking the first difference of the seven different FDI measures, the Arellano and Bond estimator removes the

TABLE 6.6   The Effect of Democracy on Inflows of FDI: Fixed Effects

Variable	FDI	FDI/GDP	Log(FDI+mini)	FDI/POP	$\log\left(\left(\frac{FDI}{GDP}\right)+\sqrt{\left(\frac{FDI}{GDP}\right)^2+1}\right)$	$\log\left(\left(\frac{FDI}{POP}\right)+\sqrt{\left(\frac{FDI}{POP}\right)^2+1}\right)$	$\log\left(FDI+\sqrt{FDI^2+1}\right)$
	Model 1	Model 2	Model 3	Model 4	Model 5	Model 6	Model 7
DEMOCRACY	9.78E+06	0.055	0.001	0.433	0.030***	0.015***	0.097**
	(1.17E+07)	(0.067)	(0.001)	(0.766)	(0.010)	(0.006)	(0.042)
ECONOMIC GROWTH	−2.20E+06	0.094**	0.001	0.401	0.019***	0.011***	0.082***
	(3.84E+06)	(0.049)	(0.001)	(0.373)	(0.006)	(0.004)	(0.024)
ECONOMIC DEVELOPMENT	1.91E+09***	0.546	0.079*	108.894***	0.737***	0.112**	0.267
	(2.94E+08)	(0.505)	(0.049)	(19.340)	(0.131)	(0.066)	(0.395)
REGIME DURABILITY	8.56E+06*	0.035	−0.001	1.294***	0.009*	0.004	0.022
	(5.35E+06)	(0.043)	(0.001)	(0.353)	(0.006)	(0.004)	(0.022)
TERRORISM	−1.27E+05	−0.001*	−0.000	−0.053*	−0.001***	−0.000**	−0.006***
	(8.09E+05)	(0.001)	(0.000)	(0.033)	(0.001)	(0.000)	(0.003)
POST–COLD WAR	3.08E+08	1.354***	0.017*	27.658*	0.801***	0.432***	2.649***
	(3.28E+08)	(0.535)	(0.036)	(19.083)	(0.175)	(0.102)	(0.533)
Constant	−1.56E+10***	5.369*	22.409***	−774.059***	−3.385**	−0.357	16.809***
	(1.91E+09)	(4.118)	(0.407)	(192.786)	(2.082)	(0.677)	(3.200)
Observations	3,452	3,452	3,452	3,452	3,452	3,452	3,452
R^2	0.22	0.10	0.96	0.17	0.26	0.18	0.15

Note: Prais-Winsten estimates and standard errors in parentheses are based on panel-corrected robust standard errors (PCSEs) with AR(1) correction. Country dummies are not reported to save space.

***$p < .01$, **$p < .05$, *$p < .10$

TABLE 6.7   The Effect of Democracy on Inflows of FDI: Dynamic Panel-Data Estimation

Variable	FDI Model 1	FDI/GDP Model 2	Log(FDI+mini) Model 3	FDI/POP Model 4	$\log\left(\left(\frac{FDI}{GDP}\right)+\sqrt{\left(\frac{FDI}{GDP}\right)^2+1}\right)$ Model 5	$\log\left(\left(\frac{FDI}{POP}\right)+\sqrt{\left(\frac{FDI}{POP}\right)^2+1}\right)$ Model 6	$\log\left(FDI+\sqrt{FDI^2+1}\right)$ Model 7
ΔLAGGED FDI	0.938***	0.088*	0.828***	0.649***	0.345***	0.407***	0.257***
	(0.051)	(0.062)	(0.066)	(0.125)	(0.038)	(0.031)	(0.030)
ΔDEMOCRACY	−1.82E+06	−0.004	−0.000	−0.486	0.032*	0.016*	0.109*
	(7.30E+06)	(0.049)	(0.000)	(1.324)	(0.020)	(0.010)	(0.068)
ΔECONOMIC GROWTH	1.45E+07*	0.112***	0.001**	1.038**	0.023***	0.017***	0.059*
	(6.46E+06)	(0.024)	(0.000)	(0.563)	(0.009)	(0.005)	(0.038)
ΔECONOMIC DEVELOPMENT	8.67E+08***	0.134	0.053***	77.175***	0.330*	−0.081	−0.344
	(2.10E+08)	(0.550)	(0.013)	(27.852)	(0.210)	(0.093)	(0.778)
ΔREGIME DURABILITY	−3.33E+05	−0.010	−0.000	0.373	0.005	0.004	−0.005
	(3.66E+06)	(0.016)	(0.000)	(0.415)	(0.006)	(0.003)	(0.028)
ΔTERRORISM	−1.58E+05	−0.003**	0.000	−0.060*	−0.003***	−0.001***	−0.010***
	(4.49E+05)	(0.001)	(0.000)	(0.042)	(0.001)	(0.000)	(0.004)
POST–COLD WAR	1.23E+08	−0.030	0.010*	10.736	0.216*	0.074	0.714
	(1.00E+08)	(0.308)	(0.006)	(11.511)	(0.142)	(0.060)	(0.609)
Constant	−1.22E+07*	0.098***	−0.000	0.090	0.022**	0.015***	0.065*
	(8.56E+06)	(0.030)	(0.000)	(0.811)	(0.011)	(0.005)	(0.046)
Sagan Test							
χ²	2985.23	3424.15	2513.21	2848.01	2383.63	2303.80	1975.33
p-value	0.0001	0.0001	0.0001	0.0001	0.0001	0.0001	0.0008

continued

TABLE 6.7   continued

Variable	FDI	FDI/GDP	Log(FDI+mini)	FDI/POP	$\log\left(\left(\frac{FDI}{GDP}\right)+\sqrt{\left(\frac{FDI}{GDP}\right)^2+1}\right)$	$\log\left(\left(\frac{FDI}{POP}\right)+\sqrt{\left(\frac{FDI}{POP}\right)^2+1}\right)$	$\log\left(FDI+\sqrt{FDI^2+1}\right)$
	Model 1	Model 2	Model 3	Model 4	Model 5	Model 6	Model 7
AB Test for AR(1)							
z	−3.40	−1.42	−3.89	−1.71	−4.66	−6.04	−6.64
p-value	0.0007	0.1544	0.0001	0.0870	0.0001	0.0001	0.0001
AB Test for AR(2)							
z	−0.33	−0.45	0.21	0.99	0.23	0.42	0.72
p-value	0.7386	0.6491	0.8341	0.3216	0.8143	0.6722	0.4695
Observations	3,036	3,036	3,036	3,036	3,036	3,036	3,036

continued

Note: Robust standard errors in parentheses except for Model 2.

***$p < .01$, **$p < .05$, *$p < .10$

time trend that is a long-term movement in my pooled data.[21] Despite the fact that the dynamic panel-data estimation takes into account endogeneity as well as trending, the results concerning the effects of democratic institutions are similar to those presented in Tables 6.4 and 6.6. Once again, DEMOCRACY is positively related with inflows of FDI in only the last three models; however, its significance level is only 0.10—a change that should not be surprising given the inclusion of the lagged dependent variable. Because the LAGGED FDI soaks up much of the variation in the dependent variable, the significance level of DE-MOCRACY is weakened (see Achen 2000).

As a last check of the robustness on the positive relationship between democracy and FDI, I perform a robust regression estimation. Choi's (2009, 159) study recommends "robust regression estimation as the most effective remedial technique to provide resistant (stable) results in the presence of outliers" (for a detailed discussion about robust regression, see also Western 1995). I expect that the use of a robust regression estimator should exert little impact on the significance of the democracy variable in Models 5 through 7 because the residuals of these models are approximately normally distributed and so are less likely to contain outlying observations. On the other hand, it is expected that a robust regression estimator will cause some significant changes to the coefficients of the democracy variable and its standard errors in Models 1 through 4 because their regression residuals do not follow a normal distribution. Table 6.8 reports the robust regression results. The democracy variable remains statistically significant at the 0.01 level across all of the models except for Model 7 (i.e., the one wherein the logged dependent variable—$\log (\text{FDI} + \sqrt{\text{FDI}^2 + 1})$—is used as a predictor), while its coefficient maintains a positive sign throughout. The robust regression results provide support for my contention that when the sample data are normally distributed, democratic institutions are positively associated with inflows of FDI.

CONCLUSION

My empirical study is the first to introduce normality tests of regression residuals into the literature of FDI (and into political science more generally). In doing so, I have investigated the empirical puzzle presented by inconclusive findings on the relationship between democracy and foreign investment. The Shapiro-Francia test statistics allow us to examine the normality of regression residuals and to compare my two newly proposed measures of FDI alongside five measures used most commonly in existing studies. My univariate analysis of normality indicates that the residuals from a linear regression model with

$$\log\left(\left(\frac{\text{FDI}}{\text{POP}}\right) + \sqrt{\left(\frac{\text{FDI}}{\text{POP}}\right)^2 + 1}\right), \log\left(\left(\frac{\text{FDI}}{\text{GDP}}\right) + \sqrt{\left(\frac{\text{FDI}}{\text{GDP}}\right)^2 + 1}\right),$$

$$\text{or } \log (\text{FDI} + \sqrt{\text{FDI}^2 + 1})$$

TABLE 6.8   The Effect of Democracy on Inflows of FDI: Robust Regression

Variable	FDI	FDI/GDP	Log(FDI+mini)	FDI/POP	$\log\left(\left(\frac{FDI}{GDP}\right)+\sqrt{\left(\frac{FDI}{GDP}\right)^2}+1\right)$	$\log\left(\left(\frac{FDI}{POP}\right)+\sqrt{\left(\frac{FDI}{POP}\right)^2}+1\right)$	$\log\left(FDI+\sqrt{FDI^2+1}\right)$
	Model 1	Model 2	Model 3	Model 4	Model 5	Model 6	Model 7
DEMOCRACY	1.41E+06***	0.036***	0.000***	0.364***	0.018***	0.015***	0.006
	(2.73E+05)	(0.005)	(0.000)	(0.038)	(0.004)	(0.003)	(0.005)
ECONOMIC GROWTH	1.77E+06***	0.039***	0.000***	0.323***	0.048***	0.031***	0.051***
	(2.66E+05)	(0.004)	(0.000)	(0.037)	(0.004)	(0.002)	(0.005)
ECONOMIC DEVELOPMENT	2.56E+07***	0.230***	0.003***	6.022***	1.202***	0.157***	1.090***
	(1.56E+06)	(0.026)	(0.000)	(0.217)	(0.021)	(0.015)	(0.030)
REGIME DURABILITY	2.69E+05***	-0.004***	0.000***	0.001	0.000	-0.003***	0.002
	(1.07E+05)	(0.002)	(0.000)	(0.015)	(0.001)	(0.001)	(0.002)
TERRORISM	1.23E+04	-0.003***	0.000	-0.022***	-0.004***	-0.002***	0.003***
	(2.75E+04)	(0.000)	(0.000)	(0.004)	(0.000)	(0.000)	(0.001)
POST-COLD WAR	4.47E+07***	0.815***	0.006***	5.284***	0.838***	0.601***	1.280***
	(3.64E+06)	(0.060)	(0.000)	(0.505)	(0.050)	(0.034)	(0.071)
Constant	-1.29E+08***	-0.609***	22.795***	-31.264***	-5.644***	-0.335***	10.632***
	(1.03E+07)	(0.171)	(0.001)	(1.431)	(0.142)	(0.097)	(0.201)
Observations	3,452	3,452	3,451	3,452	3,452	3,452	3,452

Note: Robust standard errors in parentheses.

*** $p < .01$, ** $p < .05$, * $p < .10$

deviate from a normal distribution to a lesser degree than do those from the other four measures; this finding provides an ideal basis for my subsequent significance tests. Thus, I recommend that researchers employ these three measures to ensure robust empirical analysis. I emphasize that a formal normality check should be the first step of an empirical analysis immediately upon the completion of sample data whose size is small or even moderately large. This simple univariate analysis enhances the possibility for conducting rigorous research in that it helps us avoid choosing an inappropriate measure of FDI, one that could lead to invalid estimates. In other words, univariate normality tests will help researchers understand their data better and make reliable inferences and interpretations based on subsequent multivariate analyses.

My multivariate regression analyses illustrate that when the normality assumption of the data is satisfied, democratic countries appear to attract more foreign capital than do autocratic countries. Therefore, it is unlikely that democracy is negatively associated with FDI when the regression residuals are approximately normally distributed. In terms of empirical results, by performing the Prais-Winsten regression, country fixed effects, and the Arellano and Bond GMM estimator, I discover that models using FDI, FDI/GDP, log (FDI + minimum), or FDI/POP as the dependent variable detect no significant effect of the democracy variable on foreign investment. Models that employ the dependent variable of

$$\log\left(\left(\frac{FDI}{POP}\right)+\sqrt{\left(\frac{FDI}{POP}\right)^2+1}\right), \log\left(\left(\frac{FDI}{GDP}\right)+\sqrt{\left(\frac{FDI}{GDP}\right)^2+1}\right),$$
$$\text{or } \log (FDI + \sqrt{FDI^2+1}),$$

on the other hand, are capable of predicting a significant and positive effect of democracy on foreign investment. My overall findings suggest that the four FDI measures (i.e., net FDI inflows in dollars, FDI/GDP, log (FDI + a minimum), and FDI/population) that are widely used in the literature are, in fact, not well suited for robust empirical analysis. Accordingly, I propose

$$\log\left(\left(\frac{FDI}{POP}\right)+\sqrt{\left(\frac{FDI}{POP}\right)^2+1}\right), \log\left(\left(\frac{FDI}{GDP}\right)+\sqrt{\left(\frac{FDI}{GDP}\right)^2+1}\right),$$
$$\text{and } \log (FDI + \sqrt{FDI^2+1})$$

as more desirable measures. The rationale for the recommendation should be clear now: the residuals from those respective models approximate a normal distribution, which allows researchers to obtain valid estimates and draw meaningful inferences about the democracy-FDI connection.

CHAPTER 7

Terrorism and Zero-Inflated Negative Binomial Regression

A Mismatch between Theory and Statistical Model

In any social scientific study, the implications of the theory and the observation of facts need to mesh with one another: social science conclusions cannot be considered reliable if they are not based on theory and data in strong connection with one another and forged by formulating and examining the observable implications of a theory.

GARY KING, ROBERT O. KEOHANE, AND SIDNEY VERBA,
Designing Social Inquiry: Scientific Interference in Qualitative Research

Since the September 11th attacks terrorism has been one of the most salient topics in both academic and policy circles. In particular, scholarly exploration of the causes and effects of terrorism has flourished thanks to the gathering of evidence based on empirical data. Despite this encouraging development, there is also a growing concern that certain statistical models frequently employed in studies of terrorism fail to effectively test the hypotheses put forward in their corresponding theory sections (e.g., Drakos and Gofas 2006b; see also Hall 2000). Empirical studies that do not make a direct connection between theory and data analysis violate the golden rule of King, Keohane, and Verba (1994, 29), which states that "theory and empirical research must be tightly connected." Such a failure renders many empirical findings of these studies untenable. Typically, researchers attempting to test a theory of why terror activity varies across countries employ negative binomial (NB) regression as an estimation method and operationalize the annual number of terrorist incidents as their dependent variable. NB regression is particularly useful for fitting count data, the variance of which tends to be greater than the mean. However, when a researcher's theory concerns the differences between terrorism-free and terrorism-prone countries, and when the former are observed much more often than the latter, zero-inflated negative binomial (ZINB) regression is more appropriate than NB.

Earlier studies of terrorism tended to employ NB regression as their base model and ZINB regression as one of several checks for robustness. Li (2005, 293) notes that the undesirability of ZINB as a base model is due largely to the fact that it is "lacking [in] strong theoretical priors." However, more recent studies have put ZINB at the center of their empirical analyses, and it has begun to become the preferred base model for researchers of terrorism. For example, Savun and Phillips' (2009) work theorizes, and their ZINB results support, that democratic countries are more likely than others to be terrorized by transnational terrorist groups due to their aggressive foreign policies. Relying on a different set of ZINB model specifications, Piazza (2011) offers empirical evidence that countries with high levels of minority group economic discrimination are more likely to experience domestic terrorist attacks than those countries that lack it. Hoffman, Shelton, and Cleven's (2013) study presents a theory of media freedom and media attention that explains why some countries are more vulnerable to international terrorism than others; they too present their ZINB results as evidence in support of their theoretical prediction. Santifort-Jordan and Sandler (2014) collect a unique data set for 1998–2010 of about 2,500 suicide terrorist incidents, using the Global Terrorism Database, the International Terrorism: Attributes of Terrorist Events (ITERATE) project, and the RAND Database of Worldwide Terrorism Incidents. Santifort-Jordan and Sandler apply ZINB panel estimation for country-specific variables.[1] Although to some degree these studies pave the way for a better understanding of the origins of terrorism, their empirical analyses share a common problem; that is, each of them perpetuates a mismatch between its theoretical underpinnings and its ZINB model. Thus, the purpose of the present study is to reexamine their empirical findings from the point of model selection and to make suggestions for the future of research on terrorism in particular, as well as for political science more generally.

WHAT IS ZINB FOR?

In a statistical sense, ZINB is typically used in cases where excessive zeros are present in a count data for units such as individuals or countries at a single moment, as well as when the excessive zeros consist of not-always-zeros and always-zeros.[2] As it estimates both count equation and inflation equation simultaneously, ZINB is designed to avoid underestimating the probability of excessive zeros. The count equation includes a list of independent variables that determine counts among those that are not-always-zeros; likewise, the inflation equation includes a list of inflation variables that determine whether one is in the always-zero group or the not-always-zero group. The explanatory variables in the count and inflation equations may be the same but need not be as long as adequate theoretical justification is provided.

In an effort to better illustrate the statistical properties of ZINB, this study compares it with NB by using an example of scientific productivity. NB assumes that every scientist has a positive probability of publishing any given number of papers; the probability varies across scientists according to their individual characteristics, but all scientists have some probability of publishing.[3] However, this assumption may not be applicable to those scientists who cannot publish due to certain structural restrictions (e.g., working at a secret government laboratory). Unlike NB, ZINB allows for this possibility, thereby increasing the conditional variance and the probability of zero counts (Long and Freese 2006, 394). In other words, ZINB is capable of taking into account the possible presence of scientists with no publications (i.e., the always-zero group) in cross-national data.[4]

When political researchers collect data at a single moment, it often contains individuals or countries that belong to the always-zero group. It is likely that some countries have a positive probability of experiencing political upheavals, while a majority of countries, due to their political and economic circumstances, are not potential victims. North Korea, for example, belongs to the latter group of countries because it has zero probability of experiencing international terrorist attacks—it is simply not an attractive target for the political agenda of international terrorist organizations. Having this kind of prior knowledge about a country should help researchers to correctly fit their cross-national data. In short, when political scientists collect cross-national data that include many countries with no political events or terrorism, the appropriate statistical model is ZINB.

A CLOSE EXAMINATION OF PREVIOUS STUDIES OF TERRORISM

In their article "Press Freedom, Publicity, and the Cross-National Incidence of Transnational Terrorism," Hoffman, Shelton, and Cleven (2013) investigate whether open media lead to an increase in the experience of transnational terrorism. Their theoretical argument revolves around two distinct functions of mass media—press freedom and press attention. They assert that because previous studies have failed to distinguish between the different functions of mass media (e.g., Li 2005), their reported empirical findings for the connection between media and terrorism is unreliable. On the contrary, Hoffman, Shelton, and Cleven's results point to the significant and positive effects of both press freedom and press attention on the incidence of terrorist attacks. The present study demonstrates below that because Hoffman, Shelton, and Cleven's study suffers from a mismatch between theory and statistical model, their estimated results are erroneous and, thus, their inference and conclusion are incorrect. In other words, the findings of Hoffman, Shelton, and Cleven's study result from statistical artifacts.

By focusing on country-level characteristics, Hoffman, Shelton, and Cleven (2013) assert that "the approach we use is appropriate for identifying the political institutions that serve as attractors of terrorism" (900). They emphasize that they must account for two different types of countries: one group of countries, such as North Korea, which terrorist organizations systematically avoided attacking (i.e., the always-zero country group) and a second group that eluded attack only irregularly (i.e., the not-always-zero country group). They choose ZINB as the main estimation method on the grounds that the dependent variable of international terrorist incidents is a count measure with an excessive number of zeros. This approach would be appropriate if the empirical analysis of the study were based on a cross-national data set rather than a cross-national, time-series data set. As noted above, the command zinb is programmed in Stata exclusively for a cross-national data format and, therefore, is not suitable for the cross-national, time-series data format of the study in question. When Hoffman, Shelton, and Cleven issued the Stata command zinb, excessive zeros were identified for individual *observations* and not for individual *countries*. (In fact, it is doubtful that Hoffman, Shelton, and Cleven's cross-national, time-series data set contains an excess number of countries that can be designated as the always-zero country group, but this is elaborated upon below.) The use of the command zinb mistakenly treats a large number of observations recorded as no terrorist incident as if they were individual countries in the always-zero country group.

Although Hoffman, Shelton, and Cleven's study (2013, 907n1) states that "the data, replication files, and supplemental on-line materials for these analyses can be found at http://web.ics.purdue.edu/~ahoffman," they were not available at the time of this writing. Nonetheless, based on the authors' data description, this study re-creates a data set for the same period between 1975 and 1995. Data on the incidence of transnational acts of terrorism are drawn from the ITERATE data set; the total number of observations is 3,211, which is close to the 3,441 observations of Hoffman, Shelton, and Cleven's study (2013, 902, Table 1). A quick scan of this newly created data set reveals that only two countries (i.e., Vietnam and North Vietnam) experienced zero terrorism during the entire period of study. This finding appears to be in direct contradiction with the assertion of Hoffman, Shelton, and Cleven that their data include many countries with zero terrorist incidents. However, it should be noted that the total number of zeros is 1,707 out of 3,211 (i.e., 53 percent), when each observation, as opposed to each country, in the data set is calculated. Again, when the data format is cross-national and time-series, the Stata command zinb is incapable of differentiating between the zeros that belong to the always-zero country group and those that belong to the not-always-zero country group. Thus, in the case of Hoffman, Shelton, and Cleven's terrorism data, the zinb command erroneously estimated the excessive zero counts on the basis of observation-years rather than country-years.

Because Hoffman, Shelton, and Cleven's data collection is a combination of cross-national and time-series, zinb fails to identify the systematic zeros of individual countries, and so it incorrectly picks up individual observations with no terrorist incidents as if they were individual countries with no terrorist incidents. That is, the Stata command zinb is, by default, unable to appreciate the time dimension of the cross-national, time-series data structure. This simple analysis clearly shows the mismatch between Hoffman, Shelton, and Cleven's theory and their statistical model; an incorrect data format has resulted in a lack of correspondence between their theoretical argument, which concerns the characteristics of countries, and their statistical model, which incorrectly measures attributes of individual observations instead of countries. In other words, because their theory was tested with an inappropriate estimation technique, their empirical findings are unreliable.

By dividing the targeting decisions of terrorists into two stages, Hoffman, Shelton, and Cleven's study argues that "the influence of press freedom is felt in Stage 1; the issue of press attention comes to the fore in Stage 2" (2013, 900). For this reason, the inflation equation includes press freedom as its main predictor, whereas the main predictor in the count equation is press attention. Both equations employ the same dependent variable, yet each of the two uses a completely different set of control variables, a decision for which the authors have failed to provide any theoretical justification; they do not inform readers why it is that a certain set of controls must be incorporated into the inflation equation but not into the count equation, or vice versa. It is well known that the estimated results of ZINB are highly susceptible to variation depending on the kinds of controls included in the inflation equation. This is particularly problematic for Hoffman, Shelton, and Cleven's study because the statistical method is inappropriate for their data, which is in a cross-national, time-series format. It is common practice for researchers to employ the same set of controls in both the count and inflation equations in order to increase the robustness of their estimated results (e.g., Long and Freese 2006, 309; Piazza 2011, 347, Table 2). It appears that in this case the significance of press attention and press freedom was achieved by arbitrarily selecting different control variables for each equation. A better model specification for each equation would include, all together, press freedom, Composite Index of National Capability (CINC), and all of the controls that appear in Tables 1 and 2.[5]

Hoffman, Shelton, and Cleven's study claims that press freedom is better suited to predicting why some states are never attacked rather than why the United States is attacked more than Canada. For this comparison to be true, the study should also include the press freedom variable in the count equation of Table 2 (2013, 903), and the press attention—proxied by CINC[6]—in the inflation equation of Table 1 (902); thus, the press freedom variable would appear in both count and inflation equations in Tables 1 and 2. This would allow the study in question to test, in both equations concurrently, the two queries of interest:

why some states are never attacked (in the inflation equation), and why the United States is attacked more than Canada (in the count equation). However, in Tables 1 and 2 (902, 903), Hoffman, Shelton, and Cleven do not select such a model specification. This choice raises the possibility that this error occurred because the correct model specification would have caused press freedom and press attention to become insignificant.

Other studies of terrorism are subject to the same erroneous data analysis as the work produced by Hoffman, Shelton, and Cleven. The theories of Piazza (2011), Savun and Phillips (2009), and Santifort-Jordan and Sandler (2014) pertain to how certain characteristics of countries may explain terrorist activity; however, each study chooses a statistical model—ZINB—that produces estimated results geared toward the attributes of observations rather than countries. Piazza's (2011) ZINB regression model tested the impact of Minorities at Risk (MAR) economic discrimination on domestic terrorism for the years 1970 through 2006. When the data for Model 1 in Table 2 (347) are scrutinized, only 16 out of 167 (10 percent) countries are found to belong to the always-zero country group.[7] This number does not support Piazza's claim that his model accommodates an excessive number of zero countries, because it has in fact identified an excessive number of zero observations. When Piazza's data are reanalyzed, this study notes that 1,794 out of 2,964 (61 percent) observations indeed have no terrorist incident. Simply put, because Piazza's ZINB regression model deals with excessive zeros related to observations but not countries, the estimated results have little relation to his theoretical claim.

In order to explore the relationship between democracy and terrorism, Savun and Phillips (2009) collected data on domestic terrorism during the period from 1998 to 2004, as well as data on international terrorism during the period from 1968 to 2004. According to Model 1 in Table 3 (10), the total number of countries that may be properly categorized as the always-zero country group was only 28 out of 113 (25 percent) countries, while 454 out of 777 (58 percent) observations were recorded as having no occurrence of domestic terrorism.[8] According to Model 1 in Table 5 (17), the total number of the always-zero country group was only 22 out of 163 (13 percent) countries, while 3,572 out of 5,209 (69 percent) observations have no international terrorism. In short, the estimated results from Savun and Phillips' ZINB regression model fail to provide support for their theoretical argument due to the fact that the unit of analysis for the statistical model is observation-year while, in theory, it should be the country-year.

In the effort to determine how economic, political, and military variables affect suicide terrorism, Santifort-Jordan and Sandler (2014) compiled data on domestic and transnational suicide terrorist missions for 47 countries (excluding West Bank/Gaza) during the period from 1998 to 2010. Santifort-Jordan and Sandler assert that "countries susceptible to suicide attacks are modeled by the negative binomial step of the ZINB model, while countries not susceptible to suicide attacks are modeled by the logit step of the ZINB model" (991). However, when the data for Model 1 in Table 2 (992) were analyzed, no single country (as opposed to observation) was found to be free of suicide terrorism during the study period. All of 47 sample countries experienced at least one suicide attack, so again, Santifort-Jordan and Sandler's estimates are inconsistent with their theoretical justification for the use of the ZINB model.

CONCLUDING REMARKS

The use of ZINB models and NB regression models has become the de facto standard in quantitative studies of terrorism; however, this study has pointed to the common misuse of ZINB in the literature. Even if researchers may be able to offer a convincing causal explanation, their findings are still faulty or misleading when they choose an inappropriate estimation technique that does not conform to the nature of their statistical data. This study has shown that the research designs of Hoffman, Shelton, and Cleven (2013), Santifort-Jordan and Sandler (2014), Piazza (2011), and Savun and Phillips (2009) are all flawed for this reason; that is, the results of these studies are erroneous because their choice of statistical model does not conform to their theoretical reasoning.[9] In addition, as discussed with the case of Hoffman, Shelton, and Cleven (2013), the estimates of ZINB are highly dependent on which control variables are included in the inflation equation. Arbitrary selection of controls without proper theoretical justification is an additional danger of ZINB modeling and can lead to the production of statistical artifacts. It should be noted that the potential for error with ZINB modeling looms large in other research areas as well. For example, studies done by Meernik et al. (2012) on human rights and by Moore and Shellman (2007) on refugees face the same problem. The disconnect between theory and model can be overcome either by choosing only one time period to analyze or by averaging the data. The lesson is that future researchers must be cautious and carefully consider the relevant theoretical argument, model selection, and data attributes before choosing a statistical technique. At minimum, ZINB regression should not be presented as the base estimation method but instead as a test for robustness. Furthermore, future research should refrain from citing the works in question in the effort to justify the choice of a ZINB regression model; the rationale should be clear by now—it is simply wrong.

CHAPTER 8

Democracy and Transnational Terrorism Revisited

Rule of Law

> If citizens cannot trust that laws will be enforced in an evenhanded and honest fashion, they cannot be said to live under the rule of law. Instead, they live under the rule of men corrupted by the law.
>
> DALE CARPENTER, *Flagrant Conduct: The Story of Lawrence v. Texas*

The question of how best to combat terrorism is one of today's most highly debated topics among academics, policy makers, and politicians alike. For example, the George W. Bush administration and its defenders, in their motivation to curb terrorist activities abroad, championed the advancement of democracy into terrorism-prone countries as a practical foreign policy goal (Gause 2005).[1] The Obama administration currently promotes the idea that the development of an appropriate legal framework, along with the preservation of political freedom and social justice, is a winning strategy for democratic countries in response to potential terrorist threats (Hinnen 2009). Existing empirical studies, however, present contradictory causal arguments about the possibility that democratic governance reduces terrorism. A majority of studies claim that because they promote high levels of civil liberties and legal rights for accused criminals (e.g., terror suspects), democracies leave themselves more vulnerable to potential terrorist attacks (e.g., Eubank and Weinberg 1994, 2001). In contrast, a relatively small number of studies maintain that because democracies encourage political participation and the nonviolent resolution of conflicts, their chances of experiencing illegal terrorist incidents are small (e.g., Eyerman 1998). The fact that these debates are unresolved demonstrates that current scholarship fails to offer a concrete answer to the question of whether democracies attract more terrorist attacks than do nondemocracies.

In the present study, I treat the "rule of law" as one of the most fundamental institutional characteristics of liberal democratic societies, and it is conceptualized as the synthesis of effective and impartial judicial systems alongside the recognition by ordinary citizens of the law as legitimate. I present a causal explanation in which the democratic rule of law is considered to lessen the opportunity for and willingness of ordinary citizens to engage in political violence, thereby protecting democracies from exploitation by transnational terrorists.[2] Based on negative binomial regression, population-averaged negative binomial regression, zero-inflated negative binomial regression,[3] Heckman selection models, and two-step models of one hundred countries during the period from 1984 to 1997, I find that, all other things being equal, democratic societies that maintain a strong rule of law experience notably fewer transnational terrorist incidents than do those societies with a relatively weak rule of law.

THE DAMPENING EFFECT OF THE DEMOCRATIC RULE OF LAW ON TRANSNATIONAL TERRORISM

Before exploring the link between the rule of law and transnational terrorism, we must clarify the somewhat controversial definitions of these two concepts. Terrorism is a particularly difficult concept to define because of its normative nature—as the saying goes: one man's terrorist is another man's freedom fighter. More generally, there is the persistent problem of differentiating conceptually between a terrorist attack and a military tactic. For analytical clarity, I follow Enders and Sandler's (2006, 3) definition of a terrorist attack as "the premeditated use or threat to use violence by individuals or subnational groups in order to obtain a political and social objective through the intimidation of a large audience." In spite of its bias in favor of the use of violence by national groups— note that it becomes conceptually impossible for a sovereign state to engage in terrorism, because it is an act in which only "individuals or subnational groups" can by definition engage—for the most part, this definition remains normatively neutral toward terrorist strategies. Transnational terrorism, then, is a situation in which a terrorist incident in country A involves perpetrators, victims, institutions, governments, or citizens of country B (Enders and Sandler 2006, 7). More specifically, transnational terrorist incidents may include domestic terrorist attacks against some foreign target in the terrorists' home country or in the host country, foreign terrorist attacks against some other foreign target in the host country, and foreign terrorist attacks against some domestic target of the host country (Li 2005, 280). Transnational terrorism, by definition, excludes homegrown terrorist incidents such as the Oklahoma City bombing and the Boston bombing since domestic terrorism attacks target only in the terrorists' home country.

Like the concept of terrorism, the "rule of law" is also subject to various definitional and normative disputes (see O'Donnell 2004). For analytical parsimony, I limit myself to two fundamental components that should be present in democratic societies with a high-quality rule of law: fair, impartial, and effective judicial systems, and a non-arbitrary basis in which laws and the legal system as a whole can be viewed as legitimate. As legal scholar Joseph Raz (1977, 198–201) argues, fair and impartial judicial systems require at least an independent judiciary branch with fair-minded judges, prosecutors, and lawyers, as well as a strong and stable law enforcement or police squad (for a similar view, see Fuller 1969). Institutionalizing an independent judiciary system reflects a strong commitment by government to the basic principle that all persons are equal before the law and so deserve the opportunity to have their grievances heard and their disputes settled in court; this commitment is also reflected by judges who exercise fair and impartial decision making based strictly on facts, legal arguments, and relevant laws. Furthermore, by assuring the independence of the judiciary from the other political branches, the notion of the law's sovereignty over the government is more convincing; without this independence, we would not be sure whether we have the rule of law, or simply political leaders ruling through law.

The institutionalization of a fair and independent judiciary assures citizens that they can have trust and confidence in legal norms and procedures, as well as in the courts and the police. Citizens of such societies are more likely to consult established laws and legal procedures to reconcile political and personal differences instead of resorting to physical violence as a means of resolving disputes. Because they believe in the likelihood of a fair and impartial legal ruling in court, citizens are willing to turn to the domestic judicial systems, and this brings a certain degree of order to the political and social relations of any society (Hardin 2001; O'Donnell 2004). Thus, an independent judicial system and the resulting trust of ordinary citizens in the established laws create a strong tradition of law and order in a society. Because "the rule of law" thus indicates the presence of "a strong tradition of law and order," I hereafter use these two terms interchangeably.

With these terms now clarified, we can conceptualize the effect of the liberal democratic institution of the rule of law on the rate of occurrence of terrorist activity.[4] To begin, we must understand the nature of domestic judicial systems in democracies. As a fundamental building block of any democratic society, a high-quality legal system "serves to protect people against anarchy as well as from [the] arbitrary exercise of power by public officials and allows people to plan their daily affairs with confidence" (Wilson 2006, 153). Because liberal democratic judicial systems ensure independent adjudication of legal rules, they create a fair chance for those whose interests are at stake to be heard in efficient but inexpensive legal outlets. Thus, in the presence of an effective, independent judicial system in liberal democratic societies, ordinary citizens need not resort to illegal measures to resolve complaints and grievances. Eyerman (1998, 154) makes a similar observation, saying that since democracies "increase the expected return of legal activity and offer multiple channels of non-violent expression without the threat of government retaliation," they assuage the growth of bitterness and dissatisfaction toward the administration that may potentially turn ordinary people into terrorists (see also Frey and Luechinger 2003). In contrast, where sound judicial systems are lacking, dissatisfied people are more likely to embrace the principle of retributive justice and, hence, to become involved in terrorist activity.

Second, we want to understand the nature of democratic citizens' recognition of the legal order as legitimate. Because democratic citizens are socialized to trust in the fairness and impartiality of the legal system, in the case of a dispute they are likely to follow the established laws in order to settle their political grievances. From this perspective, a turn to violence would be self-defeating, because it would ultimately undermine a legal institution that is widely seen as important and necessary. Furthermore, because democratic citizens see these institutions as generally fair and legitimate, citizens will tend to abide by the established legal order even when they disagree with an individual legal statute or ruling.[5] Democratic citizens trust that legal adjudication will produce a right and fair result, even in cases when it is not the result that they had wanted.

It is not hard to imagine, then, why ordinary citizens of democratic countries might be less likely to perpetrate acts of terrorism than those of nondemocratic countries where the legal system is tailored to suit the rich and powerful;[6] the non-arbitrary implementation of law and the distribution of punishment at the hands of a dispassionate legal system makes extralegal violence untenable or undesirable. It is important to note that, in challenging terrorism, the attitudes of law-abiding citizens in democratic societies are no less important than the presence of an independent judiciary with fair-minded judges and law enforcement officials. As we have seen, judicial institutions alone cannot produce a high-quality tradition of law and order; other factors within a society, especially the perspective of the citizenry, are actively involved. An exclusive reliance on legal authority is less likely to create and maintain safe and healthy communities when democratic citizens do not willingly cooperate with judicial institutions and serve as watchful eyes and ears for illegal terrorist activities (Garland 1996; Hogg and Brown 1998; Hardin 2001; Scraton 2004).

With the link between the rule of law and terrorism thus outlined, I now present a causal explanation of how or why ordinary people engage in activities of transnational terrorism. I argue that ordinary people have incentives to terrorize foreign facilities and citizens of foreign countries when two conditions are met: they hold grievances against formidable foreign powers that violate the political and legal rights of local citizens; and these local citizens do not believe in pursuing justice peacefully due to a poor-quality rule of law in their home country. Due to the relatively low logistics costs, the opportunity for locals to implement transnational terrorist tactics increases when foreign targets are located within the home territory. However, when local people intend to settle grievances against foreign institutions and governments abroad, they are likely to collude with transnational terrorist organizations due to the high operational costs of committing political violence in a foreign country (see Starr 1991).

Recent transnational terrorist events exemplify how it is that distressed locals are inclined to resort to terrorist violence against foreign oppressors when they lack an adequate rule of law tradition within which to air their grievances. Because many Muslim populations witnessed or experienced outlawed practices such as torture, black site prisons, and indefinite detention without due process during the George W. Bush administration, overseas U.S. citizens, soldiers, and facilities located in foreign countries have become major terrorist targets in those several countries where the rule of law is fragile. It is worth noting that such lawless procedures have not only undermined America's moral credibility and standing abroad but have also provided terrorist recruiters with some of their most effective material, resulting in a higher rate of transnational terrorist attacks in recent years (Hinnen 2009). A U.S. National Intelligence Estimate report in 2006 reveals that the indiscriminate deportation and detention of prisoners at the Abu Ghraib and Guantanamo Bay prisons caused many disgruntled Iraqi and Afghan citizens to terrorize foreign citizens and soldiers in their home country (Mazzetti 2006). Matthew Alexander (pseudonym, 2008), a senior interrogator during the second Iraq War, confirms the causal link between the abuse of the rule of law and the surge of transnational terrorist activity by stating, "I learned in Iraq that the No. 1 reason foreign fighters flocked there to fight were the abuses carried out at Abu Ghraib and Guantanamo. Our policy of torture was directly and swiftly recruiting fighters for Al-Qaeda in Iraq. [Many foreign terrorists] joined the fray because of our program of detainee abuse."

The close connection between the weak rule of law and transnational terrorist events is found in other countries as well. Sudan, for example, has come to be feared as a reservoir for and exporter of transnational terrorism not only because the sense of political community has vanished in the absence of a political order that includes fair judicial systems, but also because the public feels marginalized by foreigners and disenfranchised by the local government (Rotberg 2002). Jones et al. (2005) scrutinize nation-building activities in Panama, El Salvador, Somalia, Haiti, Bosnia, East Timor, Kosovo, Afghanistan, and Iraq and come to a similar conclusion that strong and viable judicial structures, security forces, and police are essential in the prevention of transnational terrorism, and societies that lack these structures are at much greater risk of attack. Recent remarks by Palestinian chairman Mahmoud Abbas that he is unable to curb transnational terrorism because he "cannot impose law and order in [the] West Bank" provide further evidence for this argument (*Israel Insider* 2007).

There are four main archetypal narratives that better explain the causal mechanisms underlying the relationship between the rule of law and transnational terrorism. The first causal mechanism is illustrated by a situation in which ordinary people feel desperate against foreigners who abuse the legal rights of their fellow citizens, whether at home or abroad, and who exploit their country's political and economic interests. Because these foreigners are not subject to domestic legal jurisdiction, or because they are unfairly protected by the home country's justice system, citizens are more likely to take justice into their own hands and to engage in locally coordinated terrorist attacks against the foreigners and their facilities. Iraqi suicide attacks against U.S. forces are cases in point. Because many young Iraqis feel mistreated by U.S. soldiers but are unable to turn to Iraqi domestic courts for resolution, they often, for lack of any other recourse, become perpetrators of violent terrorist activities. This same phenomenon is seen in the insurgency of Iraqi civilians against the armed private soldiers who operate with virtual immunity from law, whether it is that of Iraq or that of their own countries (see Pape 2005; Broder and Risen 2007; Singer 2007; Shanker and Myers 2008). Still another example is a series of suicide attacks that Hezbollah launched against American, French, and other allied troops in Lebanon in the 1980s. Hezbollah believed that these terrorist acts would help bring justice and liberty to all Lebanese people (Qassem 2005).

The second causal mechanism is an extension of the first, where hopeless citizens become transnational terrorists as a strategy to push forward their domestic agendas. In this case, discontented citizens who are frustrated with a low-quality rule of law at home go abroad to carry out attacks against foreign targets of the host country as an attempt to rectify foreign exploitation of their home country. This is done either because foreign targets are more vulnerable to attack, or because there is some strategic advantage in putting the attack on an international, as opposed to domestic, stage. In the latter case, the purpose of transnational terrorist attacks is to evoke domestic opposition in the host country in the hopes that it will bring an end to the foreign presence. Either way, discontented citizens of one country become foreign terrorists in another, determined to attack its institutions, citizens, or property. The suicide car bombing of the UN headquarters in Baghdad on August 19, 2003, is an archetypal example because the followers of the late Abu Musab al-Zarqawi, a Jordanian militant Islamist, intentionally targeted the UN and killed at least eight Iraqis and fourteen foreigners including Sérgio Vieira de Mello, a Brazilian UN diplomat (Enders and Sandler 2006).

The third causal mechanism of transnational terrorism is one in which discontented people are angry at politically influential foreign targets within their own country. However, in these situations the citizens possess no readily available means to retaliate against those foreigners or their well-guarded facilities.

Feelings of powerlessness among disgruntled people may lead them to seek the support of transnational terrorists, seeing it as the best or only strategy to redress their frustrations (Tessler and Robbins 2007). Such circumstances provide an ideal opportunity for transnational terrorist groups to build a relationship with disaffected locals, a relationship that ultimately offers these groups safe havens, easier access to material resources, and better channels through which to execute militant operations against foreign targets in the host country (i.e., foreign terrorist attacks on some other foreign target). Essentially, a discontented local citizenry provides the strategic opportunity for transnational terrorist groups to carry out attacks against foreign targets in a country. For example, many Iraqis welcome and support Al Qaeda operatives from countries such as Pakistan to help them fight against U.S. forces.

The fourth causal mechanism is illustrated by a situation in which citizens have grievances against their own corrupt government but lack any avenue for redress. Because there is a breakdown of the necessary social support that allows for a stable rule of law tradition, the possibility of "mob rule" and lawlessness becomes acute. However, because the citizens themselves are too weak to revolt, they are more likely to turn to outside sources of help, such as transnational terrorist groups that can take action on their behalf (i.e., foreign terrorist attacks on a domestic target). Possessing global financial resources and disciplined members who operate in autonomous terrorist cells, transnational terrorist organizations are capable of attracting local people who feel disadvantaged and using them to help carry out their own terrorist plots. It should not be surprising that underprivileged people and ethnic minority groups are especially vulnerable to recruitment by transnational terrorists who suggest radical violence against domestic institutions and officials as a solution to their frustrations and grievances. Disgruntled Pakistani tribesmen, for example, join together with foreign Al Qaeda members, Uzbek militants, and Taliban fighters to initiate terrorist attacks against the people and places most significant to the Musharraf government (Gall and Rohde 2008; Masood 2008).

In all of the above cases, transnational terrorists are able to carry out attacks because their targets are in countries that lack a strong tradition of the rule of law. This indicates the importance of establishing, and consistently enforcing, the democratic rule of law in order to curtail the actions of organized terrorist groups as well as to discourage ordinary people from becoming perpetrators of transnational terrorism. Because liberal democratic countries maintain a strong tradition of law and order built upon independent judicial systems and legitimate, non-arbitrary law, it is less likely that their citizens will resort to transnational terrorism in order to resolve disputes. However, it should be noted that when a country abandons the rule of law for the sake of expedience, it no longer adheres to the principle of democratic governance and thus puts its overseas citizens and soldiers in danger of becoming victims of transnational terrorism. One may claim that it is not necessary for a government to exhibit both law and order, since some autocratic countries may have order without law and appear to experience only a small number of terrorist incidents. However, it should be stressed that the political and social order that results from oppressive measures such as the use of a secret police force, mass murder, or genocide under a dictator is clearly not an order based on fair and impartial legal systems leading to citizens' adherence to established laws based on their belief that the system is just. Because authoritarian leaders justify the threat of punishment and violence with the support of corrupt domestic legal authorities, ordinary citizens have incentives to challenge the legitimacy of authoritarian rule by promoting terrorist violence under the auspices of transnational terrorist groups. For example, Chechen fighters have garnered support from Muslim sympathizers around the world to terrorize the authoritarian Russian government. The BBC's online Q&A on the conflict states that "it has been known for years that Muslim volunteers have traveled to Chechnya to join the fight, reportedly after attending training camps in Afghanistan or Pakistan" (Reuters AlertNet 2008). In this sense, my conceptualization of "democratic order" should be distinguished from "autocratic order." The former is a key component of the truly liberal democratic rule of law that contributes to a decrease in transnational terrorist incidents, whereas the latter is more likely to be a temporary or short-lived manifestation in the absence of popular support and may actually manifest support for transnational terrorism.[7]

To recap, the rule of law reinforces a political system's legitimacy by protecting the rights of citizens and foreigners and by providing them with the means to settle disputes in nonviolent ways. Thus, the rule of law acts as a cornerstone for liberal democracies, making it unlikely that average citizens will seek outside support from transnational terrorist organizations; it essentially preempts their engagement in illicit transnational terrorist violence. An independent judiciary with fair-minded judges and police officers who enforce laws widely seen as legitimate are foundational to an environment in which the public can use the established laws to settle disputes because they consider the system to be fair and just; thus, the combined impact of impartial judicial systems and the recognition among ordinary citizens of the law as legitimate is likely to reduce transnational terrorism in democratic countries. Therefore, I state my hypothesis as follows:

H_1: The democratic rule of law has a dampening effect on the incidence of transnational terrorism: fair and impartial judicial systems along with the public's recognition of the law as legitimate will discourage transnational terrorist events.

RESEARCH DESIGN

To test the democratic rule of law hypothesis, I conduct a cross-sectional, time-series data analysis with a sample of one hundred countries during the period from 1984 to 1997. Given several analysts' criticism that the different model specifications and statistical methods in existing studies may be responsible for having produced conflicting findings regarding the democracy-terrorism link (e.g., Sandler 1995; Enders and Sandler 2006), I use Li's (2005) research design as a frame of reference.[8] Li presented his first three models (288, Table 1) as the main empirical analysis to test the effects of three different democratic features on transnational terrorism: democratic participation and government constraint in Model 1; press freedom in Model 2; and democratic participation, government constraint, and press freedom together in Model 3. He hypothesized that democratic participation would be shown to decrease transnational terrorism and projected that government constraint and press freedom would increase it. The present study differs from Li's models in two respects: the inclusion of the rule of law variable; and the shorter study period of 1984–1997. The former is self-explanatory; the latter is necessary due to the limited availability of data for the rule of law variable. Li's study spans the years from 1975 to 1997, but data on the rule of law are available only as far back as 1984, so I have used data from that point onward to 1997, which is the endpoint of Li's study. Despite the shorter study period, the empirical analysis takes an important step toward determining whether the maintenance of a high-quality rule of law leads to a decrease in transnational terrorist incidents.

The dependent variable is the annual total number of transnational terrorist events that occurred in a country, operationalized with Mickolus et al.'s (2006) International Terrorism: Attributes of Terrorist Events (ITERATE) database.[9] Consistent with the theoretical discussion in the previous section, transnational terrorist events are recorded if domestic terrorists attack any foreign target in a home or host country, if foreign terrorists attack any domestic target in a country, or if foreign terrorists attack some other foreign target in a country. It should be noted that although the ITERATE data set is a widely used source of transnational terrorist activity, it does contain some limitations and inherent shortcomings due to the fact that its sources come from newspaper accounts. This fact may introduce underreporting bias as autocratic regimes tend to limit freedom of the press.[10] In addition, the ITERATE database has been criticized for the inclusion of some incidents that may be considered domestic terrorism. In fact, the codebook of the ITERATE data set (Mickolus et al. 2006, 9) observes that in some cases, the data are not entirely clear on the distinction between transnational and domestic terrorism: "While many of these attacks [committed by separatists or irredentists] are considered to be domestic terrorism, such attacks are included if the terrorists traverse a natural geographical boundary to conduct attacks on the metropole, e.g. Northern Irish attacks on the main British island, Puerto Rican attacks outside of the island, and attacks within Israel by Palestinian refugees."[11]

The rule of law variable measures the coexistence of the two democratic features conceptualized in the previous section: the strength and impartiality of the legal system and the degree of popular observance of law as a fair and legitimate way to settle claims. The source of this variable is the International Country Risk Guide (ICRG) compiled by the Political Risk Services (PRS) Group.[12] The ICRG first assesses each of these two features on a scale of 0 to 3. For example, a country may enjoy a high rating of 3 in terms of its judicial system, but a low rating of 1 if the law is routinely ignored by the public without effective sanction (for example, by widespread rioting or looting). The ICRG then combines the two scores from each feature to produce a seven-point scale with 0 indicating a weak law and order tradition where citizens depend on physical force or illegal means to resolve grievances, and 6 denoting a strong law and order tradition where the established law enforcement and judicial channels are effectively used by citizens to settle disputes. According to the rule of law hypothesis, a high rating on this scale should produce a dampening effect on the number of transnational terrorist incidents; a low score would indicate a much higher likelihood of transnational terrorism. It should be noted that the ICRG releases for public use only the aggregated measure, which is sufficient to test the combined effect of the two democratic features on transnational events.

The explanation for the three democracy-related variables and other controls is summarized from Li's (2005) study (see also Li and Schaub 2004). The democratic participation variable captures the exacerbating effect of democracy on transnational terrorism and is measured as the percentage of the population in democratic countries who voted in general elections. The voting rates for non-democratic countries are coded as 0 and come from Vanhanen's (2000) Polyarchy data set, while the regime type of each country is derived from the Polity data set (on Polity, see Marshall and Jaggers 2007). The government constraint variable measures the level of the checks and balances imposed on the executive and should capture the detrimental effect of democracy on transnational terrorism. It is based on the executive constraints measure of the Polity data set, where it is coded on a seven-point scale, with 1 denoting unlimited executive authority and with 7 indicating executive parity or subordination. The press freedom variable, theoretically conceived as being epiphenomenal to the degree of executive constraints, also detects the detrimental effect of democracy on transnational terrorism. It is a dichotomous variable, with 1 indicating the existence of free news media capable of functioning as an area of political competition or debate and with 0 indicating otherwise. Van Belle's (1997, 2000b) media openness data collection is used for this variable.

The remaining control variables are as follows: the income inequality variable is anticipated to attract more terrorist attacks and is operationalized with the Gini coefficient on a scale of 0 to 100.[13] The economic development variable is expected to decrease transnational terrorism and is measured by the logged real GDP per capita, adjusted for purchasing power parity. The regime durability variable is expected to reduce transnational terrorism and measures the number of years since the most recent regime change. The country size variable, measured by the logged total population, is projected to increase transnational terrorism due to the difficulty of successfully policing a larger population. The government capability variable is expected to thwart transnational terrorism and is measured by the logged national capability index of a state's share of the world's total population, industry, and military forces. The past incident variable is anticipated to increase transnational terrorism and is measured by the logged average annual number of terrorist incidents within each country since 1968, or since independence if after 1968. The post–Cold War variable is coded as 1 since 1991 and as 0 otherwise. The military conflict involvement variable is coded as 1 for military conflict or war involvement and as 0 otherwise. Five regional dummies are created: Europe, Africa, Asia, and America, with the Middle East being the comparison region.

Because the dependent variable (i.e., the total number of transnational terrorist incidents) is a nonnegative count measure, a negative binomial maximum-likelihood regression is employed with robust standard errors clustered by country. To further confirm the robustness of the main findings reported below, four other advanced estimation techniques are used: population-averaged negative binomial regression, zero-inflated negative binomial regression, Heckman selection models, and two-step models. All independent variables are lagged one year to ensure that they cause changes in the dependent variable rather than vice versa.

EMPIRICAL RESULTS

Table 8.1 includes seven negative binomial regression models and compares the dampening effect of the rule of law variable with the three democracy-related variables and the thirteen control variables. Because the theoretical expectations are directional, a one-tailed test is employed at the 0.10, 0.05 and 0.01 levels.[14] To save space, the discussion is limited to only the theoretically interesting variables of democratic institutions, while the results of the other controls are omitted.

Model 1 presents the replicated results of Li's (2005, 288) Model 1 in Table 8.1, where the democratic participation and government constraint hypotheses are tested concurrently. The results were obtained after the original data set was limited to the study period from 1984 to 1997 and adjusted for the available data

TABLE 8.1 Effects of the Rule of Law on Transnational Terrorist Incidents within Countries, 1984–1997

Variable	Negative Binomial Regression						
	Model 1	Model 2	Model 3	Model 4	Model 5	Model 6	Model 7
Rule of law		−0.121 (2.10)	−0.126 (2.10)		−0.125 (2.03)		−0.119 (1.99)
Democratic participation	−0.007 (1.26)	−0.006 (1.16)				−0.007 (1.07)	−0.006 (0.94)
Government constraint	0.024 (0.69)	0.026 (0.76)				0.017 (0.46)	0.017 (0.50)
Press freedom				0.092 (0.43)	0.115 (0.58)	0.094 (0.41)	0.114 (0.55)
Income inequality	0.002 (0.16)	−0.001 (0.02)	−0.001 (0.06)	−0.001 (0.05)	−0.004 (0.27)	−0.001 (0.04)	−0.003 (0.25)
Economic development	−0.238 (2.09)	−0.112 (1.05)	−0.132 (1.24)	−0.277 (2.40)	−0.139 (1.27)	−0.243 (2.01)	−0.115 (1.03)
Regime durability	−0.051 (0.87)	−0.031 (0.56)	−0.030 (0.51)	−0.074 (1.06)	−0.054 (0.85)	−0.072 (1.04)	−0.055 (0.89)
Country size	0.075 (1.67)	0.099 (2.17)	0.102 (2.32)	0.078 (1.74)	0.102 (2.25)	0.073 (1.57)	0.097 (2.07)
Government capability	0.294 (2.07)	0.281 (2.06)	0.284 (2.06)	0.286 (1.87)	0.274 (1.86)	0.284 (1.85)	0.271 (1.84)
Past incident	0.578 (12.98)	0.548 (12.41)	0.547 (12.57)	0.568 (11.93)	0.538 (11.55)	0.575 (12.97)	0.543 (12.11)
Post–Cold War	−0.647 (6.72)	−0.538 (4.87)	−0.524 (4.42)	−0.427 (4.34)	−0.324 (2.90)	−0.432 (4.52)	−0.334 (3.17)
Military conflict	−0.345 (2.72)	−0.339 (2.59)	−0.331 (2.56)	−0.368 (2.79)	−0.365 (2.69)	−0.372 (2.77)	−0.370 (2.68)
Europe	0.188 (0.92)	0.264 (1.35)	0.239 (1.21)	0.122 (0.61)	0.214 (1.06)	0.170 (0.82)	0.245 (1.21)
Asia	−0.143 (0.57)	−0.150 (0.61)	−0.113 (0.47)	−0.140 (0.55)	−0.146 (0.59)	−0.158 (0.61)	−0.166 (0.65)
Americas	−0.342 (1.93)	−0.316 (1.77)	−0.264 (1.40)	−0.280 (1.42)	−0.244 (1.25)	−0.314 (1.70)	−0.282 (1.49)
Africa	−0.417 (1.77)	−0.323 (1.38)	−0.325 (1.34)	−0.464 (1.84)	−0.350 (1.38)	−0.441 (1.78)	−0.339 (1.37)
Constant	0.568 (0.35)	−0.436 (0.28)	−0.329 (0.21)	1.027 (0.65)	−0.074 (0.05)	0.852 (0.54)	−0.187 (0.12)
Observations	1,254	1,254	1,254	1,052	1,052	1,052	1,052
Dispersion = 1	4.32	4.22	4.26	4.33	4.22	4.28	4.18
Wald chi-squared	620.52	676.66	504.88	436.44	461.69	553.41	634.34
Prob > chi-squared	0.001	0.001	0.001	0.001	0.001	0.001	0.001

Note: Robust z-statistics, adjusted over countries, in parentheses.

of the rule of law. However, the results here do not corroborate Li's main findings with respect to the significance of those two democratic features. Neither the beneficial effect of democratic participation nor the detrimental effect of government constraint emerges, but the effects of the other control variables do appear to be consistent with Li's findings except in the cases of regime durability and Asia.[15] According to the results of Model 1, it appears that neither of those two democratic features has significant explanatory power when it comes to predicting the total number of transnational terrorist incidents.

There are a few possible reasons for the insignificance of the two democracy variables. One is that the truncated time period that I have used (1984–1997) has an unexpected effect on the two democracy-related variables.[16] Another plausible explanation for the insignificance of those two variables is that there are logical flaws or errors of measurement in Li's study. Democratic participation (through voting) may have been misconstrued as a feature that leads to a decrease in transnational terrorism when it may in fact have only a spurious effect. Li's study conceptualizes that the higher the voting rate in democracies, the less likely transnational terrorism is to occur. However, because political nonparticipation (i.e., not voting) is common in many full-fledged democracies, including the United States, and scarce in emerging democracies, the high level of political participation may not necessarily be associated with the low level of transnational terrorist incidents (DeLuca 1995). More importantly, as G. Bingham Powell (1982) properly points out, the voter turnout rate is affected by many institutional and attitudinal factors and may have little to do with whether citizens have a reasonable chance to have their interests represented through elections. Simply put, the actual patterns of democratic participation through voting may be quite complex and may vary from country to country.

In addition, because Li's study measures the government constraint variable in terms of the level of executive constraints (i.e., the XCONST variable in Polity), it may be subject to measurement error, meaning that it may fail to capture democratic governments' policy behavior in response to transnational terrorism. According to Marshall and Jaggers (2007), the level of executive constraints increases if the influence of *any* accountability group—such as the legislature or judiciary in Western democracies, the military in coup-prone polities, the ruling party in a one-party state, and councils of nobles or powerful advisers in monarchies—increases. Regardless of the type of accountability group—that is, democratic or nondemocratic—"the concern is therefore with the checks and balances between the various parts of the decision-making process" (23). In this sense, a state with a high score on government constraints should not be considered a democracy by default because it could, in fact, be an autocracy.

Model 2 in Table 8.1 expands Model 1 and tests my main hypothesis by introducing the rule of law variable into the analysis. The rule of law variable is shown to be statistically significant at the 0.05 level. As hypothesized, the existence of a high-quality rule of law tradition is likely to correspond to a reduced number of transnational terrorist incidents. In contrast, both democratic participation and government constraint[17] remain insignificant in this model. What happens to the rule of law variable if the other two democracy-related variables are excluded from Model 2? As it stands, the reason that the rule of law variable is significant while democratic participation and government constraint are not may have had something to do with the fact that these three variables are conceptually related to one another (i.e., the presence of multicollinearity). Model 3 takes this possibility into consideration by keeping the rule of law variable and excluding the other two democracy-related variables from Model 2. The coefficient sign for the rule of law variable remains negative and, again, is significant at the 0.05 level, indicating that democracies with fair and impartial judicial systems in which citizens follow established laws to settle their claims are likely to see a lower rate of occurrence of transnational terrorist incidents.[18]

Model 4 displays the replicated results of Li's (2005, 288) Model 2 in Table 8.1, where the press freedom hypothesis alone is tested. The results were produced after having adjusted the original time frame of Li's study period to 1984–1997 to accommodate the data availability of the rule of law variable, and after having included the past incident variable. The reasons for the first condition are noted above. The second condition is incorporated in order to conduct a more rigorous empirical test to account for the potentially confounding effect of past terrorist incidents. By and large, my replicated results shown under Model 4 in Table 8.1 are not consistent with Li's previous findings regarding the effect of press freedom; the existence of a free press, in this instance, seems to have little relation to the occurrence of transnational terrorism.

It turns out that the significance of the press freedom variable changes depending on the inclusion of the past incident variable in the model. When the past incident variable is left out of the model, press freedom is statistically significant, but when the past incident variable is incorporated, press freedom becomes insignificant.[19] Li's (2005, 290) study did not include the past incident variable in Model 2, referring to its confounding effect on press freedom as the reason for the decision. But Li's study included both press freedom and past incident in his Model 3 along with democratic participation and government constraints.[20] It is important to note that the failure to take into consideration a confounding variable can lead one to unjustifiably conclude that the explanatory variable has a causal relationship with the dependent variable (see Greene 2003; Gujarati 2003). Indeed, due to the exclusion of the confounding past incident variable in Li's study, the relationship between press freedom and transnational terrorism appears to be spurious: press freedom should not have been reported as an important cause of terrorism in the absence of the past incident variable. In addition, a robust statistical analysis requires the same sets of controls for consistency, a test that necessitates the inclusion of the past incident variable from the start. Put differently, the hypothesis testing for the rule of law in the presence of the past incident variable poses a more rigorous and fair test for this study.

Model 5 extends Model 4 by incorporating the rule of law variable with press freedom and the other controls. This model shows that a sound law and order tradition appears to produce a dampening effect on the occurrence of transnational terrorism that is supported statistically at the 0.05 level. When the past incident variable is excluded from the model, the significance of the rule of law is stronger at 0.01.

Model 6 presents the replicated results of Li's (2005, 288) Model 3 in Table 8.1, where the democratic participation, government constraint, and press freedom hypotheses are tested together. None of the three democracy-related variables turn out to be significant in Model 6. Model 7 extends Model 6 by including the rule of law variable with the other 15 control factors. Again, this variable is significant at the 0.05 level, indicating that a strong rule of law tradition is likely to produce a deterrent effect on the number of transnational terrorist incidents.[21]

Mousseau's (2011) recent work implies that contract-intensive economies are less likely to experience terrorism than contract-poor economies and perhaps more likely to promote the high quality of the rule of law.[22] If these relationships hold true, contract-intensive economies should also affect international terrorism. This is a speculation that needs to be tested in the context of the democracy and terrorism model built in this study. The estimated results are shown in Table 8.2 in which Mousseau's contract-intensive economy measure is tested.[23] In contract-intensive societies, most individuals obtain livable incomes, goods, and services through interacting with strangers in a market, while the government makes an active effort to ensure widespread availability of economic opportunities. The measure of contract-intensive economy (CIE) is referred to as third-party (state) enforced contracting in economic security, measured as the natural log of U.S. dollars of life insurance contracting per capita with missing data imputed (for more details, see Mousseau 2012, 2013a). Mousseau (2013b, 191) asserts that "life insurance contracting is an ideal measure of CIE because, unlike other contracts, life insurance contracts must rely on third-party enforcement, since the commitment of the insurer can take place only after the death of the policyholder." It appears that the contract-intensive economy fails to achieve statistical significance across models in Table 8.2, while the rule of law remains as a significant and negative predictor in Models 3, 5, 8, and 11.

For further empirical verification of the results in Table 8.1, I report the substantive effects of the variables. Table 8.3 shows the substantive effects of the rule of law variable and six other variables that show statistical significance in a consistent manner across Models 2, 3, 5, and 7 in Table 8.1. It is apparent that

TABLE 8.2   Effects of Contract-Intensive Economy and the Rule of Law on Transnational Terrorist Incidents within Countries

Variable		Model 1	Model 2	Model 3	Model 4	Model 5	Model 6	Model 7	Model 8	Model 9	Model 10	Model 11
							Negative Binomial Regression					
Contract-intensive economy	coef	-0.058	-0.050	-0.047	-0.041		-0.056	-0.049		-0.071	-0.061	
	(z)		(0.83)	(0.75)	(0.67)			(0.73)			(0.90)	
Rule of law	coef			-0.118		-0.125			-0.123			-0.116
	(z)			(2.12)		(2.12)			(2.06)			(2.01)
Democratic participation	coef	-0.007	-0.008	-0.007						-0.007	-0.008	-0.007
	(z)	(1.29)	(1.37)	(1.27)						(1.09)	(1.21)	(1.08)
Government constraint	coef	0.025	0.025	0.028						0.018	0.014	0.016
	(z)	(0.72)	(0.75)	(0.82)						(0.49)	(0.40)	(0.47)
Press freedom	coef						0.095	0.125	0.143	0.095	0.143	0.154
	(z)						(0.44)	(0.57)	(0.70)	(0.42)	(0.61)	(0.72)
Income inequality	coef	0.001	-0.005	-0.007	-0.004	-0.006	-0.002	-0.007	-0.009	-0.002	-0.008	-0.010
	(z)	(0.09)	(0.28)	(0.40)	(0.24)	(0.39)	(0.15)	(0.43)	(0.60)	(0.14)	(0.49)	(0.63)
Economic development	coef	-0.233	-0.161	-0.047	-0.209	-0.080	-0.272	-0.208	-0.078	-0.237	-0.148	-0.034
	(z)	(2.06)	(1.21)	(0.36)	(1.52)	(0.58)	(2.37)	(1.52)	(0.55)	(1.98)	(1.08)	(0.25)
Regime durability	coef	-0.051	-0.034	-0.018	-0.040	-0.019	-0.074	-0.063	-0.044	-0.072	-0.057	-0.043
	(z)	(0.87)	(0.58)	(0.32)	(0.69)	(0.33)	(1.06)	(0.93)	(0.71)	(1.04)	(0.84)	(0.70)
Country size	coef	0.070	0.062	0.086	0.068	0.091	0.072	0.065	0.090	0.067	0.057	0.083
	(z)	(1.55)	(1.40)	(1.93)	(1.57)	(2.09)	(1.61)	(1.47)	(2.03)	(1.45)	(1.26)	(1.81)
Government capability	coef	0.285	0.281	0.267	0.285	0.272	0.275	0.273	0.259	0.273	0.269	0.255
	(z)	(2.01)	(1.97)	(1.95)	(1.98)	(1.97)	(1.80)	(1.76)	(1.74)	(1.78)	(1.73)	(1.71)
Past incident	coef	0.572	0.581	0.550	0.575	0.547	0.562	0.567	0.537	0.569	0.579	0.546
	(z)	(12.84)	(12.24)	(11.76)	(11.87)	(11.72)	(11.82)	(11.39)	(11.11)	(12.88)	(12.46)	(11.85)

Post–Cold War	−0.649	−0.648	−0.542	−0.638	−0.525	−0.429	−0.425	−0.324	−0.435	−0.429	−0.335
	(6.75)	(6.84)	(4.98)	(6.46)	(4.46)	(4.37)	(4.37)	(2.91)	(4.56)	(4.56)	(3.22)
Conflict	−0.340	−0.338	−0.334	−0.332	−0.326	−0.364	−0.361	−0.359	−0.367	−0.362	−0.362
	(2.66)	(2.70)	(2.57)	(2.67)	(2.53)	(2.75)	(2.79)	(2.69)	(2.73)	(2.78)	(2.69)
Europe	0.180	0.204	0.268	0.150	0.237	0.113	0.124	0.209	0.160	0.191	0.252
	(0.89)	(1.00)	(1.40)	(0.76)	(1.21)	(0.56)	(0.61)	(1.04)	(0.78)	(0.92)	(1.27)
Asia	−0.149	−0.133	−0.144	−0.104	−0.108	−0.145	−0.131	−0.140	−0.165	−0.140	−0.154
	(0.59)	(0.52)	(0.59)	(0.42)	(0.45)	(0.57)	(0.51)	(0.57)	(0.64)	(0.54)	(0.61)
Americas	−0.345	−0.318	−0.300	−0.274	−0.249	−0.282	−0.260	−0.230	−0.318	−0.287	−0.264
	(1.95)	(1.69)	(1.63)	(1.36)	(1.27)	(1.43)	(1.26)	(1.14)	(1.72)	(1.48)	(1.38)
Africa	−0.425	−0.324	−0.251	−0.359	−0.266	−0.473	−0.384	−0.285	−0.450	−0.335	−0.257
	(1.81)	(1.16)	(0.92)	(1.23)	(0.93)	(1.88)	(1.29)	(0.96)	(1.82)	(1.16)	(0.90)
Constant	0.714	0.613	−0.349	0.818	−0.220	1.201	1.095	0.022	1.023	0.839	−0.140
	(0.45)	(0.38)	(0.23)	(0.50)	(0.14)	(0.76)	(0.68)	(0.01)	(0.66)	(0.53)	(0.09)
Observations	1,227	1,227	1,227	1,227	1,227	1,029	1,029	1,227	1,029	1,029	1,227
Dispersion = 1	4.34	4.33	4.23	4.39	4.28	4.35	4.34	4.23	4.30	4.28	4.18
Wald chi-squared	605.11	635.34	686.40	480.70	526.07	425.54	459.12	498.80	535.81	567.41	646.45
Prob > chi-squared	0.001	0.001	0.001	0.001	0.001	0.001	0.001	0.001	0.001	0.001	0.001

Note: Robust z-statistics, adjusted over countries, in parentheses.

TABLE 8.3   Marginal Effects of Statistically Significant Variables

Variable	Negative Binomial Regression			
	Model 2	Model 3	Model 5	Model 7
Rule of law				
1 standard deviation	−18%	−18%	−19%	−19%
2 standard deviations	−32%	−33%	−34%	−33%
Country size				
1 standard deviation	16%	17%	17%	16%
2 standard deviations	35%	36%	36%	35%
Government capability				
1 standard deviation	25%	25%	23%	23%
2 standard deviations	56%	57%	53%	52%
Past incident				
1 standard deviation	139%	138%	132%	134%
2 standard deviations	471%	469%	446%	456%
Post–Cold War	−42%	−41%	−28%	−28%
Military conflict involved	−29%	−28%	−31%	−31%
Africa	−28%	−28%	−30%	−29%

Note: The baseline values are as follows: mean for continuous variables and 0 for dummy variables.

regardless of model specification, the combined effect of well-functioning legal systems and ordinary citizens' willingness to observe the law notably reduces the likelihood of transnational terrorism. For example, as shown in the shaded rows, the risk that any country will experience a transnational terrorist incident decreases by 18 percent if the quality of its rule of law increases by one standard deviation; the likelihood of transnational terrorist events decreases by 32 percent if the rule of law quality increases by two standard deviations. While the post–Cold War period, conflict involvement, and African region variables all appear to decrease the likelihood of a transnational terrorist incident, the country size, government capability, and history of past incidents variables seem to increase the possibility.

It is plausible that alternative statistical estimation techniques might cause the significance of the rule of law variable to disappear if it is not sufficiently robust. Table 8.4 evaluates the robustness of the results of Models 2, 3, 5, and 7 reported in Table 8.1 by performing four other advanced statistical estimations: population-averaged negative binomial regression, zero-inflated negative binomial regression, Heckman selection models, and two step models. Models 1 through 4 show the results where a population-averaged negative binomial regression is used, allowing for an AR(1) correlation structure. Overall, the dampening effect of the rule of law on transnational terrorist events is confirmed. Model 1 includes the rule of law, democratic participation, government

TABLE 8.4 Marginal Effects of Statistically Significant Variables: Robustness Tests

Variable	Population-Averaged				Zero-Inflated				Heckman Selection				Two Step			
	Model 1	Model 2	Model 3	Model 4	Model 5	Model 6	Model 7	Model 8	Model 9	Model 10	Model 11	Model 12	Model 13	Model 14	Model 15	Model 16
Rule of law	-0.144 (2.61)	-0.156 (2.87)	-0.137 (2.31)	-0.126 (2.10)	-0.162 (2.29)	-0.180 (2.71)	-0.150 (2.03)	-0.153 (2.19)	-0.847 (3.39)	-0.809 (3.54)	-0.937 (3.55)	-0.868 (3.27)	-0.122 (2.11)	-0.127 (2.11)	-0.126 (2.03)	-0.120 (2.00)
Democratic participation	-0.007 (1.31)			-0.006 (0.97)	-0.010 (1.09)			-0.009 (1.06)	-0.049 (1.89)			-0.061 (2.23)	-0.006 (1.18)			-0.006 (0.97)
Government constraint	-0.003 (0.08)			-0.026 (0.59)	-0.028 (0.61)			-0.043 (1.02)	0.265 (1.59)			-0.018 (0.10)	0.026 (0.76)			0.017 (0.50)
Press freedom		0.145 (0.86)	0.200 (1.08)			-0.027	0.153 (0.12)			1.599	1.924 (2.16)			0.115	0.114 (0.57)	
Income inequality	0.020 (1.35)	0.019 (1.27)	0.020 (1.23)	0.022 (1.35)	0.014 (0.92)	0.012 (0.79)	0.013 (0.85)	0.016 (1.03)	0.042 (0.58)	0.044 (0.64)	0.046 (0.61)	0.035 (0.47)	-0.001 (0.10)	-0.002 (0.14)	-0.005 (0.37)	-0.005 (0.35)
Economic development	-0.047 (0.34)	-0.090 (0.66)	-0.080 (0.53)	-0.037 (0.24)	0.071 (0.49)	0.006 (0.05)	0.044 (0.31)	0.096 (0.62)	2.050 (1.70)	1.355 (1.24)	1.087 (1.02)	1.492 (1.38)	-0.227 (2.06)	-0.253 (2.37)	-0.259 (2.31)	-0.228 (1.94)
Regime durability	-0.081 (1.64)	-0.082 (1.66)	-0.098 (1.67)	-0.100 (1.69)	-0.049 (0.73)	-0.054 (0.79)	-0.084 (1.19)	-0.076 (1.11)	-0.120 (0.56)	-0.135 (0.68)	-0.330 (1.34)	-0.348 (1.39)	-0.031 (0.55)	-0.029 (0.50)	-0.053 (0.84)	-0.054 (0.88)
Country size	0.209 (4.46)	0.222 (4.92)	0.259 (4.94)	0.247 (4.59)	0.182 (3.16)	0.196 (3.43)	0.197 (3.16)	0.189 (3.10)	0.510 (2.46)	0.500 (2.67)	0.723 (3.25)	0.664 (2.96)	0.094 (2.05)	0.097 (2.20)	0.097 (2.12)	0.092 (1.94)
Government capability	0.333 (2.10)	0.334 (2.12)	0.368 (2.12)	0.371 (2.13)	0.079 (0.43)	0.095 (0.55)	0.118 (0.63)	0.101 (0.51)	-0.411 (0.87)	-0.440 (0.95)	-0.429 (0.77)	-0.516 (0.93)	0.272 (1.99)	0.275 (2.00)	0.263 (1.78)	0.260 (1.76)
Past incident	0.586 (9.95)	0.581 (10.51)	0.577 (9.38)	0.593 (9.06)	0.646 (10.31)	0.635 (11.76)	0.634 (11.23)	0.644 (10.06)	1.629 (7.03)	1.703 (8.31)	1.746 (7.24)	1.830 (7.26)	0.542 (12.28)	0.540 (12.43)	0.531 (11.43)	0.536 (12.03)

continued

TABLE 8.4   continued

Variable	Population-Averaged				Zero-Inflated				Heckman Selection				Two Step			
	Model 1	Model 2	Model 3	Model 4	Model 5	Model 6	Model 7	Model 8	Model 9	Model 10	Model 11	Model 12	Model 13	Model 14	Model 15	Model 16
Post–Cold War	−0.419	−0.388	−0.167	−0.192	−0.610	−0.551	−0.313	−0.384	−2.352	−1.768	−1.140	−1.413	−0.645	−0.635	−0.435	−0.440
	(3.71)	(3.49)	(1.37)	(1.54)	(4.02)	(3.51)	(1.94)	(2.46)	(2.65)	(2.32)	(1.01)	(1.23)	(6.58)	(6.25)	(4.37)	(4.55)
Conflict	−0.315	−0.324	−0.447	−0.448	−0.472	−0.465	−0.508	−0.515	−1.826	−1.772	−2.057	−2.002	−0.333	−0.325	−0.361	−0.365
	(1.80)	(1.85)	(2.42)	(2.42)	(2.57)	(2.57)	(2.74)	(2.68)	(1.67)	(1.74)	(1.79)	(1.74)	(2.54)	(2.51)	(2.65)	(2.64)
Europe	0.664	0.595	0.530	0.627	0.451	0.334	0.397	0.465	2.680	2.728	2.797	3.242	0.256	0.230	0.203	0.235
	(2.72)	(2.57)	(2.07)	(2.34)	(1.72)	(1.28)	(1.58)	(1.83)	(2.25)	(2.60)	(2.30)	(2.60)	(1.31)	(1.17)	(1.01)	(1.17)
Asia	−0.212	−0.233	−0.250	−0.192	−0.184	−0.230	−0.114	−0.126	−0.214	0.207	−0.326	−0.314	−0.156	−0.121	−0.154	−0.173
	(0.84)	(0.98)	(0.97)	(0.71)	(0.64)	(0.82)	(0.42)	(0.47)	(0.18)	(0.20)	(0.27)	(0.26)	(0.64)	(0.51)	(0.62)	(0.68)
Americas	−0.305	−0.300	−0.250	−0.219	−0.425	−0.436	−0.312	−0.305	−1.175	−0.731	−0.973	−1.024	−0.320	−0.268	−0.248	−0.286
	(1.68)	(1.80)	(1.31)	(1.08)	(1.81)	(1.78)	(1.30)	(1.32)	(1.34)	(0.95)	(1.06)	(1.08)	(1.79)	(1.42)	(1.26)	(1.51)
Africa	−0.540	−0.547	−0.442	−0.431	−0.627	−0.635	−0.506	−0.518	0.073	0.353	0.589	0.667	−0.331	−0.332	−0.358	−0.348
	(1.99)	(2.03)	(1.49)	(1.46)	(2.05)	(2.06)	(1.67)	(1.74)	(0.07)	(0.36)	(0.51)	(0.58)	(1.42)	(1.37)	(1.41)	(1.41)
Constant	−3.975	−3.772	−4.769	−5.043	−2.984	−2.682	−3.260	−3.544	−20.711	−14.389	−15.037	−16.733	0.329	0.463	0.743	0.598
	(2.23)	(2.13)	(2.39)	(2.50)	(1.69)	(1.55)	(1.74)	(1.88)	(1.54)	(1.18)	(1.23)	(1.37)	(0.22)	(0.30)	(0.49)	(0.41)
Observations	1,075	1,075	882	882	697	697	633	633	1,397	1,397	1,199	1,199	1,227	1,227	1,029	1,029
Wald chi-squared	431.85	440.12	364.19	361.07	416.30	422.78	395.52	376.70	240.94	268.16	272.07	277.52	659.91	495.10	451.87	615.02
Prob > chi-squared	0.001	0.001	0.001	0.001	0.001	0.001	0.001	0.001	0.001	0.001	0.001	0.001	0.001	0.001	0.001	0.001
chi-squared	0.001	0.001	0.001	0.001	0.001	0.001	0.001	0.001								

Note: Robust z-statistics, adjusted over countries, reported in parentheses, except for the Heckman selection and population-averaged regression models.

constraint, and the other controls. It shows that the rule of law is a contributing factor in the reduction of transnational terrorist incidents. Model 2 is built to test an independent explanatory role for the rule of law by excluding the two conceptually related variables of democracy (i.e., democratic participation and government constraint) from Model 1. The dampening effect of the rule of law remains unchanged; the variable is supported at the 0.01 level. In Model 3, the rule of law is in competition with press freedom and the other control factors but still does not lose its statistical significance. Model 4 includes all four democracy-related variables. While the rule of law is statistically significant at the 0.05 level, none of the remaining three democratic factors is shown to have any bearing on transnational terrorism.

Negative binomial and population-averaged negative binomial regression models assume that all countries are equally vulnerable to transnational terrorism. Yet, the reality is that many countries experience no transnational terrorist attacks due to the absence of political or security interests for terrorist groups. Zero-inflated negative binomial regression models take this fact into account. Models 5 through 8 show the results when the observations for terrorism-prone countries are used for estimation. On the whole, the dampening effect of the rule of law is confirmed with the zero-inflated count modeling: if there is no rule of law, there is no law and order, resulting in an increase in transnational terrorist incidents (Adame 2007). A strong law and order tradition in democratic societies appears to produce a terrorism-reducing effect in all four models: Model 5, where the rule of law is in competition with democratic participation and government constraint; Model 6, where the independent influence of the rule of law alone is tested; Model 7, where the rule of law is competing with press freedom; and Model 8, where the rule of law is tested against all three of the other democracy-related factors.[24]

Due mainly to the data availability of the rule of law in the ICRG data set, the sample includes one hundred countries rather than all possible nation-states; this may require some analysis of the factors that cause a country to be included in the ICRG data set. To this end, I employ a Heckman selection analysis, modeling the factors that cause a country to be included in the ICRG data set at the first stage and then the causes of transnational terrorism at the second stage. Models 9 through 12 show the results of the second stage of the Heckman selection model. Interestingly, with the implementation of the Heckman selection model, the significance of the rule of law variable turns out to be higher than in the previous models. The beneficial effect of the rule of law is confirmed in a consistent manner against all four different model specifications.

Finally, it is possible that the causal arrow may also point in the opposite direction of that which was hypothesized; in other words, it may be the case that events of transnational terrorism also cause a decline in the rule of law, specifically in cases where a state chooses to stop observing constitutionally established institutional rights in the face of terrorist threats by imposing martial law or by waiving basic rights (e.g., the United States after September 11, the U.K. in the 1970s, and Russia after the mid-1990s). To account for the possibility of mutual causality (i.e., endogeneity), I use a two-step negative binomial regression model. The rule of law is first modeled as a function of transnational terrorism, and then the likelihood of transnational terrorism is predicted by the rule of law at the second step. The results from the second step of the model are consistent with those of the previous model estimations and can be seen in Models 13 through 16. Again, we see that the rule of law has a preventive effect on the rise of transnational terrorism.

Because my theoretical discussion focuses on the frequency of terrorist events, the dependent variable of all the empirical tests has been measured by the number of transnational terrorist incidents. However, it would be worthwhile to investigate alternative ways of measuring transnational terrorism since the use of the total number of terrorist incidents as a dependent variable indiscriminately amalgamates terrorist events of differing magnitude (in terms of resulting deaths and injuries). This is an important point since it has been observed that a "new terrorism"—characterized by a drop in the number of incidents but an increase in lethality—has replaced the "old terrorism" of the 1970s and 1980s. Recognizing these limitations, Frey and Luechinger (2005, 144) propose the number of persons killed and the number of persons injured in terrorist attacks as alternative measures to total event counts because they are capable of capturing the unequal degree of severity in each terrorist incident (see also Crain and Crain 2006; Frey, Luechinger, and Stutzer 2007).

Table 8.5 evaluates the robustness of the results of Models 2, 3, 5, and 7 reported in Table 8.1 by replacing the dependent variable of the total number of transnational terrorist incidents with that of the number of individuals who are either wounded or killed, calculated and tested separately. The empirical results with these two alternative measures reveal that the democratic rule of law is a contributing factor in preventing severe terrorist casualties. Interestingly, regardless of the choice of the measure of the dependent variable, the magnitude of the coefficient for the rule of law and its significance in Table 8.5 turn out to be stronger than those in Table 8.1, providing further support for my theoretical arguments.

CONCLUSION

Most existing studies claim that liberal democracies experience more transnational terrorist attacks than other regime types, while a small number maintain that democratic institutions are less vulnerable to terrorism. I have argued that the rule of law is an essential feature of liberal democratic governments;

TABLE 8.5   Effects of the Rule of Law on Transnational Terrorist Casualties within Countries, 1984–1997

	Negative Binomial Regression							
	Total number of individuals wounded				Total number of individuals killed			
Variable	Model 1	Model 2	Model 3	Model 4	Model 5	Model 6	Model 7	Model 8
Rule of law	−0.210	−0.228	−0.247	−0.226	−0.236	−0.234	−0.242	−0.242
	(3.21)	(3.27)	(3.71)	(3.40)	(3.36)	(3.17)	(3.31)	(3.44)
Democratic participation	−0.012			−0.014	−0.001			0.001
	(1.91)			(2.17)	(0.17)			(0.16)
Government constraint	0.035			0.009	0.059			0.028
	(0.80)			(0.22)	(1.33)			(0.57)
Press freedom			0.001	0.027			0.142	0.102
			(0.00)	(0.12)			(0.79)	(0.53)
Income inequality	−0.013	−0.013	−0.019	−0.019	−0.004	−0.006	−0.011	−0.011
	(0.66)	(0.67)	(0.97)	(0.95)	(0.15)	(0.24)	(0.42)	(0.41)
Economic development	−0.213	−0.251	−0.216	−0.155	−0.172	−0.128	−0.142	−0.164
	(1.25)	(1.43)	(1.20)	(0.87)	(1.00)	(0.71)	(0.82)	(0.94)
Regime durability	−0.001	−0.003	0.012	0.003	−0.009	−0.004	−0.010	−0.008
	(0.01)	(0.03)	(0.14)	(0.04)	(0.13)	(0.06)	(0.12)	(0.10)
Country size	0.051	0.060	0.075	0.059	0.080*	0.065	0.072	0.079
	(0.78)	(0.88)	(1.15)	(0.92)	(1.38)	(1.07)	(1.20)	(1.36)
Government capability	0.120	0.132	0.125	0.111	0.307	0.300	0.318	0.320
	(0.60)	(0.67)	(0.60)	(0.53)	(1.39)	(1.38)	(1.42)	(1.42)
Past incident	0.616	0.610	0.621	0.645	0.612	0.650	0.662	0.645
	(9.45)	(8.97)	(9.32)	(9.89)	(8.66)	(9.26)	(8.77)	(8.66)
Post–Cold War	−0.233	−0.186	−0.082	−0.125	−0.308	−0.306	−0.135	−0.138
	(1.50)	(1.18)	(0.52)	(0.75)	(1.76)	(1.69)	(0.71)	(0.74)
Conflict	−0.341	−0.311	−0.402	−0.427	−0.057	−0.045	−0.123	−0.127
	(1.36)	(1.25)	(1.47)	(1.53)	(0.24)	(0.18)	(0.51)	(0.52)
Europe	0.256	−0.308	−0.316	−0.225	0.116	−0.048	−0.107	−0.138
	(0.58)	(0.76)	(0.84)	(0.54)	(0.32)	(0.13)	(0.31)	(0.40)
Asia	−0.407	−0.359	−0.477	−0.472	−0.423	−0.299	−0.409	−0.460
	(1.26)	(1.14)	(1.38)	(1.38)	(1.37)	(0.92)	(1.20)	(1.41)
Americas	−0.786	−0.697	−0.657	−0.723	−0.659	−0.588	−0.565	−0.590
	(2.87)	(2.51)	(2.36)	(2.61)	(2.99)	(2.42)	(2.35)	(2.64)
Africa	−0.302	−0.303	−0.260	−0.234	−0.425	−0.371	−0.452	−0.473
	(1.04)	(1.00)	(0.83)	(0.77)	(1.25)	(0.99)	(1.31)	(1.45)
Constant	2.933	3.003	2.718	2.560	1.420	1.371	1.476	1.551
	(1.28)	(1.31)	(1.23)	(1.14)	(0.46)	(0.44)	(0.49)	(0.51)
Observations	1,254	1,254	1,052	1,052	1,254	1,254	1,052	1,052
Dispersion = 1	36.80	36.88	33.35	33.28	80.30	80.52	76.45	76.43
Wald chi-squared	236.51	224.97	197.72	212.40	349.99	308.60	298.63	314.77
Prob > chi-squared	0.001	0.001	0.001	0.001	0.001	0.001	0.001	0.001

Note: Robust z-statistics, adjusted over countries, in parentheses.

accordingly, I have hypothesized that the synergistic effect of fair and impartial judicial systems and legitimate non-arbitrary law helps to discourage ordinary citizens from engaging in transnational terrorist violence and so protects democracies from being exploited by transnational terrorists. That is, the democratic rule of law is conceptualized to diminish the opportunity for and willingness of ordinary citizens to engage in activities of transnational terrorism. The empirical results show that, more than any other democratic feature (e.g., political participation), a strong tradition in the rule of law produces a dampening effect on transnational terrorism.

This finding is important for future policy making. Although the thrust of American foreign policy has been toward democratization, the empirical findings presented here suggest that the cultivation of the rule of law is more likely to reduce the occurrence of transnational terrorist acts. For this reason, emphasis should not simply be put on democratic procedures such as voting and legislative debate, but rather on judicial and legal training. In fact, the empirical findings suggest that the significance of the role of the U.S. Agency for International Development (USAID) and similar agencies in the European Union is critical, as one of their primary missions is to fund independent judiciaries in developing countries (see USAID 2008). These kinds of agencies should work together to find more financial resources to help establish a sound rule of law tradition in terrorism-prone countries.

PART II

Searching for New Ideas and Empirical Evidence

CHAPTER 9

Old Habits Die Hard

Leaders' Prior Military Experience, Repression, and Civil War

Prior military experience should make a leader more comfortable discussing the possibility of using military force and weighing the pros and cons of military force.

MICHAEL C. HOROWITZ AND ALLAN C. STAM, "How Prior Military Experience Influences the Future Militarized Behavior of Leaders"

Parochial motives, socialized values, and sheer familiarity with the instruments of armed coercion create conditions that may predispose military leaders in favor of using force.

TODD S. SECHSER, "Are Soldiers Less War-Prone Than Statesmen?"

Although existing studies of civil conflict recognize mass mobilization as a critical element for the rebellion of any small dissent group to succeed (e.g., Gurr 1970, 1986; Davenport 2007), they fail to explain how exactly it is that a relatively small number of armed dissenters can gain the amount of popular support needed to launch a military campaign against an incumbent government. Scholars consider that repressive state structures will prohibit dissident groups from forming viable armed organizations capable of posing a challenge to the government. Yet, they fail to see another crucial possibility that when the state's repressive tools are used indiscriminately against ordinary citizens, this will backfire, angering a wider group of people and strengthening opposition to the regime. This kind of indiscriminate repression leads to a substantial loss of human lives and property, often turning a rebellion that is small in size into one that has acquired mass participation (Davenport, Armstrong, and Lichbach 2008). The important question, however, is why some leaders are more inclined than others to use indiscriminate repression against popular uprisings when they are presumably aware that these actions may drive ordinary citizens to participate in the violence, thus escalating its scale.

In the effort to explain why it is that some leaders are more repressive than others in this context, the present study relies on two suggestions put forward by Peter D. Feaver (1999, 235–36), a leading researcher into civil-military relations: "scholars should explore more fully the linkages between patterns of civil-military relations and the propensity to use force," and "the literature offers a rich resource of civil-military case studies but relatively few rigorous attempts to test hypotheses against these data." Specifically, this study collects longitudinal data in order to examine whether prior military experience causes a leader to be more or less likely to employ indiscriminate violence against his or her own population, which, in turn, strengthens opposition to the regime and potentially provokes rebel movement that was initially small in size to develop into the first stages of a civil war. Based on the assumption that political leaders' beliefs and attitudes (which are themselves reflections of their experiences and memories) affect the likelihood of civil war, this study argues that one's prior military experience is key to an explanation and understanding of the origins of civil violence. This study asserts that a leader's past military professionalization crucially factors into his or her decision to enact security policies that mistreat civilian populations (i.e., use of indiscriminate repression), and that this is a much less common course of action chosen by leaders who do not have prior military experience. Indiscriminate repression escalates public perceptions of injustice and so is likely to increase civilian opposition to the regime. As civilian populations feel threatened and angry in the face of repression, they become sympathetic to and supportive of subversive groups and their antigovernment initiatives. Civilians become more willing to take up arms and join with these groups in the effort to avenge their grievances, a process that may ultimately lead to the outbreak of civil war.[1]

This study builds two-stage statistical models in order to examine whether leaders with a military background are more repressive than those who lack this background; it then examines whether such repression is related to the onset of civil war. The two-stage logistic regression models of 157 countries during the period from 1976 to 2007 ultimately produce evidence that, all other things being equal, top national executives with prior military experience are more likely than those with none to anger large groups of citizens through the use of indiscriminate political violence; the countries they rule are, therefore, more vulnerable to experiencing civil war than are those countries whose leaders do not have a military background.

This study proceeds in four sections. The first elucidates the causal linkages between a leader's military experience and the onset of civil war, as well as presenting three historical case studies to illustrate this phenomenon; the second offers an explication of the research design with statistical model building, operationalization, and data sources; this is followed by a discussion of the empirical results and several robustness tests in part three and then a concluding section to summarize the main findings and advance some important policy implications.

WHY IS A LEADER'S MILITARY BACKGROUND
A CAUSE OF CIVIL WAR ONSET?

This section draws a hypothesis from the conceptual linkages between a leader's military background and the onset of civil war; it then illustrates the argument by briefly discussing three historical case studies.

Conceptualizing the Link between a Leader's Military
Background and the Onset of Civil War

Domestic political protests have been ubiquitous throughout human history. National leaders prefer to respond to such events, if possible, through the use of security police forces rather than through the deployment of military personnel; this is due to the fact that soldiers, insofar as they are trained for wartime scenarios, are less suitably prepared to deal with civilian violence. However, this study posits that this policy preference is not necessarily consistent among all leaders. That is, in some cases leaders may push for a military option or for a mixture of security police and military forces in their attempts to suppress dissidents and protesters. In this scenario, they expect that the use of military force will have a deterrent effect on domestic political violence, ensuring that it will not develop into a full-fledged civil war (Tullock 1971; Rasler 1996). However, the present study contends that the desired deterrence is attained only in cases where the use of military violence is restricted to dissident groups and is not employed indiscriminately against a large proportion of the civilian population. When the use of repressive measures is aimed against the latter group, on the other hand, it is expected to generate a backlash against the regime, thus providing an opportunity for what may be initially small opposition movements to recruit large numbers of disgruntled individuals (Kalyvas 2006; Thoms and Ron 2007; Jacobsen and de Soysa 2009).

When leaders deploy military forces to tamp down popular unrest, they understand that there is always a possibility that this will result in the use of excessive force, irrespective of the identity of the intended targets.[2] Furthermore, military operations are unlikely to distinguish between subversives and civilian bystanders because soldiers are not as well trained for these particular scenarios, a situation that may result in the total destruction of the lives and living conditions of the latter group (Fearon and Laitin 2003, 80). Because many civilian victims are the rural poor or people who work with them, the additional burdens resulting from destructive military operations contribute to insurmountability of their economic suffering. An appreciation of these conditions as unjust will, naturally, generate a significant degree of resentment toward the government among members of the population; these people may then sympathize with dissident causes and join opposition movements in order to express their frustration and anger at their perceived lack of alternatives (Gurr 1970, 1986; Petersen 2002). In this context we see how indiscriminate military violence may drive civilians who would otherwise be neutral to join dissident groups out of the desire for self-defense. This logic is consistent with Mason and Krane's (1989, 176) argument that "what is required to convert normally risk-aversive peasants into revolutionary soldiers is a high level of indiscriminately targeted repressive violence" (see also Stanley 1996; Thoms and Ron 2007; Jacobsen and de Soysa 2009).

Whenever military repression is used indiscriminately against innocent civilians, it tends to backfire, generating sizable sympathy for the opposition both at home and abroad. Civilian victims of excessive military violence have every psychological incentive to supply food, hideouts, intelligence, and recruits for antigovernment activists. Generally, after having witnessed the abuse and murder of civilians, the international community will condemn such military atrocities, delegitimize the political authority of the sitting government, and offer moral and material support to dissident groups. In such a scenario, opposition movements gain a popular and international base that enables them to become a legitimate force of antigovernmental resistance equipped with relatively competitive combat capabilities; it would seem that, at this point, a military confrontation is difficult to avoid. Simply put, the use of indiscriminate repression by a government will often anger or awaken a large portion of an otherwise neutral civilian population, thus precipitating the outbreak of civil war by inciting citizens to join small rebel groups out of either vengefulness or fear.[3]

This discussion raises the following important question: what kind of national leader is inclined to employ indiscriminate violence against his or her own citizens? To answer this question, this study turns to the literature of civil-military relations, which maintains that because of their military professionalization, training, and skills, military leaders—in contrast to civilian leaders—are predisposed to use violence against their own citizens. This is an assumption implied by the conventional wisdom that "where you stand depends on where you sit" (Gray 1975, 86; see also Allison 1971).[4] Students of civil-military relations have put forward the idea that with an increase in militarism (i.e., the increasing influence of military leaders over the decision-making process), a state is more likely to act with aggression and belligerence (e.g., Nordlinger 1970; Finer 1975; Wayman 1975; McKinlay and Cohan 1976; Janowitz 1981; Wolpin 1983; Snyder 1984; Van Evera 1984; Whitten and Bienen 1996; Desch 1998, 2001; Feaver 1999; Choi and James 2005; Pickering 2011). Because military leaders are what Lasswell (1941, 1997) refers to as "specialists on violence," they are generally less averse than are civilian leaders to the use of military violence. Morgan (1993, 246) asserts that military leaders who participate in the decision-making process "are likely to urge or endorse the use of force and regard it as a proper and feasible step." Similarly, Brecher (1996, 220) contends that "[when the military is] in power . . . [it is] likely to employ violence or more severe violence, even if alternative techniques of crisis management are available." The epigraphs from Horowitz and Stam (2012) and Sechser (2004) likewise highlight the significance of a military leader's inclination to recommend the use of force as a response to external threats.

It is also important to note that the military mentality, which proliferates under military rule, does not allow much room for political compromise, but instead encourages total victory over one's enemies at all costs (Sechser 2004; Davenport 2007); this tendency naturally translates into a justification for the use of brutal violence against presumably innocent civilian bystanders, in that their lives are worth sacrificing for the sake of military success. Dent's (1970, 92) study on the military in the Nigerian Civil War points to this military mentality: "[for a military soldier,] 'military government' means power in military hands, including his own, and the rule of the law of the gun." Davenport's (1995) pooled cross-sectional, time-series data analysis of fifty-seven countries from 1948 to 1982 confirms such arguments and the findings of previous studies on civil-military relations (e.g., Lasswell 1941; Hibbs 1973; Ziegenhagen 1986; Gurr 1986), namely, that military influence increases political repression out of sheer habit.[5] In their recent study, Wayman and Tago (2010, 9) contend that "a military regime, by its definition, is more likely to have stronger armed forces and a lower threshold for using them"; these authors go on to present evidence supporting the positive relationship between military rule and the onset of democide (that is, the intentional killing of people committed by government). The studies of Davenport (2007) and Fjelde (2010) provide empirical evidence that military regimes are more prone to armed conflict than are regimes with civilian institutions.[6]

The overall findings of previous studies of civil-military relations support the idea that a leader's prior military experience plays an important role in explaining his or her indiscriminate use of repression, and that a potential consequence of repression is the outbreak of civil conflict. Leaders with a military background are more likely to exhibit violent behavior because of their military mentality and their military training and culture; they often resort to the use of force as a first choice for conflict resolution—as they say, "old habits die hard." The mentality of leaders who have made the military their profession is often that of victory at all costs, and the military knowledge and skills they have acquired may lead them to prioritize the use of military violence over other means. As the primary mission of soldiers is to defeat or kill uniformed enemy combatants, they are not properly trained to deal with civilian uprisings or to accommodate civilian demands. Because many leaders with prior military experience were, in fact, career military people, their preferred method of conflict resolution is likely to relate to their habit of employing military violence. Simply put, the military repression of civilians is more likely to feel like a natural choice for leaders with a military background. The literature of socialization in general and of military socialization in particular is consistent with the above discussion (see Lupton and Wilson 1959; Janowitz 1971; Parry 2005). All "human beings perceive what goes on about them within a frame of reference determined by their total previous experience" (Matthews 1954, 3); no differently, then, should we understand leaders' security decisions as being based on prior life experiences during which their beliefs and attitudes were formed. In particular, as Janowitz (1971) points out, soldiers' perspectives are shaped by their social background and military professionalization, which could potentially cause them to favor indiscriminate repression as a response to civil disorder.

Of course, in response to civic unrest leaders with a military background may have a number of options available (they could use discriminate or indiscriminate force, or they could choose to use no violence at all), but in the absence of alternative democratic political institutions designed to manage popular demands (e.g., political parties), these leaders are more likely to deal with civilian populations in the same way they do with small armed groups. Because leaders with military professionalization are less familiar than civilian leaders with the concept of co-opting political opposition and retaining popular supporters, they are less likely to devise political mechanisms capable of peacefully channeling popular demands for change (Davenport 2007; Fjelde 2010). Moreover, most leaders who assume the position of top national executive by exploiting their military muscle find that their political power is dependent on a small winning coalition; thus, they are less concerned about political fallout than are those leaders who require a broad base of popular support; accordingly, the former have less incentive to engage with a large swath of the population and feel more free to use military force against both dissidents and civilian bystanders (Bueno de Mesquita et al. 2003). Indiscriminate repression, then, infuriates the public, strengthens the opposition movement, and precipitates the outbreak of civil violence. Specifically, when countries are ruled by leaders who have prior military professionalization (i.e., when civilian supremacy in civil-military relations is not established), there is an increase in militarism generally; that is, brutal military tactics come to be widely perceived as the best (or only) option for the repression of both dissident and civilian protests.[7] In sum, indiscriminate repression potentially enrages a large number of ordinary citizens, leaving permanent scars on too many civilian victims and, therefore, motivating many of them to support domestic opposition to the incumbent regime; these factors often serve to precipitate civil war.

From the above theoretical conceptualization of a leader's military background comes the following hypothesis:

H₁: Prior military experience makes a leader prone to the use of indiscriminate violence that consequently should turn a popular uprising into the first stage of a civil war.

Illustrative Civil War Cases: Guatemala, Nigeria, and El Salvador

By briefly examining three historical case studies regarding the onset of civil war (i.e., Guatemala in 1960, Nigeria in 1967, and El Salvador in 1979), this study draws further causal connections between a leader's military background and the likelihood of civil war onset. The Guatemalan Civil War lasted thirty-six years—from 1960 to 1996. This civil war is often presumed to originate as a popular response to an authoritarian civilian leader's oppression of the population; however, the outbreak of the war did not actually occur until two years after José Miguel Ramón Ydígoras Fuentes (1958–63) assumed the presidency and began to repress the civilian population through the use of military force. Before he came to power, Ydígoras was a military general disciplined by the relevant mind- and skill-set. As his political support came mainly from the white-skinned descendants of European immigrants, he did not hesitate to discriminate against the darker-skinned, native Mayan people who constituted more than half of the nation's populace; he employed brutal military violence in response to domestic political protests.

This former general had acquired, during the course of his military professionalization, a certain familiarity and comfortableness with the use of military force as a tool of political repression. The indigenous Maya, though, were not passive inhabitants but longtime activists, demonstrated by their instrumentality in the election of several reformist presidents from the Revolutionary Action Party (PAR)—namely, Juan José Arévalo (1945–51) and Jacobo Árbenz Guzmán (1951–54)—until the time when U.S. Central Intelligence Agency intervention overthrew President Árbenz Guzmán in 1954 (Woodard 2006, 90). Considered a threat because of the success of their previous activist and reformist programs, Mayan civilians were tortured, maimed, and killed, and their property was destroyed. An early campaign of military repression, targeted at reformist elites and the popular classes, which included the Mayan people, appeared to have effectively smothered the popular demand for socioeconomic change (Grandin 2004, 196). However, as the brutal military violence continued under the presidency of former general Ydígoras, the opposition movement gained momentum and mobilized many committed civilian supporters who were provoked by the regime's indiscriminate violence to join dissident groups such as the urban Guatemalan Labour Party (Jonas 1991; Grandin 2000, 2004). This process led to an increase in insurgent violence and, ultimately, to the first stage of the Guatemalan Civil War in 1960. If civilian bystanders had not been brutalized by Ydígoras' forces, it seems less likely that so many would have joined the rebel groups out of their desire to avenge the specific harms done to their families, friends, and neighbors.

The Nigerian Civil War, which ran from July 6, 1967, to January 15, 1970, occurred under the leadership of General Yakubu "Jack" Dan-Yumma Gowon, who was head of the Federal Military Government from August 1, 1966, to July 29, 1975. Gowon ascended to power following a military coup d'état in July 1966 that overthrew the previous president, General Johnson Aguiyi-Ironsi, an Igbo who had himself gained power as the result of a coup that took place only five months prior. General Gowon did not hesitate to kill many Igbo officers and civilians; it is likely that his military expertise, training, and skills had demonstrated to him the effectiveness of military violence as a tool of political repression.

For example, following the orders of the military dictator, the 4th Battalion in the North ruthlessly put down the popular uprisings that had broken out on September 29, 1966. This military brutality, which included rape, looting, and the wholesale executions of Igbo soldiers and innocent civilians in the North, caused widespread outrage, fueled the public outcry for justice, and was met with a violent popular reaction (Dent 1970; Panter-Brick 1970; Luckham 1974). This study expects that if the military violence had been carried out selectively against uniformed soldiers who were directly involved in the coup, Igbo officers and secessionists would not have been able to garner the popular support necessary to pose a legitimate challenge to the sitting government; in that case, the Nigerian Civil War of 1967 might have been avoided. Because it threatened the very existence of the Igbo people, the regime's use of indiscriminate military violence served only to intensify political opposition to military dictator Gowon, which led to the onset of civil war.

Before the civil war broke out in El Salvador in 1979, Carlos Humberto Romero Mena served as president from 1977 to 1979; before coming to power, he too served as a military general. The way General Romero seized the presidency—that is, through bloodshed (and electoral fraud)—was consistent with his military training. More importantly, his leadership style was characteristically that of a military dictator; the use of military violence during his tenure, which featured periods of escalation, was the norm rather than the exception. Despite intense domestic and international pressures, the former military general was eager to criminalize antigovernment activity and continued to use indiscriminate military violence against the noncombatant civilian population, thus intensifying his own mass opposition. In February 1978, for example, he ordered soldiers to shoot hundreds of civilians who were engaged in peaceful protests against electoral fraud (Americas Watch 1982, 39).

Romero was deposed by a reformist coup d'état led by military officers and civilians who on October 15, 1979, formed the Revolutionary Government Junta;

the junta made what were ultimately empty promises to initiate land reform and create a new constitution. The (new) antigovernment movement made an effort to win the hearts and minds of the rural and urban poor by providing them with food and shelter, but it is likely that they gained the majority of their popular support as a reaction to the violent repressive tactics by the junta. Unfortunately, military leaders in the Revolutionary Government Junta, like those of the previous regime, did not hesitate to torture, assassinate, and mutilate thousands of innocent civilians (Mason and Krane 1989, 186–89). These prolonged military atrocities in El Salvador angered a significant portion of the civilian population; many of these individuals joined guerrilla groups, which were eventually unified under the name Farabundo Martí National Liberation Front (FMLN). Later on, the FMLN launched a successful military campaign against the government, leading to a twelve-year civil war (Mason and Krane 1989; Stanley 1996; Wood 2003).

RESEARCH DESIGN

This study collects statistical data on 157 countries during the period from 1976 to 2007; thus, the country-year is the appropriate unit of analysis. As the military experience hypothesis is drawn from two stages of the civil violence process (first from leaders' prior military experience to the use of indiscriminate violence, and then from indiscriminate violence to the onset of civil war), its empirical tests require a two-stage statistical analysis. By modeling indiscriminate military violence as a function of leaders' military experience, violent dissent, civil war, per capita income, and population, the first stage examines whether leaders' military experience is linked to their use of indiscriminate military violence. The first stage is used to generate predicted values for indiscriminate violence, which serves as a main predictor of the onset of civil war at the second stage. The second stage incorporates a one-year lagged term of the predicted values for indiscriminate violence along with several control variables such as per capita income, democracy, and ethnic fractionalization. The second stage is built to explore whether indiscriminate military violence, while controlling for other causal factors, indeed precipitates the onset of civil war.

Building a Model for the First Stage

At the first stage, the dependent variable is indiscriminate military violence while the independent variables include leaders' prior military experience, violent dissent, civil war, per capita income, and population. Unfortunately, there exists no statistical data that directly captures the level of indiscriminate military violence against ordinary citizens, across countries, before the emergence of a civil war.[8] This study argues that the status of state repression acts as a good proxy for indiscriminate military violence because we can understand the former as the most likely outcome of the latter. To increase the credibility of the findings reported below, this study measures indiscriminate violence from two different repression data sources: the Political Terror Scale (PTS) and the Cingranelli-Richards (CIRI) index of physical integrity rights.[9] The physical integrity rights measure is an additive index based on the occurrence of torture, extrajudicial killings, political imprisonment, and disappearances, which represent the most extreme dimensions of political repression. It ranges from 0 (no government respect for these four rights) to 8 (full government respect for these four rights). To facilitate an easy interpretation of the estimated coefficient, the original ranking from 0 to 8 is reversed here with 0 corresponding to the lowest repression and 8 corresponding to the highest repression.

The PTS ranges from 1 to 5, with 1 indicating a country with the highest quality of human rights protections, and 5 denoting a country where the government employs unrestrained political terror against its entire population. The PTS relies on the same source materials as the physical integrity rights measures in the CIRI index and "in most instances use of either data set will result in the same or similar findings" (Wood and Gibney 2010, 395). A feature that is dissimilar between the two data sets is related to coding procedures. The CIRI index reports the combined scores for human rights by using the U.S. Department of State's (USDS) Country Reports on Human Rights Practices as its primary source and Amnesty International's (AI) Annual Report as a secondary source; the PTS, on the other hand, provides two separate scores of human rights violations, one from each of the previously named sources. Accordingly, the correlation between the two measures is high—approximately 0.79 between the USDS and the CIRI, and 0.75 between the AI and the CIRI during the time period of this study. However, Wood and Gibney's (2010, 394) study claims that "the PTS better captures the relative severity of abuse across countries"; also, the PTS measures conditions or structures, while the CIRI focuses on types of abuse. However, because the estimates produced by both the USDS and the AI scores are virtually identical, the empirical analysis reported below relies on the former to save space.

The military experience variable must capture whether a country is ruled by a chief executive who has had substantial military professionalization, and who exercises primary influence in the shaping of most major decisions affecting the nation's internal security affairs. This study relies on two different data sources in an effort to verify the robustness of the findings reported below. The first source is Besley and Reynal-Querol's (2011) data on the occupational background of leaders; the second source is Cheibub, Gandhi, and Vreeland's (2010) data collection, which identifies whether the effective head of state has experienced a significant degree of military professionalization. Besley and Reynal-Querol classify the occupation of political leaders in each country and year by consulting the Archigos data compiled by Goemans, Gleditsch, and Chiozza (2009) and then supplementing it with Ludwig (2002) as well as with their own raw materials. Besley and Reynal-Querol categorize top national executives into the following broad groups: royalty, civil servant, professor, scientist, military professional, businessperson, and other. In this study, the first military experience variable is operationalized with Besley and Reynal-Querol's classification; it is a dichotomous measure, recorded as 1 if the leader was in the military immediately before holding office (i.e., military professional) and as 0 if otherwise.

The second military experience variable is operationalized with Cheibub, Gandhi, and Vreeland's (2010) data collection. It is also a dichotomous measure, recorded as 1 if the effective head is, or at any point was, a member of the military by profession and as 0 if a civilian. It is important to note that retired members of the military are recorded as 1 because the shedding of a uniform is not enough to indicate the civilian character of a leader, and because retired soldiers holding positions as executive leaders remain "specialists on violence" given their previous military training, socialization, and mindset (Lasswell 1941, 1997). This coding procedure is consistent with this study's earlier conceptualization regarding a leader's prior military experience. If top executives come from a branch of the government other than the regular military forces—such as one of the secret services (e.g., CIA and Mossad), paramilitary forces (e.g., Iran's Revolutionary Guard and Basij militia), or gendarmerie (e.g., former French colonies in Africa)—they are not recorded as leaders with a military background.

The argument that leaders with prior military experience are more likely than those without to indiscriminately repress ordinary citizens is probabilistic rather than deterministic. That is, this study does not claim that all leaders prefer to use military repression after having been exposed to military professionalization. The military experience data compiled by Besley and Reynal-Querol and by Cheibub, Gandhi, and Vreeland accurately capture the dimensions of this argument as the data include information indicating that, in some cases, leaders are not predisposed to use military repression despite their military background (e.g., Eisenhower and de Gaulle). Of course, this variation is to be expected in the context of a liberal democratic tradition where civilian rule over the military is the norm, even when a nation's leader has an exclusively military background. In these cases, the tradition of civilian rule likely overrides the background of any particular leader (Huntington 1957; Feaver and Gelpi 2004; Choi and James 2005).

In line with the standard model used within the literature of repression and human rights violations (e.g., Davenport 2007), this study includes four additional variables in its statistical model. It measures political dissent by two different indicators: violent dissent (i.e., riots and guerrilla warfare) as operationalized by Banks (2010), and civil war as operationalized by the Uppsala and PRIO (Peace Research Institute Oslo) groups.[10] It might not be that the mere presence of a leader with a military background leads directly to high levels of repression and thus to an increased risk of civil war; one could argue, rather, that the critical element is the propensity of such a leader to use violence when under threat. To discern whether it is military rule in and of itself, or whether it is a matter of how military rulers rule the state, the violent dissent variable is included in the statistical model. This study also examines the possibility that leaders with a military background are more likely to use repressive measures to maintain civil order when they face an internal challenge from antigovernment armed forces. We may find that leaders with a military professionalization background are more likely to come to power in unstable states, those where civil war is already a more likely possibility. To account for such an issue, this study relies on the Uppsala and PRIO Armed Conflict Dataset. A civil war is defined as a contested incompatibility between a government and one or more opposition groups that results in at least twenty-five battle deaths in a year. The civil war onset variable is coded as 1 when a new civil war occurs; it is also coded as 1 when two years elapse after the beginning of the civil war. Per capita income and population are introduced in order to consider the main tenets of modernization theories. Leaders of countries in which poverty and greater population are major political issues are more likely to repress their citizens in the hope of reducing high levels of socioeconomic stress. Per capita income is measured in thousands of 1985 U.S. dollars as collected from Penn World Tables and World Bank data. Data on population size are gathered from World Bank figures; this is a logged term of the total population in thousands.

Because the dependent variable of state repression is rank ordered and ordinal, this study employs an ordered logit model with robust standard errors (Greene 2003; Gujarati 2003). When an OLS regression model is used instead, the estimated results coincide with those with ordered logit; they are not reported below in order to save space. To help mitigate problems of reverse causality, all of the predictors are lagged one year in the statistical model.

Building a Model for the Second Stage

At the second stage, the dependent variable is the onset of civil war and the main independent variable is predicted values for indiscriminate violence as measured by the form of state repression (see Thoms and Ron 2007; Jacobsen and de Soysa 2009). To help ensure the robustness of the findings reported below, this study introduces two measures of civil war onset collected from the Uppsala and PRIO Armed Conflict Dataset, which has emerged as the "gold standard" for civil war data. The first variable is the same dichotomous measure of civil war onset that is discussed above (called "onset2"). The second variable includes the onset of intrastate conflict with at least twenty-five battle deaths per annum, or with a five-year lapse since the last observation (called "onset5"). The second onset variable differs from the first one with respect to the minimum intermittency period allowed before a new onset is coded. Because a country with an ongoing armed conflict can experience an outbreak of a new conflict, all country-year observations following the onset of a conflict are kept in the data set. This approach has been widely used in previous studies of civil war using the Uppsala and PRIO Armed Conflict Dataset; this is exemplified in the recent works of Fjelde (2010) and Bergholt and Lujala (2012). As noted above, the predicted values for state repression generated in the first stage are then used as a main predictor of the onset of civil war at the second stage; this variable should capture how the use of indiscriminate violence against civilian populations precipitates the outbreak of civil war.

To avoid the risk of omitted variable bias, this study includes seven control variables, all of which commonly appear in the civil war literature (e.g., Fearon and Laitin 2003; Salehyan and Gleditsch 2006; Salehyan 2009; Taydas, Peksen, and James 2010). Per capita income is introduced to measure some financial and bureaucratic aspects of state capacity. Countries with fragile financial, military, and political institutions are more likely to experience internal wars due to weak local policing and corrupt counterinsurgency practices. Per capita income is measured in thousands of 1985 U.S. dollars; it is collected from Penn World Tables and World Bank data and lagged one year to ensure that it affects the likelihood of the onset of internal warfare rather than vice versa.[11]

Population size is controlled since civil violence is more likely to occur in highly populated countries due to the difficulties of policing; gathered from World Bank figures, it is a logged term of the total population, in thousands, from the previous country-year. It has been argued that because mountainous countries provide rebels with natural sanctuaries such as swamps, caverns, and jungles, they have a higher risk of the onset of internal war than other countries; therefore, this study includes a logged term of an estimated percentage of mountainous terrain according to the coding of geographer A. J. Gerard. Because civil war is more likely to occur when potential rebels reside in a territorial base that is separated from the country's center by water or a significant distance (e.g., Angola from Portugal), countries are coded as 1 for noncontiguous countries and as 0 otherwise. Oil-exporting countries provide rebels with a material incentive to compete for control of state power. Based on World Bank data, a country is coded as 1 if it is a major oil producer, making at least one-third of its export revenues from fossil fuels, and as 0 otherwise.

Democracy is a variable that should capture a lower risk of the onset of internal warfare. The institutional and civil rights framework of democracies helps to discourage discrimination and repression along cultural or other lines. The

Polity IV data set provides the basis for this variable, as it captures the general quality of democratic institutions. Polity evaluates countries on an eleven-point scale, ranging from 0 to 10. An overall polity score from full autocracy (−10) to full democracy (+10) is calculated by subtracting the autocracy score from the democracy score (see Marshall and Jaggers 2007). This study also tests the effect of anocracy. Fearon and Laitin (2003, 81) hypothesize that anocracy should increase the risk of civil war, as it reflects "political contestation among competing forces and, in consequence, state incapacity." Fearon and Laitin report supporting evidence for the positive effect of anocracy. In this study, anocratic regimes are ones that score between 5 and 5 on the composite democracy index. For empirical tests, anocracy is operationalized as a dichotomous measure with 1 indicating an anocratic regime. This study finds that anocracy is statistically insignificant, so its results are not reported in order to save space. Ethnic fractionalization, which is believed to instigate internal war, is based on estimates of ethnic group population from the *Atlas Narodov Mira* (1964) and has been updated for some newer countries using Fearon and Laitin's (2003) study. Ethnic fractionalization can be interpreted as representing the probability that two randomly drawn individuals in a country are from different ethnolinguistic groups.

Since the dependent variable, civil war onset, is dichotomous, this study employs a logistic regression model for estimation. It is well known that countries within a particular group or context tend to be more similar to each other in terms of an outcome variable than they are to countries in a different group or context. For example, any several countries that constitute a group sharing similar historical contexts may produce similar outcomes. As pointed out by many econometricians (e.g., Wooldridge 2002; Greene 2003), standard logit models fall short of accounting for the dependence of the outcome variable within countries from the same context; therefore, this study employs logistic regression models that consider this cluster effect whereby the observations are independent across but not necessarily within countries.

The estimated results from logit with clustering may be biased, as they are obtained without a consideration of temporal dependence in the dichotomous dependent variable, civil war onset. For example, if a country has civil peace for five years and then a civil war erupts, the onset of civil war variable is recoded as 0 during each of the five peace years, followed by a 1 in the year when the civil war erupted. The presence of temporal dependence may require special attention. Students of political methodology have suggested at least two estimation methods. The first one is Beck, Katz, and Tucker's (1998) logit splines, and the second one is Carter and Signorino's (2010) cubic polynomial of time. In both of these methods, the data are assumed to have an underlying temporal dimension, and the binary observations are assumed to represent grouped duration data. In order to take advantage of the method recently proposed by Carter and

Signorino, the cubic polynomial of time is included in the logit model as a way to control for temporal dependence.[12]

EMPIRICAL RESULTS

Table 9.1 presents estimated results using ordered logit at the first stage and logit with both clustering and cubic polynomial of time at the second stage. The hypotheses are directional, so a one-tailed test at the 0.05, 0.01, and 0.001 levels is performed. To save space, the subsequent discussion is confined to the theoretically interesting variables of this study, while the results for the control variables are only minimally explained. Model 1 tests the main hypothesis regarding whether a leader's prior military experience is positively associated with a higher risk of civil war onset. When the first stage of Model 1 regresses state repression on the military background of leaders, it produces results in which the military experience variable is statistically significant at the 0.001 level and in the hypothesized direction. These results indicate that when a country is ruled by leaders with prior military experience, its citizens are more likely to become the victims of indiscriminate repression. The second question pertains to whether this increase of indiscriminate violence contributes to the outbreak of civil war. The second stage of Model 1 is built to answer this question by regressing the onset of civil war variable on a one-year lagged term of the predicted values for state repression as well as seven control variables. As expected, the predicted repression variable achieves significance with a positive sign indicating that as state repression increases, the onset of civil war is more likely to result. The impact of the seven control variables corroborates the findings of previous civil war studies; namely, that civil wars are more likely to occur in those countries that are poor and highly populated, are surrounded by rough terrain, are oil-exporting countries, and are ethnically diverse; democracy seems to have no bearing on civil war onset.[13]

When the results from stages one and two are evaluated simultaneously, it appears that indiscriminate military violence has the tendency to provoke civilians to support or even join dissident groups in the effort to avenge their grievances when it is initiated by leaders with a history of past military professionalization. As a consequence, the dissident movement grows to such a formidable size that it has the capacity to pursue military action against the incumbent government. Most importantly, as my hypothesis predicted, a leader's prior military experience is a contributing factor to the likelihood of civil conflict.

In an attempt to avoid the potential bias that may stem from omitted variables, Model 2 modifies its first stage model by adding four additional factors of state repression but keeps the same model specification at the second stage. Despite this modification, the military experience variable at the first stage still

TABLE 9.1   Leaders' Prior Military Experience, Political Terror, and Civil War Onset

Variable	Besley and Reynal-Querol								Cheibub, Gandhi, and Vreeland	
	Model 1	Model 2	Model 3	Model 4	Model 5	Model 6	Model 7	Model 8	Model 9	Model 10
First Stage: Repression$_t$			Repression measured by Political Terror Scale							
Military experience$_{t-1}$	1.029*** (0.196)	0.540** (0.202)			1.029*** (0.196)	0.540** (0.202)			0.825*** (0.191)	0.825*** (0.191)
Violent dissent$_{t-1}$		0.816*** (0.236)				0.816*** (0.236)				
Civil war$_{t-1}$		1.180*** (0.220)				1.180*** (0.220)				
Per capita income$_{t-1}$		-0.162*** (0.027)				-0.162*** (0.027)				
Population$_{t-1}$		0.299*** (0.073)				0.299*** (0.073)				
Wald chi^2	27.59	120.20			27.59	120.20			18.66	18.66
Prob > chi^2	0.001	0.001			0.001	0.001			0.001	0.001
Log pseudolikelihood	-4991.96	-4361.41			-4991.96	-4361.41			-5142.36	-5142.36
Observations	3,490	3,444			3,490	3,444			3,567	3,567
Second Stage: Civil War$_t$	onset2	onset2			onset5		onset2	onset5		
Repression_Predicted$_{t-1}$	0.540* (0.247)	0.359** (0.153)			0.479* (0.259)	0.487** (0.170)			0.610* (0.341)	0.669** (0.288)
Military experience$_{t-1}$			0.556* (0.254)	0.427* (0.185)			0.493* (0.266)	0.379* (0.186)		
Per capita income$_{t-1}$	-0.081* (0.043)	-0.017 (0.056)	-0.081* (0.043)	-0.089** (0.033)	-0.103* (0.047)	-0.011 (0.062)	-0.103* (0.047)	-0.120*** (0.036)	-0.095** (0.040)	-0.115** (0.043)

Population$_{t-1}$	0.151*	0.015	0.151*	0.239***	0.111	-0.102	0.111	0.214***	0.166*	0.121
	(0.088)	(0.124)	(0.088)	(0.053)	(0.087)	(0.131)	(0.087)	(0.050)	(0.086)	(0.085)
Mountainous terrain$_t$	0.175*	0.132*	0.175*	0.179***	0.135	0.102	0.135	0.175***	0.172*	0.143*
	(0.085)	(0.076)	(0.085)	(0.058)	(0.084)	(0.074)	(0.084)	(0.057)	(0.086)	(0.082)
Noncontiguous state$_t$	0.505*	0.321	0.505*	0.083	0.491	0.242	0.491	0.054	0.469	0.470
	(0.283)	(0.286)	(0.283)	(0.191)	(0.318)	(0.349)	(0.318)	(0.222)	(0.286)	(0.324)
Oil exporter$_t$	0.464*	0.526*	0.464*	0.521*	0.314	0.382	0.314	0.422*	0.486*	0.327
	(0.272)	(0.250)	(0.272)	(0.234)	(0.251)	(0.248)	(0.251)	(0.235)	(0.274)	(0.253)
Democracy$_{t-1}$	0.009	-0.006	0.009	0.018	0.013	-0.002	0.013	0.028*	0.008	0.015
	(0.020)	(0.019)	(0.020)	(0.012)	(0.021)	(0.021)	(0.021)	(0.013)	(0.020)	(0.020)
Ethnic fractionalization$_t$	1.359***	1.180***	1.359***	0.996***	1.023**	0.843***	1.023**	0.973***	1.251***	0.950**
	(0.364)	(0.371)	(0.364)	(0.257)	(0.365)	(0.358)	(0.365)	(0.257)	(0.361)	(0.345)
Constant	-5.272***	-5.157***	-5.272***	-5.988***	-5.053***	-4.925***	-5.053***	-6.213***	-5.290***	-5.134***
	(0.846)	(0.837)	(0.846)	(0.554)	(0.793)	(0.817)	(0.793)	(0.527)	(0.818)	(0.760)
Wald chi²	74.36	213.89	74.36	118.44	48.70	140.57	48.70	94.29	72.04	49.88
Prob > chi²	0.001	0.001	0.001	0.001	0.001	0.001	0.001	0.001	0.001	0.001
Log pseudolikelihood	-497.46	-495.16	-497.46	-854.53	-390.11	-390.11	-384.68	-715.22	-498.97	-390.28
Observations	3,194	3,190	3,194	6,681	3,194	3,194	3,194	6,681	3,265	3,265

Notes: The estimates for the cubic polynomial of time (i.e., t, t^2, and t^3) are omitted to save space.

Robust standard errors are in parentheses.

*$p < .05$, **$p < .01$, ***$p < .001$, one-tailed tests

turns out to be statistically significant at the 0.01 level and in the hypothesized direction; the predicted repression variable at the second stage remains significant at the 0.01 level with a positive sign. These findings provide further evidence that a leader's prior military experience is a causal factor related to the development of civil war.

Next, to examine how the military experience variable directly affects the likelihood of civil war, Model 3 presents results obtained after the civil war onset is regressed on the military experience variable and the seven control variables. Because the military experience variable achieves significance with a positive sign, it is reasonable to assume that when a country is ruled by a leader with prior military experience, its risk of a civil war is likely to increase. This finding suggests that the military experience variable may be considered a useful proxy for a leader's expertise in and preference for the use of violent force (i.e., it captures a leader's proclivity for resorting to the use of indiscriminate violence against domestic political opposition). With that in mind, this study extended the time period of the sample data back to 1945 (i.e., it added thirty-two more years) and tested the direct relationship between military experience and civil war onset during the period from 1945 to 2007. Model 4 replicates Model 3 with the extended data. The results are consistent with those in Model 3, again verifying the assertion that a leader's military background matters.

In addition to reporting their statistical significance, a calculation of the substantive effects of the variables is a crucial step in any data analysis (see Greene 2003; Gujarati 2003). To calculate a baseline probability of civil war against which to make comparisons, this study sets the continuous variables at their means and the dichotomized variables at 0. It then adjusts the variables of greatest interest, one at a time, to see the change in the predicted probability of civil war. To illustrate, when a substantive analysis is performed with Model 3, this study finds that the substantive effect of the military experience variable is consistent with its statistical significance; the civil war risk among countries that are ruled by leaders with prior military experience will increase approximately 71 percent, indicating once more that indiscriminate military violence considerably heightens the likelihood of internal warfare. It is also worth noting that given the high human and financial costs associated with such a conflict, even small changes in the predicted probability of political violence should not be dismissed. Increasing the annual probability of a civil war by 71 percent is hardly trivial when we recognize that even a single, relatively short incidence of civil war could cost thousands of human lives and result in millions of dollars of infrastructure damage.

Models 1 through 4 of Table 9.1 recorded the civil war onset variable as 1 when a new civil war occurs as well as in cases where two years have elapsed after the beginning of the civil war (called "onset2"). However, an onset variable that differs from the one used in the previous three models with respect to the minimum intermittency period may produce different estimates. Models 5 through 8 investigate this possibility by replicating Models 1 through 4 after having replaced "onset2" with "onset5," which is defined as the onset of intrastate conflict with a five-year lapse since the last observation. The results in Models 5 through 8 are consistent with those in Models 1 through 4, confirming that, all other things being equal, countries under military leadership are more vulnerable to civil war onset than are countries under civilian leadership. Countries ruled by leaders with a history of military professionalization (countries in which civilian control over the military is unlikely to be enforced) are the same countries where domestic political protests teeter toward the brink of civil war; this study has argued that this tendency is caused by the propensity of these leaders to rely on indiscriminate military violence against not only dissidents but innocent civilians as well.

The estimated results discussed so far were obtained with a military experience variable whose operationalization is based on Besley and Reynal-Querol's (2011) data on the occupational background of leaders. In order to verify the robustness of its findings, however, this study introduces an additional leadership background variable collected from Cheibub, Gandhi, and Vreeland's (2010) dataset. In particular, Cheibub, Gandhi, and Vreeland's effective head variable is used (i.e., "emil" in the data set). After replacing Besley and Reynal-Querol's variable with Cheibub, Gandhi, and Vreeland's variable, Model 9 replicates Model 1, and Model 10 replicates Model 5. The rationale for replicating Models 1 and 5 is that these models produce predicted values for state repression after an exclusive consideration of the effect of a leader's prior military experience. Given the focus of this study, it makes sense that an increased level of state repression should be solely the outcome of a leader's proclivity to use violence, rather than the result of factors such as violent dissent and per capita income. In other words, because the main purpose of building the first stage model is not to explain as much variance in the state repression variable as possible, but to gauge the influence of a leader's prior military experience, the control factors are less relevant. The results from Models 9 and 10 are virtually the same as those from Models 1 and 5, confirming the hypothesis that countries ruled by leaders with a military background are at a greater risk of civil war onset. When the second and sixth models, which incorporated the four additional controls at the first stage, are replicated, the results (shown in Models 1 and 2 in Appendix Table 9.1) are similar to those in Models 9 and 10.

The state repression variable used in Table 9.1 comes from the PTS. What would happen if the variable was measured with a different data source? Models 1 through 4 in Table 9.2 address this question by employing the CIRI index of physical integrity rights. Models 1 through 4 replicate Models 1, 5, 9, and 10

TABLE 9.2   Leaders' Prior Military Experience, Physical Integrity Rights, and
Civil War Onset

| Variable | Besley and Reynal-Querol | | Cheibub, Gandhi, and Vreeland | |
	Model 1	Model 2	Model 3	Model 4
First Stage: Repression$_t$	Repression Measured by Physical Integrity Rights			
Military experience$_{t-1}$	1.020***	1.020***	0.798***	0.798***
	(0.200)	(0.200)	(0.195)	(0.195)
Wald chi²	25.90	25.90	25.90	25.90
Prob > chi²	0.001	0.001	0.001	0.001
Log pseudolikelihood	−6110.22	−6110.22	−6110.22	−6110.22
Observations	2,919	2,919	2,979	2,979
Second Stage: Civil War$_t$	onset2	onset5	onset2	onset5
Repression_Predicted$_{t-1}$	0.747**	0.768**	0.590	0.875**
	(0.258)	(0.319)	(0.391)	(0.353)
Per capita income$_{t-1}$	−0.068	−0.093	−0.087*	−0.112*
	(0.043)	(0.057)	(0.041)	(0.051)
Population$_{t-1}$	0.197*	0.170*	0.224**	0.192*
	(0.089)	(0.097)	(0.083)	(0.094)
Mountainous terrain$_t$	0.175*	0.146	0.151	0.142
	(0.093)	(0.095)	(0.095)	(0.094)
Noncontiguous state$_t$	0.439	0.260	0.374	0.204
	(0.303)	(0.431)	(0.292)	(0.432)
Oil exporter$_t$	0.350	0.003	0.378	0.031
	(0.308)	(0.335)	(0.299)	(0.336)
Democracy$_{t-1}$	0.018	0.032	0.011	0.031
	(0.023)	(0.026)	(0.024)	(0.025)
Ethnic fractionalization$_t$	1.364***	1.064**	1.148***	0.900*
	(0.374)	(0.430)	(0.374)	(0.396)
Constant	−5.717***	−5.934***	−5.590***	−5.960***
	(0.888)	(1.060)	(0.856)	(1.006)
Wald chi²	77.60	40.71	69.87	39.04
Prob > chi²	0.001	0.001	0.001	0.001
Log pseudolikelihood	−380.08	−293.18	−383.39	−294.29
Observations	2,659	2,659	2,714	2,714

Notes: The estimates for the cubic polynomial of time are omitted to save space.

Robust standard errors are in parentheses.

*$p < .05$, **$p < .01$, ***$p < .001$, one-tailed tests

of Table 9.1, respectively. The overall results in Table 9.2 agree with those in Table 9.1, providing further indication that a leader's military background matters in predicting the likelihood of civil war.[14]

Do alternative statistical models cause the significance of the theoretically interesting variables to disappear? Tables 9.3 and 9.4 reevaluate the robustness of the results reported in Tables 9.1 and 9.2 by employing two additional statistical estimation techniques: generalized estimating equations (GEEs) and rare event logit.[15] The change in the estimation technique applies only to the models that appear at the second stage, while the first stage models are again estimated with ordered logit. The Woolldridge test for autocorrelation and a likelihood-ratio test for heteroskedasticity are conducted against the civil war data set of this study; the null hypothesis of the former test is no first-order correlation, and that of the latter test is no heteroskedasticity (Wooldridge 2002; Drukker 2003). The test results indicate that the null hypotheses are rejected; therefore, the achievement of unbiased estimates will require correction for both panel heteroskedasticity and temporally correlated errors. As discussed in Zorn's (2001) study, GEEs are a suitable estimator used to correct for first-order autocorrelation as well as for heteroskedasticity. Models 1 through 4 of Table 9.3 replicate Models 1, 5, 9, and 10 of Table 9.1, and Models 5 through 8 of Table 9.3 replicate Models 1 through 4 of Table 9.2. The GEEs results of Table 9.3 are similar to those in Tables 9.1 and 9.2 with respect to the significance levels and the coefficient signs. The results confirm that a leader's prior military experience is indeed a cause of civil war onset.

This study found its civil war data to have an excessive number of zero counts (the occurrence of civil war onset is found to be 4.01 percent with onset2 [battle deaths >= twenty-five or two years elapsed] and 2.89 percent with onset5 [battle deaths >= twenty-five or five years elapsed]), which suggests that GEEs may lose some of their effectiveness, resulting in biased estimates. A rare event logit— originally developed by Tomz, King, and Zeng (1999), expanded upon by King and Zeng (2001), and recently used in Choi's (2010b) study on terrorism—addresses this issue. Table 9.4 shows the results of the rare event logit models. The significance of the military experience variable is once again confirmed in a consistent manner, regardless of the different possibilities for operationalizing a leader's military background, political repression, and civil violence, respectively.

CONCLUSION

In order to better understand how some domestic political protests develop into armed civil conflict while others do not, this study probes the possibility that a political leader's prior military experience is linked to a higher risk of civil

TABLE 9.3 Leaders' Prior Military Experience, Repression, and Civil War Onset: Generalized Estimating Equations

Variable	Besley and Reynal-Querol	Cheibub, Gandhi, and Vreeland	Besley and Reynal-Querol	Cheibub, Gandhi, and Vreeland	Besley and Reynal-Querol	Cheibub, Gandhi, and Vreeland	Besley and Reynal-Querol	Cheibub, Gandhi, and Vreeland
	Model 1	Model 2	Model 3	Model 4	Model 5	Model 6	Model 7	Model 8
First Stage: Repression$_t$	Political Terror Scale				Physical Integrity Rights			
Military experience$_{t-1}$	1.029***	0.825***	1.029***	0.825***	1.020***	0.798***	1.020***	0.798***
	(0.196)	(0.191)	(0.196)	(0.191)	(0.200)	(0.195)	(0.200)	(0.195)
Wald chi^2	27.59	18.66	27.59	18.66	25.90	25.90	25.90	25.90
Prob > chi^2	0.001	0.001	0.001	0.001	0.001	0.001	0.001	0.001
Log pseudolikelihood	−4991.96	−5142.36	−4991.96	−5142.36	−6110.22	−6110.22	−6110.22	−6110.22
Observations	3,490	3,567	3,490	3,567	2,919	2,979	2,919	2,979
Second Stage: Civil War$_t$	onset2		onset5		onset2		onset5	
Repression_Predicted$_{t-1}$	0.602*	0.671*	0.497*	0.682**	0.838**	0.688	0.796**	0.899**
	(0.267)	(0.367)	(0.260)	(0.290)	(0.297)	(0.443)	(0.325)	(0.358)
Per capita income$_{t-1}$	−0.091*	−0.105**	−0.106*	−0.117**	−0.084*	−0.105**	−0.095	−0.114*
	(0.045)	(0.043)	(0.048)	(0.043)	(0.048)	(0.045)	(0.058)	(0.052)
Population$_{t-1}$	0.165*	0.182*	0.111	0.121	0.219*	0.251**	0.168*	0.191*
	(0.100)	(0.096)	(0.089)	(0.088)	(0.105)	(0.099)	(0.102)	(0.099)
Mountainous terrain$_t$	0.185*	0.181*	0.135	0.141*	0.195*	0.169	0.147	0.141
	(0.093)	(0.094)	(0.085)	(0.083)	(0.107)	(0.110)	(0.097)	(0.095)

Noncontiguous state$_t$	0.650*	0.607*	0.499	0.473	0.643*	0.577*	0.289	0.230
	(0.303)	(0.304)	(0.316)	(0.320)	(0.332)	(0.320)	(0.430)	(0.429)
Oil exporter$_t$	0.458	0.477	0.298	0.313	0.357	0.391	−0.021	0.007
	(0.302)	(0.305)	(0.253)	(0.252)	(0.357)	(0.353)	(0.340)	(0.339)
Democracy$_{t-1}$	0.004	0.003	0.012	0.014	0.017	0.009	0.029	0.028
	(0.021)	(0.022)	(0.020)	(0.019)	(0.024)	(0.024)	(0.024)	(0.023)
Ethnic fractionalization$_t$	1.422***	1.308***	1.037**	0.965**	1.491***	1.268**	1.077**	0.905*
	(0.391)	(0.387)	(0.372)	(0.352)	(0.426)	(0.425)	(0.436)	(0.405)
Constant	−6.002***	−6.019***	−5.361***	−5.407***	−6.760***	−6.691***	−6.133***	−6.137***
	(0.912)	(0.899)	(0.809)	(0.794)	(0.987)	(0.959)	(0.995)	(0.963)
Wald chi²	62.93	59.99	43.00	42.41	57.62	46.79	34.40	32.09
Prob > chi²	0.001	0.001	0.001	0.001	0.001	0.001	0.001	0.001
Observations	3,193	3,265	3,193	3,265	2,657	2,712	2,657	2,712

Note: Semirobust standard errors are in parentheses.

*p < .05, **p < .01, ***p < .001, one-tailed tests

TABLE 9.4 Leaders' Prior Military Experience, Repression, and Civil War Onset: Rare Event Logit

Variable	Political Terror Scale				Physical Integrity Rights			
	Besley and Reynal-Querol	Cheibub, Gandhi, and Vreeland	Besley and Reynal-Querol	Cheibub, Gandhi, and Vreeland	Besley and Reynol-Querol	Cheibub, Gandhi, and Vreeland	Besley and Reynal-Querol	Cheibub, Gandhi, and Vreeland
	Model 1	Model 2	Model 3	Model 4	Model 5	Model 6	Model 7	Model 8
First Stage: Repression$_t$								
Military experience$_{t-1}$	1.029***	0.825***	1.029***	0.825***	1.020***	0.798***	1.020***	0.798***
	(0.196)	(0.191)	(0.196)	(0.191)	(0.200)	(0.195)	(0.200)	(0.195)
Wald chi^2	27.59	18.66	27.59	18.66	25.90	25.90	25.90	25.90
Prob > chi^2	0.001	0.001	0.001	0.001	0.001	0.001	0.001	0.001
Log pseudolikelihood	−4991.96	−5142.36	−4991.96	−5142.36	−6110.22	−6110.22	−6110.22	−6110.22
Observations	3,490	3,567	3,490	3,567	2,919	2,979	2,919	2,979
Second Stage: Civil War$_t$	onset2		onset5		onset2		onset5	
Repression_Predicted$_{t-1}$	0.599**	0.668**	0.498*	0.682*	0.836***	0.692*	0.797**	0.902**
	(0.214)	(0.265)	(0.255)	(0.295)	(0.247)	(0.313)	(0.301)	(0.344)
Per capita income$_{t-1}$	−0.087*	−0.101**	−0.100*	−0.111*	−0.080*	−0.100**	−0.089	−0.107*
	(0.039)	(0.038)	(0.051)	(0.048)	(0.043)	(0.042)	(0.059)	(0.055)
Population$_{t-1}$	0.165**	0.183**	0.112	0.122	0.219***	0.250***	0.169*	0.192*
	(0.065)	(0.066)	(0.078)	(0.079)	(0.070)	(0.070)	(0.086)	(0.088)
Mountainous terrain$_t$	0.183**	0.179**	0.132	0.139*	0.192*	0.167*	0.144	0.139
	(0.074)	(0.074)	(0.084)	(0.083)	(0.085)	(0.085)	(0.096)	(0.094)
Noncontiguous state$_t$	0.652**	0.609**	0.510*	0.482*	0.645**	0.580*	0.309	0.250
	(0.231)	(0.231)	(0.280)	(0.284)	(0.274)	(0.269)	(0.361)	(0.364)

Oil exporter$_t$	0.463*	0.480*	0.310	0.323	0.368	0.401	0.009	0.036
	(0.225)	(0.225)	(0.280)	(0.280)	(0.265)	(0.264)	(0.361)	(0.362)
Democracy$_{t-1}$	0.004	0.003	0.012	0.014	0.017	0.009	0.028	0.027
	(0.016)	(0.016)	(0.020)	(0.019)	(0.018)	(0.018)	(0.023)	(0.022)
Ethnic fractionalization$_t$	1.408***	1.293***	1.024**	0.951**	1.464***	1.246***	1.052**	0.885*
	(0.327)	(0.313)	(0.382)	(0.364)	(0.360)	(0.345)	(0.440)	(0.414)
Constant	−5.963***	−5.985***	−5.323***	−5.374***	−6.704***	−6.645***	−6.084***	−6.096***
	(0.717)	(0.716)	(0.834)	(0.837)	(0.798)	(0.796)	(0.962)	(0.967)
Observations	3,194	3,265	3,194	3,265	2,659	2,714	2,659	2,714

Note: Robust standard errors are in parentheses.

*$p < .05$, **$p < .01$, ***$p < .001$, one-tailed tests

war onset. Drawing on the existing civil-military relations literature—which has provided useful insights into armed conflict since the writings of Sun Tzu (1971) and Carl von Clausewitz (1976), but the potential utility of which has long been underused in scholarly debates over the causes of civil war onset—this study began by putting forward an intuitive argument: leaders with a military background are inclined to use indiscriminate military violence, which inculcates feelings of anger, bitterness, and despair among their civilian populations and thus helps to consolidate a popular base for opposition movements; if this base is large enough, it may be capable of launching a successful military campaign against the sitting government. This conceptualization is a response to critical reviews of the "grievance" school of thought in civil war studies. For example, Fearon and Laitin (2003) contend that grievances cannot explain civil war because grievances exist everywhere whereas civil wars are rare; however, this study argues that not all grievances are the same. Although grievances may exist in all states, the severity of those grievances varies a great deal. Violent and indiscriminate repression of innocent civilians by a military ruler is qualitatively different from, say, overtaxation or disenfranchisement. The former is likely to spark armed resistance, while the latter is less likely to do so.

Three historical civil war examples (Guatemala, Nigeria, and El Salvador) illustrate the positive relationship between a leader's prior military experience and the onset of civil war. For a large-N analysis, this study collected statistical data on 157 countries during the period from 1945/1976 to 2007. Four different statistical techniques were employed for estimation; namely, ordered logit, standard logit with clustering, GEEs, and rare event logit. To further verify the robustness of the findings, this study employed at least two different measures of each of the main variables: military background, state repression, and civil war onset. The empirical results provide evidence that irrespective of estimation technique or differing operationalizations, the military experience variable is consistently and positively associated with a greater risk of civil war. This finding supports the theoretical logic of civil violence that was put forward in this study: a country ruled by leaders with prior military experience is more likely to engage in indiscriminate repression and, in doing so, is more likely to precipitate the onset of civil war.

The empirical findings reported in this study present several important implications for future foreign policy making. U.S. foreign policy should aim to help to establish or bolster civilian regimes in other countries. The United States has historically paid little attention to the type of leadership that exists in allied countries when a security exigency for world peace has to be prioritized. As long as U.S. national interests are not compromised in a country, the military has been allowed to enjoy control of the state—for example, those U.S. institutional and development projects that purported to strengthen the agencies and factions of the Salvadoran military despite its continuing use of violence against civilians (Stanley 1996, 8). However, political dynamics have changed since the collapse of the former Soviet Union as international security threats have become relatively infrequent and domestic threats have increased; thus, it seems that military preferences tend to prevail over civilian preferences if civilian control over the military is not already firmly established and vigilantly maintained (Desch 1998, 2001). This means that the U.S. foreign policy tailored to the Cold War security environment needs to be adjusted for the post–Cold War period in order to prevent unintended negative consequences such as the outbreak of civil war as a response to abusive military force. More importantly, when the United States provides economic and military assistance to foreign countries (as they do, for example, through the USAID), it can be more selective of which type of leadership regimes receive its support, as such aid should be used to contribute to regional peace and to further reduce the risk of future civil war.

APPENDIX TABLE 9.1   Leaders' Prior Military Experience, Repression, and Civil War Onset: More Controls at the First Stage

	Cheibub, Gandhi, and Vreeland		Besley and Reynal-Querol		Cheibub, Gandhi, and Vreeland	
Variable	Model 1	Model 2	Model 3	Model 4	Model 5	Model 6
First Stage: Repression$_t$	Political Terror Scale		Physical Integrity Rights			
Military experience$_{t-1}$	0.416*	0.416*	0.446*	0.446*	0.327*	0.327*
	(0.189)	(0.189)	(0.201)	(0.201)	(0.189)	(0.189)
Violent dissent$_{t-1}$	0.818***	0.818***	0.880***	0.880***	0.894***	0.894***
	(0.239)	(0.239)	(0.260)	(0.260)	(0.263)	(0.263)
Civil war$_{t-1}$	1.197***	1.197***	0.807***	0.807***	0.840***	0.840***
	(0.220)	(0.220)	(0.190)	(0.190)	(0.197)	(0.197)
Per capita income$_{t-1}$	−0.165***	−0.165***	−0.165***	−0.165***	−0.175***	−0.175***
	(0.025)	(0.025)	(0.026)	(0.026)	(.025)	(.025)
Population$_{t-1}$	0.295***	0.295***	0.378***	0.378***	0.382***	0.382***
	(0.072)	(0.072)	(0.071)	(0.071)	(0.071)	(0.071)
Wald chi^2	126.54	126.54	142.74	142.74	151.85	151.85
Prob > chi^2	0.001	0.001	0.001	0.001	0.001	0.001
Log pseudolikelihood	−4455.00	−4455.00	−5475.67	−5475.67	−5568.46	−5568.46
Observations	3,520	3,520	2,883	2,883	2,943	2,943
Second Stage: Civil War$_t$	onset2	onset5	onset2	onset5	onset2	onset5
Repression_Predicted$_{t-1}$	0.341*	0.488*	0.287*	0.447**	0.246	0.422*
	(0.151)	(0.175)	(0.171)	(0.187)	(0.158)	(0.186)

	(1)	(2)	(3)	(4)	(5)	(6)
Per capita income$_{t-1}$	-0.029	-0.020	-0.020	-0.013	-0.035	-0.024
	(0.055)	(0.061)	(0.062)	(0.075)	(0.060)	(0.073)
Population$_{t-1}$	0.035	-0.090	0.079	-0.045	0.107	-0.026
	(0.121)	(0.131)	(0.143)	(0.154)	(0.135)	(0.152)
Mountainous terrain$_t$	0.128*	0.097*	0.117	0.096	0.114	0.092
	(0.075)	(0.073)	(0.086)	(0.090)	(0.086)	(0.090)
Noncontiguous state$_t$	0.324	0.233	0.235	-0.069	0.256	-0.054
	(0.288)	(0.350)	(0.307)	(0.488)	(0.305)	(0.483)
Oil exporter$_t$	0.538*	0.398*	0.409	0.105	0.413	0.118
	(0.252)	(0.248)	(0.290)	(0.330)	(0.292)	(0.331)
Democracy$_{t-1}$	-0.007	-0.003	-0.004	0.009	-0.004	0.008
	(0.020)	(0.021)	(0.023)	(0.026)	(0.024)	(0.026)
Ethnic fractionalization$_t$	1.131***	0.780***	1.087**	0.783*	1.048**	0.729*
	(0.373)	(0.358)	(0.395)	(0.435)	(0.398)	(0.432)
Constant	-5.186***	-4.954***	-5.387***	-5.715***	-5.407***	-5.726***
	(0.834)	(0.814)	(0.921)	(1.184)	(0.922)	(1.174)
Wald chi²	206.54	206.54	229.18	130.07	212.93	127.59
Prob > chi²	0.001	0.001	0.001	0.001	0.001	0.001
Log pseudolikelihood	-496.69	-496.69	-381.47	-291.68	-382.87	-292.62
Observations	3,261	3,261	2,655	2,655	2,710	2,710

Notes: The estimates for the cubic polynomial of time are omitted to save space.

Robust standard errors are in parentheses.

*$p < .05$, **$p < .01$, ***$p < .001$, one-tailed tests

CHAPTER 10

Democracy, Status Quo, and Military Manpower Systems

> Justifying conscription to promote the cause of liberty is one of the most
> bizarre notions ever conceived by man! Forced servitude, with the risk
> of death and serious injury as a price to live free, makes no sense.
> RON PAUL, "Conscription—The Terrible Price of War"

The choice between conscription and volunteer enlistment can be thought to
indicate the balance of political power between civilians and the military in
domestic politics; it may also determine how it is that a state responds to external threats in international politics. Conscripted soldiers, for example, may
be more readily available than are volunteers for mobilization and deployment;
this may in turn be associated with a higher likelihood of conflict involvement
and even "some of history's greatest catastrophes such as the two world wars"
(Møller 2002, 300–301).[1]

In fact, debate over this issue revolves around both domestic imperatives and
the international environment. In Canada, for instance, a conscription crisis
developed during World War I because nationalists in the province of Quebec
argued against the practice as a manifestation of an unwanted allegiance to the
British Empire (Archer et al. 2002, 364). At the other extreme, some states avoid
conscription altogether because of the perceived unreliability of their domestic
population, even in cases where aggressive external intentions exist; some examples, at various times, include Pakistan, Saudi Arabia, and Nigeria. In still
other instances, states may seek conscription to undermine potentially threatening domestic counter-elites; such was the case with France prior to World
Wars I and II, Allende's Chile, and Nicaragua. A greater understanding of how
the choice is made of one system over another will thus have relevance for both
domestic and international political processes.

Although the choice of a military manpower system is an important issue,
research on it generally remains out of the "spotlight" for students of international relations.[2] The reasons for this apparent shortage of interest vary. Yet,
one of the main reasons can be attributed to lack of data. Although some descriptive and historical treatments exist, no integrated research project grants

centrality to a cross-national, time-series analysis. More importantly, the majority of studies have been carried out, not by political scientists, but by economists, who conduct cost-benefit analyses of conscripted versus volunteer military systems. Thus, research so far focuses mainly on the domestic implications of military manpower structure such as budget analysis for conscription and volunteer service, but not on the international political determinants. In other words, a military manpower system tends to appear as a causal variable in relation to economic matters, rather than as something to be explained from a political science perspective.[3]

Analysis of interstate dyads is used widely in studies of international relations but is at quite some distance from the literature on civil-military relations in general and on conscription in particular. Because a state's choice between the use of conscripted versus volunteer forces depends on its political-military position vis-à-vis that of other states, a dyadic rather than monadic analysis is preferred. Any research on the choice of military manpower system must pay heed to pairs of states (dyads) over time because of its inherently relational character (Oneal, Russett, and Berbaum 2003, 372). The foundation for this belief is the classic concept of the "security dilemma," namely, as one state takes action to enhance its security, the effect is often that of decreased security for one or more others (Jervis 1978; see also Glaser 1997). While the effects noted above are not in the strict sense limited to the dyad as a unit of analysis, this is the most direct way to investigate the security dilemma; thus, the present study follows in this tradition.

To broaden the scope of investigation with respect to military manpower systems, this study combines both domestic and international factors from political as well as economic categories. A multinomial logit model is tested on a pooled cross-national, time-series data set that spans over a hundred years. The unit of analysis is the interstate dyad-year. This study goes beyond scholarship on international conflict in terms of method, where generally either simple ordinary least squares or logistic regression is employed for a single or few nations in a particular year;[4] and military manpower systems in terms of substance, where it is typical for issues of economic rather than international political significance to predominate. In doing so, this study indicates some causal factors that may explain any particular regime's decision between either a conscripted force or a volunteer military manpower system.

Four additional sections appear below. The second section consists of a literature review that sets the context for an attempt to explain conscription. Hypotheses, measurement, data, and model building are discussed in the third section. The fourth section reports empirical results about determinants of military manpower systems: conscripted versus volunteer. The fifth and final section summarizes the implications of the empirical findings.

THE POLITICAL ECONOMY OF MILITARY MANPOWER SYSTEMS

Existing literature on military manpower systems focuses mainly on the domestic impact of the choice between conscripted and volunteer military forces—factors, for example, such as social opportunity costs and military preparedness. Paul Russell Anderson's (1945) "Universal Military Training and National Security," published by the *Annals of the American Academy of Political and Social Science*, appears as a foundational work in the field, dealing with military history, military and cultural considerations, and manpower alternatives for Great Britain, the Soviet Union, and France. Manpower studies in the United States began to pick up in the middle of the Vietnam War, during which the antiwar social climate resulted in open and sometimes violent confrontations over the military draft. In response to these political situations, several prominent economists—interestingly enough, not political scientists—built, in the late 1960s and early 1970s, a theoretical framework from the perspective of labor economics. Various related articles appeared in top economic journals including the *American Economic Review* and the *Quarterly Journal of Economics* (see Altman and Fechter 1967; Hansen and Weisbrod 1967; Oi 1967; Miller 1968; Fisher 1969; Friedman 1972).

Although economic theorization at the time focused on identifying which manpower systems produced more desirable defense outcomes, discussion followed a normative direction and tended to favor professional soldiers over conscripted ones. For example, Hansen and Weisbrod (1967), Miller (1968), and Friedman (1972) constructed a formal model in which volunteers are superior to conscripts due to their greater economic efficiency (i.e., lower social costs). Other studies, though, came to the opposite conclusion. For instance, based on the percentage of the eligible population recruited into the military and the deadweight loss associated with conventional taxation, Lee and McKenzie (1992) and Warner and Asch (1995) developed an economic model in which the draft, under certain conditions, is more cost-efficient than volunteer service. Numerous empirical studies have tested various economic theories concerning the preferred type of military manpower system. Altman and Fechter (1967), Oi (1967), and Fisher (1969) found that, to maintain a military force of 2.65 million soldiers in the early 1970s, the United States would have to accept significantly higher budgetary payroll costs. These costs, according to their estimates, would vary from $4 billion to $8.3 billion per annum. Comparing the two manpower systems in terms of issues of allocative efficiency and equity in the case of Belgium, Kerstens and Meyermans (1993) conclude that the mixed manpower system produces allocative inefficiency (i.e., too many able young men are drafted) and that the draft is a second-best policy due to inequality (i.e., the draftees pay implicit taxes much higher than the observed average income tax rates). Based on an economic analysis of manpower procurement in the Dutch military, Du-indam (1999) contends that since the economic cost of conscription outweighs the benefits, eligible men are less willing to serve. These studies, taken together, would seem to favor a volunteer system, at least in terms of economic criteria.

Aside from the economically oriented studies just noted, some political, historical, sociological, and cultural studies do exist. Martin Anderson's (1982) edited volume, *The Military Draft: Selected Readings on Conscription*, provides an excellent collection. With a focus on various aspects of the policy debate over conscription, it deals with the history, philosophy, constitutionality, and economics of conscription; universal national service; the practices of other nations; and powerful, emotional arguments from both advocates and opponents. In addition, several policy-oriented studies have come out. For example, *In Pursuit of Equity* (1967, called the "Marshall Report"), prepared by the National Advisory Commission on Selective Service, along with *The Report of the President's Commission on an All-Volunteer Armed Force* (1970, labeled the "Gates Report"), paved the way for the introduction of an all-volunteer force in the United States in 1973. Bowman, Little, and Sicilia's (1986) edited book, *The All-Volunteer Force after a Decade: Retrospective and Prospect*, concluded that the U.S. all-volunteer force was in good shape at the end of fiscal year 1983, but it also predicted that due to rising costs, sophisticated new weapons systems, and a smaller recruitment pool, serious manpower procurement challenges could occur in the future. In the same vein, Gilroy, Phillips, and Blair (1990) argue that despite the less favorable recruiting environment during the fifteen years since its inception, the all-volunteer army has succeeded primarily because of the systematic development of the Army College Fund.

Sociologically oriented works on conscription have expanded the agenda considerably, in a way that is somewhat relevant to the present study. The potential end of conscription (especially in Europe, where it still predominates) has stimulated a profusion of scholarship in recent years (Haltiner 1998; Jehn and Selden 2002; Møller 2002; Leander 2004). Other studies have probed the origins and evolution of military service and the effects of conscription, most notably in connection to democracy (Barkawi 2002; Kestnbaum 2002; Dolman 2004). The result of these works, taken together, is a more nuanced and multifaceted conceptualization of conscription and an appreciation for the way it may, depending on the social scientific context, be theorized as either a cause or effect.

RESEARCH DESIGN: HYPOTHESES, MEASUREMENT, DATA, AND MODEL BUILDING

This section formulates hypotheses, explains measurement issues and data sources, and builds a statistical model for hypothesis testing.

Hypotheses

Because the determinants of military manpower systems have not yet been studied systematically, the causal mechanism is a matter of question. In answer, this study adopts hypotheses derived from some findings that are well established in the field of international relations, most notably, from the study of conflict processes. Both international and domestic factors are included in an initial model of the choice between military manpower systems.

Based on said findings, one would expect that two types of states rely on conscripted soldiers as opposed to volunteers: states that perceive a strong external threat, and states that seek to overturn the status quo. States choosing conscription are likely to do so because national leaders perceive external threats to national security (i.e., the likelihood of war) in the future. For example, because of the continuous threat represented by the Cold War bipolar security regime, the United States maintained its manpower largely by means of a conscription force up until 1973; South Korea, with its sizable and wealthy capital so near the border it shares with hostile North Korea, even still does. However, the United States chose to move to an all-volunteer force in the wake of the Vietnam War and with the waning of the Cold War more generally. After the fall of the U.S.S.R. and the consequent reduction in the risk for a general war, European states also moved toward all-volunteer forces (Anderson, Halcoussis, and Tollison 1996, 189). Based on a sample of 143 countries for the year 1984, White (1989) reports that war involvement is positively associated with conscripted soldiers. Thus, the following hypothesis is both intuitive and based on theory and evidence gleaned from the relevant literature:

> H_1: A relatively high risk of war is likely to lead to conscription within an interstate dyad.

Evidence from the literature also indicates that it is rational for states to choose conscription if they seek to overturn the status quo; that is, to facilitate the launch of a military attack. In this context, conscription can be considered a driving force behind at least some international conflict.[5] National leaders are likely to be more interventionist insofar as conscripted soldiers reduce the relative cost of pursuing the option of launching an attack against an external enemy (Beukema 1982, 489; Brigance 1945, 198–99). In other words, conscripted soldiers are simply more readily available for use than volunteers. Mussolini's Fascist Italy, Hitler's Nazi Germany, and Tojo's Japan took conscription to its extreme end of application in World War II. Thus, the hypothesis about satisfaction with the status quo is as follows:

> H_2: Satisfaction with the status quo is unlikely to lead to conscription within an interstate dyad.

Military expenditure and the number of military personnel in uniform impact the choice of a military manpower structure. High military expenditures effectively encourage conscription because a large standing army becomes more feasible. At this point, one would expect that a military prefers to maintain more soldiers for the purposes of contingency planning so that it can maintain its status as a player in the bureaucratic political game (Choi 2002). It appears that use of conscription also creates lower per unit cost to the military than does the recruitment of volunteer soldiers, who must be paid at a level that more closely approaches market wages (Altman and Fechter 1967; Oi 1967; Fisher 1969). Thus, the hypothesis about military expenditure is as follows:[6]

H_3: An increase in military expenditure is likely to lead to conscription within an interstate dyad.

A conscripted army within a military infrastructure would be more usable than would a smaller professional force in the ongoing struggle for influence within government. Hansen and Weisbrod (1967, 401) claim that "with a draft the military is readily able to secure whatever men are needed, whenever they are needed." Size, after all, would seem to matter, at least in principle. Furthermore, relative costs for conscription are lower than for volunteer soldiers, meaning that a larger army should be more likely to use conscription. Among seventy-eight countries for 1983, Thomas W. Ross (1994) finds that the size of a military produces a positive effect on the decision to use conscripted soldiers. Thus, the hypothesis about the size of the military is as follows:

H_4: An increase in the number of military personnel is likely to lead to conscription within an interstate dyad.

Given the centrality of neo-Kantianism in the study of international conflict, it is interesting to assess the impact of the three basic variables—democracy, economic interdependence, and joint memberships in international organizations—on the choice between military manpower systems. Because these variables show persistent pacifying effects in relation to conflict processes, such as militarized interstate disputes and wars (Russett and Oneal 2001), it is reasonable to expect that their effects might carry over to a security-oriented national attribute such as military manpower systems.

Conscription is not entirely consistent with the notion of individual freedom. While a volunteer army preserves the freedom of an individual to choose whether to serve in the armed forces, conscription "is absolutely opposed to the principles of individual liberty which have always been considered a part of American democracy" (Senator Robert A. Taft, quoted in Nixon 1982, 604). It is less legitimate, therefore, for a democracy to require its citizens to be conscripted; the phenomenon of conscientious objection, for example, is not unknown in such societies (Horeman and Stolwijk 1998). Thus, the hypothesis about democracy is as follows:

> H_5: A higher level of democracy is unlikely to lead to conscription within an interstate dyad.

Economic interdependence is also likely to discourage interstate conflicts (Oneal and Russett 1999a; Russett and Oneal 2001). States with extensive economic ties should be more likely to choose volunteer service over conscription in that they have a lower chance, all other things being equal, of becoming involved in interstate disputes. Such disputes, after all, should be more likely to occur in the presence of conscripted forces because of their higher military preparedness in comparison to all-volunteer forces (T. Ross 1994). Thus, the hypothesis about economic interdependence is as follows:

> H_6: A higher level of economic interdependence is unlikely to lead to conscription within an interstate dyad.

Joint memberships in international organizations are likely to increase collective security (Oneal and Russett 1999b; Russett and Oneal 2001). States within such networks—for example, states within a non-aggression treaty organization—should have a lower incentive to employ conscription in anticipation of violent conflict. Thus, the hypothesis about joint memberships is as follows:

> H_7: A higher number of joint memberships in international organizations is unlikely to lead to conscription within an interstate dyad.

Measurement and Data

The dependent variable, military manpower system, is coded as 2 if both states in a dyad-year adopt a conscription system for active duty military personnel, as 1 if either state in a dyad-year has conscripts, and as 0 otherwise.[7] No aggregate data on manpower exist over an extended spatial and temporal domain, so this study has consulted with both Horeman and Stolwijk (1998) and Prasad and Smythe (1968), two of the most comprehensive sources with respect to each state's military manpower system. For either cross-checking or complementing military manpower data with respect to reliability and validity, numerous sources have also been used as follows: International Institute for Strategic Studies (1970 through 2000); M. Anderson (1976); Keegan (1979, 1983); Stockholm International Peace Research Institute (1985); Pope (1987); and Schumacher et al. (1989).

War is coded as 1 if both states in a dyad-year become involved in an international war, and as 0 otherwise. This study has recorded Zeev Maoz's standard five categories (i.e., 1 for no militarized action; 2 for a threat to use force; 3 for a display of force; 4 for a use of force; and 5 for war) for the level of hostility in each dyad-year into two values (i.e., 0 and 1).[8]

Satisfaction with the status quo is a measure of how each state views its current situation based on the correspondence between its own portfolio of alliances and that of the hegemon, as indicated by the tau-b measure of statistical association; 1 is added to each state's tau-b score to make it positive; it is then multiplied by the score of the two states in a dyad to create a measure of joint satisfaction. Each state's tau-b score is from Oneal and Russett's (1999b) data set.

Military expenditure is calculated as follows: First, an annual growth rate for military expenditure is calculated for each state in a dyad for a given year. Second, the larger value of the percentage expenditure between the two states in each dyad-year becomes the recorded value.[9] The data come from Bennett and Stam's EUGene data set (Bennett and Stam 2000). Bennett and Stam's military expenditure data originally come from the 1993 update to the Correlates of War (COW) National Capabilities data file, which is the standard among students of international conflict. Since the original military expenditure is recorded as a nominal value (i.e., not inflation-adjusted), it is converted into a real value using Sahr's Inflation Conversion Factors for 1700 to Estimated 2010.[10] The year 2000 is the base year for the Consumer Price Index (CPI).

The variable for military personnel is calculated as follows: First, the number of soldiers as a percentage of population is determined for each state. Second, the weak link assumption is used to derive a score for the dyad-year. Like the military expenditure data, the data for this variable are obtained from Bennett and Stam's data set, EUGene, which includes military personnel and total population in the form of the national capabilities data file.

The measurements and data for democracy, economic interdependence, and joint memberships in international organizations use Oneal and Russett's (1999b) pioneering work. Democracy is based on the weak link assumption; that is, the score for the less democratic state in a dyad is taken to be the stronger determinant of conscription. Economic interdependence also assumes the weak link in that the score for the less interdependent state in a dyad is taken to be the stronger determinant of conscription. The number of joint memberships held by a state determines its international organization variable; that is, the more joint memberships a state claims in intergovernmental organizations, the less likely it is to engage in a dispute and, in turn, its dyad is regarded as less likely to adopt conscription.

Building a Multinomial Logit Model

Since the dependent variable is categorical—not ordered, but nominal—this study chooses a multinomial logistic regression model to test the hypotheses. Multinomial logit models are multiequation models; since the dependent variable has three categories, the multinomial logit model will generate two equations. Each of these equations is like a binary logistic regression comparing a group with the reference group (i.e., no conscription). This study uses Stata statistical software to carry out maximum-likelihood multinomial logistic regression.

For the multinomial logit model, all independent variables are lagged by one year and are therefore not affected by a choice of conscription. Equation 1 includes one dependent variable and seven independent variables as follows:

$$(1) \quad Y_t = \alpha + \beta_1 X_{1t-1} + \beta_2 X_{2t-1} + \beta_3 X_{3t-1} + \beta_4 X_{4t-1} + \beta_5 X_{5t-1} + \beta_6 X_{6t-1} + \beta_7 X_{7t-1} + \varepsilon$$

Here,

Y_t: military manpower with conscripted soldiers
X_{1t-1}: war
X_{2t-1}: satisfaction with the status quo
X_{3t-1}: military expenditure
X_{4t-1}: military personnel
X_{5t-1}: democracy
X_{6t-1}: economic interdependence
X_{7t-1}: joint memberships in international organizations
ε: error term

Because this study includes over 130 states during the period from 1886 to 1992, it employs a pooled cross-national, time-series analysis. As mentioned earlier, the data analysis focuses on dyad-years due to the fact that it must assess the effect of relations of pairs of states over time on military manpower. Since all of the hypotheses are directional, this study employs a one-tailed test for each variable.

EMPIRICAL RESULTS

Table 10.1 shows the empirical results for predicting the likelihood of conscription during the study period. The first column lists the variable names; the second and third columns present the results when either one or both states have conscripted soldiers, respectively.

The second column reveals what factors determine the use of conscription by either state, as compared with the choice of a volunteer military manpower

TABLE 10.1   Predicting the Likelihood of Conscription, 1886–1992

Independent Variable	Conscription versus Voluntary Service	
	Conscripted Soldiers, either A or B	Conscripted Soldiers, both A and B
War	−0.5927	0.2446
	(−0.7689)	(0.7536)
Satisfaction with the status quo	0.3207***	0.6336***
	(0.0755)	(0.0795)
Military expenditure	0.0623	0.1383***
	(0.0409)	(0.0426)
Military personnel	1.8507***	3.8362***
	(0.2042)	(0.2183)
Democracy	−0.0053	−0.0272***
	(0.0071)	(0.0075)
Economic interdependence	−8.9646	−0.4121
	(11.6006)	(9.5874)
International organizations	−0.0127***	−0.0087***
	(0.0027)	(0.0028)
Constant	0.9314***	−0.3246**
	(0.1212)	(0.1310)
Chi²	696.58	
P of Chi²	(0.001)	
Log likelihood	−107,389.52	
Pseudo R²	0.075	
Observation	120,680	

Note: *p <.05; **p <.01; ***p <.001, one-tailed tests

system. The war variable shows no statistical significance, indicating that although one of the two states in a dyad-year perceives a strong external threat, an adoption of conscription within an interstate dyad is not guaranteed. This result is consistent with Thomas W. Ross' (1994, 125) recent study that reports no significant effect for war on the presence of conscription. Satisfaction with the status quo is statistically significant at the 0.001 level, suggesting that when either state is satisfied with the distribution of benefits achieved under the leadership of the most dominant state, the dyad is likely to maintain conscripted soldiers. This result is counterintuitive, so its implications are discussed in detail in the conclusion.

The military expenditure variable is not statistically significant, indicating that an expenditure increase has no bearing on conscription. The military personnel variable is statistically significant at the 0.001 level; therefore, as the number of soldiers increases in either state in a dyad-year, one of those states becomes more likely to employ conscription. This result agrees with White's (1989, 779) empirical study on the relationship between conscription and military size.

The democracy variable is not statistically significant, so it appears that the presence or absence of this regime type does not affect the military manpower structure of either state in a dyad-year. The economic interdependence variable also turns out to be statistically insignificant, suggesting that trade volume does not necessarily reduce the likelihood of conscription. Joint memberships in international organizations are negatively associated with conscription, making it the single component of the neo-Kantian triad that works in this context. Of course, it should be pointed out that the present research design is an especially challenging one for neo-Kantianism; it includes a dependent variable that is a national attribute as opposed to being a form of direct action by states, such as participation in a militarized interstate dispute or war. For this reason, the performance of the neo-Kantian variables at this stage of the analysis should not be regarded as irredeemable. Instead, the results suggest that the neo-Kantian triad, like any other successful theoretical framework, will eventually find a limit to its applicability.

The third column shows which factors are associated with use of conscription by both states in a dyad. The war variable again shows no statistical significance. Satisfaction with the status quo again is statistically significant at the 0.001 level. It is more likely that conscripted soldiers will be maintained by both states in a dyad-year under greater satisfaction with the status quo.

The military expenditure variable is statistically significant at the 0.001 level, meaning that an increase in spending is likely to lead to conscription on the part of both states in a dyad-year. The variable for military personnel again shows statistical significance at the 0.001 level; as the number of soldiers in either military force increases, both states in a dyad-year become more likely to resort to conscripted soldiers.

The coefficient on the democracy variable is, this time, statistically significant at the 0.001 level and in the hypothesized direction. It appears that as both states become more democratic, in a given dyad-year, they are likely to employ volunteer soldiers over conscripts to protect their national security; this result agrees with Anderson, Halcoussis, and Tollison's (1996, 198) recent study. The economic interdependence variable continues to show no statistical significance. Joint memberships in international organizations again are associated negatively with conscription. It appears that with an increase in joint memberships, both states in a given dyad-year are less likely to maintain conscripted soldiers.

CONCLUSION

Employing a multinomial logit model, this pooled cross-national, time-series data analysis stands as an initial effort to identify what factors may distinguish the choice between conscription and volunteer military service for the dyad-years from 1886 to 1992. Given the fact that existing political literature on the determinants of military manpower systems is almost nil, this study should be regarded as an attempt to broaden its scope and method, especially by incorporating international political factors and by analyzing interstate dyads. This study seeks to address an understudied and neglected area of international relations: the choice of military manpower systems within the increasingly paradigmatic level of analysis represented by interstate dyads.

The empirical results show that a larger number of military personnel, along with satisfaction with the status quo, are positively associated with the likelihood of conscription, and joint memberships in international organizations are negatively associated; yet, war and economic interdependence seem to have little to do with conscription. The data analysis also reveals that both states in a dyad-year become more likely to employ conscripted soldiers as military expenditure increases, and become less likely to maintain conscripts as they become more democratic.

It is interesting that satisfaction with the status quo turns out to have a counterintuitive effect. Considering the realist perspective that "if you want peace, prepare for war," this result may be regarded as affirmative. It seems that states may be choosing to increase their security in an anarchical world by maintaining conscription when their preferences are in line with those of the leading superpower—a puzzle that will certainly need further attention, given its apparent intuitive and theoretical inconsistency with hegemonic stability theory and existing research findings. It appears that as the quality of democratic governance increases, both states in a dyad are likely to move away from use of conscripted soldiers. This implies that the world may become a more democratic place in which the right of an individual to choose to serve is greatly respected in proportion to the increased number of democratic countries.

It is also worth bearing in mind that the world continues to change in sometimes step-level or qualitative ways. Consider, for example, the shift in attitudes toward conscription and military service in general throughout the 1990s; the very future and meaning of these institutions appear to be in question (Haltiner 1998; Leander 2004). While it seems unlikely that conscription will disappear altogether, the evolution of its meaning and the implications for potential state aggression should warrant our special caution in terms of the ability to draw implications from a data analysis that goes no further than the year 1992. Additional data collection and analysis, along with a more nuanced measurement of conscription, will be essential elements of a greater practical understanding of the contemporary world.

Along those lines, the multinomial logit model, which incorporates international and domestic factors, captures only part of the whole story with respect to military manpower systems; future research should include other aspects, such as civic duty. As Choi and James (2003) indicate, the choice of military manpower structure may be based on the concept of civic duty (i.e., to serve the state) more than it is on national security concerns in response to external threats. If so, this would suggest that a combination of variables from comparative political studies, rather than from international relations research, might prove promising at the next stage of research.

CHAPTER 11

Selectorate Theory, Democracy, and Terrorism

Null Results

> We need to incentivize the publication of replications and null re-
> sults. . . . With null results on well-established expectations appearing in
> our leading disciplinary review, the current publication bias would be
> reduced.
>
> DAVID D. LAITIN, "Fisheries Management"

Drawing on Morrow et al.'s (2008) selectorate theory and empirical model, this study weighs in on the debate over whether democracies experience more or less terrorist attacks than do nondemocracies.[1] In doing so, this research also tests the general applicability of the selectorate theory, which, it has been claimed, is "surprisingly broad in its implications" (Bueno de Mesquita et al. 2003, xi). Although the deterrence of terrorism is an essential requisite of the enhancement of general public welfare that democratic governments typically provide for reasons of national security, students of the selectorate theory have to this point neglected to examine its empirical application and implications (Bueno de Mesquita et al. 2003; Kennedy 2009).[2] At the same time, students of terrorism have offered no discussion of the success of the selectorate theory in terms of predicting terrorist events, though they consider the concept and measurement of democracy to be critically related to the debate over regime type and terrorist activity (Enders and Sandler 2006; Wade and Reiter 2007; Choi 2010b). Unfortunately, the selectorate theory, which has been deemed one of the most influential theories of democracy in the contemporary era, has not yet been incorporated into the discussion. The present study fills this gap by investigating which type of democratic institution is more effective in reducing the incidence of terrorist attacks—the size of the winning coalition (W) or executive constraints.

Morrow et al.'s selectorate theory stipulates that W selects political leadership and, furthermore, that this variable predicts the provision of public goods and private benefits better than any other aspect of democratic institutions. They postulate that other features of democracy may help to facilitate various protections of public welfare, but that the effect of W should be the strongest. Separating out the effect of W from other elements of democracy is critical for their empirical analysis not only because "a large proportion of the variance in Democracy is the larger size of the winning coalition in such systems," but also because "both Democracy and W are constructed from some of the same indicators" (2008, 394). They then introduce institutional constraints on the chief executive as another key attribute of democracy because "the checks and balances [they] associate with diffusion of power in a democracy play no role in [the selectorate] theory" (395). They report that for twenty-five out of thirty-one different national policies, W explains more of the variance than does executive constraints.

Built on negative binomial regression, population-averaged negative binomial regression, zero-inflated negative binomial regression,[3] and rare event logit models of 158 countries during the period from 1970 to 1999, the present study compares the relative importance of W and executive constraints, each of which is hypothesized to reduce the likelihood of a country's experiencing terrorist attacks. However, the results of the tests are mixed at best. All else being equal, W is statistically significant in the theoretically predicted direction (i.e., it reduces terrorism), while the executive constraints variable is statistically significant but in a counterintuitive direction (i.e., they increase terrorism). Interestingly, the absolute size of the coefficient of the former turns out to be smaller than that of the latter, which is contrary to the prediction of the selectorate theory. More importantly, when region, country, and year fixed effects are taken into consideration for robustness checks, the effect of W fades away while that of executive constraints remains the same. Ultimately, this empirical analysis leads to null results: democratic countries with large winning coalitions or greater executive constraints do not prove to be more successful in their efforts to enhance national security in response to potential terrorist threats.

SELECTORATE THEORY, DEMOCRACY, AND TERRORISM

Understanding the effect of democracy on public policies remains an important issue for political scientists as well as for policy makers. In particular, interesting are the recent exchanges among Bueno de Mesquita et al. (2003), Clarke and Stone (2008), and Morrow et al. (2008), who debate whether the effect of the size of the winning coalition (W) on the production of particular policy outcomes is stronger than other features of democratic institutions. Bueno de Mesquita et al. (2003) present evidence that W outperforms a residualized democracy variable. Clarke and Stone (2008), however, find that W shows no significance in their empirical analysis when it is tested against the democracy variable (instead of Bueno de Mesquita et al.'s residualized democracy variable). Morrow et al. (2008, 394) offer an alternative selectorate model, emphasizing the importance of controlling for aspects of democracy that fall outside of the parameters of the selectorate theory. Specifically, they decide to use executive constraints against W in place of Clarke and Stone's measure of democracy. They find that for twenty-five out of thirty-one public policies, W possesses more explanatory power than do executive constraints.

This study uses Morrow et al.'s alternative selectorate model to evaluate the relative importance of W and executive constraints in predicting the incidence of terrorist attacks. In doing so, this study adopts the central prediction of the selectorate theory: because democratic countries tend to have large winning coalitions, leaders have increased incentive to shift public policies away from private benefits. For example, democratic leaders may, for electoral reasons, shift their focus from the provision of private benefits such as grants of monopoly to the provision of public goods such as national security, education, and health care. Democratic countries with large winning coalitions are expected to actively engage in attempts to reduce the incidence of terror attacks; otherwise, their leaders are likely to face public disapproval for failing to secure the nation from harm, which will put their own political survival in jeopardy. A more detailed theoretical reasoning follows.

Morrow et al.'s selectorate theory assumes that a political leader's ultimate goal is to retain power (see also Bueno de Mesquita et al. 2003; Kennedy 2009). Political leaders thus have enormous incentive to satisfy the domestic constituencies that keep them in office. Morrow et al.'s study attempts to make a cross-national generalization of the selectorate theory with a special focus on three institutional characteristics of political systems that determine the retention and selection of leaders: the selectorate, the winning coalition, and the support coalition. The selectorate is composed of individuals within the state who have a say in policy outcomes by selecting a leader (i.e., the voting public); the winning coalition is the portion of the selectorate sufficient to make the choice to keep or put a leader in office (i.e., a majority of the voting public); and the support coalition is a subset of those selectors who support the current leader (i.e., those who, in fact, voted for the victorious candidate). In order to remain consistent with Morrow et al., the present study focuses only on variations in winning coalition size in its examination of the selectorate theory and terrorism.

The selectorate theory offers a simple hypothesis: as winning coalitions become larger, leaders suffer from limited revenue resources, making the distribution of private goods increasingly difficult; accordingly, a democratic leader's political survival is dependent on the distribution of public goods. In this context, leaders in democratic societies should make every effort to deliver public goods to members of the winning coalition, which is often as large as 51 percent of the selectorate. However, leaders who preside over small winning coalitions, as is more often the case in an autocracy, have little incentive to implement policies to deliver public goods because they are able to maintain power by efficiently targeting private benefits to key supporters in their ruling coalition. That is, autocratic leaders have the capacity to survive in office despite the consequences of failed national policies (e.g., ongoing economic crises, war defeats, and deteriorating health care systems).

According to the logic of the selectorate theory, we should expect democratic countries to fight harder against terrorism because leaders subject to large winning coalitions are more likely to be ousted from power if these efforts fail. The assumption is that because the deterrence of terrorism represents an important and general public good in a democratic society, the leaders of these countries should put forth a greater effort to discourage both domestic and international terrorist activity. In particular, it is expected that these leaders will try harder to reduce the total number of terrorist attacks due to the fact that an increase in the frequency of terrorist activity is likely to reduce public support for the incumbent government.[4] Thus, democratic leaders with large winning coalitions are more likely to benefit from a decrease in the incidence of terrorism.[5] This assumption is exemplified by the U.S. government's extended efforts to prevent the recurrence of terrorist incidences after September 11, 2001.

Although Morrow et al.'s (2008) study offers no specific theoretical arguments regarding the effect of executive constraints on policy outcomes, they do make clear that the theoretical predictions of W and other aspects of democratic regimes run in the same direction. They argue that democratic countries with greater executive constraints should also work harder than nondemocratic countries to provide public goods for reasons other than the one offered by the selectorate theory. Accordingly, when W is expected to increase the quality of a public policy in Morrow et al.'s selectorate model, executive constraints are also predicted to exert a positive effect. This study remains consistent with Morrow et al.'s predicted relationship between executive constraints and public goods by hypothesizing that high levels of executive constraints within a democratic country will lessen the incidence of terrorism.

It is essential to bear in mind that although both W and executive constraints are supposed to decrease the number of terrorist attacks, the effect of the former should be stronger than that of the latter. That is, as Morrow et al. argue, executive constraints not specified in the selectorate theory are expected to explain less of the variance in the rate of terrorism than does the theory's core factor, winning coalition size.

As noted earlier, this study defines terrorism as an act in which only nonstate actors can engage. In general, terrorism is classified as either domestic or international. Domestic terrorism includes homegrown terrorist incidents such as the Oklahoma City bombing and occurs only against domestic targets in a terrorist's home country; international terrorism, then, is a situation in which a terrorist incident in country A involves perpetrators, victims, institutions, governments, or citizens of country B (Enders and Sandler 2006; Dugan 2010). In evaluating the effects of the two relevant features of democracy (i.e., *W* and executive constraints), this study refers to both domestic and international terrorist events. The rationale for this decision is based on a simple intuition: for the sake of their political survival, democratic leaders will do their best to deter all kinds of terrorism, whether domestic or international. This intuition is in line with Martha Crenshaw's (2002, 31) observation that "the distinction between 'international' terrorism and 'domestic' terrorism is artificial and has been so for some time." Dugan's (2010, 4) recent study confirms Crenshaw's observation: "the divide between domestic and international terrorism has become more artificial as cultures become more global." Falkenrath (2001, 164) also argues along the same line that a domestic-international distinction is "an artifact of a simpler, less globally interconnected era."

RESEARCH DESIGN

For empirical testing, cross-sectional, time-series data are collected for a sample of 158 countries during the period from 1970 to 1999.[6] Consistent with the theoretical discussion in the previous section, the dependent variable is the annual total number of domestic and international terrorist incidents occurring in a given country.[7] It should be noted that this study refers to terrorist events as those carried out either by individual terrorists or by terrorist groups because democratic leaders are unlikely to differentiate between the two in their general effort to decrease the frequency of terrorist events. In other words, the unit of analysis in this study is country-year, not terrorist groups.[8] The data source is the Global Terrorism Database (GTD) Explore. This web-based interactive visual exploratory tool has gathered systematic data on all types of terrorist incidents (more than 85,000 cases) since 1970 (Lee 2008).[9] Although there are other widely used data sets on terrorism (e.g., Mickolus et al.'s [2006] data on international terrorism), the GTD is the most comprehensive insofar as it includes data on domestic as well as international terrorism (see LaFree and Dugan 2007; LaFree, Dugan, and Fahey 2007; LaFree and Ackerman 2009).[10]

Two Democracy-Related Independent Variables: The Winning Coalition and Executive Constraints

Morrow et al.'s (2008) study operationalizes the key concept of the winning coalition size based on three individual components of the Polity composite index—competitiveness of executive recruitment, openness of executive recruitment, and competitiveness of political competition (for a detailed discussion on Polity, see Marshall and Jaggers 2007)—as well as on an indicator of the nature of the regime that comes from Arthur Banks (2010). W is a normalized ordinal measure ranging from 0 to 1 (i.e., 0, 0.25, 0.50, 0.75, and 1).

The executive constraints variable is introduced in Morrow et al.'s study under the theoretical condition that "any test of selectorate theory against a measure of democracy must parse out elements of democracy that lie outside that theory from those within it" (394). It is also a normalized ordinal measure with 0 for its smallest value and 1 for its greatest.[11] As Morrow et al. point out, the normalization of W and executive constraints makes it easy for the reader to compare their relative importance in explaining the variance in terrorist activity.[12]

Other institutional features of democracy are not included in this study because their theoretical arguments are not discussed in Morrow et al.'s study and because their conceptualizations overlap with that of W. The inclusion of both W and any other democratic feature in the same selectorate model demonstrates the failure to separate out the effect of the latter from that of the former. For instance, because Chenoweth (2010) finds evidence that intergroup competition motivated by the competition of the political regime is related to an increase in terrorist incidents, one could argue that the political competition component of the Polity dataset (i.e., Chenoweth's proxy measure of intergroup competition) should be included in this study. However, since Morrow et al.'s measure of W already treats the competitiveness of political competition as one of its key components, testing W and political competition in the same statistical model would obscure the estimated results due to the presence of severe multicollinearity.

Although Li (2005) reports that freedom of the press and political participation have some bearing on the incidence of international terrorism, these factors are not part of this study's empirical testing due to not only a lack of data but also a lack of theoretical justification. While this study covers the period from 1970 to 1999, Van Belle's (2000a) press freedom data point ends in 1995.[13] Li hypothesizes that the higher the voting rate in a democracy, the less likely it is to be the site of an international terrorist attack. However, because political nonparticipation (i.e., not voting) is ubiquitous in many full-fledged democracies—including or even especially the United States—but less widespread in emerging democracies, high levels of political participation may not necessarily be associated with higher levels of democracy and thus lower levels of terrorist incidents (see Powell 1982; DeLuca 1995).

Controlling for Commonly Used Terrorism-Related Variables

To control for alternative explanations, this study includes nine control variables that frequently appear in existing studies of terrorism: regime durability, economic development, government capability, population, surface area, failed state, international conflict, post–Cold War, and past incidents.

Regime Durability: Previous studies show that terrorists find fewer opportunities to engage in attacks against countries with a long history of regime stability in comparison to countries that experience frequent regime changes (e.g., Eyerman 1998; Eubank and Weinberg 2001); thus, longer regime durability is expected to decrease the likelihood of terrorism. Based on Marshall and Jaggers' (2007) Polity data set, regime durability is measured by the number of years a country has gone without experiencing a regime change; a regime change is measured as a three-point shift in a country's Polity score for a given year.

Economic Development: Due to the pervasiveness of feelings of relative economic deprivation among the public in less developed countries, there tend to be more individuals willing to resort to terrorist tactics as an expression of their grievances (Kahn and Weiner 2002; Choi and Luo 2013). Accordingly, the economic development variable is included as a control for reducing terrorism. Data for this variable are derived from Gleditsch (2002), and the variable is measured by the logged GDP per capita, adjusted for purchasing power parity.

Government Capability: Terrorists are less likely to terrorize countries that have sufficient means to enact antiterrorist measures; they instead target those countries with lesser material means (Li 2005). In this context, high levels of government antiterror capabilities are expected to exert a dampening effect on terrorism. The government capability variable is measured through a logged composite indicator of a state's share of the world's total population, industry, and military forces. The data are drawn from the Correlates of War's National Material Capabilities data set (Singer 1987).

Population: Because of the inherent difficulty of policing a large population, such countries tend to be more vulnerable to potential terrorist plots and attacks (Eyerman 1998). Thus, the population variable, measured by the logged total population, is projected to increase the likelihood of terrorism. Data for this variable are taken from the U.S. Census Bureau (2008).

Surface Area: Previous studies find that countries with a vast territory are more likely to provide terrorist hideouts; potential terrorists may be discontented minority ethnic groups harboring political and economic grievances against the government (Abadie 2004). This variable is taken from the World Bank's (2010) *World Development Indicators* and is measured as the logged square kilometers of a country's territory.

Failed State: Failed states—countries where the central government is too weak to exercise legal authority over much of its territory—are bound to attract terrorists. Iraq, Syria, and Sudan, for example, have come to be feared as reservoirs and exporters of terrorism (Rotberg 2002). Some recent studies provide empirical evidence for the link between failed states and terrorism (e.g., LaFree, Dugan, and Fahey 2007; Piazza 2008). The failed state variable ranges from 0 to 17 by combining the severity of ethnic wars (0–4), revolutionary wars (0–4), adverse regime changes (1–4), and genocides and politicides (0–5). Data come from the Political Instability Task Force (2007).

International Conflict: Involvement in international conflict makes a country unstable and opens it to terrorist plots aiming to sabotage its political and economic systems and to create tension between the domestic population and an enemy abroad (J. Ross 1993). Based on data from Gleditsch et al. (2002), the international conflict variable is coded as 1 for involvement in militarized interstate disputes or war and as 0 otherwise.

Post–Cold War: Enders and Sandler's (2006) study discovers the systemic decrease in terrorist activity that took place after the end of the Cold War. Accordingly, this study includes the post–Cold War variable as a control; it is coded as 1 since 1991 and as 0 otherwise.

Past Incidents: Past terrorist incidents affect the potentiality for current terrorist events. However, as noted in Li's (2005) study, simply adding a one-year lagged dependent variable on the right side of the equation is equivalent to ignoring a much longer history of past terrorism.[14] To avoid this problem, the past incident measure records the annual average number of past terrorist incidents.

Finally, because the dependent variable (i.e., the total number of terrorist incidents) is a nonnegative count measure, a negative binomial maximum-likelihood regression method is employed with robust standard errors clustered by country. All independent variables are lagged one year to ensure that they cause changes in the dependent variable rather than vice versa. To confirm the robustness of the main findings reported below, three other advanced estimation techniques are implemented: population-averaged negative binomial regression, zero-inflated negative binomial regression, and rare event logit.

EMPIRICAL RESULTS

Table 11.1 reports the results of four different statistical estimations in order to compare the dampening effects of the size of the winning coalition and executive constraints while controlling for the nine terrorism-related factors. A one-

TABLE 11.1   Size of the Winning Coalition, Executive Constraints, and
Terrorism, 1970–2000

Variable	Model 1 Negative Binomial	Model 2 Population-Avged	Model 3 Zero-Inflated	Model 4 Rare Event Logit
W	−0.964**	−1.367*	−0.997**	−0.751***
	(0.578)	(0.897)	(0.574)	(0.248)
Executive constraints	1.103**	1.387**	1.097**	1.195***
	(0.498)	(0.610)	(0.493)	(0.202)
Regime durability	−0.011***	−0.008***	−0.011***	−0.006***
	(0.002)	(0.003)	(0.002)	(0.002)
Economic development	0.626***	0.335***	0.595***	0.602***
	(0.189)	(0.139)	(0.189)	(0.070)
Government capability	−0.264	−0.177	−0.245	−0.239***
	(0.210)	(0.222)	(0.207)	(0.072)
Population	0.885***	0.893***	0.875***	0.617***
	(0.216)	(0.265)	(0.212)	(0.094)
Surface area	−0.132**	−0.141*	−0.137**	−0.023
	(0.072)	(0.088)	(0.072)	(0.027)
Failed state	0.381***	0.135**	0.378***	0.343***
	(0.064)	(0.076)	(0.065)	(0.039)
International conflict	−0.217	0.161**	−0.202	−0.021
	(0.194)	(0.094)	(0.215)	(0.202)
Post–Cold War	0.184	0.343*	0.075	0.773***
	(0.168)	(0.212)	(0.216)	(0.086)
Past incidents	0.033***	0.022***	0.031***	0.102**
	(0.007)	(0.004)	(0.007)	(0.050)
Constant	−18.304***	−15.172***	−17.550***	−16.762***
	(5.964)	(6.172)	(5.907)	(2.314)
Wald chi-squared	453.08	477.24	416.60	n/a
Prob > chi-squared	0.0000	0.0000	0.0000	n/a
Observations	3,927	2,842	2,016	3,927

Note: Robust standard errors, adjusted over countries, in parentheses.

*p < .10, **p < .05, ***p < .01, one-tailed tests

tailed significance test at the 0.10, 0.05, and 0.01 levels is employed because the theoretical expectations are directional. As shown in Model 1, the hypothesis about W is supported; it is statistically significant at the 0.05 level. As W increases, democratic leaders are more likely to seek to secure their populace against terrorist attacks for the sake of their own political survival. This results in a reduction of the total number of domestic and international terrorist incidents. In this context, democracies with large winning coalitions appear to be successful in their efforts to deter terrorism.

The hypothesis regarding executive constraints is also supported, but its direction is counterintuitive; that is, it appears democratic countries with greater executive constraints experience higher levels of terrorist activity. Although this result is inconsistent with Morrow et al.'s theoretical expectations, it is in line with those existing studies of terrorism that report a positive relationship between executive constraints and international terrorism (see Li 2005; Chenoweth 2010). It is plausible that because the liberal dilemma is balancing the need to provide security with a protection of the liberal principles upon which democracy rests, democratic leaders are less likely than autocratic leaders to implement prompt and harsh antiterror measures; this, then, may result in a failure to adequately prevent terrorist attacks. One aspect of the argument for increased executive power in the United States is that it allows the president to more effectively enforce antiterror measures. It was interesting to see, in 2008, the reluctance of newly elected President Obama to give up some of the same executive powers that Democrats had criticized during the Bush years. In this context, it is reasonable to argue that democratic countries with high levels of executive constraints make timely counterterrorism efforts less likely to begin.

When we set aside the counterintuitive results regarding executive constraints in order to compare the relative importance between W and executive constraints in absolute terms of their coefficients, the former (0.964) is weaker than the latter (1.103). This finding is inconsistent with the prediction of Morrow et al.'s theoretical arguments.

Among the nine control variables, four display statistical significance in the hypothesized directions: regime durability, population, failed state, and past terrorist incidents. The hypothesis about economic development is supported, but in a counterintuitive direction; it appears that industrialized economies are more exposed to domestic and international terrorism than those that are underdeveloped. It has been argued that countries with greater economic resources may inadvertently facilitate the cultivation of skills that could be used for terrorist activity due to the prevalence of their educational institutions; that is, it has been argued that more educated individuals are better able to plot and execute terrorist activities (see Krueger and Maleckova 2002). The effect of the surface area variable is also counterintuitive. It could be the case that the more expansive the territory, the more people are able to live in a less stressful and more peaceful environment due to the fact that they avoid a struggle for scarce political resources. Government capability, international conflict, and post–Cold War do not achieve statistical significance. It is likely that the effects of these three variables are washed out by the other variables, including W, executive constraints, and past terrorist incidents.

Substantive Effects of Statistically Significant Variables

Because statistical significance does not necessarily ensure a meaningful finding in a practical sense, the substantive effects of variables must also be reported for empirical verification. To calculate a baseline probability of a terrorist incident against which to make comparisons, this study sets the continuous variables at their means and the dichotomized variables at 0. It then adjusts the variables of greatest interest one at a time to see the change in the predicted probability of terrorism. Table 11.2 shows the substantive effects of the W and executive constraints variables, as well as of the six other variables that show statistical significance in Model 1 in Table 11.1. It is evident that while W reduces the likelihood of terrorism, executive constraints notably increase the likelihood of terrorism. As shown in the shaded rows, the risk that any country will experience any type of terrorism decreases by 26 percent if the size of the winning coalition increases by one standard deviation; the likelihood of terrorism decreases by 45 percent if the size of the winning coalition increases by two standard deviations. In contrast, the risk that any country will experience any type of terrorism increases by 55 percent if the level of executive constraints increases by one standard deviation; the likelihood of terrorism increases by 141 percent if the level of executive constraints increases by two standard deviations.

Employing Three Alternative Statistical Estimation Methods

One may assert that if the estimates are not robust, alternative statistical estimation techniques will cause the significance of W and executive constraints to disappear. Models 2 through 4 in Table 11.1 evaluate the robustness of the results of the negative binomial regression in Model 1 by performing three other advanced statistical estimations: population-averaged negative binomial regression, zero-inflated negative binomial regression, and rare event logit. Model 2 shows the results of the population-averaged negative binomial regression. By allowing for an AR(1) correlation structure, the population-averaged negative binomial regression may produce more robust estimates than the standard negative bino-

TABLE 11.2   Substantive Effects of Statistically Significant Variables

Variable	Negative Binomial Regression
W	
1 standard deviation	−26%
2 standard deviations	−45%
Executive constraints	
1 standard deviation	55%
2 standard deviations	141%
Regime durability	
1 standard deviation	−27%
2 standard deviations	−47%
Economic development	
1 standard deviation	104%
2 standard deviations	313%
Population	
1 standard deviation	298%
2 standard deviations	1,482%
Surface area	
1 standard deviation	−22%
2 standard deviations	−39%
Failed state	
1 standard deviation	75%
2 standard deviations	206%
Past incidents	
1 standard deviation	151%
2 standard deviations	530%

Note: The baseline values are as follows: mean for continuous variables and 0 for dummy variables.

mial regression. Overall, the new estimation method confirms the dampening effect of *W* on terrorism as well as the detrimental effect of executive constraints.

The empirical tests employed so far—negative binomial and population-averaged negative binomial regression models—assume that all countries have an equal chance of experiencing a terrorist attack. However, in reality there are countries that are much less likely to experience terrorist activity because they offer no political or security interest for terrorists. The estimated coefficients reported may be biased, then, because they were calculated without accounting for this difference in characteristics between terrorism-prone and terrorism-free countries. There is, of course, an excess of non-events in the distribution of the dependent variable because few countries are actually victims of terrorism events (Zorn 1998). Because the prevalence of zero counts in the data can pose a statistical challenge if not estimated separately, a standard negative binomial regression estimation loses some of its effectiveness. A zero-inflated negative binomial regression model is designed to address this issue by assuming that there are two latent groups in the data. It assumes that a country in the Always-0 group (i.e., a terrorism-free country) has an outcome of 0 with a probability of 1, whereas a country in the Not Always-0 group (i.e., a terrorism-prone country) might have a zero count, but that there is a nonzero probability that it has a positive count (see Long and Freese 2006). For an illustration of this innovative method, see Ivanova and Sandler's (2007) recent study on chemical, biological, radiological, and nuclear terrorism.

Model 3 shows the results when the observations appearing in the Not Always-0 group are used for estimation. On the whole, the dampening effect of *W* is confirmed with the zero-inflated count modeling: as the size of the winning coalition increases, there will be a lower incidence of terror attacks because democratic leaders, for the sake of their own political survival, will work harder at deterrence. Once again, the detrimental effect of executive constraints is confirmed.

Another method capable of dealing with the excessive zeros problem is the rare event logit that was developed by Tomz, King, and Zeng (1999), expanded upon by King and Zeng (2001), and more recently used in Wade and Reiter's (2007) study on suicide terrorism. For this technique, the event count dependent variables are redefined as a dichotomous measure, coded as 1 if any attacks are recorded and as 0 otherwise. Model 4 shows the results of the rare event logit. As expected, the significance of *W* is confirmed and that of executive constraints remains significant but in the counterintuitive direction.

Robustness Tests: Region, Country, and Year Fixed Effects

Because this study has yet to account for fixed effects that control for omitted variables that differ between countries while remaining constant over time, it may have reported biased and inconsistent estimates. In their "Dirty Pool" article, Green, Kim, and Yoon (2001, 442) argue that "analyses of pooled cross-section data that make no allowance for fixed unobserved differences between [regions, countries, and years] often produce biased results." Because terrorism is not evenly spread throughout the world, this longitudinal study must pay heed to the methodological insights of Green, Kim, and Yoon. We know that some regions, such as the Middle East, are more prone to terrorist attacks than others.[15] To control for the regional differences, six regional dummies have been created: Americas, Europe, Asia, Oceania, and Africa, with the Middle East being the comparison region. In addition, this study accounts for country and year fixed effects, given that some countries are more vulnerable to terrorism due to their unique political environment, and that some years appear to show more frequent terrorist events than others.

TABLE 11.3   Size of the Winning Coalition, Executive Constraints, and
Terrorism, 1970–2000: Fixed Effects

Variable	Model 1 Region Dummies	Model 2 Region and Country	Model 3 Region and Year	Model 4 Region, Country, and Year
W	−0.314 (0.485)	−0.118 (0.177)	−0.414 (0.435)	−0.147 (0.181)
Executive constraints	1.019*** (0.412)	0.941*** (0.133)	1.001*** (0.382)	1.013*** (0.135)
Regime durability	−0.009*** (0.003)	−0.001 (0.001)	−0.008*** (0.002)	−0.003*** (0.001)
Economic development	0.481*** (0.152)	0.519*** (0.062)	0.483*** (0.146)	0.417*** (0.065)
Government capability	−0.379** (0.209)	−0.350*** (0.073)	−0.366** (0.199)	−0.185*** (0.079)
Population	1.127*** (0.217)	0.439*** (0.083)	1.086*** (0.208)	0.288*** (0.090)
Surface area	−0.201*** (0.072)	0.033 (0.032)	−0.150** (0.068)	−0.003 (0.033)
Failed state	0.426*** (0.064)	0.206*** (0.014)	0.402*** (0.061)	0.191*** (0.014)
International conflict	−0.251 (0.204)	0.054 (0.100)	−0.246 (0.198)	−0.048 (0.097)
Post–Cold War	0.335** (0.148)	0.340*** (0.053)	1.836*** (0.286)	1.845*** (0.184)
Past incidents	0.025*** (0.006)	−0.000 (0.001)	0.025*** (0.007)	−0.003*** (0.001)
Americas	0.190 (0.377)	−0.170* (0.119)	0.116 (0.340)	−0.021 (0.128)
Europe	−0.893*** (0.347)	−0.084 (0.123)	−0.674** (0.335)	−0.210* (0.131)
Asia	−1.246*** (0.399)	−0.523*** (0.143)	−1.176*** (0.373)	−0.482*** (0.155)
Oceania	−1.122** (0.507)	−0.866*** (0.295)	−1.155*** (0.474)	−0.812*** (0.313)
Africa	−1.034*** (0.394)	−0.353*** (0.140)	−1.048*** (0.363)	−0.449*** (0.149)
Constant	−20.718*** (5.502)	−15.340*** (2.043)	−21.798*** (5.195)	−11.051*** (2.212)
Wald chi-squared	603.62	814.86	1,360.00	1,433.04
Prob > chi-squared	0.0000	0.0000	0.0000	0.0000
Observations	3,927	3,865	3,927	3,865

Note: Robust standard errors, adjusted over countries, in parentheses.

*$p < .10$, **$p < .05$, ***$p < .01$, one-tailed tests

The results in Table 11.3, which are obtained with negative binomial regression, show the effects of W and executive constraints after accounting for region, country, and year fixed effects. Model 1 considers regional differences only. Compared to the Middle East region, Europe, Asia, Oceania, and Africa experience less terrorism. Model 2 considers region and country fixed effects together, while Model 3 reports region and year fixed effects, and Model 4 accounts for all three fixed effects together in a single selectorate equation. This analysis reveals that when controlling for each of those four combinations of fixed effects, the W hypothesis is no longer supported across models; the executive constraints hypothesis is supported, but again in the counterintuitive direction. Simply put, the use of fixed effects causes the robustness of W to disappear, indicating that leaders with large winning coalitions fail to work harder to improve national security in response to growing terrorist threats.

CONCLUSION

This study has relied on one of the most authoritative contemporary theories of democracy—the selectorate theory—in an attempt to explore the effects of different democratic institutions on the rate of terrorist activity. In doing so, it has made three contributions. First, while existing studies that rely on the selectorate theory employ Bueno de Mesquita et al.'s (2003) original selectorate model (with the residualized democracy variable), this study implements Morrow et al.'s (2008) alternative selectorate model (with the executive constraints variable). Second, this study extends the application of the alternative selectorate model to studies of terrorism. Third, this study investigates the controversial issue of the democracy-terrorism connection by comparing the effects of W and executive constraints on domestic and international terrorism. Unfortunately, the empirical analysis leads to null results. The basic statistical results indicate that democracies with large winning coalitions may deter terrorism whereas democracies with more executive constraints fail to do so. However, when the robustness of these mixed findings is further scrutinized according to fixed effects of region, country, and year, the dampening effect of W dissipates, and the detrimental effect of executive constraints remains with a wrong sign. These results indicate that neither democratic countries with large winning coalitions nor those with greater executive constraints are successful in their efforts to fight terrorism.

Because the deterrence of terrorism is a primary and general effort of national security, and because the political survival of domestic leadership depends on this effort, the lack of empirical evidence in this study is disappointing to students of the selectorate theory.[16] However, the inconclusive results of this study may be attributed to the "crude and primitive" measure of W rather than to the formal logic of the selectorate theory itself. Fortunately, since Morrow et al. "are working on more sensitive, contextual, and . . . accurate measures of the sizes of the winning coalition" (2008, 399), future research should be able to offer a better understanding of the causes of the provision of public goods, including national security in general and the fight against terrorism in particular.

CHAPTER 12

The Political Economy of Foreign Direct Investment

Democracy, Economic Crisis, and
Domestic Audience Benefits

> When jobs are scarce, the instinct for self-preservation is strong, and the temptation to blame foreign competitors is all but irresistible.
> ALAN S. BLINDER, *Hard Heads, Soft Hearts: Tough-Minded Economics for a Just Society*

The effort to determine why it is that multinational corporations are attracted to democratic countries has long been a subject of inquiry among students of international political economy (e.g., Oneal 1994; Feng 2001; Jensen 2003; Li and Resnick 2003; Ahlquist 2006; Jakobsen and de Soysa 2006; Blanton and Blanton 2006, 2007; Choi and Samy 2008; Choi 2009). The general consensus that has emerged in the existing literature is that because democratic institutions provide financial policy consistency, they reduce the political risks of expropriation, thereby making democracies more attractive for multinational corporate investment. More specifically, the literature considers domestic audience *costs* as a means of understanding this policy credibility: the presence of audience costs creates a political structure in which democratic leaders are held accountable for their inconsistent foreign direct investment (FDI) policies, including reneging on a promise or threat (e.g., Jensen 2003, 595). Therefore, regardless of domestic political and economic conditions, democratic leaders tend to avoid making arbitrary policy changes or reversals, which offers a more favorable investment environment for multinationals. However, the literature has yet to consider the possibility of domestic audience *benefits*. It is possible that during times of economic crisis, leaders of democratic countries will encounter incentives to change FDI policies and scapegoat foreign firms in the effort to boost their own political popularity among domestic constituents; it is likely, though, that this would result in a decreased inflow of FDI (see Lewis-Beck 1988; Lewis-Beck and Stegmaier 2000; Weede 2003, 2005; Caplan 2007). Using a cross-sectional, time-series data analysis for seventy countries during the period from 1980 to 1995, this study finds that, ceteris paribus, democratic developing countries in economic crisis are associated with decreased FDI inflows.

This study is structured as follows: after outlining the ongoing debates over the impact of democracy on foreign investment, it develops a conceptual framework explaining how domestic audience benefits are linked to reversals of fortune for foreign investors. The next section, research design, describes the multiplicative regression model and variable operationalization, which is followed with a discussion of the empirical results. The concluding section offers a brief summary and makes suggestions for future research.

LITERATURE REVIEW

Existing studies of the democracy-FDI link present conflicting expectations in which democratic institutions are found as often to encourage as to discourage inflows of FDI. Li and Resnick (2003) provide the logic for both sides of this debate. On the one hand, democratic institutions may deter foreign investment because they are designed to protect domestic markets from multinationals' oligopolistic or monopolistic behaviors; on the other hand, democracies may provide a better investment climate for multinational corporations by improving the quality of property rights protection. Li and Resnick's statistical findings provide empirical evidence for the negative effect of democratic institutions (measured in the Polity data) and for the positive effect of property rights protection on FDI. Likewise, Jensen's (2003) study advances the FDI literature by highlighting the beneficial effect of democracy on FDI inflows. He reasons that democratic political systems are more credible and less risky due to the institutional credibility that results from the presence of multiple veto players and domestic audience costs, both of which help to attract large amounts of foreign investment. Jensen produces a pooled data analysis demonstrating that democracies attract more FDI than do autocracies (see also Feng 2001). Interestingly, Jensen (2003, 595), in trying to explain the credibility of democratic political systems, asserts that the audience cost argument is "more strongly supported than the veto player argument." Blanton and Blanton's (2007) argument is consistent with Jensen's findings insofar as their claim is that respect for human rights (a traditionally democratic trait) seems to enhance political stability and to decrease the likelihood of public outcry over human rights abuses. Insofar as we can conflate respect for human rights with democratic politics, Blanton and Blanton's study suggests that democracies attract more FDI than do autocracies.

The fact that findings are mixed with regard to the effects of democracy on FDI has urged several researchers to conduct further empirical investigations. Yang's (2007) econometric models, for instance, show no evidence of a systematic relationship between democratic governance and foreign investment; this indicates that simply being a democracy is not enough to attract higher levels of inflows of FDI (see also Oneal 1994; Harms and Ursprung 2002). Jakobsen and de Soysa (2006), on the other hand, reanalyze the negative link between democratic institutions and FDI that was originally reported in Li and Resnick's (2003) study. Jakobsen and de Soysa produce empirical evidence showing that once the sample size studied by Li and Resnick is expanded to include all available developing countries, democratic institutions (measured in the Polity data) are, in fact, positively correlated with inflows of FDI. Upon a comparison of the empirical results of Li and Resnick (2003) with those of Jensen (2003), Choi and Samy (2008) report that while the former is sensitive to the scale effect of heterogeneous countries, the latter is not. Thus, Choi and Samy corroborate the argument that democratic institutions are positively associated with FDI inflows. Using outlier diagnostics and robust regression, Choi (2009) finds a significant and positive relationship between democracy and FDI. Furthermore, economists Busse and Hefeker (2007), who also conducted a rigorous empirical analysis, concluded that the high rate of accountability in democratic governments is one of the most significant determinants in attracting foreign investment.

In sum, having explored the effect of different aspects of democracy and having implemented rigorous hypothesis testing methods, many FDI studies find evidence that democracies attract more FDI than do autocracies. In particular, by applying the core arguments of domestic audience costs (which is borrowed from studies of international conflict) to the foreign investment policies of democratic leaders, several scholars assert that in anticipation of the potential electoral costs that come with inconsistent policy statements, democratic leaders tend to provide high levels of policy credibility to foreign investors (e.g., Jensen 2003, 2006; Blanton and Blanton 2007; Choi and Samy 2008). Students of audience costs underscore that irrespective of domestic political and economic conditions, the policy-making behavior of democratic leaders is consistently in favor of foreign investors. However, these arguments overlook a potentially negative effect of democratic accountability on foreign investment and ignore the question of why democratic leaders sometimes act against the interests of foreign investors. Especially during times of economic crisis, democratic leaders whose domestic economic performance is perceived as unsatisfactory by the public will have incentive, for the sake of their own political survival, to blame multinational corporations for the poor economic circumstances; this action could discourage future inflows of FDI.

EXPLAINING DEMOCRATIC LEADERS' FDI POLICY BEHAVIOR

This section begins by introducing a brief definition of domestic audience costs and identifying a potential flaw in the theoretical argumentation of audience costs in the existing FDI literature. With this understanding in hand, it then presents a causal explanation of how domestic audience benefits can affect inflows of FDI.

The idea of domestic audience costs has been popularized by students of international relations over the past decade as a means of understanding international conflict situations wherein a leader of one country makes threats against another country before ultimately backing down. In this context, domestic audience costs refer to the electoral cost that a democratic leader must pay after backing down from the initial security threats that were made against another country; assuming that potential voters will view this as a major policy failure, the audience cost argument predicts that leaders will be punished for it at the polls (Reiter and Stam 2004; Slantchev 2005; Tomz 2007). Leeds's (1999) study narrows the focus of this hypothesis, arguing that domestic audiences in democracies are more capable of punishing elected leaders for reneging on international agreements or alliances than are audiences in autocracies.

As noted above, FDI researchers have appropriated the concept of domestic audience costs to explain the policy credibility of democratic systems, arguing that because citizens are capable of inflicting political costs on their leaders, democracies produce more consistent FDI policies. Just as international relations scholars have made assumptions regarding how politicians will be judged by voters, FDI scholars assume that voters are capable of understanding the investment deals made by their governments along with the relevant cost-benefit analyses of multinationals' economic activities (e.g., Jensen 2003, 595). That is, these arguments rest on the premise that citizens are competent evaluators of the financial scene and economic policies. This assumption provides some basis for the argument that democratic leaders make reliable deals with foreign investors in order to avoid the risk of electoral punishment. However, this line of reasoning also entails a number of implicit premises that are less obvious and thus warrant discussion. Specifically, the notion that democratic leaders take potential audience costs into account when considering FDI policies is based on two assumptions: that the public has a working knowledge of policy issues enabling them to inflict these costs, and that leaders are themselves able to competently perceive and reliably predict these costs. Prior studies have used the concept of audience costs without explaining in precise terms how it is that they are generated by the public and perceived by political leaders. Upon closer scrutiny, the question shifts from "what is the effect of domestic audience costs?" to "what are the factors that give rise to these costs?" The present study responds to the second question by positing that the open media within most democracies serve as an intermediary, creating and transmitting domestic audience costs between the public and its leaders at the domestic level.[1] Therefore, when free and open media are present, we would expect to see the effect of audience costs; when such conditions are not present, audience costs should not exert a substantial effect on foreign investment.

The role of the media in determining the effect of audience costs can be understood in both negative and positive terms. If mass media are controlled by the state (as is the case in most autocratic regimes), ordinary citizens may easily be misled or manipulated in such a way that there will appear to be no vocal opposition to a leader's misconduct. Due to the absence of independent mass media that would potentially question leaders about inappropriate policy changes, it is relatively easy for autocratic leaders to maintain power even after reneging on multinational contracts. In this sense, the lack of open media in an autocracy actively negates the possibility that we will see an effect from domestic audience costs on the rate of foreign investment. By contrast, the high degree of media openness typical in democracies provides the public with an opportunity to gather objective information and to scrutinize more closely its government's investment policies. Therefore, it is more difficult for democratic leaders to engage in arbitrary policy making without it being publicized, a fact that reinforces the effectiveness of domestic audience costs and contributes to the credibility and consistency of their foreign investment policies.[2] The presence of an open domestic media is positive in the context that it provides democratic citizens with the opportunity to inflict political costs on their leaders for their perceived wrongdoings. Li and Resnick's (2003, 182) study makes a similar observation, noting that "open media bring about relatively better monitoring of elected politicians." Because multinational corporations are aware that the domestic audience costs created by high levels of media openness constrain democratic leaders from violating agreed FDI policies (e.g., expropriation), they are likely to seek better business opportunities by moving into democratic countries (see Thomas and Worrall 1994; Van Belle 2000a, 2000b; Slantchev 2005; Choi and James 2007).

While we can understand the role of the media in both positive and negative terms, we should note that so far we have only discussed the potential effect of audience costs, thereby casting the public in a purely watchdog role. However, we can see the public in another light by recognizing the possibility that leaders may also reap domestic audience *benefits*. For instance, it is plausible that democratic leaders may breach previous policy commitments if they expect to see political gains as a result. In this context, domestic audience benefits refer to the potential boost in electoral popularity that a democratic leader might receive by making and subsequently breaking foreign investment deals. The reasoning is similar to that of the domestic audience costs argument but, followed to its logical conclusion, assumes that elected political officials will always act in ways to minimize costs or maximize benefits. That is, even if making investment deals with multinational corporations is electorally beneficial in the long term, democratic leaders may break their promises at a later date if to do so would once again benefit them at the polls. From this perspective, there is no a priori reason to assume that honoring prior agreements is categorically the most politically beneficial strategy; indeed, it is not hard to imagine a scenario in which the rational calculus would motivate a democratic leader to change course on a previous FDI policy stance.[3]

In his book *The Myth of the Rational Voter*, Caplan (2007) analyzes public opinion data on economic attitudes and makes the empirical claim that voters in democracies tend to blame foreign corporations for their economic difficulties. Consequently, public outcry likely offers the political opportunity for elected leaders to take advantage of domestic audience benefits by breaking their potentially long-term relationship with one or several multinational corporations;[4] "after all, *no* politician benefits from the affection of [foreign investors] who cannot vote" (Weede 2003, 312; emphasis in the original). Deteriorating conditions in the domestic economy provide a particularly good pretext for pursuing this strategy.[5] If democratic leaders suffer from low popular support due to a sluggish national economy, they may attempt to increase their own job approval ratings by scapegoating multinational corporations (see Davies 1981; James and Hristoulas 1994; James and Rioux 1998; Pickering and Kisangani 2005). Furthermore, because ordinary citizens already have a propensity to blame foreign companies—which they perceive as ruthless, profit-seeking entities getting rich at the expense of the "little man's" economic well-being—especially during an economic crisis, this strategy is likely to be a successful one. Under such conditions, disgruntled citizens no longer value the benefits of foreign ownership and may demand an immediate end to the perceived exploitation of foreign capital in order to, at least symbolically, satisfy their frustrations and financial misery. Thus, when domestic constituents demand action, elected political officials would be wise to respond at the expense of multinational corporations. In fact, Henisz (2002) argues that projects that were nationalized under International Monetary Fund (IMF) programs are the same investments that were nationalized during periods of economic downturn. Specifically, democratically elected Venezuelan president Carlos Andres Perez's 1975 nationalization of the oil industry and the action taken by the then-democratic government of Nigeria against the oil industry in 1979 provide two specific cases in point (Davies 1981).[6]

Because economic crises often affect citizens on very personal levels—such as through the loss of a job or a wage cut—their demands for policy solutions tend to be urgent. Elected political leaders must face these voters in upcoming elections, so those demands are likely to be answered. Because political leaders are aware that their constituents have stronger psychological reactions to personal economic losses than they do to gains, and that they "act largely on their perceptions of the national economy" (Lewis-Beck and Stegmaier 2000, 212; see also Lewis-Beck 1988), these politicians have incentives to divert those constituency pressures onto multinational corporations (e.g., through the confiscation of current output or capital). Thus, if personal economic grievances have reached the point where public resentment threatens an elected official's goals for reelection, politicians are likely to scapegoat foreign firms by characterizing them as the principal culprits of the crisis and force them to divest through forced sale, ownership transfer, direct expropriation, or extra-legal acts (see Kahneman and Tversky 1979; Kobrin 1980; Remmer 1991; Thomas and Worrall 1994; Blinder 1996; Bueno de Mesquita et al. 2003; Weede 2003, 2005). Simply put, when their political survival is at stake due to a slumping economy, democratic leaders are unlikely to admit fault or blame domestic forces; rather, they are inclined to blame and scapegoat nonvoting foreign investors. Domestic audience costs, which under normal economic conditions act to constrain the incentives democratic leaders have to break multinational deals, are likely to transform into domestic audience benefits in cases where foreign investors are blamed for a nation's economic crisis.

In contrast, autocratic leaders are less likely to blame and scapegoat foreign firms in times of economic crisis because the maintenance of their position does not depend on their appeal to a large electoral segment of society. Because autocratic leaders can use the powers of the executive (security police, censorship, physical implementation of the election mechanism, etc.) to stay in office even in instances where popular opinion favors their removal, they do not need foreign firms to take the fall for them. Even so, it is likely that an autocratic regime is in control of the news media and so will deflect the audience costs that would otherwise potentially affect their FDI policy behavior. Moreover, since most autocracies are underdeveloped economies where financial resources are scarce, they are less likely to expel the foreign firms that play a crucial role in their economic development plan by bringing in new technologies, capital, products, management skills, and so on.

To summarize, the selectorate in a democracy is larger than that in an autocracy, so democratic leaders have to appeal to a larger segment of society than do autocratic leaders (Bueno de Mesquita et al. 2003). Thus, those democratic leaders who need popular votes for reelections are more likely to breach their FDI deals in response to public outcry over ongoing economic hardship. By breaking these investment contracts at opportune times, democratic leaders are likely to boost their own electoral popularity (i.e., gain domestic audience benefits) while discouraging foreign investment.

H$_1$: In times of economic crisis, democratic leaders are likely to seek domestic audience benefits, thereby resulting in a decrease of FDI inflows.

RESEARCH DESIGN

To test the effect of the domestic audience benefits, a multiplicative regression model is built with the following econometric equation:

$$FDI\ inflows_{it} = \alpha + \beta_1\ (audience\ costs_{it-1}) + \beta_2\ (economic\ crisis_{it-1})$$
$$+ \beta_3\ (audience\ costs_{it-1} * economic\ crisis_{it-1}) + \beta_4\ (institutional\ democracy_{it-1})$$
$$+ \beta_5\ (political\ instability_{it-1}) + \beta_{6\ to\ k}\ (other\ economic\ variables_{it-1}) + \varepsilon$$

By implementing a cross-sectional, time-series regression analysis, this study accounts for the variation across countries and over time in the FDI data. The sample consists of seventy developing countries[7] and, due to limited data availability, covers the time period from 1980 to 1995; most reliable FDI data start in 1980, and audience costs (measured via media openness) data are currently available only up to 1995. The pooled data are fitted by the following three estimation methods for the purpose of robustness tests: random effects by assuming the effects of "country" as a random sample of the effects of all the countries in the full population of countries;[8] generalized estimating equations (GEEs) to take within-group correlation into account; and Prais-Winsten models with panel-corrected standard errors (PCSEs). All independent variables are lagged one year to ensure that the independent variables determine dependent variable outcomes rather than vice versa.

The unit of observation for the dependent variable is net FDI inflows as a percentage of total GDP. Net FDI inflows are calculated as total FDI inflows less total FDI outflows; thus, net FDI inflows can be either positive or negative, with negative inflows indicating disinvestment by multinational corporations (World Bank 2010). Although there are at least two additional ways of measuring the activities of foreign firms, they are not employed in this study for the reasons laid out by Choi and Samy (2008). First, as compared to the FDI/GDP, the FDI inflows do not account for the scale effect of sample countries and thus are subject to the outlier problem that violates the normal i.i.d. assumption about residual errors in ordinary least squares regression models; as a result, the estimated results are likely to lead to incorrect inferences. Second, the log of the FDI inflows is also not recommended because FDI inflows can be either zero, positive, or negative, and taking the log of zero or negative FDI inflows does not make mathematical sense.

Because the hypothesis about domestic audience benefits is conditional (i.e., depending on the presence of economic crisis), it requires that we include three terms in the same model: audience costs, economic crisis, and audience costs * economic crisis. As expressed in the econometric equation, the last variable is an interaction term of the first and second constitutive terms. The interaction term is introduced to fully capture the effect that democracies in economic crisis have on inflows of FDI.

Because democratic countries are regarded as generating high levels of audience costs via open and free media, the presence of domestic audience costs is identified with Van Belle's (2000a, 137–48) global press freedom data.[9] Van Belle provides a five-category coding scheme: 0 for no news media (e.g., Vanuatu), 1 for clearly free news media (e.g., the United States), 2 for imperfectly but relatively free news media (e.g., Finland and Mexico), 3 for restricted news media that are not directly controlled by the government (e.g., Jordan), and 4 for government controlled or strictly censored news media (e.g., North Korea). Keeping in mind Van Belle's warning that "categorical coding used for this analysis does *not* produce a five-point interval scale" (140; emphasis in the original), audience costs are operationalized in this study as a dichotomous variable. The variable is coded as 1 if a country has free or imperfectly free news media capable of functioning as an arena of political competition or debate (i.e., observations in categories 1 and 2); otherwise it is coded as 0 (i.e., observations in categories 0, 3, and 4).

To the best of my knowledge, there is no precise measure of economic crisis across time and across the range of developing countries on which scholars and policy makers have agreed to conduct empirical analyses. However, Frankel and Rose's (1996, 362) study appears to be a seminal work in the identification of economic crises. These two economists report that "the proportion of external debt accounted for by FDI is consistently, strongly and significantly associated with [economic] crash incidence." A ratio of FDI to debt for all countries is calculated and ranked according to this key finding. Countries are classified as experiencing an economic crisis if they belong to the tenth percentile of the sample.[10] That is, the economic crisis variable is a dichotomous measure that is equal to 1 if a country falls into the bottom 10 percent and to 0 otherwise.[11]

One might express the concern that, despite the conceptual distinction between economic crisis and inflows of FDI, their measures capture similar phenomena. Because economic crisis is operationalized as the ranking of the ratio of FDI to debt, it does not eliminate FDI as part of the definition and so in this way includes the lagged value of the dependent variable on the right-hand side of the equation. If this concern were justified, one would expect to see a high correlation between the two variables; however, the fact that the correlation coefficient is only 0.19 casts doubt on the possibility that the economic crisis variable and the dependent variable of FDI inflows measure similar economic events.

To test the conditional hypothesis that democracies with open domestic media are likely to discourage FDI inflows in their efforts to reap audience benefits during times of economic crisis, an interaction term between audience costs and economic crisis is also included in the econometric model. It is coded as 1 only if a country enjoys a high degree of media openness (i.e., a numerical category of 1) and is simultaneously experiencing an economic crisis (i.e., a numerical category of 1); it is coded as 0 otherwise. (The correlation coefficient between the interaction term and FDI inflows is only 0.12, which again relieves us of the concern that the operational definitions of the two measures are too similar.)

At this point in the analysis, it is useful to examine the presence of domestic audience benefits in competition with institutional democracy, one of the most widely used democracy variables in the literature. The institutional democracy variable, which is obtained from the Polity data set, captures five different institutional aspects of democratic systems—competitiveness of participation, regulation of participation, competitiveness of executive recruitment, openness of executive recruitment, and constraints on the executive—but it does not measure any aspect of open and free media (for a detailed explanation on Polity, see Gurr, Jaggers, and Moore 1991). According to Diamond (1999, 9), Polity "acknowledges civil liberties [such as media openness] as a major component of democracy but, because of the paucity of data, does not incorporate them." Because institutional democracy is not conceptually related to media openness, each of these two variables is expected to exert an independent effect on FDI. The institutional democracy variable is operationalized on a scale of 0 (least democratic) to 20 (most democratic).

Seven other commonly used FDI-related control variables are also incorporated into the econometric model to avoid the production of spurious statistical results: political instability, economic size, economic development, economic growth rates, economic openness, government budget deficit, and government consumption.[12] Since the effects of these seven variables are well documented in various existing studies (e.g., Jensen 2003; Li and Resnick 2003; Blanton and Blanton 2006, 2007; Jacobsen and de Soysa 2006; Choi and Samy 2008), this study provides only a brief overview of their theoretical arguments in the interest of space. Because foreign firms are less likely to enter a country that experiences frequent political disorder, political instability should lead to a lower rate of FDI inflows. For example, autocratic China has been the recipient of billions of dollars in FDI over the past twenty years, likely as a result of its political stability. The political instability variable is obtained from Banks' (2010) Cross-National Time-Series Data Archive and is measured by the weighted conflict index of assassinations, general strikes, guerrilla warfare, government crises, purges, riots, revolutions, and antigovernment demonstrations. Big economies lure more FDI due to the expectation of higher future returns, so economic size is expected to be positively related to FDI inflows; the economic size variable is measured by the log of GDP. Since advanced economies attract more FDI due to their high levels of consumer purchasing power and capital endowment, economic development should also increase FDI inflows; the economic development variable is measured by the log of GDP per capita. Fast-growing

economies provide foreign investors with a plethora of future market opportunities, so a positive relationship between economic growth and FDI inflows
is expected. As highly open economies attract more FDI, economic openness
should encourage more FDI inflows; the economic openness variable is measured by the sum of exports and imports divided by GDP. Economies with high
levels of budget deficit may be financed by inflows of foreign capital, and, consequently, a government with a large budget deficit should seek to increase its FDI
inflows; the government budget deficit variable is measured by the total amount
of deficit as a percentage of GDP. Because economies with excessive government
consumption are perceived as weak by multinational corporations, government
consumption should be negatively related to FDI inflows; the government consumption variable is measured as government expenditure as a percentage of
GDP. All the economic variables are obtained from World Bank's (2010) World
Development Indicators, 2010.

EMPIRICAL FINDINGS

Table 12.1 shows the multiplicative regression results where the conditional hypothesis of domestic audience benefits is tested with three of the most commonly used estimation methods in the FDI literature: random effects, GEEs,
and PCSEs.[13] One-tailed significance tests are reported at the 0.10, 0.05, and
0.01 levels because the theoretical expectations are directional. Jensen (2003,
600, 604) and Li and Resnick (2003, 195), two prominent works in the FDI literature, employ the same significance levels. To save space, this discussion of
the findings focuses on the main theoretical concern of this study—the impact
of democratic institutions (in terms of domestic audience costs/benefits) on inflows of FDI, conditional to the occurrence of economic crisis.

According to Model 1 with random effects, the audience costs variable is
statistically insignificant and therefore does not support the argument that democracies are likely to attract more FDI inflows when there is no economic
crisis. Put differently, democratic domestic audiences do not contribute to the
FDI policy credibility of democratic systems. It is important to note that although existing studies refer to audience costs as a key aspect of democratic
institutions, they have failed to design an accurate measure for the existence
and magnitude of this variable and instead rely on a proxy to conduct their
empirical analyses. While a positive relationship between audience costs and
FDI has been reported in existing studies, the theoretical arguments are not
supported by precise measurement indicators, rendering the empirical results
unconvincing (Choi and Samy 2008). When domestic audience costs are operationalized through a direct measure, media openness, it is found to have no
bearing on inflows of FDI.

TABLE 12.1   The Effect of Domestic Audience Costs on FDI Inflows as
Economic Conditions Change

Variable	Model 1 Random Effects	Model 2 GEEs	Model 3 PCSEs
Audience costs	−0.572	−0.587	−0.367
	(0.536)	(0.721)	(0.346)
Economic crisis	−0.595**	−0.591***	−0.035
	(0.295)	(0.222)	(0.260)
Audience costs * economic crisis	−0.859**	−0.860**	−0.573**
	(0.437)	(0.475)	(0.326)
Political instability	2.30e-06	2.43e-06	5.69e-07
	(0.001)	(0.001)	(8.27e-06)
Institutional democracy	0.081**	0.083	0.058**
	(0.047)	(0.067)	(0.029)
Economic size	0.001	0.001	0.006
	(0.068)	(0.089)	(0.059)
Economic development	0.012	0.012	0.087
	(0.188)	(0.184)	(0.176)
Economic growth	0.051***	0.051***	0.034***
	(0.014)	(0.013)	(0.014)
Economic openness	0.021***	0.021***	0.021***
	(0.005)	(0.005)	(0.005)
Government budget deficit	0.042**	0.041*	0.034**
	(0.024)	(0.028)	(0.019)
Government consumption	−0.001	−0.001	0.007
	(0.032)	(0.040)	(0.024)
Constant	−0.488*	−0.456	−1.082**
	(1.320)	(1.790)	(1.220)
Wald chi-squared	126.05	57.76	116.89
Prob > Wald chi-squared	0.001	0.001	0.001
R-squared			0.11
within	0.11	n/a	
between	0.42	n/a	
overall	0.20	n/a	
N	752	752	752

Note: In parentheses, robust standard errors for random effects and GEEs, and panel-corrected standard errors for PCSEs.

$*p < .10, **p < .05, ***p < .01$

Based on the finding that the coefficient of the interaction term (audience costs * economic crisis) is significant with a negative sign, we can conclude that democratic leaders are more likely to disrupt FDI inflows when their country is experiencing an economic crisis. However, the coefficient of the interaction term only indicates the average effect of the interaction between audience costs and economic crisis on FDI, not the marginal effect of domestic audience benefits on FDI. That is, the interaction term does not allow us to predict the impact of democratic domestic audiences as economic conditions change. To fully test the conditional hypothesis regarding domestic audience costs, we need to calculate the marginal effect of audience costs on FDI inflows as economic conditions change (i.e., the added effect of both audience costs and audience costs * economic crisis). The added magnitude of the coefficients is 1.432, and its adjusted standard error is 0.630.[14] These findings, and the fact that the joint coefficient is significant at the 0.05 level with a negative sign, provide evidence that democratic leaders do indeed reap domestic audience benefits by scapegoating foreign investors in an effort to gain political popularity among their domestic constituents. Figure 12.1 further illustrates the marginal effect of audience benefits: democratic institutions have a strong reductive effect on FDI inflows in times of economic crisis.[15] A democratic country whose national economy undergoes a crisis is likely to turn its back on multinational corporations in response to public outcry, thus discouraging the future inflow of FDI.

FIGURE 12.1   Marginal Effect of Audience Costs on FDI Inflows as Economic Conditions Change

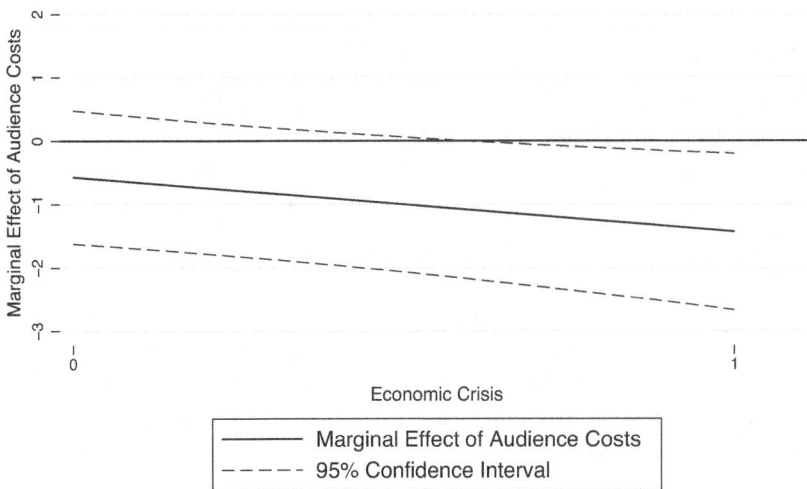

A similar level of significance is indicated by the other two statistical estimation methods. According to GEEs in Model 2, the joint coefficient, which is estimated by testing the conditional hypothesis about domestic audience benefits, is 1.447 with a standard error of 0.822; it is significant at the 0.05 level. According to PCSEs in Model 3, the joint coefficient is 0.940 with a standard error of 0.428; it is also significant at the 0.05 level. These results corroborate the hypothesis that domestic audience benefits in democracies do exist, and that foreign firms are forced to divest by democratic leaders who suffer low job approval ratings due to a depressed economy. Regardless of the statistical method used, it is found that democratic leaders profit politically from the audience benefits gained by scapegoating foreign companies during times of economic crisis.

Among the control variables, political instability finds no support in any of the three models. Its insignificant coefficient may be attributed to the fact that coups, revolutions, assassinations, riots, and strikes happen infrequently. Because such events do not necessarily lead to policy changes that have any relevance to the operation of multinational corporations, foreign investors may not consider them to be investment risk factors (Jakobsen and de Soysa 2006). The institutional democracy variable is significant in the models with random effects and PCSEs; however, it fails to attain significance when tested with GEEs. Economic growth, economic openness, and government budget deficit consistently contribute to an increase of FDI, regardless of estimation method. It appears that developing countries with high growth rates attract more foreign firms, that economic openness is vital for attracting foreign investment, and that a decrease of budget deficit will have a positive effect on FDI inflows.[16]

CONCLUSION

Previous studies have provided evidence that regime type is an important political factor in the explanation of FDI inflows; it has been argued that democracies attract more FDI than do autocracies. Given their policy implications, these studies have generated constructive debates among academics and policy makers alike. In their theory sections, several existing studies have discussed domestic audience costs as a uniquely democratic political constraint. They have argued that the constraining role played by democratic domestic audiences on the potential for elected leaders to make arbitrary policy changes results in high levels of credibility with regard to foreign investment, thus attracting more multinational corporations. However, this conceptualization fails to recognize the presence of domestic audience benefits, a concept that indicates the political profit accrued by democratic leaders who, in the event of ongoing economic depression, are compelled to please their electoral constituents by scapegoating nonvoting foreign investors. This study has conducted a cross-sectional, time-series data analysis and found supporting evidence that democratic developing countries are related to decreased inflows of FDI during periods of economic crisis. This finding suggests that democracies are not in and of themselves magnets for FDI. Rather, because leaders of democratic countries can divert public attention from the domestic economy's poor performance by putting the blame on foreign firms, democracies—at least in times of crisis—may actually be less efficient than autocracies in terms of attracting the investment of multinational corporations.

Potentially, one could argue that foreign investors stop providing FDI in the case of economic crisis of their own accord, even in situations where democratic leaders do not scapegoat them; however, barring a worldwide economic recession, this is an unlikely scenario. Because FDI is generally defined as a company from one country making a physical investment into building a factory in another country, it does not include foreign investment in the stock markets. In other words, from the perspective of the multinational corporations, FDI is a long-term investment in plants, equipment, and infrastructure that will be durable and generally useful irrespective of the host country's market conditions. In response to an unfavorable economic situation in any particular host country, multinational corporations—which typically possess global financial resources—are more likely to initiate an aggressive marketing strategy to protect their long-term investment than they are to immediately discontinue or divest their financial assets. Although it would be interesting to explore the case of equity investments, which are potentially "hot money" and can leave at the first sign of economic troubles, it is beyond the scope of this study and is therefore left for future research.

CHAPTER 13

The United States' Use of Military Force and Terrorism

> If there is one lesson for U.S. foreign policy from the past 10 years, it is surely that military intervention can seem simple but is in fact a complex affair with the potential for unintended consequences.
>
> FAREED ZAKARIA, "Islam, Democracy, and Constitutional Liberalism"

The claim is often made by the United States that it deploys its armed forces abroad in order to preserve world peace and prosperity, but it is possible that these interventions may instead undermine those very objectives. For example, when U.S. military force is used to neutralize domestic disputes in foreign countries, it may incite retaliatory terrorist attacks coordinated by disadvantaged local groups or international terrorists (Piazza 2007, 2008). This study examines the impact of U.S. military intervention on a rise in potential terrorist activity. It is argued that military interventions stimulate an increase in terrorist incidents by undermining domestic security systems in target states and providing targets for terrorist groups (James and Oneal 1991; James and Hristoulas 1994; James and Rioux 1998). Here, a cross-national, time-series data analysis with a sample of 166 countries during the period from 1970 to 2005 shows that U.S. military action is indeed counterproductive, as it tends to inflame terrorist activity in the states in which intervention has occurred.

At the outset, it should be clear that the purpose of this study is not to compare the net benefits of conducting a particular intervention mission (e.g., neutralizing domestic disputes in the target country) with the net costs (e.g., the cost of the mission and any increase in terrorist attacks). This empirical research simply explores the question of whether U.S. military interventions as a whole led to a rise of terrorism as an "unintended" consequence, irrespective of the desired results of a particular intervention mission. Yet, each individual mission may have different desired results. For example, the U.S. military intervention in Iraq was carried out in order to remove the Saddam Hussein regime (the claim was that Iraq possessed weapons of mass destruction and supported international terrorism). Whatever the primary objective of an intervention mission, it may still be achieved despite an increase in terrorist activity. In this case, an

increase in terrorist attacks might be a price (or, rather, an "acceptable" negative consequence) that the United States has to pay if the primary mission is to
be accomplished. In other words, a cost-benefit analysis of whether different
intervention missions led to different desired results is left for future research,
as it would be at least a book-length project on its own.

The rest of this study is organized into several parts. After defining key
conceptual terms, this study presents a conceptual framework in which U.S.
military intervention is linked to a rise in terrorist incidents. Next, a negative
binomial regression model is built in order to test the impact U.S. military operations have on occurrences of terrorism. Then, a two-step model is offered
to take into account endogeneity bias: although U.S. military intervention may
increase the incidence of terrorism, such an intervention may also be a result
of preexisting terrorist activity in the target country. This section is followed by
a discussion of the empirical results. Finally, this study concludes by summing
up the key findings, putting forward policy implications, and suggesting some
possible avenues for future research.

DEFINING MILITARY INTERVENTION AND TERRORISM

For analytic clarity, this study begins by defining the terms *military intervention*
and *terrorism*. As Little (1987, 49) puts it, "intervention has always been and
remains an imprecise and extremely ambiguous concept." This implies that a
researcher's scientific inquiry and causal inference may be distorted by a vague
definition of military intervention. For the purposes of this study, the definition
used by Pearson and Baumann (1993) is employed, since it is one of the most
authoritative definitions to be found in the literature on military intervention;
for these researchers, the phrase *military intervention* refers to the movement of
regular troops or forces of one country into the territory or territorial waters of
another country, or to the forceful military exploits by troops already stationed
inside one country by another country. In order to differentiate full-fledged
military interventions from minor border encounters and shooting incidences,
the term *regular troops* does not include paramilitary forces, and the term *military exploits* does not include actions taken by border guards or police; this
definition attempts to avoid conflating the effects of small-scale border skir-
mishes or actions undertaken by paramilitary forces with the consequences of
sustained military interventions.

Terrorism is a particularly difficult concept to define due to its value-laden
nature; that is, one country's terrorist may be another country's freedom fighter.
This study follows LaFree and Dugan's (2007) definition of terrorism as an intentional threat or act of violence by a nonstate actor in order to attain a political,
economic, religious, or social goal.[1] Domestic terrorism includes incidents such

as the Oklahoma City bombing in April 1995 and the nerve gas attack on the Tokyo subway in March 1995, because these were directed at only domestic targets in the terrorists' home country. International terrorism, on the other hand, is a situation in which a terrorist incident in country A involves perpetrators, victims, institutions, governments, or citizens of country B (Enders and Sandler 2006, 7; Dugan 2010). It is important to note that the category *international terrorism* does not require that terrorists go across national borders when engaging in attacks, nor does it necessitate involvement on the part of notorious international terrorist organizations such as Al Qaeda. As long as the origin of the victims, targets, or perpetrators of this form of political violence can be traced back to at least two different countries, it is regarded as international terrorism. For instance, the destruction of the Al Khubar Towers (housing U.S. airmen in June 1996 near Dhahran, Saudi Arabia) is considered an international terrorist act because there were at least two different nationalities involved (for a more detailed discussion, see Enders and Sandler 2006). Simply put, when a local population or international terrorist group targets U.S. interests, the incident is classified as international terrorism.

WHY U.S. MILITARY INTERVENTION INFLAMES TERRORISM

According to U.S. Department of Defense statistics from September 30, 2011, U.S. armed forces are deployed in more than 150 countries around the world, with more than 205,118 of its 1,425,113 active-duty personnel serving outside of the United States and its territories.[2] The missions vary from regime change to territorial conquest to humanitarian intervention.[3] Whatever the primary mission of any particular U.S. military intervention may be, it will produce certain ramifications for the country in which the intervention takes place. This study argues that one of those ramifications is the creation of an environment favorable to domestic and international terrorist events—an unintended and negative consequence.[4] Two explanations are offered in this section, the first as a lead-in to the second.

To begin, a rise in terrorist attacks may be attributed to the fact that military campaigns by U.S. armed forces undoubtedly destabilize a target country's domestic security apparatus, thereby pushing the country into political disorder. A weakened security system in the chaotic aftermath of a military assault offers local rebel and terrorist groups a favorable opportunity to achieve their political goals through terrorist violence (Piazza 2007, 2008). If a local population or an incumbent government becomes the victim of terror, domestic terrorism is likely to arise. That is, even if the purpose of a particular U.S. military intervention is to compel a target government to cease certain of its activities (as is the case in regime change and humanitarian interventions), it may simultaneously diminish that government's capacity to provide adequate security measures against domestic terrorist threats. In this case, the affected country's security apparatus may have fewer means to devote to the policing of its population and thus become less capable of curbing terrorist activity. Domestic terrorist groups are likely to find this a favorable environment in which to build up clandestine operations and terrorize local targets. In this context, U.S. military intervention has produced an unintended and negative effect in the target state, having potentially acted as "a lightning rod for terrorism" (Eland 2007, 13).

The first explanation informs the second, and the second highlights processes of political maneuvering and the motives of rogue leaders in the affected states. When dealing with U.S. military interventions, rogue leaders understand and estimate the political risks that stem from the terrorist challenge at the domestic front. To put it another way, when rogue leaders are confronted with a high risk of attack from local rebels or terrorists, they have enormous incentives to deflect these attacks in order to maintain power. The deployment of U.S. soldiers and the consequent increase in local terrorist activity often drive rogue leaders to resort to scapegoating (Levy 1989; James and Oneal 1991; James and Hristoulas 1994; James and Rioux 1998). That is, for their political survival, rogue leaders will make the local population, or terrorist sympathizers, feel as if they are being unjustly subjugated and oppressed by an imperialist United States, rather than acknowledge the misconduct of their own government that may have prompted U.S. military intervention in the first place. State-owned media further help sensationalize the image of U.S. military assaults as an illegitimate intrusion in the eyes of the local population; this tends to provoke moral backlash and motivate opposition. Accordingly, these leaders are able to shift the blame for their wrongdoings rather than admit that their misguided policy actions may have been the root cause of the military intervention. The politically manipulative act of scapegoating enables them to incite the local population to adopt tactics of violent resistance, often taking the form of terrorist attack.

It is not hard to imagine that given their limited options for holding on to power, rogue leaders are inclined to manipulate public opinion and to urge their citizens to take up arms against U.S. interests rather than against the government. Although not all the citizens who have grievances against their fellow citizens and the government switch their targets to U.S.-related personnel and objects, many of them are likely to be influenced by the political propaganda of rogue leaders; thus, they become agents of international terrorism against U.S. soldiers, private contractors, and foreign journalists. In other words, states in which an intervention occurs may be subject to both domestic and international terror simultaneously, depending on the target chosen by the local population. Terrorist groups may target local people who collaborate with U.S. military forces (domestic terrorism) or American journalists or soldiers (international terrorism). The scapegoating tactic also helps domestic and international terrorist groups increase their recruitment and initiate future terrorist attacks.[5] For example, by portraying their position as that of David standing up to the American Goliath, and by exaggerating the civilian collateral damage from U.S. actions, rogue leaders invoke antagonistic feelings against the United States. As evidenced by the retaliation carried out by Hezbollah in Lebanon, rogue leaders may characterize U.S. military intervention as an unjust interference into their nation's domestic affairs, urging citizens to turn to terrorism in defense of their territory (for a similar argument, see Crenshaw 1990; Pape 2003). For instance, in response to U.S. military assaults, Islamic fundamentalists have shown themselves capable of indoctrinating young people to resort to terrorism in the name of Jihad (Chowdhury 2010). In this case, terrorist activity is perceived as a feasible option in defense of the state and is adopted as a form of national security against a foreign invader.[6] In fact, Vasquez (1993, 124) believes that humans are "soft-wired" to occupy and, if necessary, defend territory when it is threatened; this "human territoriality" helps explain why individuals may resort to terror when they believe their homeland to be in danger. Of course, these kinds of ill-perceived beliefs reflect political manipulation on the part of rogue leaders whose ulterior motive is political survival.

The motive-based explanation is similar to the "tool" approach to terrorism that is rooted in the psychology of goal-means relations. According to Kruglanski and Fishman (2006, 194), the tool perspective "views terrorism as a means to an end, a tactic of warfare that anyone could use. . . . Its major concern is the conditions under which an individual or a group would opt for a given course of action versus its possible alternatives, given these actors' objectives." Within the context of this study, rogue leaders intend for their publics to perceive terrorist tactics as a viable tool in the effort to force foreign invaders out of occupied territory. But why choose terrorism over other potential tactics that could be used to achieve this goal? This study argues that terrorism is the most logical "tool" in these situations. When faced with the possibility of political fallout resulting from U.S. military intervention and local terrorist attacks, rogue leaders often employ strategic tactics such as scapegoating the United States and justifying as a permissible response the proliferation of terrorist acts aimed at repelling the military assaults. In the effort to promote their own political influence, rogue leaders are likely to portray U.S. military intervention as an illegitimate form of political violence; they do their best to manipulate public opinion and ensure that terrorism is perceived by the local people or by terrorist sympathizers as an appropriate and effective tool for fighting off foreign invaders. Several existing studies make a similar observation. For instance, Crenshaw (1990, 31) notes: "if [local populations] perceive [the intervening power] as unjust, morally corrupt, and violent, then terrorism may seem legitimate and justified." Blumenthal et al. (1975, 110) also find that "the stronger the perception of an act as violence, the more violence is thought to be an appropriate response."

Chalmers A. Johnson's (2000, 2004) studies, in particular, illustrate how the U.S. overseas military presence often drives terrorists to fight back against what they perceive to be acts of American imperialism. The term *blowback* in Johnson's studies refers to a situation in which U.S. overseas military assaults cause local people or terrorist sympathizers to turn to terrorist strategies to preserve their territorial integrity against U.S. interests. The work by Ivan Eland (1998), the former director of Defense Policy Studies at the Cato Institute, is in line with Johnson's blowback argument. Eland discusses approximately sixty terrorist incidents that were considered to be in response to various U.S. military interventions. He concludes that "all of the examples of terrorist attacks on the United States can be explained as retaliation for U.S. intervention abroad" (21). The possible linkage between U.S. military intervention and a rise in terrorist attacks is also discussed by the Defense Science Board (1998, 15): "Historical data show a strong correlation between U.S. involvement in international situations and an increase in terrorist attacks against the United States." These previous studies, then, lend credence to the theoretical argument put forth in this study; namely, that rogue leaders tend to portray the U.S. armed forces as representative of an expansionist or imperialist power, thereby encouraging local populations and terrorist sympathizers to defend against and expel these forces by adopting terrorist activity.

It is important to note that this study conceptualizes the United States' use of military force as "a lightning rod for terrorism" without differentiating among the various types of intervention missions. This study asserts that the net effect of various military missions on terrorist activity is detrimental—a contention that may be thought incompatible with some of the core intended policy outcomes of military intervention in post-9/11 America. However, because this study focuses on the impact of military interventions "as a whole," rather than that of particular classes of intervention missions, an analysis of this potential incompatibility is left for future research. In fact, a full theorization of the multiple forms of military intervention and a performance of the necessary empirical tests would require significantly more space than this chapter.[7]

RESEARCH DESIGN

To test the theoretical prediction about the overall effect of U.S. military interventions, this study collects cross-national, time-series data for 166 countries during the period from 1970 to 2005. The number of sample countries and the study period are restricted by the available terrorism data, which begin only in 1970 (LaFree and Dugan 2007), and by the U.S. military intervention data, which end in 2005 (Pickering and Kisangani 2009).

Consistent with the theoretical expectation about a rise in both domestic and international terrorism, in response to U.S. military interventions, the dependent variable, terrorism, is operationalized as the total number of domestic and international terrorist events that occurred in a country per year. The data are collected from the Global Terrorism Database (GTD) Explorer, a Web-based interactive visual exploratory tool that deals with systematic data about all types of terrorist incidents.[8] The GTD Explorer was originally built using data from 1970 to 2004, but it has now been expanded to include data up to the year 2011 and includes over 104,000 cases of terrorist incidences (Lee 2008).[9] It should be noted that the GTD does not distinguish between threats and actual terrorist incidents. To justify the inclusion of threats of force, LaFree and Dugan (2007, 186) cite Bruce Hoffman's (1998, 38) contention that "terrorism is as much about the threat of violence as the violent act itself"; this argument is relevant, for example, in the case of aerial hijackings ("I have a bomb and I will use it unless you follow my demands"). The lack of a distinction between verbal utterances and physical acts of terrorism in the data set may raise a concern, as the severity of each terrorist incident is not the same. To account for this concern, this study creates another dependent variable that counts only the terrorist attacks that result in casualties. Furthermore, it is worth noting that the GTD categorizes the general type of terrorist target into twenty-two categories including military targets such as army units, patrols, barracks, convoys, and jeeps.

The main independent variable, U.S. military interventions, measures the total number of U.S. military interventions per year that took place within a country's borders. Every intervention experienced by a host government increases the value of this variable by 1 for that specific year, ranging from 0 to 3. It should be noted that since the military intervention variable intends to capture the overall effect of interventions on the emergence of potential terrorist activity, it is an aggregated measure of multiple missions that occurred in the same year; the data come from two different but related sources. Simply put, the variable does not differentiate between types of intervention missions led by U.S soldiers. The Pearson and Baumann (1993) data cover the period from 1946 to 1988, while the data by Pickering and Kisangani (2009) cover the period from 1989 to 2005. Besides splitting up the temporal domain, the two data sets conceptualize and operationalize military interventions using identical criteria.

To avoid omitted variable bias, this study includes seven control variables, namely, economic development, regime durability, total population, democracy, failed state, post–Cold War, and a lagged term of terrorism. Some studies argue that when a national economy is performing poorly, many financially underprivileged people are likely to feel intensified economic deprivation, effectively giving them an excuse to engage in terrorist activity (e.g., Kahn and Weiner 2002). However, other studies show that developed economies are more vulnerable to terrorism. Because industrialized countries produce more highly educated individuals, they may supply a relatively large number of potential terrorists who are better able to plot and carry out terrorist events. In fact, several studies find evidence that terrorists tend to come from relatively wealthy and educated family backgrounds (see Krueger and Maleckova 2002, 2003; Bloom 2005). More importantly, Choi's (2010b) recent study reports that economic development is positively associated with terrorism. This study, in fact, supports the hypothesis that economic development has a detrimental effect on terrorist activity, as disgruntled people are less likely to become terrorists when they cannot access sufficient economic resources to master tactics and skills in preparation for more sophisticated attacks. Economic development is measured by the logged yearly value of a country's gross domestic product (GDP) per capita, adjusted for purchasing power parity (PPP). Data for this variable are derived from Gleditsch (2002), whose updated data include fewer missing observations than other sources such as the World Bank.

Countries with stable regimes may experience fewer terrorist attacks because they are more capable of consistently monitoring the movement of terrorists within their borders. Previous empirical studies support this claim and show that countries experiencing regime change are more vulnerable to terrorist attacks than those countries that do not suffer from abrupt shifts in regime characteristics (e.g., Eubank and Weinberg 1998; Eyerman 1998). The regime durability variable measures the number of years that a country has gone without experiencing a regime change, as measured by a three-point shift in a country's Polity score for a given year; data for this variable are collected from Marshall and Jaggers' (2007) Polity data set. It is expected that regime durability will have an attenuating effect on terrorism.

Countries with a large population will probably find it more difficult to monitor their entire citizenry than would a country with a smaller population. This lack of oversight may provide terrorists with the ideal conditions for the planning and implementation of their campaigns (Eyerman 1998). Total population, in this study, is measured by the country's annual logged total population and is expected to correlate with an increase in terrorism; data for this variable are taken from the U.S. Census Bureau (2008).

The connection between democracy and terrorism is controversial. Some studies claim that democracy provides peaceful channels for conflict resolution, through which individuals can settle their grievances without resorting to illegal terrorist activity (e.g., Eyerman 1998; Li 2005; Choi 2010b). However, others argue that democracies promote the proliferation of terrorist activity by providing populations with greater civil liberties (e.g., Chalk 1995; Eubank and

Weinberg 2001). For example, the right to a free and fair trial and the right to free association make it harder for a government to detect and monitor suspected terrorists and terrorist organizations. Regarding the controversy, this study sides with those who argue that democratic government may in some ways promote terrorist activity; the promotion of personal civil liberties within many democracies may help facilitate the undisturbed planning of attacks, thus making them ideal settings for terrorist activity. The democracy variable is coded as 1 for democracies and 0 for autocracies, and the data are taken from Cheibub, Gandhi, and Vreeland's (2010) study. When a continuous measure from the Polity data collection is used instead, the results do not deviate from those reported below.

Some recent studies suggest that failed states are particularly prone to becoming breeding grounds for terrorism (e.g., Piazza 2007, 2008); the lack of central authority and the presence of porous borders make it harder for these countries to curb terrorist activity once it does materialize. The failed state variable ranges from 0 to 17 by combining the severity of ethnic wars (0–4), revolutionary wars (0–4), adverse regime changes (1–4), and genocides and politicides (0–5); the data come from the Political Instability Task Force (2007). The failed state variable is expected to exert a positive effect on the emergence of terrorist activity.

Enders and Sandler (1999, 2006) provide evidence that the total number of terrorist attacks has decreased with the end of the Soviet funding of left-wing groups. To account for a systemic decrease in terrorist activity after the end of the Cold War, a post–Cold War variable is included. This variable is coded 0 from 1968 to 1990 and 1 thereafter. Since countries with a large number of terrorist incidents in one year are likely to have similar levels in the following year, this study controls for the effect of past terrorist attacks by adding a lagged dependent variable on the right-hand side of the equation. It is worth noting that a lagged dependent variable is often omitted on the right-hand side of an equation since it tends to account for a large portion of the dependent variable's variation (Achen 2000).

Because the dependent variable is operationalized as the total number of terrorist events per year, this study employs a negative binomial maximum-likelihood regression model with Huber-White robust standard errors, clustered by country; this estimation method is chosen over Poisson regression since the variance of the terrorism data is much larger than the mean. Negative binomial regression adds a dispersion parameter in order to model the unobserved heterogeneity among observations; thus, this method allows the variance to exceed the mean, which essentially corrects for the overdispersion found in Poisson regression models (Hilbe 2007). Because no excessive zeros are found in the dependent variable, this study does not employ zero-inflated negative binomial regression. This is not surprising given the fact that this study's dependent variable measures both transnational and domestic terrorism, the prevalence of which drastically reduces the number of zeros in the data. To ensure that the predictors cause the outcome variable, as opposed to the other way around, all of the predictors are lagged one year behind the outcome variable.

EMPIRICAL FINDINGS

Table 13.1 reports empirical results. Model 1 provides evidence that U.S. military intervention is a cause of terrorism because its coefficient is significant at the 0.001 level and the sign is positive.[10] As hypothesized, U.S. military intervention creates undesirable consequences, regardless of its intentions. As recent U.S. military intervention in Pakistan and Yemen illustrates, it may backfire; that is, it may inflame new terrorist activity as well as strengthen existing terrorist networks. Furthermore, by providing an opportunity for rogue leaders to demonize the United States, it may damage America's carefully honed image of itself as an international defender of freedom and democracy, resulting in increased levels of terrorist recruitment and actual attacks within the target country.

Although Model 1 looks into the overall effect of U.S. military interventions, readers may think of its estimated results in terms of individual missions. This way readers can easily envision the positive effect of an intervention mission on terrorist activity, whether it is regime change or territorial conquest. At the same time, the results may also cast doubt on whether the same repercussions apply to humanitarian missions. Therefore, a discussion of a historical case of U.S. humanitarian military intervention is in order as a way to help readers visualize the positive relationship between interventions and terrorism. The 1992 U.S. humanitarian intervention into Somalia—a country torn apart by famine and civil war—is a relevant example. It is well known that in this scenario U.S. military forces sided with one of the local factions against the other, ultimately bombing a neighborhood in Mogadishu. As a result, enraged crowds, backed by foreign Arab mercenaries, killed eighteen U.S. soldiers (Eland 1998, 2007); the United States then was forced to withdraw completely from Somalia. Although the U.S. military was dispatched for a strictly humanitarian mission, its very presence provoked a retaliatory attack against U.S. soldiers after Somali warlords were able to transform the local perception of the intervention; ordinary Somali people saw it less as a humanitarian effort aimed at bringing peace and stability to the country, and more as an unwelcome intrusion into domestic affairs.

In this study, all of the control variables, with the exception of post–Cold War, achieve significance. As hypothesized, citizens of developed countries are more likely to have access to the economic resources needed to facilitate terror-

TABLE 13.1   The Effect of U.S. Military Interventions on Terrorism, 1970–2005

Variable	Negative Binomial Regression Model 1	NBR with Distributed Lags Model 2
U.S. Military intervention$_{t-1}$	0.479***	0.562***
	(0.199)	(0.092)
U.S. Military intervention$_{t-2}$		0.254***
		(0.080)
U.S. Military intervention$_{t-3}$		0.218***
		(0.076)
U.S. Military intervention$_{t-4}$		0.246***
		(0.056)
U.S. Military intervention$_{t-5}$		0.138*
		(0.095)
U.S. Military intervention$_{t-6}$		0.074
		(0.109)
U.S. Military intervention$_{t-7}$		0.105
		(0.102)
U.S. Military intervention$_{t-8}$		−0.051
		(0.101)
U.S. Military intervention$_{t-9}$		−0.141
		(0.173)
U.S. Military intervention$_{t-10}$		0.200
		(0.195)
Economic development$_{t-1}$	0.301***	0.223***
	(0.049)	(0.048)
Regime durability$_{t-1}$	−0.005**	−0.004**
	(0.002)	(0.002)
Population$_{t-1}$	0.322***	0.315***
	(0.032)	(0.031)
Democracy$_{t-1}$	0.419***	0.408***
	(0.109)	(0.113)
Failed state$_{t-1}$	0.157***	0.147***
	(0.016)	(0.019)
Post–Cold War$_{t-1}$	0.046	−0.100
	(0.088)	(0.082)
Terrorism$_{t-1}$	0.006***	0.006***
	(0.000)	(0.000)
Constant	−5.829***	−4.926***
	(0.660)	(0.628)
Wald chi-squared	721.06	920.39
Prob > chi-squared	0.001	0.001
Log pseudolikelihood	−11672.15	−8858.46
Dispersion = 1	47.45	48.61
Observations	5,092	3,573

Note: Robust standard errors are in parentheses.

*$p < .10$, **$p < .05$, ***$p < .01$, one-tailed tests

ist attacks. Also, countries that do not see frequent regime changes are less likely to experience terrorist events. Population is an obvious factor simply because a higher population provides terrorists with more targets. Democratic political systems, it turns out, are more vulnerable to terrorist attacks than nondemocratic regimes because they provide a favorable environment for terrorist activity. As predicted, failed states are associated with a higher risk of terrorism, and countries that have experienced terrorist attacks in the year prior are more likely to see their recurrence in the next. The lack of significance for the post–Cold War variable may be explained by the fact that while this study relies on both "domestic and international" terrorism data, findings of previous studies are based on "international" terrorism data only. It is also plausible that the U.S. military intervention variable attenuates the significance of the post–Cold War variable.

Since statistical significance does not necessarily ensure a meaningful finding in a practical sense, the substantive effects of variables should be reported for empirical verification. In order to calculate a baseline probability of a terrorist incident, against which we may make comparisons, this study sets the continuous variables at their means and the dichotomized variables at 0. It then adjusts the variables of greatest interest one at a time to gauge the change in the predicted probability of terrorism. The substantive analysis indicates the risk that any particular country will experience terrorism increases by an astonishing 62 percent if the United States intervenes once per year, by 161 percent if the intervention occurs twice per year, and by 321 percent if it intervenes three times per year. Thus, it is fair to say that the substantive effects reflect the statistical significance.

It is important to note that a temporary increase in the number of terrorist attacks may actually signal a long-term decline. For example, during the Surge, as Al Qaeda fought for control over the population, Iraq experienced a short-term increase in attacks; the level subsequently declined, however, as U.S. military forces successfully secured civilian areas, gathered intelligence, and deprived insurgents of resources and shelter. Simply put, since the average counterinsurgency lasts nearly a decade, a mission may take years before it is deemed a success. To account for the possibility of short-term versus long-term trends in terrorist activity, this study introduces negative binomial regression models with distributed lags examining the effect of U.S. military intervention during the past ten years. Model 2 in Table 13.1 reports estimated coefficients and standard errors. Since the model demonstrates the positive effect of military interventions on terrorism over the ten-year period, there is little indication of a long-term decline in the incidence of terrorist attacks. Model 2 clearly shows that, on average, U.S. military intervention provokes a period of increased terrorist activity lasting at least five years.[11]

This study has so far developed a plausible set of reasons as to why we may expect U.S. military intervention to increase the likelihood of incidents of terror and has provided systematic empirical evidence supporting this expectation. It is possible that a complex reciprocal relation exists between U.S. military intervention and terrorist activity, with each reinforcing the other. That is, although we have seen that U.S. military intervention tends to incite terrorist attacks, the presence of terror cells in a target country is presumably what prompted U.S. action in the first place (Azam and Thelen 2010).[12] In fact, one of the nine intervention missions (listed in note 3) aims to catch and kill rebel or terrorist forces. Along this line, Betts (1998, 28) notes that "today, as the only nation acting to police areas outside its own region, the United States makes itself a target for states or groups whose aspirations are frustrated by U.S. power." In fact, as exemplified by the invasion of Afghanistan, the United States often considers military power to be a legitimate foreign policy tool in the effort to eliminate terrorist networks in those countries thought to harbor them. In other words, U.S. military intervention may be endogenous to terrorist activity in the target country.

The best way to account for the endogeneity bias noted above is to build simultaneous equations models. However, standard simultaneous equations models rely on the assumption that two endogenous variables are continuous measures. Since the endogenous variables of this study are count measures, standard simultaneous equations models are inappropriate. For this reason, after my having consulted Russett, Oneal, and Davis (1998), this study develops two steps in the model-building process. The first step evaluates the impact of four factors on U.S. military intervention, namely, terrorism, veto players, failed state, and a lagged term of U.S. military intervention. This first step produces predicted values for U.S. military intervention to be used in the second step. The second step then incorporates a one-year lagged term of the predicted values for U.S. military intervention plus the same seven predictors employed in the models in Table 13.1 (i.e., economic development, regime durability, population, democracy, failed state, post–Cold War, and terrorism).[13]

The predicted values for U.S. military intervention from step one are estimated by taking into account terrorism at time t–1, veto players at time t–1, failed state at time t–1, and U.S. military intervention at time t–1. These four lagged independent variables ensure the appropriate causal relationship between independent and dependent variables. Of the independent variables, U.S. military intervention, terrorism, failed state, and a lagged term for U.S. military intervention were discussed in the previous section. Accordingly, this section is limited to an explanation of the veto players variable. The existing literature shows that democracies tend to have more legislative veto players able to place checks and balances on arbitrary executive power than do nondemocratic regimes (Tsebelis 2002). Accordingly, the existence of multiple veto players is a key feature of democratic political systems. In this case, it is expected that the

United States, being one of the most democratic countries in the contemporary world, would not execute hostile military action against another democracy, as it is presumed that two democratic countries with high veto constraints rarely engage in a conflict (Dunne 2009; Choi 2010c). This study uses Henisz's (2000) data collection on veto players.[14] Henisz measures the level of institutional constraints produced by the three key veto players in each country's policy-making process: the executive, the lower legislative chamber, and the upper legislative chamber. Regardless of the specific policy issues, the Henisz measure captures the political constraints imposed on the executive by the lower and upper legislative chambers. The measure is continuous and employs a scale of 0 (least constrained) to 1 (most constrained).

In step one, to estimate the U.S. military intervention model, whose dependent variable is a nonnegative count measure, this study uses Poisson regression with Huber-White robust standard errors clustered by country. The choice of Poisson regression is based on the evidence that the mean and the variance of the dependent variable are approximately equal in the data. To deal with the presence of many zeros in "international" terrorism data, some studies use zero-inflated Poisson regression (e.g., Li 2005). However, the Vuong test of zero-inflated Poisson versus Poisson indicates that the basic Poisson model better fits the "domestic and international" terrorism data collected for this study. As stated in the previous section, step two estimates the terrorism model using a negative binomial regression model. To account for the endogeneity bias, estimation is based on the predicted values for U.S. military intervention, instead of the original variable.

Table 13.2 reports the results of the two steps of model building regarding the U.S. military intervention–terrorism connection. The top part reports the estimated coefficients and standard errors from the U.S. military intervention equation of step one, while the bottom part displays the estimates from the terrorism equation of step two. Model 1 predicts terrorist incidents, while Model 2 employs terrorist casualties as the dependent variable. Model 1 shows results for the overall consequences of U.S. military intervention. The first step of Model 1 supports the theoretical expectations regarding determinants of U.S. military intervention. The likelihood of intervention against a country increases if terrorist events become active and visible, if the central government loses political authority over its territory, and if at least one terrorist attack occurred during the previous year. In contrast, the United States is less likely to intervene in countries with well-established political institutions where the chief executive's political power is checked by a legislature. The second step in Model 1 provides evidence that U.S. military intervention does, in fact, increase the likelihood of terrorist activity among the target population; the coefficient for the predicted values of U.S. military intervention is statistically significant at the 0.001 level

Variable	Terrorist Incidents Model 1	Terrorist Casualties Model 2
First Step: U.S. Military Intervention$_t$		
Terrorist incident$_{t-1}$	0.002** (0.001)	
Terrorist casualty$_{t-1}$		0.140*** (0.050)
Veto player$_{t-1}$	−0.823* (0.594)	−1.128** (0.578)
Failed state$_{t-1}$	0.178*** (0.054)	0.157*** (0.061)
U.S. military intervention$_{t-1}$	1.652*** (0.324)	1.816*** (0.346)
Constant	−4.308*** (0.218)	−4.432*** (0.229)
Wald chi-squared	333.35	359.18
Prob > chi-squared	0.001	0.001
Log pseudolikelihood	−412.96	−408.95
Observations	5,092	5,092
Second Step: Terrorism$_t$		
PV_U.S. military intervention$_{t-1}$	0.167*** (0.038)	−0.020 (0.137)
Economic development$_{t-1}$	0.293*** (0.049)	0.219*** (0.047)
Regime durability$_{t-1}$	−0.005** (0.002)	−0.004*** (0.001)
Population$_{t-1}$	0.319*** (0.032)	0.217*** (0.034)
Democracy$_{t-1}$	0.421*** (0.110)	0.193*** (0.078)
Failed state$_{t-1}$	0.162*** (0.016)	0.068*** (0.019)
Post–Cold War$_{t-1}$	0.016 (0.089)	−0.221*** (0.053)
Terrorist incident$_{t-1}$	0.006*** (0.000)	
Terrorist casualty$_{t-1}$		0.302*** (0.017)

TABLE 13.2   continued

Variable	Terrorist Incidents Model 1	Terrorist Casualties Model 2
Constant	−5.684*** (0.671)	−5.921*** (0.624)
Wald chi-squared	801.15	1023.02
Prob > chi-squared	0.001	0.001
Log pseudolikelihood	−11416.57	−5683.30
Dispersion = 1	48.11	2.12
Observations	4,923	4,923

Note: Robust standard errors are in parentheses.

$*p < .10, **p < .05, ***p < .01$, one-tailed tests

and is in the hypothesized direction. It appears that an interventionist American foreign policy actually escalates the number of retaliatory terrorist attacks on American troops, as well as on local targets. Again, all of the control variables, except for post–Cold War, achieve significance.

To check the robustness of the results reported for Model 1 in Table 13.2, this study also employs the annual number of casualties from terrorism, as measured by the number of people wounded and killed by terrorist attacks, in place of the annual number of terrorist incidents. This alternate measure is preferred for the following three reasons: (1) it examines whether terrorists are more willing to inflict mass casualties in response to U.S. military intervention; (2) instead of indiscriminately amalgamating terrorist events without regard for destructiveness or lethality, it takes the severity of the consequence into account, allowing this study to avoid the assumption that terrorist incidents producing no casualties are commensurable with events killing or wounding hundreds of people; and (3) it is capable of capturing what has been identified as a recent trend in international terrorism—the overall number of attacks decreases as lethality increases (Crain and Crain 2006; Frey, Luechinger, and Stutzer 2007).

If the above explanations are correct, U.S. military intervention should, in general, continue to exert a positive effect over the alternate casualty measure noted above. The results of Model 2 in Table 13.2 show that military intervention on the part of the United States is often prompted by an increase in terrorist casualties (see top part); however, the intervention itself appears to have little relation to an increase in terrorist-related casualties (see bottom part).

This study has not yet distinguished domestic terrorism from international terrorism for two reasons. First, as conceptualized here, U.S. military interven-

TABLE 13.3 Domestic versus International Terrorism, 1970–2005

	Domestic Terrorism	International Terrorism
Variable	Model 1	Model 2
First Step: U.S. Military Intervention$_t$		
Terrorism$_{t-1}$	0.003	0.007
	(0.002)	(0.010)
Veto player$_{t-1}$	−0.753*	−0.653
	(0.586)	(0.627)
Failed state$_{t-1}$	0.181***	0.185***
	(0.055)	(0.053)
U.S. military intervention$_{t-1}$	1.671***	1.633***
	(0.320)	(0.362)
Constant	−4.303***	−4.302***
	(0.217)	(0.217)
Wald chi-squared	356.19	349.22
Prob > chi-squared	0.001	0.001
Log pseudolikelihood	−414.04	−414.80
Observations	5,092	5,092
Second Step: Terrorism$_t$		
PV_U.S. military intervention$_{t-1}$	0.150**	0.271***
	(0.069)	(0.041)
Economic development$_{t-1}$	0.266***	0.321***
	(0.060)	(0.057)
Regime durability$_{t-1}$	−0.005**	−0.005***
	(0.003)	(0.002)
Population$_{t-1}$	0.340***	0.310***
	(0.037)	(0.039)
Democracy$_{t-1}$	0.510***	0.596***
	(0.133)	(0.122)
Failed state$_{t-1}$	0.168***	0.188***
	(0.019)	(0.023)
Post–Cold War$_{t-1}$	−0.002	−0.472***
	(0.095)	(0.099)
Terrorism$_{t-1}$	0.008***	0.028***
	(0.000)	(0.003)
Constant	−6.352***	−7.471***
	(0.773)	(0.795)
Wald chi-squared	867.61	700.39
Prob > chi-squared	0.001	0.001

TABLE 13.3   continued

Variable	Domestic Terrorism Model 1	International Terrorism Model 2
Log pseudolikelihood	−8656.38	−6397.14
Dispersion = 1	45.56	7.90
Observations	4,923	4,923

Note: Robust standard errors are in parentheses.

$^*p < .10, ^{**}p < .05, ^{***}p < .01$, one-tailed tests

tion is related to an increase in both domestic and international terrorism. Second, as Crenshaw points out, "the distinction between 'international' terrorism and 'domestic' terrorism is artificial and has been so for some time" (quoted in Schmid 2004, 59). Dugan's (2010, 4) recent study confirms Crenshaw's observation, namely, "the divide between domestic and international terrorism has become more artificial as cultures become more global." However, it would be intriguing to see the results of separate analyses for domestic versus international terrorism representing the total number of domestic or international terrorist incidents that occurred in any particular country per year. For empirical tests, this study turns to the worldwide terrorism data collection of Enders, Sandler, and Gaibulloev (2011), which systematically separated LaFree and Dugan's (2007) Global Terrorism Database (GTD) into domestic and international terrorist incidents. Enders, Sandler, and Gaibulloev (2011, 3) underscore that "no other article provides such a complete partitioning of domestic and transnational incidents." Table 13.3 replicates Model 1 in Table 13.2 in the light of domestic versus international terrorism; this disaggregation of terrorism does not eliminate the unfavorable effect of U.S. military intervention. Indeed, it finds that there is a trivial difference between domestic and international terrorism in this respect. The overall results in Table 13.3 agree with the theoretical expectation linking intervention and terror and confirm the unintended effect of U.S. military intervention, regardless of the type of terrorism.

When trying to determine the consequences of U.S. military intervention, it is useful to distinguish between terrorist attacks on the homeland and terrorist attacks in a foreign country. In 2004, President George W. Bush implied just such an assumption when he declared that "we are fighting these terrorists with our military in Afghanistan and Iraq and beyond, so we do not have to face them in the streets of our own cities." We may or may not believe that the

TABLE 13.4 Terrorism within versus Terrorism outside the Intervened
Country, 1970–2005

	Homeland	Foreign Country
Variable	Model 1	Model 2
First Step: U.S. Military Intervention$_t$		
Terrorism$_{t-1}$	0.003**	0.004
	(0.001)	(0.006)
Veto player$_{t-1}$	−0.830*	−0.618
	(0.589)	(0.608)
Failed state$_{t-1}$	0.177***	0.186***
	(0.056)	(0.054)
U.S. military intervention$_{t-1}$	1.679***	1.642***
	(0.323)	(0.354)
Constant	−4.306***	−4.302***
	(0.217)	(0.217)
Wald chi-squared	349.42	348.75
Prob > chi-squared	0.001	0.001
Log pseudolikelihood	−412.96	−414.85
Observations	5,092	5,092
Second Step: Terrorism$_t$		
PV_U.S. military intervention$_{t-1}$	0.159***	−0.068
	(0.067)	(0.057)
Economic development$_{t-1}$	0.250***	0.330***
	(0.053)	(0.066)
Regime durability$_{t-1}$	−0.005*	−0.004**
	(0.003)	(0.002)
Population$_{t-1}$	0.325***	0.284***
	(0.032)	(0.038)
Democracy$_{t-1}$	0.434***	0.589***
	(0.122)	(0.122)
Failed state$_{t-1}$	0.166***	0.196***
	(0.017)	(0.019)
Post–Cold War$_{t-1}$	0.163**	−0.319***
	(0.096)	(0.114)
Terrorism$_{t-1}$	0.006***	0.029***
	(0.000)	(0.003)
Constant	−5.634***	−7.306***
	(0.686)	(0.807)
Wald chi-squared	631.80	1238.45
Prob > chi-squared	0.001	0.001

TABLE 13.4   continued

Variable	Homeland Model 1	Foreign Country Model 2
Log pseudolikelihood	−10203.09	−6101.89
Dispersion = 1	54.19	7.26
Observations	4,923	4,923

Note: Robust standard errors are in parentheses.

$^*p < .10, ^{**}p < .05, ^{***}p < .01$, one-tailed tests

strategy is worthwhile, but the logic that we will knowingly accept an increase in foreign attacks for a reduction in those at home is steadfast. One could make the case that it is a strategy of attrition—wear down the enemy abroad, so he or she no longer has the capacity to fight us at home. By treating those terror events occurring within the country targeted for military action separately from events occurring outside the country in question, Table 13.4 addresses this concern. While Model 1 is concerned with terrorist attacks on the homeland, Model 2 examines those that take place on foreign soil. The overall pattern of homeland terrorism in Model 1 resembles that of domestic terrorism in Table 13.3, verifying the positive relationship between U.S. military intervention and the terrorist reaction. The foreign terrorism variable in Model 2 somewhat deviates from the international terrorism variable in Table 13.3, since it fails to indicate significance for the military intervention variable. This analysis of homeland versus foreign terrorism indicates that international terrorists may be less interested in crossing borders than in staying put in order to respond to U.S. military campaigns; more importantly, it shows that international terrorist groups are less influenced by the political manipulation of rogue leaders in the intervened states. Since U.S. military intervention affects local populations considerably more than it does foreign populations, the finding that most retaliatory terrorist attacks take place within, as opposed to outside of, the targeted country is by no means surprising.

CONCLUSION

The current literature on terrorism pays little attention to the possibility that U.S. military intervention could act as a catalyst for further terrorist violence. Empirical studies of U.S. military intervention overlook its potential impact on the number of terrorist events, despite the fact that the past four decades have shown a high proportion of terrorist activity aimed at U.S. targets in foreign countries (e.g., U.S. soldiers, embassies, or multinational corporations) (see La-Free, Yang, and Crenshaw 2009). This study makes three contributions to the literature by bridging two research areas (i.e., terrorism and military intervention). First, it examines this underdeveloped area by conceptualizing the U.S. military intervention-terrorism connection and by employing single equation models followed by two-step models to account for reverse causality. Second, it examines the short-term versus long-term trends in terrorist attacks. Third, it underscores the categorical difference between terrorist incidents and terrorist casualties and distinguishes between events of homeland and foreign terrorism in response to U.S. military intervention.

The empirical results indicate that U.S. military intervention is liable to increase the frequency of terrorist incidents, whether or not it leads to more terror-related casualties. Rather than providing global security and economic prosperity for the world, U.S. military action tends to result in blowback. When the United States, through the use of military force, meddles in the internal affairs of other nations, the result is often retaliatory terrorist attacks against U.S. interests as well as local targets. As conceptualized in this study, the interventions apparently provide a window of opportunity for a rogue leader, in the effort to preserve his or her regime amid a domestic terrorist challenge, to strategically scapegoat the United States (e.g., Lebanon in the 1980s, Somalia in the early 1990s, and Pakistan and Yemen in the late 2000s). An implication of this finding is that the United States should help train and provide intelligence information, weapons, and equipment to counterterrorism units in terrorism-prone countries, rather than directly intervene in the domestic affairs of such countries. This way, the United States can avoid direct military involvement and the potential that its missions will backfire.

Future research should explore more detailed consequences of the different types of U.S. military intervention. For example, it might be interesting to examine some nuanced case studies to determine why even humanitarian interventions are associated with an increase in terrorism. In other words, it is plausible that the impacts of the various types of military intervention may differ in terms of their provocation of retaliatory terrorist activity; however, as shown in Appendix Table 13.1, the preliminary results of this study do not support this conjecture.[15] Although this study focuses solely on the United States, as it has been the most dominant player in international politics for the past several decades, future research should also examine the effect of military interventions by other major powers including the United Kingdom, France, and Russia. It is possible that other major powers may fare better or worse than the United States with respect to potential blowback; if this is the case, then accounting for these differences would make for an interesting project on its own.

APPENDIX TABLE 13.1   The Effect of Each Type of U.S. Military Mission on Terrorism, 1970–2005

Variable	Regime Change Model 1	Territorial Model 2	Economic Model 3	Strategic Model 4	Domestic Political Model 5	Social Model 6	Terrorist Pursuit Model 7	Humanitarian Model 8	Diplomatic Model 9
U.S. Military interventions$_{t-l}$	0.503*	1.487***	0.894**	0.484**	0.511*	0.937***	-0.619	0.681***	0.219
	(0.374)	(0.133)	(0.455)	(0.289)	(0.325)	(0.242)	(0.649)	(0.159)	(0.508)
Economic development$_{t-l}$	0.307***	0.306***	0.306***	0.309***	0.308***	0.307***	0.307***	0.309***	0.307***
	(0.048)	(0.048)	(0.049)	(0.048)	(0.049)	(0.048)	(0.048)	(0.048)	(0.048)
Regime durability$_{t-l}$	-0.005**	-0.005**	-0.005**	-0.005**	-0.005**	-0.005**	-0.005**	-0.005**	-0.005**
	(0.002)	(0.002)	(0.002)	(0.002)	(0.002)	(0.002)	(0.002)	(0.002)	(0.002)
Population$_{t-l}$	0.304***	0.303***	0.302***	0.305***	0.304***	0.303***	0.302***	0.305***	0.303***
	(0.032)	(0.032)	(0.032)	(0.032)	(0.032)	(0.032)	(0.032)	(0.033)	(0.032)
Democracy$_{t-l}$	0.404***	0.406***	0.409***	0.406***	0.406***	0.406***	0.404***	0.407***	0.404***
	(0.108)	(0.108)	(0.107)	(0.108)	(0.107)	(0.108)	(0.108)	(0.108)	(0.108)
Failed state$_{t-l}$	0.167***	0.170***	0.170***	0.166***	0.169***	0.169***	0.171***	0.164***	0.169***
	(0.016)	(0.016)	(0.016)	(0.016)	(0.016)	(0.015)	(0.016)	(0.016)	(0.015)
Post–Cold War$_{t-l}$	0.075	0.071	0.071	0.077	0.078	0.072	0.069	0.066	0.071
	(0.088)	(0.088)	(0.088)	(0.088)	(0.087)	(0.088)	(0.088)	(0.086)	(0.088)
Terrorism$_{t-l}$	0.006***	0.006***	0.006***	0.006***	0.006***	0.006***	0.006***	0.006***	0.006***
	(0.000)	(0.000)	(0.000)	(0.000)	(0.000)	(0.000)	(0.000)	(0.000)	(0.000)
Constant	-5.511***	-5.481***	-5.466***	-5.557***	-5.524***	-5.500***	-5.474***	-5.551***	-5.497***
	(0.669)	(0.672)	(0.674)	(0.662)	(0.664)	(0.673)	(0.672)	(0.673)	(0.673)
Wald chi-squared	527.23	534.53	526.76	533.18	561.46	534.58	564.59	578.32	532.40
Prob > chi-squared	0.001	0.001	0.001	0.001	0.001	0.001	0.001	0.001	0.001
Log pseudolikelihood	-11750.63	-11752.39	-11748.52	-11745.94	-11749.95	-11750.22	-11752.96	-11741.44	-11753.51
Dispersion = 1	52.53	52.67	52.39	52.04	52.24	52.35	52.65	51.89	52.61
Observations	4,995	4,995	4,995	4,995	4,995	4,995	4,995	4,995	4,995

Note: Robust standard errors are in parentheses.

*p < .10, **p < .05, ***p < .01, one-tailed tests.

Conclusion

When we publish in peer-reviewed books and journals, we expect that our scholarship will be read closely and discussed by our fellow researchers. That is, we publish our scientific findings in the hopes of transmitting knowledge within a scientific community so that others may use it as a starting point from which to construct their own theories and build their own empirical models. The accumulation of scientific knowledge is integral to future fact-finding and is always the first step toward scientific progress and even revolution. However, when scientific discoveries reported in publication outlets are flawed or biased, they become obstacles to the progress of empirical political research. How can we avoid or minimize the likelihood of these unfortunate events? A particularly simple solution would be to require researchers to publicly disclose their data and statistical programs for the purposes of replication, thereby allowing others to discuss, scrutinize, and, if necessary, rectify the findings. Furthermore, an essential part of graduate training and scholarly activity should be to learn how to constructively criticize and correct by practicing critical replication projects. Replication projects encourage the future generation of researchers to conduct more cautious and rigorous empirical testing by "act[ing] as police patrol on common misdemeanors such as omitted variables and results presented that were infected by cherry-picked covariates" (Laitin 2013, 46; for a similar view, see also Carsey 2014; Dafoe 2014; Ishiyama 2014). By conveying the lessons from replication projects (as well as new research programs) to advanced undergraduate and graduate students as well as quantitative scholars, this book contributes to the scientific progress of empirical political studies in the four major areas of democracy, foreign investment, terrorism, and conflict.

Certainly though, replication is not a panacea for all that ails us in terms of the publication of erroneous empirical research; however, it does, at least, meet the standards of good research activity as laid out by the two epigraphs at the beginning of this book. Karl Popper points out that "science is perhaps the only human activity in which errors are systematically criticized and, in time, corrected"; David L. Goodstein likewise reminds us that "the only way that science can make progress is by showing that theories are wrong." Ideally speaking, replication should facilitate scholarly exchange between established and up-and-coming scholars; however, this possibility can be realized only when all involved are receptive to new ideas and differing opinions, and when established scholars possess a strong desire to move the discipline forward by abstaining from defending their work at the expense of knowledge accumulation and scientific truth. Yet, the reality is that the practice of replication in the discipline of political science and the field of international relations is not as appreciated as any enthusiastic empiricist would hope. The appropriate replication materials for many empirical studies, especially those published in top journals and presses—including the *American Political Science Review, International Organization,* Oxford University Press, and Cambridge University Press—are often unavailable for scrutiny. Sometimes even when replication materials are publicly accessible, they are not replicable. For example, in their *International Studies Quarterly* article, Oneal and Tir (2006, 757) lament that "Davies (2002) reports a link between domestic strife and the initiation of interstate disputes, but his results cannot be reproduced with his posted data, and they contain substantial errors."[1] My own replication experiences have been irregular. For example, I was excited when, with their editors' help, I was able to obtain the replication data and statistical programs for Maoz and San-Akca's (2012) *International Studies Quarterly* article; however, my excitement was short-lived upon discovering that my replicated results did not correspond to those reported in the study.

What would be the best way to help political researchers pursue scientific discoveries and revolution while minimizing the risk of falling victim to potential errors, fraud, and misconduct? The following two quotes might point us in the right direction:

> If we are serious about promoting research transparency and scholarly integrity via access to replication files, we must also, as a community, provide a venue for this material to be made public (and published). Given the challenges associated with publishing replication attempts, researchers now have little incentive to conduct such studies . . . an outlet for the publication of replication studies that appear in APSA journals is needed (although not necessarily exclusively on articles that appear in APSA journals), that APSA should publish. (Ishiyama 2014, 82-83)

> If replication is critical to the progress of knowledge, scholarly journals should be encouraged to publish replication studies. . . . Doing this would encourage more scholars to engage in such activities. (Carsey 2014, 73)

The first quote comes from John Ishiyama, the lead editor of the *American Political Science Review;* the second is from Thomas M. Carsey, a researcher with a strong interest in research methods, including issues of model building, pooled panel data, and Monte Carlo simulation and resampling. The message should be loud and clear: the posting of replication materials for public use is not sufficient for the establishment of a genuinely rigorous scientific paradigm in empirical political research; rather, it requires that the most prestigious outlets, including the *American Political Science Review* and *International Organization*, begin publishing replication studies on a regular basis without prejudice. Additionally, in order to provide a fair and impartial review environment, editors of top-tier journals and presses should avoid sending replication papers to the original authors at the initial stage of the review process. Original authors have an incentive to discourage the publication of replication studies that are critical of their empirical models and results, a bias that undeniably distorts the review process at the initial stage. If the original authors choose to offer a rejoinder, it should be encouraged but also held to the same degree of rigorous review.

Importantly, this book has no intention of destroying well-established research programs by pointing out mistakes and errors embedded in their empirical analyses. In fact, this book insists that the presence of mistakes and errors should be treated as part of the scholarly voyage into the universe of scientific truth, as unintended errors are integral to future fact-findings because they push us to seek better models and more accurate conceptualizations. We understand in the hard sciences, for example, how the wrong concept of geocentrism was the necessary precursor to heliocentrism, before the latter became accepted as scientific truth. Similarly, in our own field many international relations scholars were less keen to explore alternative theories before witnessing the failure of Kenneth Waltz's neorealism to predict or explain the end of the Cold War and the collapse of the former Soviet Union. Accordingly, this book hopes that those researchers whose work has been—thanks to their willingness to share their data—replicated in its chapters will engage in a constructive exchange of ideas and criticisms rather than hasten to assert that the replications are fundamentally flawed or contain statistical and reporting errors. Of course, when defensive assertions produce further scholarly debates via formal publication outlets, they too may lead us another step closer to scientific truth and hopefully revolution in the twenty-first century.

Chapters 1 through 8 in part 1 of this book reexamine major empirical studies in the discipline of political science in general and the field of international relations in particular. The results of these efforts appear to cast serious doubt on several widely accepted theories and empirical findings across various research areas. Chapter 1 scrutinizes Fearon and Laitin's (2003) statistical model, which predicts that democracy, ethnicity, and religion have no explanatory power in the context of the occurrence of civil war. However, by employing a simultaneous equations model in which mutual causality is taken into consideration, the chapter actually overturns Fearon and Laitin's findings: that is, while well-established democratic countries or religiously diversified countries are exposed to fewer civil war onsets, ethnically diverse countries are more likely to experience this type of violence. Chapter 2 looks into Gartzke's (2007) capitalist peace model, which is built to demonstrate that capitalism—rather than democracy—leads to interstate peace. Yet, the reanalysis uncovers that the capitalist peace model suffers from model misspecification, observation omission, and sample selection bias. When these errors are corrected, the capitalist model loses its effectiveness, predicting that democracy, not capitalism, exerts a pacifying effect on international conflict.

Chapter 3 reexamines Morrow et al.'s (2008) selectorate model with fixed effects. The chapter contends that the fixed effects of the selectorate model are misspecified because they fail to control separately for the effects of geographic regions and years. The data analysis shows that when fixed effects are implemented separately for region, country, and year, and when heteroskedasticity and autocorrelation are corrected for, the size of the winning coalition (W) is either insignificant or in the counterintuitive direction in twenty-seven out of thirty-one (87 percent) selectorate models. By presenting a novel theoretical claim that civil liberties are a better predictor of public policy outcomes than is W, chapter 4 questions the validity of Morrow et al.'s (2008) selectorate theory. The replication results offer evidence that the inclusion of a variable to account for a high level of civil liberties contributes to a loss of the robustness, if not the significance, of W in more than 62 percent of the selectorate models. The chapter concludes that countries with high levels of civil liberties do a better job of providing public goods to their citizens than do countries with large winning coalitions.

Chapter 5 reevaluates and compares two classical works of foreign direct investment (FDI) by Li and Resnick (2001) and Jensen (2003). Despite the fact that the research designs of the two studies resemble each other closely, their results regarding the effect of democracy on the activities of foreign investors point in opposite directions. The chapter starts with a simple simulation to illustrate how outlying observations drastically affect the estimated coefficients and standard errors of linear OLS regression analysis. The logic of the simulation is then applied to the two published studies to demonstrate that once outlier problems are mitigated, democratic regimes actually foster more foreign investment than authoritarian regimes. Relying on new data and new diagnostic techniques, chapter 6 more deeply investigates the controversial relationship between democracy and inflows of FDI. The new data analysis demonstrates that when the fundamental assumption of normality in regression residuals of foreign investment data is upheld, democracies tend to attract more foreign capital than autocracies.

Chapter 7 discusses the utility of zero-inflated negative binomial (ZINB) regression, an estimation method that has been employed incorrectly in the terrorism literature. ZINB regression is used to test the theoretical argument that due to their unique political and economic circumstances, many countries experience no terrorist attacks at all, while others remain vulnerable. For empirical estimation of a ZINB regression model, the existing studies collect cross-national, time-series data on terrorism; however, ZINB regression is designed exclusively for a *cross-sectional* data set. As such, ZINB regression is unable to capture the uniqueness of terrorism-free countries in contrast to terrorism-prone countries, as its estimation process incorrectly treats individual *observations* with no terrorism as individual *countries* with no terrorism. Because existing studies have implemented the wrong statistical model, their estimates are biased, and their findings are statistical artifacts.

Chapter 8 presents a causal mechanism in which the presence of a high-quality democratic rule of law is considered to diminish the opportunity and willingness for ordinary citizens to engage in political violence, thereby insulating democracies from international terrorist attacks. Built off of Li's (2005) research design, it conducts a cross-sectional, time-series data analysis of a hundred countries for the years 1984–1997. It appears that, ceteris paribus, promoting a strong rule of law tradition markedly reduces the risk of international terrorism, while other democratic features such as political participation and government constraints fail to achieve significance.

These eight replication chapters challenge the major findings of several authoritative empirical political studies. A close examination of these studies reveals that their estimated results are insufficiently robust to pass various validity tests; their inferences and conclusions, then, have been put into doubt. When their statistical models are corrected and reanalyzed, they fail to show the same estimated results, instead producing very different empirical regularities. The fact that these eight chapters have generated findings so dissimilar to those of the original studies reminds us of the importance of replication projects and of their potential contributions to the process of scientific discovery. As previously noted, many top journals and book publishers do not require that authors post replication materials publicly; as a result, almost all of those published works escape from the scrutiny of the research community. Given the significance of the findings that have emerged in the eight chapters of part 1, there can be no doubt that the danger posed by a lack of scientific replication activity is too serious — and common—to ignore. The "no replication" culture in the major publication outlets must be challenged in order to help future researchers learn the kind of rigorous research tools necessary for scientific progress.

Scientific results are meant to improve our knowledge about politics and inform us how political factors such as wars and terrorism influence and are influenced. Thus, we political scientists do not seek knowledge for our own sake, but to improve our political environments. The benefit of scientific findings exists in their ability to make a positive difference for our societies, countries, and international communities. However, in the absence of rigorous, scientific information, national leaders do not have sufficient knowledge to make informed decisions; thus, their decision-making practices become little more than exercises in ideology and the use of power. More importantly, scientific findings from erroneous data analysis can potentially be used to justify bad policy. Consider Fearon and Laitin's (2003) study on the causes of civil war. The study could lead policy decision makers to emphasize the role of economic development or state capacity as a way to reduce the risk of the outbreak of civil war while completely ignoring the real danger that stems from the unaddressed grievances of politically disadvantaged ethnic groups. Similarly, Li and Resnick's (2003) findings could entice democratic leaders into implementing repressive investment policies as an effort to increase inflows of foreign capital for economic development. The point is that when top journals and presses are encouraged to publish replication projects, the risk of producing misleading policy recommendations in empirical political studies should decrease, thus increasing the potential for our national leaders to engage knowledgeably in domestic and international affairs.

Chapters 9 through 13 in part 2 of this book switch gears, seeking to identify some heretofore unnoticed empirical patterns in the same political issue areas from chapters 1 through 8. Note that chapters 9 through 13 explore new research ideas with original research designs and data collection. They uncover new empirical regularities and offer new generalizations regarding the underlying fundamental processes of democracy, foreign capital, terrorist activity, and civil warfare, as well as discuss relevant policy implications in the context of the role of democratic governance.

Chapter 9 addresses the recurrent question of how it is that domestic political opposition becomes strong enough to initiate civil war in some, but not all, countries. The empirical analysis tests and confirms the argument that when leaders with prior military experience use indiscriminate violence to repress their citizens, they increase the number of opposition sympathizers, producing a sizable opposition movement that has then likely gained the momentum necessary to instigate a civil war. It appears that in an effort to stem the proliferation of civil war, American foreign policy agents should focus their efforts on encouraging countries to institutionalize civilian control over the military, which is an essential feature of democratic institutions. In the past, the United States was tolerant of allied countries under military dictatorship for an international security exigency (e.g., El Salvador). However, in order to prevent the wider negative consequences of military rule, Washington should emphasize the establishment of civilian supremacy. When the U.S. Agency for International Development provides economic and military assistance to foreign countries, it should be more selective of the type of regime that receives its support, as such aid is intended to contribute to national and regional peace.

Combining commonly discussed domestic and international factors from the literature—both political and economic—of international conflict, chapter 10 seeks to pinpoint the determinants of military manpower systems. An original data set of military manpower systems spanning over a hundred years is collected and used for hypothesis testing. The empirical results show that higher levels of military personnel and expenditure, as well as a general satisfaction with the status quo, are associated with conscription. Yet, note that satisfaction with the status quo is counterintuitive. This finding seems to provide support for the realist perspective that "if you want peace, prepare for war"; it may be that states choose to increase their security in an anarchical world by maintaining a large number of conscripted soldiers even when their preferences *are* in line with those of the leading superpower. The empirical analysis also indicates that democracy and joint memberships in international organizations are linked to the choice of volunteer military system. It appears that as the quality of democratic governance increases, both states in a given dyad are likely to move away from the use of conscripted soldiers. This implies that the world may become a more democratic place in which the right of an individual to choose to serve is greatly appreciated in proportion to the increased number of democratic countries.

Chapter 11 produces null results when Morrow et al.'s (2008) selectorate model is tested in the context of the democracy and terrorism connection. The first set of testing indicates that while W exerts a dampening effect on terrorism, executive constraints fail to produce the same effect; yet, the second set of testing fails to find the same deterrent effect of W. That is, when regional differences, country, and year fixed effects are all accounted for, the positive effect of the W variable disappears while the counterintuitive effect of executive constraints remains the same. This chapter finds, then, that democratic countries with these two institutional features have a more difficult time, in general, challenging international terrorism. Because the deterrence of terrorism is a primary effort of national leaders, and because the political survival of democratic leaders depends on this effort, the lack of empirical evidence in this chapter is disappointing to students of the selectorate theory and terrorism. The null results may indicate that U.S. foreign policy decision makers should rethink the effectiveness of promoting democracy abroad.

Chapter 12 introduces the concept of domestic audience benefits—that is, the possibility that a democratic leader will use a national economic crisis to his or her electoral advantage by exploiting foreign firms as scapegoats (i.e., reneging on investment deals or expropriating output or capital); this act would likely discourage inflows of FDI over time. Built on a cross-sectional, time-series data analysis for seventy developing countries during the period from 1980 to 1995, this chapter produces evidence that democratic developing countries are, in times of economic crisis, likely to experience decreased inflows of FDI. This finding implies that because democratic leaders are capable of diverting public attention from a deteriorating domestic economy by blaming foreign firms, democracies may actually be less efficient than autocracies in terms of inducing foreign capital from multinational corporations. Potentially, one could argue that foreign investors choose to stop providing FDI in the case of economic crisis for entirely different reasons, having nothing to do with democratic leaders attempting to scapegoat them; however, barring a worldwide severe economic recession, this is an unlikely scenario. Because FDI is generally defined as a company from one country making a physical investment into building a factory in another country, foreign investment in the stock markets is not part of my investigation. Furthermore, in response to an unfavorable economic situation in any particular host country, foreign investors with global financial resources are more likely to initiate an aggressive marketing strategy to protect their long-term investment than they are to immediately discontinue or divest their financial assets.

Chapter 13 looks into the impact of U.S. military intervention on the emergence of terrorist activity abroad. This chapter argues that U.S. military action inadvertently increases the number of terrorist incidents by undermining the domestic security apparatus in the target state and by providing opportune targets for terrorist groups. A cross-national, time-series data analysis of 166 countries during the period from 1970 to 2005 indicates that U.S. military intervention is liable to increase the frequency of terrorist incidents and casualties. Rather than providing global security and economic prosperity for the world, U.S. military action tends to result in blowback by providing a window of opportunity for a rogue leader to strategically scapegoat the United States in an effort to preserve the existing regime amid a domestic terrorist challenge (e.g., Lebanon in the 1980s, Somalia in the early 1990s, and Pakistan and Yemen in the late 2000s). This finding leads to a clear foreign policy recommendation: Washington should help train and provide intelligence information, weapons, and equipment to counterterrorism units in terrorism-prone countries, rather than directly intervene in the domestic affairs of such countries. In this way, the U.S. government can avoid direct military involvement and the potential that its missions will backfire.

The overall empirical findings of chapters 9 through 13 demonstrate the ambivalence of democratic governance for world leaders who are interested in engaging in data-based policy decision making. On the one hand, there is evidence that democratic countries are more resilient to domestic and international political turmoil than are their counterparts. Democratic countries are less likely to experience the onset of civil war when the tradition of civilian supremacy—a primary pillar of democracy—is well established and cultivated (chapter 9); democratic countries are also more likely to maintain volunteer military systems in responding to external threats (chapter 10). (Note that the volunteer service reflects the democratic principle of equality better than conscription does because it preserves the freedom of an individual to choose whether to serve in the armed forces.) Without a doubt, these findings do justice to the worldwide campaign for the promotion of democracy, one of the core foreign policy agendas of the U.S. government. On the other hand, democratic countries seem to be vulnerable to terrorist threats on the domestic front. Neither democratic countries with large winning coalitions nor those with a greater degree of the separation of powers appear to be successful in their efforts to challenge growing terrorist threats (chapter 11). The United States, one of the most powerful democracies in the contemporary world, turns out to be a lightning rod for inciting terrorism abroad (chapter 13). Furthermore, when democratic leaders suffer from an economic downturn, they are likely to scapegoat foreign investors for the sake of their own political benefit, thus reducing future FDI inflows and dampening long-term economic growth (chapter 12). These findings raise a challenging question: Is it possible to insulate democratic political systems from those destructive forces? Perhaps the best policy choice lies in the particular political circumstances of individual countries. For example, if the priority of the incumbent leadership is to avert civil conflict in the near future, an obvious policy choice would be to institutionalize civilian control over the military. However, if a country becomes a victim of frequent terrorist attacks, its leaders might need to consider rebalancing national security and civil liberties.

In closing, this book hopes to serve as a stepping-stone toward scientific progress and, if possible, the next big idea of scientific revolution. The replication projects in chapters 1 through 8 have raised serious doubts regarding several widely accepted findings in the field of international relations by showing the presence of statistical artifacts. As is asserted in this book, scientific breakthrough is unlikely to happen as long as the findings of the most widely read political studies are insulated from scrutiny by journal editors and book publishers who discourage replication studies. The "next big idea" can only be developed in a scholarly environment where new concepts are relentlessly tested on the basis of trial and error prior to being published. Although any number of experiments may turn out to be wrong, we simply cannot know until we try repeatedly. Indeed, chapters 9 through 13 present some suggestions for new research ideas that may lead us to a crucial clue regarding the big idea of the next scientific revolution. Simply put, the empirical work done in this book should be regarded as "the end of the beginning" rather than, as Winston Churchill said, "the beginning of the end."

NOTES

Introduction

1. The *AER* is among the nation's oldest and most respected scholarly journals in the discipline of economics.

2. Economist Paul Krugman (April 18, 2013) describes a prime example of replication in a *New York Times* op-ed piece as follows:

> Ms. Reinhart and Mr. Rogoff allowed researchers at the University of Massachusetts to look at their original spreadsheet—and the mystery of the irreproducible results was solved. First, they omitted some data; second, they used unusual and highly questionable statistical procedures; and finally, yes, they made an Excel coding error. Correct these oddities and errors, and you get what other researchers have found: some correlation between high debt and slow growth, with no indication of which is causing which, but no sign at all of that 90 percent "threshold."

3. Laitin's (2013, 46) recent suggestion is, however, encouraging: "we need to incentivize the publication of replications and null results. . . . With null results on well-established expectations appearing in our leading disciplinary review, the current publication bias would be reduced . . . it would through replications act as a police patrol on common misdemeanors such as omitted variables and results presented that were infected by cherry-picked covariates." Another encouraging development is a *PS: Political Science & Politics* symposium on data access and research transparency (Lupia and Elman 2014).

Chapter 1. Democracy, Ethnicity, Religion, and Civil War

1. Hegre and Sambanis (2006, 513–14), for instance, acknowledge that "a concern with our approach as well as with all studies of civil war onset is that some of the variables included in civil war models may be endogenous . . . we assume exogeneity for all variables (as do almost all the studies that we surveyed in this literature). . . . Since very few of the papers in the literature on civil war deal with the issue of endogeneity, we also ignore it and simply try to reduce the risk by lagging independent variables."

2. Two-stage probit least squares, as its name implies, carries out a two-stage process. At the first stage, the endogenous variable is regressed on all of the exogenous variables, and the predicted values of this regression are computed. At the second stage, the predicted values replace the original endogenous variables in the equation for estimation. Since detailed econometric explanations are laid out in Keshk (2003) and Keshk, Reuveny, and Pollins (2010), its operation is not described here to save space (see also Maddala 1983; Greene 2003).

3. Elbadawi and Sambanis (2002, 309) make the same conjecture: "democracy may be endogenous to civil war."

4. The data set is publicly available at https://web.stanford.edu/group/fearon-research/cgi-bin/wordpress/.

5. This practice is consistent with Beck, Katz, and Tucker's (1998, 1266) study in which they argue that "no one model is perfect for all situations."

6. Bueno de Mesquita et al.'s (2004, 378) study on international war applies the same approach with only a minimum number of predictors: "while we recognize that other variables exert an independent impact on the dependent variables, our objective is not to explain as much variance as possible but to test the predictions of the theory."

7. In order to fill in as many missing observations of each variable as possible, Fearon and Laitin searched for a variety of primary and secondary sources. These efforts enabled them to compile a complete and comprehensive data set of civil war for 161 countries during the period from 1945 to 1999.

8. It should be noted that while Fearon and Laitin include a lagged term of democracy in their single equation logit model, this study employs the original term in order to test its simultaneous relationship with civil war onset at the same year t.

9. It is plausible that political grievances exist in many countries, both democratic and nondemocratic. However, Fearon and Laitin argue that "other things being equal, political democracy should be associated with less discrimination and repression along cultural or other lines, since democracy endows citizens with a political power (the vote) they do not have in dictatorship" (2003, 79).

10. The data and the codebook can be found at http://dvn.iq.harvard.edu/dvn/dv/epr /faces/study/StudyPage.xhtml?globalId=hdl:1902.1/11796&tab=files&studyListingIndex=0 _038423516cef4f8d7855ab866ca5.

11. Stata 11.0 is used for estimation. The Stata command for Fearon and Laitin's single equation logit model is logit and for Keshk's simultaneous equations model is cdsimeq.

12. The pseudo R^2 is 0.092; this is slightly smaller than Fearon and Laitin's (i.e., 0.108) due to a different total number of observations. This study uses 6,214 observations, 113 less observations than Fearon and Laitin's. The data availability for the national capabilities variable, which is used at the first stage of simultaneous equations in Models 2 and 3, lessens the number of observations.

13. Fixed-effects models can examine the determinants of within-country variability. When country fixed effects are considered for Model 1, the results are drastically changed. For example, per capita income becomes insignificant while ethnicity becomes significant with a wrong sign. This is because more than 58 percent of the total observations are dropped in the estimation process, resulting in a biased logit analysis. This is not surprising given the warning of Schneider, Barbieri, and Gleditsch (2003, 22): fixed-effects logit "does not seem ideal for binary dependent variables whose one outcome represents a rare event," thereby leading to a dramatic loss of observations. For this reason, the rest of this study does not employ country fixed effects.

14. If any instrumental variable is not exogenous, then simultaneous equation models will be inconsistent in large samples. If simultaneous equation models are inconsistent, then they will fail to produce estimates that are close to the true value of the population parameter, even if the sample size is large. See Greene (2003) and Wooldridge (2009) for a detailed discussion of tests for instrument exogeneity.

15. If the instruments are irrelevant or weak, then simultaneous equation models will be inconsistent in large samples. Also, they will not have an asymptotic normal distribution; therefore hypothesis tests will not be valid (Staiger and Stock 1997; Stock 2002).

16. To check for instrument relevance, Miguel, Satyanath, and Sergenti's (2004, 735) study relies on the F-statistic and cites Staiger and Stock's study (1997).

17. Vreeland's X-POLITY variable is a sum of XCONST, XRCOMP, and XROPEN, leaving out PARCOMP and PARREG.

18. Since there is no substantive difference between democracy and X-POLITY, the subsequent analysis in this study is confined to democracy in order to be consistent with Fearon and Laitin's original study; this choice should assuage the concern that different results are due to the use of X-POLITY over democracy.

19. The democracy variable in Model 1 is set at time $t-1$, which is the same as in Fearon and Laitin's model specification. When democracy at time t is used instead of $t-1$, no substantive changes are reported with respect to the significance level and the coefficient sign.

20. The onset of the civil war variable in the ethnicity equation of the first stage is significant with a positive sign. This finding is in line with Fearon's (2006, 856) contention that "[civil] violence can have powerful effects on the politicization of ethnicity." The inclusion of the per capita income variable is based on Easterly and Levine's (1997, 1237–39) findings that income is negatively associated with ethnicity and is operationalized with the 1964 *Atlas Narodov Mira*. As expected, the per capita income variable achieves significance with a negative sign.

21. However, Mousseau's (2001) study finds that ethnic divisions alone are not enough to increase the risk of political violence.

22. The data set is publicly available at http://www-management.wharton.upenn.edu /henisz/.

23. Due to the presence of multicollinearity, the legislative veto players measure is not included in the democracy equation of the first stage in Models 2 and 3 in Table 1. Because both veto players and democracy are operationalized with the same data source (Polity) the correlation is 0.84. A severe multicollinearity problem is suspected when the correlation exceeds 0.80 (see Greene 2003).

24. Due to the data availability of legislative veto players, the total number of observations in Model 2 is reduced from 6,214 to 6,002.

25. Fearon, Kasara, and Laitin's (2007) single equation logit Model 6 is replicated because it is pointed to as the most problematic model of Cederman and Girardin's (2009) study. Fearon, Kasara, and Laitin's rejoinder to Cederman and Girardin states: "Worse, Model 6 shows that when we recode Syria as having a minority EGIP, which seems at least as plausible as CG's coding, the estimate for N* falls by a factor of three and is statistically insignificant" (189).

26. The total number of observations in Model 5 is 3,160 because the sample is a subset of Fearon and Laitin's original data set. Cederman and Girardin (2009, 178) explain that "due to the limited data availability for the N* index, we focus on the Eurasian and North African cases only."

27. The 18 countries are Bahamas, Barbados, Cape Verde, Comoros, Dominica, Grenada, Hong Kong, Iceland, Luxembourg, Malta, Samoa, Seychelles, Solomon Islands, St. Lucia, St. Vincent and the Grenadines, Suriname, Tonga, and Vanuatu.

28. The correlation between ethnic polarization and fractionalization is 0.45.

29. Bueno de Mesquita (2005) argues that because religion is endogenous to civil war, a single equation model produces biased and inconsistent estimates that make correct inference impossible.

30. For the purposes of comparison, Model 10 in Table 1.2 uses the same model specification as Model 1 in Table 1.2 and Model 3 in Table 1.1. When the variable for legislative veto players is included in Table 1.2 in place of that representing national capabilities in Model 10, its coefficient sign is negative, and it is statistically significant at the 0.001 level.

31. Blattman and Miguel (2009, 2) suspect endogeneity between per capita income and internal political conflict (see also Sobek 2010). When per capita income is excluded from Models 2, 4, 6, and 8 in Table 1.4 to account for Blattman and Miguel's concern, democracy, religion, and ethnicity are all significant at the 0.001 level. The sign of the coefficient for each

of the first two variables is negative, and that for the last is positive, again verifying the main findings of the present study. To save space, the detailed results are not reported.

32. Similar arguments are made in Kaufmann (1996) and Fearon and Laitin (2000).

33. As noted earlier, this study conducts several empirical tests to establish the existence of endogeneity, as well as to verify the validity of the instrumental variables used within the simultaneous equations systems.

Chapter 2. Capitalist Peace, Democratic Peace, and International War

A slightly different version of this chapter appeared in Seung-Whan Choi, "Re-Evaluating Capitalist and Democratic Peace Models," *International Studies Quarterly* 55, no. 3 (2011): 759–69.

1. Other challenges to the democratic peace have emerged (e.g., Choi 2010a; Choi and James 2007). A recent exemplar is Mousseau (2013b), who argues that contract-intensive economies create societal norms that promote peace better than democratic institutions. However, Dafoe, Oneal, and Russett (2013) and Ray (2013) refute the findings of Mousseau for theoretical and empirical reasons and confirm the significance of the democratic governance.

2. One may argue that the democratic peace is primarily concerned with the escalation of disputes and not their onset (see Chan 1997); however, this study follows Gartzke's step to allow for a comparison between the findings.

3. Gartzke's replication data file is available at http://dss.ucsd.edu/~egartzke/.

4. Beck, Katz, and Tucker's warning is that "the costs of incorrectly imposing duration dependence are, at a minimum, inefficiency and incorrect standard errors, and in some complicated cases may even lead to inconsistent parameter estimates" (1998, 1269).

5. Although the other variables in the democratic peace model might be measured with error, the possibility is not discussed in this study because they do not directly alter the significance of the democracy variable.

6. When the measurement error is corrected, Oneal and Russett's basic result appears to remain significant, though not as much as before. Note that in response to Mousseau's (2013b) economic peace model, Dafoe, Oneal, and Russett (2013) and Ray (2013) make a similar discussion of the measurement error.

7. Appendix 2.1 shows a replication of Gartzke's Models 1 through 4 in Table 1 (2007, 177). There is a discrepancy between the replication and Gartzke's reporting. The replication shows that the Trade Dep.(Low) variable is significant at the 0.01 level in Model 1, at the 0.05 level in Model 2, and at the 0.05 level in Model 3. On the contrary, Gartzke's study reports the insignificance of the Trade Dep.(Low) variable and contends that the introduction of Fin. Open. (Low) causes Trade Dep.(Low) to become statistically insignificant. However, the replication results should not be given too much credit because all the models are misspecified due to the absence of a peace year variable. Appendix 2.2 corrects the omitted variable bias by adding a complete set of peace years (i.e., peace years, spline1, spline2, and spline3). Unsurprisingly, the Democracy(Low) variable becomes significant across all four models, as noted earlier.

8. To isolate the effect of wealth on likely subjects of territorial aggression, Gartzke's study employs an interaction term between economic development and contiguity. Economic development is expected to increase the likelihood of a dispute and is noted as GDPPC(Low), which measures the lower of the two populations weighted by gross domestic product statistics for a given dyad. Contiguity is hypothesized to increase the likelihood of a dispute and is represented by a dichotomous variable with "1" for dyadic partners that share a land border or

that are separated by fewer than 150 miles of water. The interaction variable, GDPPC * Contig., is expected to decrease the likelihood of a dispute. Thus, GDPPC(Low) and GDPPC * Contig. should both be significant but in opposite directions.

9. Interestingly, the regional dummies are not included in Gartzke's most complete capitalist model (i.e., Model 5) "to show that the combined influence of liberal economic variables does not depend on the presence of controls for regional heterogeneity" (178).

10. To avoid confusion of the significance level, the magnitude of the coefficient on the GDPPC * Contig. variable and its standard error is reported in five decimal places, −0.00027 and 0.00022, respectively. The p value is 0.210.

11. The Stata command, "intgph," is used to draw Figure 2.1. The command estimates a selected nonlinear model that includes a multiplicative interaction term and uses simulated parameters generated by King, Tomz, and Wittenberg's (2000) "estsimp" command (part of the "Clarify" suite of commands) to evaluate and graphically portray the effect of one interacted variable conditional on different values of the other interacted variable (Zelner 2009).

Chapter 3. A Reanalysis of the Selectorate Model

1. Bueno de Mesquita et al.'s (2003) *The Logic of Political Survival* has emerged as one of the most influential works in the discipline of political science (see Kennedy 2009).

2. Democracy refers to the democracy-autocracy variable of Polity (i.e., the composite democracy score on the 21-point scale). The residuals of democracy are created by regressing the democracy variable on the size of the winning coalition (and the size of the selectorate) and then saving the residuals (see Clarke and Stone 2008, 388n3).

3. Although changes in suffrage can be another democratic concept, Polity oddly fails to consider this. Svolik (2008, 156), for example, considers a country to be a democracy if at least 50 percent of adult men have the right to vote, if free multiparty elections are held to elect the legislature, and if the executive is elected in popular elections and is directly accountable to voters or an elected legislature.

4. Another important assumption of the fixed-effects model is that such time-invariant characteristics are unique to the individual unit and should not be correlated with other individual characteristics. More specifically, fixed effects are used to consider the fact that each country or region has its own unique characteristics that impact or bias the predictor or outcome variables. Of course, as they are unobservable, unique characteristics are not easily quantifiable and, thus, are left within the error term. The political system of a particular country or within a particular region could, for example, have some impact on W or health care quality. Because fixed effects discern the unobserved but constant characteristics of the error term, they allow researchers to assess a predictor's net effect without worry about a potential correlation between predictor and error term (Green, Kim, and Yoon 2001; Wooldridge 2002; Greene 2003).

5. Similar applications can be found in Equation 2 in Acemoglu et al. (2005, 46) and in Equation 1 in Acemoglu et al. (2008, 814).

6. The selectorate model identifies six geographic regions: Europe, South and Central America, North America and the Caribbean, Asia, the Middle East, and Africa.

7. Morrow et al.'s Stata do-file indicates that the selectorate model for education expenditures, for instance, is issued in the following way: xtreg educexpend w exconstal, fe i(regyr) where i(regyr) controls for fixed effects of an interaction of region and year (see http://politics .as.nyu.edu/object/retesting_smith.html).

8. All the empirical results in this section are obtained by using Morrow et al.'s replication materials. Stata 11.0 is used for estimation.

9. Interestingly, among the 31 original selectorate models, the war (interstate or civil) model alone is built to control for country fixed effects instead of region-year interaction fixed effects. Bueno de Mesquita et al. (2003, 184) contend that since most wars "occur within the specific context of a region-year" (i.e., between neighboring countries), region-year fixed effects would, by construction, remove all of the variance of interest. This contention is contradictory to their previous claim: the rationale for region-year fixed effects was to "[make their] tests especially demanding [by removing] any temporal and spatial factors that might be the actual explanation for shifts in the values of [their] dependent variables" (Bueno de Mesquita et al. 2003, 137). As expected, when this study implements region-year interaction fixed effects instead of country fixed effects, W fails to achieve significance.

10. In their "Dirty Pool" article, Green, Kim, and Yoon (2001, 442) also argue that "analyses of pooled cross-section data that make no allowance for fixed unobserved differences between [countries] often produce biased results."

11. For an application of three-way fixed effects, see Abowd, Kramarz, and Margolis (1999).

Chapter 4. Examining the Predictability of the Selectorate Theory

1. At the outset, it should be clear that the introduction of civil liberties does not claim to directly address all concerns about the selectorate model. Other institutional and cultural factors may affect the provision of public goods, including but not limited to existing laws, norms, and whether social welfare is viewed as a public or a family responsibility.

2. Thomson et al. (2012) find that the extent to which parties fulfill specific electoral manifestos in ten countries varies cross-country, and that within-country variation exists according to the status and composition of government, type of pledges, and socioeconomic conditions.

3. Bueno de Mesquita, Smith, et al. (2003, 73) point out that "democracy is generally associated with a variety of characteristics, of which coalition size is but one." Bueno de Mesquita, Morrow, et al.'s (2004, 364) footnote goes a step further, stating that "we use the phrase large coalition and the term democracy interchangeably to improve readability."

4. The contrasting concepts of policy demanders and policy suppliers were originally developed by political economists in an attempt to explain the choice of economic institutions. For more details, see Bernhard, Broz, and Clark (2002).

5. The statistic of 29 percent is calculated by identifying all the observations whose Polity composite score is smaller than 6 and whose executive constraint level ranges from 5 (i.e., substantial limitations) to 6 (i.e., intermediate category) to 7 (i.e., executive parity or subordination). The cutoff value of 6 for the Polity composite indicator follows the conventional practice (e.g., Dixon 1994). The choice of the three highest levels of executive constraint follows Marshall and Jaggers's (2007) criterion for the presumed democratic checks and balances that should exhibit a *substantial* degree in each polity. Marshall and Jaggers operationally define "a mature and internally coherent democracy" in which "(a) [its] political participation is fully competitive, (b) [its] executive recruitment is elective, and (c) [its] constraints on the chief executive are *substantial*" (14).

6. All the empirical results in this section are obtained with the use of Morrow et al.'s replication materials, which are available at http://politics.as.nyu.edu/object/retesting_smith.html.

7. The note can be found in "Why Do Clarke and Stone Find What They Do," http://politics.as.nyu.edu/docs/IO/8146/clarke_stone.pdf.

8. As noted, both executive constraints and civil liberties are measured on a seven-point scale, while *W* is on a five-point scale. Interestingly, although both executive constraints and civil liberties are on the same scale, the former fails to outperform *W*, while the latter outweighs *W* in Model 2 in Table 4.1. The conceptual distinction between executive constraints and civil liberties may have contributed to the difference in results. Since executive constraints are not an ideal measure of democracy, Morrow et al.'s analysis may have found no empirical evidence.

9. Categories 5, 6, and 7 include fewer countries than do the other categories.

10. The statistic of 0.5 percent is calculated by identifying all the observations whose Polity composite score is smaller than 6 and whose civil liberties range from 0.83 to 1 on a scale of 0 to 1.

Chapter 5. Democracy, Foreign Direct Investment, and Outliers

This chapter is a revised and expanded version of Seung-Whan Choi, 2009, "The Effect of Outliers on Regression Analysis: Regime Type and Foreign Direct Investment," *Quarterly Journal of Political Science* 4, no. 2 (2009): 153–165.

1. For more FDI studies, see Chan and Mason (1992); Oneal (1994); Ahlquist (2006); Blanton and Blanton (2006, 2007); Choi and Samy (2008).

2. The use of simulated data to demonstrate the impact of influential observations is also found in Belsley, Kuh, and Welsch (1980); Agresti and Finlay (1997); and Hamilton (2004).

3. The numbers in parentheses are standard errors.

4. Like many other major political science journals including *American Political Science Review* and the *Journal of Politics, International Organization* does not require the authors to deposit or post their data and statistical programs on the official website. However, both Li and Jensen were kind enough to provide me with their data for replications.

5. When country fixed effects are instead used for estimation, the results are similar to the main findings reported below.

6. The choice of Li and Resnick's model specification and estimation method is also intended to assuage the potential criticism that the use of a different research design is what has led to my conclusion in favor of Jensen's findings.

7. Component-plus-residual plots and CERES plots are, however, both regarded as superior tools for the detection of nonlinearity.

8. The grid lines in the plotting region help to gauge the distance from the mean of the residuals to each outlier.

9. This means that the 1992–1995 observations are not the only ones that could have led to the negative relationship; other observations could have contributed to it as well, but the 1992–1995 observations were large enough to do it on their own.

10. Other influential outlier diagnostics such as DFITS, Cook's Distance, and Welsch Distance led to a similar conclusion but are not discussed here to save space (see Welsch and Kuh 1977; Cook 1977; Welsch 1982).

11. The level of democracy in Botswana for 1978 is 18 on a scale of 0 (least democratic) to 20 (most democratic).

12. In order to save space, I do not discuss detailed estimation methods about robust regression. More information can be found in Western (1995); Rogowski and Kayer (2002); Hamilton (2004).

13. The Stata program for robust regression does not produce R^2.

14. The FDI data in the two original studies were obtained from the same source, World Bank, World Development Indicators, 1999.

15. Again, both studies use Polity as the data source for their democracy variables.

16. One may contend that in Li and Resnick's original model, the sign of LEVEL OF DEMOCRACY turns out to be negative after controlling for property rights protection. Li and Resnick's model was reexamined without PROPERTY RIGHTS PROTECTION. Appendix 5.1 reports the results that corroborate findings in Tables 5.3, 5.4, and 5.5; democracy is positively related with FDI.

17. The following analogy should be helpful in further understanding the choice of the FDI/GDP ratio over the FDI/dollar measure. I hypothesize that girls like chocolate pies more than boys do and so build a statistical model using the number of pies eaten and gender. Unfortunately, I report counterintuitive results that boys eat more chocolate pies than girls do, so I conclude that boys, not girls, like pies more. One might argue that the research design is flawed because without considering the average stomach size of each gender group, I cannot be certain of the relationship. It may be that boys eat more pies than girls simply because their stomachs can hold more pies. Whether I can accept the gender difference (i.e., regime type) is directly related to whether a control for the difference of stomach size (i.e., GDP) is taken into account. By looking into the mere number of pies eaten (i.e., FDI dollar amounts), I cannot be sure of the real impact of gender.

Chapter 6. Explaining the Foreign Direct Investment-Democracy Controversy: Normality of Regression Residuals

1. For a counterargument to Choi's conclusion, see Li's (2009) study.

2. In Jarque and Bera's (1987, 164) words, "in all, violation of the normality assumption may lead to the use of suboptimal estimators, invalid inferential statements and to inaccurate conclusions, highlighting the importance of testing the validity of the assumption."

3. When the effect of democracy using other data sources such as the Freedom House (2009) and Cheibub, Gandhi, and Vreeland (2010) is tested, I find no substantive change, so the results are not reported below in the interest of saving space.

4. The publication of the Polity data set has made it possible for the researcher to overcome the limitation of a dichotomous measure of democracy, which, due to the lack of more refined measures, was a common practice in the not so distant past (Oneal and Ray 1997, 754).

5. FDI net inflows are defined as the net inflows of investment that acquire a lasting management interest in a business firm operating in a country other than that of the investor.

6. Normal distribution is defined as a continuous probability density function roughly characterizing a random variable that is the sum of a large number of independent random events; it is usually represented by a smooth bell-shaped curve symmetric about the mean (Gujarati 2003).

7. However, Li and Resnick (2003, 200) are critical of the use of FDI/GDP because they believe that it measures the relative importance of FDI to a country's economy rather than FDI inflows per se.

8. Although Li (2009) advocates the utility of the log transformation with a minimum constant value, Choi (2009) counters that the strategy is not well conceived because it is contrary to the nature of FDI data, which can assume either positive, negative, or zero values; it also fails to account for the scale of an economy.

9. Following Li's (2009, 174) contention that "a model of FDI/GDP does not allow us to separate the respective effects of an independent variable on FDI and GDP," I do not include

a market-size variable (i.e., log of GDP). Further, according to Jakobsen and de Soysa's (2006) study, the effect of exchange rate volatility is not robust across different model specifications. For this reason, I exclude exchange rate volatility as a control. When market size and exchange rate are included, the results do not substantively deviate from those reported below.

Achen (2002) proposes a "rule of three" for a more precise empirical analysis. Too many independent variables in regression analyses tend to produce results that are not robust from one model specification to another. Thus, researchers should use no more than three variables on the right-hand side of a regression equation in the absence of a formal theory. According to the rule of three criterion, the results reported in existing studies of FDI may be considered spurious. As a robustness check, I limit myself to three key independent variables (e.g., democracy, economic growth, and terrorism) and find results similar to those reported in the next section. The results are not reported here to save space, but they can be obtained from the author upon request.

10. I also operationalize political instability with the composite index from Banks' (2010) data set of political events that include coups, revolutions, assassinations, riots, and general strikes. Because it turns out to be insignificant, it is not reported in this study. Li and Resnick (2003, 197) also find that "political instability has the expected negative sign in all four models in Table 1, but is not statistically significant in any of them." Büthe and Milner (2008, 749) report that "POLITICAL INSTABILITY is estimated to reduce FDI, though the effect is in model 2 not quite significant at conventional levels." The insignificance of political instability is not surprising given Jakobsen and de Soysa's (2006, 392) observation that "political risk analysts have consistently questioned the value of focusing too heavily on political instability on the grounds that such instability happens infrequently, does not necessarily lead to policy changes of relevance to foreign investors, and hence does not always pose a significant risk to MNCs (multinational corporations) (Kobrin 1979, Oseghale 1993, Poynter 1985, Schneider and Frey 1985)."

11. As noted in note 19, I also control for year and decade dummies.

12. Simple regression models show the positive effect of FDI on economic growth or economic development, which indicates a potential endogeneity bias.

13. Stata 11 is used for empirical analysis.

14. These two tests are performed for the full model. For example, when the dependent variable is net FDI inflows in dollars, the independent variables are democracy, economic growth, economic development, regime durability, terrorism, and post–Cold War.

15. The Stata command is "xtpcse" with two options: pairwise and corr(ar1).

16. A Pearson product-moment correlation analysis shows that regardless of the operational measure of FDI, none of the seven measures is negatively associated with the democracy variable. This implies that as the quality of democratic institutions improves, foreign investors tend to invest more because democratic countries offer credible and consistent investment policies that facilitate business operations for the maximization of profits (see Jensen 2003).

Multicollinearity may be suspected among the independent variables. This study has conducted three sets of rigorous diagnostic tests for multicollinearity: variance inflation factors, R^2 statistics, and eigenvalues and condition index (see Belsley, Kuh, and Welsch, 1980; Gujarati, 2003). None of these tests indicates severe multicollinearity. These results are not surprising given that a simple correlation analysis indicates a low strength of relationship between any two key variables. For instance, the correlation between democracy and economic growth is −0.0043; that between democracy and economic development is 0.3321; and that between economic growth and development is 0.0455.

17. Although the smallest value is −0.308, the second smallest value turns out to be 21.923, which is very close to the mean, 22.885.

18. One may claim that the presence or absence of China in the sample is a related issue since it attracts a huge amount of FDI. When rerunning the seven regression models after excluding the China observations, I found virtually the same results: the beneficial effect of democracy is revealed in only the last three models.

19. As a robustness check, I also use fixed-effects linear models with an AR(1) disturbance. The Stata command for the within estimator for fixed-effects models is "xtregar" with fe. The results are similar to those in Table 6.6 and can be obtained from the author upon request. When year and decade fixed effects are tested to account for the unique effect of the time period on FDI, the results are similar to those of country fixed effects as far as the effect of democracy is concerned.

20. As shown at the bottom of Table 6.7, the consistency of the Arellano-Bond GMM estimator is verified insofar as there is no second-order serial correlation in the residuals of the differenced specification. The overall appropriateness of the instruments is also confirmed by a Sargan test of over-identifying restrictions.

21. Drawing on Fisher-type tests, which take as their null hypothesis the assumption that all the panels contain a unit root (Choi 2001), I find that net FDI inflows in dollars, log (FDI + a minimum), and FDI/population violate the assumption of stationarity. Taking the first difference of these three measures resolves the violation (Wooldridge 2002; Gujarati 2003).

Chapter 7: Terrorism and Zero-Inflated Negative Binomial Regression

1. The four studies of Savun and Phillips (2009), Piazza (2011), Hoffman, Shelton, and Cleven (2013), and Santifort-Jordan and Sandler (2014) are mentioned here because they use ZINB regression as the main empirical models.

2. This study refrains from using statistical notations and proofs for purposes of parsimonious presentation. For technical details, see Lambert (1992); Cameron and Trivedi (1998); Hall (2000); Long and Freese (2006); Hilbe (2007).

3. The Stata command is "nbreg" for cross-national data and "xtnbreg" for cross-national, time-series data.

4. The Stata command is "zinb" for cross-national data; however, no Stata command is found for cross-national, time-series data. The latter is also an indication that zinb is not programmed to handle longitudinal data. Yet, previous studies of terrorism invoked the Stata command zinb to fit their longitudinal data without any precautionary measures.

5. However, it would be questionable to include executive constraints and democratic participation in the same model, as their correlation is 0.84, according to Table 2 (38). Given their high correlation, these two variables are virtually the same measure and so cannot exert independent effects on the outcome variable. The present study notes that in Table 2, where the two variables appear in the same model, Hoffman, Shelton, and Cleven's study claims to follow Li's (2005) approach. However, Li's executive constraints and democratic participation are not highly correlated (0.56) in his empirical models.

6. Using CINC as a proxy for press attention is odd because "CINC is not normally used as a proxy for press attention" (Hoffman, Shelton, and Cleven 2013, 901) and because the composite index for national material capabilities is likely to pick up politico-military factors rather than press attention.

7. Piazza's replication materials can be found at http://www.prio.org/JPR/Datasets/.

8. Replication materials were obtained from the authors.

9. To borrow Drakos and Gofas' (2006b, 81) phrase, "the applicability of a Zero-Inflated model could be defended simply on the basis of statistical reasoning."

Chapter 8. Democracy and Transnational Terrorism Revisited

Some parts of this chapter appeared in Seung-Whan Choi, "Fighting Terrorism through the Rule of Law?," *Journal of Conflict Resolution* 54, no. 6 (2010b): 940–66.

1. Ironically, the Bush administration and its defenders simultaneously argued in favor of some undemocratic practices, such as secret wiretapping of American citizens, as effective tools with which to challenge terrorist activity.

2. It should be noted that I do not discuss whether market civilization respects or disrespects the rule of law (on market civilization, see Mousseau 2002/3, 2011), because the focus of this study is on how the rule of law, as a predictor, affects international terrorism.

3. Estimation problems related to zero-inflated negative binomial regression are discussed in chapter 7.

4. The reader will notice my insistence on the use of the term *liberal* when referring to the "liberal democratic rule of law." This is done in anticipation of concerns about the controversial nature of the rule of law in respect to democratic decision making. It is not hard to imagine a theory of democracy in which popular sovereignty is seen as ruling supreme over any codified or traditional sense of governing law; indeed, it is the sovereignty of popular decision making over law that defines the radical democratic ideal, following in the tradition of Rousseau. By using the term *liberal democracy*, I refer both to the dominant practice of constitutional democratic governance in the twentieth century and to a theoretical account of democracy in which the rule of law is seen as an integral component.

5. This is an important and nuanced point that deserves clarification. On the one hand, the subjects of law cannot be seen as completely voluntary adherents. If law were a completely voluntary obligation, then it would not need the coercive dimension that we understand it to have; without coercion, law is rendered a mere suggestion, or, as Thomas Hobbes (1985, 223) famously put it: "Covenants, without the sword, are but Words." On the other hand, as Rawls (1971/1999, 211) pointed out, we cannot take the authoritarian account of law offered by Hobbes wholesale: "While a coercive mechanism is necessary, it is obviously essential to define precisely the tendency of its operations." That is, if laws were simply the whim of the sword wielder, there would be no reason to follow these laws except for the threat of punishment; we would eventually find the incentives to revolt against such tyranny overwhelming. Therefore, the democratic rule of law cannot simply mean the legal coercion of citizens but must also imply some public understanding and acknowledgment of the "tendency of law's operations." For the purposes of this study, I contend that this is achieved when the coercive element of law is somehow linked up with, and justified by, a notion of public autonomy relevant to our intuitions concerning democracy. In this sense, an effective and legitimate rule of law obtains when there is a middle ground between, or coexistence of, pure voluntary adherence to law and pure submission to legal coercion. In this middle ground, laws are seen as legitimate; this entails the recognition of, if not the voluntary subscription to, laws as sovereign in political and social proceedings insofar as they are produced in some non-arbitrary fashion and are adjudicated and processed by fair and impartial judicial systems. In short, the democratic rule of law means that citizens voluntarily subscribe to the legal system even when they are coerced to act in accord with individual laws.

6. One may argue that democratic citizens and elected officials may be heavily implicated in terrorism abroad, especially in nondemocratic countries regarded as illegitimate and dangerous. Although this possibility appears to be at odds with my line of reasoning, it is exceptional because only a few major powers like the United States could carry out such "preventive or extreme measures" (see Barber 2003; Hobsbawm 2007). More importantly, this possibility should be referred to as state or state-sponsored terrorism, which is beyond

my conceptualization of terrorism since I only focus upon those transnational terrorist acts committed by individuals or subnational groups.

7. A few exceptional cases may be found in some countries such as Singapore, where a stable authoritarian rule is the norm, but where the level of transnational terrorism is relatively low. This is because the trust between the government and its citizens (including its Muslim citizens) has been built over time (OnIslam & News Agencies 2009). That is, Singaporeans believe that they can rely on the domestic legal systems to settle claims and so do not feel the need to turn to political violence.

8. Li's statistical programs and data are available at http://jcr.sagepub.com/content/vol49 /issue2/.

9. Although the University of Maryland–based Global Terrorism Database at http://jcr .sagepub.com/content/vol49/issue2/ may be considered an alternative source, it does not distinguish transnational terrorism from domestic terrorism, and it has no reliable data for 1993 due to a mismanaged data transfer (Global Terrorism Database 2009).

10. For a more general discussion about underreporting bias, see Drakos and Gofas (2006a). It should be noted that the ITERATE database is not used in Drakos and Gofas' analysis. They instead examine the National Memorial Institute for the Prevention of Terrorism (MIPT) Knowledge Base and conclude that it may represent an understatement of the true number of terrorist incidents.

11. Although it is important to learn how large a percentage of the incidents in the ITERATE data set potentially falls into the category of domestic terrorism, there is no clear way of identifying these incidences because of the ambiguity of the coding rule. Mickolus (1982, 20) states, "sources are often vague regarding the actual name of the [terrorist] organization responsible, or unclear about the amount of legally acceptable evidence pointing to responsibility." Despite these drawbacks, I believe that the ITERATE data set is adequate to test the rule of law hypothesis because the effect of a few domestic incidents is likely to be marginal and because the data have been widely used in the existing terrorism literature (see Li and Schaub 2004; Enders and Sandler 2006). In fact, if all the terrorist incidents that occurred within Israel, Puerto Rico, and the UK are treated as missing data in empirical tests on the suspicion of the measurement error, my preliminary results indicate that the significance level of the democratic rule of law variable actually turns out to be higher than what is reported in the next section.

12. Although the World Bank's (2008) Worldwide Governance Indicators provide another source of a rule of law measure, its data collection is limited, as it begins in 1996.

13. Unlike Li's hypothesis, recent studies of Mousseau (2011, 2002/3) argue that feelings of income inequality are unlikely associated with support for terrorism.

14. Note that if the $p < 0.05$ level were used as the minimal standard for the significance tests, the main hypothesis about the rule of law would still be supported across all the models in the results that follow. Note that robust z-statistics are reported in parentheses below each coefficient.

15. Li reported that while the democratic participation variable is statistically significant at the 0.05 level, the government constraint variable is statistically significant at the 0.01 level (288). As in Li's findings, the government capability and conflict variables are significant, but not in the predicted direction.

16. When I reran Li's (2005, 288) Model 1 with his original data from 1984 to 1997, the democratic participation variable was statistically significant at the 0.10 level, but the government constraint variable was not.

17. The correlation between the rule of law and democratic participation is 0.61. A severe multicollinearity problem is suspected if and only if the correlation exceeds 0.80 (see Greene

2003; Gujarati 2003). The correlation between the rule of law and government constraint is 0.53.

18. Among the control variables, the changing effect of the economic development variable is intriguing because it is significant in Model 1 but not significant in Models 2 and 3. It may be that economic development, which is dependent on a stable legal environment, is subsumed by the rule of law variable. The correlation between the rule of law and economic development is 0.69.

19. The same results are also found with Li's (2005, 288) Model 2 during the original study period from 1975 to 1997.

20. Li's (2005, 288) Model 3 in Table 1 shows that both democratic participation and government constraints are statistically significant, while press freedom is not. However, when the past incident variable is excluded from Li's Model 3, democratic participation and press freedom are no longer supported, while government constraint is.

21. One may argue that there are collinearity problems among the four democracy-related variables. To alleviate this concern, I run another model where the rule of law variable is included, but the other three democracy-related variables are excluded. The magnitude of the negative coefficient and the z-score for the rule of law variable are slightly increased, at the same time showing the beneficial effect of the rule of law for the decrease of transnational terrorism. The correlation matrix shows the strength of 0.61 between the rule of law and democratic participation, 0.53 between the rule of law and government constraint, and 0.56 between the rule of law and press freedom.

22. I am grateful to the reviewer for the comment. However, it should be noted that the relationship between contract-intensive economies and rule of law is found to be statistically insignificant according to the study of Beck and Webb (2003, 66–67), the original compiler of the life insurance contracting data.

23. Due to the missing values in Mousseau's (2013a) data collection, Table 8.2 includes 1,227 total observations, which is 27 fewer than in Table 8.1.

24. To address the excessive zeros problem, another robustness test is performed with rare event logit developed by Tomz, King, and Zeng (1999), expanded upon by King and Zeng (2001), and recently used in Wade and Reiter's (2007) study on suicide terrorism. The results are similar to those of zero-inflated negative binomial regression.

Chapter 9. Old Habits Die Hard

1. At the outset, it should be clear that the focus of this study is indiscriminate political violence that takes place before the outbreak of civil war; it does not discuss brutality at the hands of the government or rebel forces during the internal war period. For determinants of state repression during civil war, see Kalyvas (2006) and Kim (2010).

2. There are also, of course, examples in which a domestic police force uses excessive force against its civilian population. For instance, SAVAK, Iran's secret police, systematically suppressed Pahlavi's opponents before the Iranian Revolution. Although security policemen sometimes employ unnecessary violence against dissident groups, their use of force is usually not as harsh as that of the military.

3. Some case studies may, however, beg to differ with this contention. While repression may drive civilians away from the regime, they only become rebels once the group has amassed the resources sufficient to offset a civilian's risk of participation in the dissident group and to demonstrate an ability to effectively challenge the regime (Wood 2003).

4. Looking at American civil-military relations, some studies suggest the opposite relationship, i.e., civilian hawks and military doves (e.g., Huntington 1957; Betts 1991; Feaver and Gelpi 2004). The American case may be an exception due to its long history of civilian supremacy over the military. In other words, this study emphasizes the overall tendency, across countries and over a long time period, for military leaders to act hawkishly and for civilian leaders to act dovishly.

5. In Davenport's (1995) work, political repression measures the limitation of the news media and the political restrictions imposed upon citizens and political parties.

6. Gurses and Mason's (2010, 148) empirical research, however, shows that personalist or neopatrimonial regimes are more prone to civil war onset than are any other type, including military regimes.

7. The argument does not deny that some civilian leaders will also commit political violence against civilian populations by ordering the military to do so. However, this occurs much less frequently in the case of civilian leadership than that of military leadership.

8. To be specific, data on the number of civilian deaths are currently unavailable for the purposes of this study. Although some data sources for civilian deaths, such as genocide and politicide from the Political Instability Task Force (2007), are available, they are not useful for this study since they provide information on the number of people killed during, rather than prior to, civil wars.

9. The PTS is available online at http://politicalterrorscale.org/ (see Wood and Gibney 2010; Gibney, Cornett, and Wood 2011). The CIRI index of physical integrity rights is available online at http://www.humanrightsdata.com/ (see Cingranelli and Richards 1999, 2010a, 2010b).

10. See the official UCDP/PRIO Armed Conflict Dataset v4-2008 at http://www.prio.no/CSCW/Datasets/Armed-Conflict/UCDP-PRIO/Old-Versions/4-2007/.

11. As Sobek's (2010) study provides useful insights, several recent studies explore different state capacity variables such as government share of consumption and total revenue.

12. The estimated results obtained from logit splines do not substantively deviate from those using a cubic polynomial of time. To save space, the results are not reported here.

13. It is possible that multicollinearity may be suspect among the independent variables. When three sets of rigorous diagnostic tests for multicollinearity (i.e., R^2 statistics, variance inflation factors, eigenvalues, and condition index) are conducted (see Belsley, Kuh, and Welsch 1980; Gujarati 2003), none of the tests indicates severe multicollinearity.

14. Models 3 through 6 in Appendix Table 9.1 show results obtained after having included four additional predictors at the first stage. The significant, positive effect of the repression predicted variable at the second stage remains the same.

15. Following the warning of Schneider, Barbieri, and Gleditsch (2003, 22) that fixed-effects logit "does not seem ideal for binary dependent variables whose one outcome represents a rare event," this study does not employ fixed-effects logistic regression models. Because of this shortcoming, the fixed-effects logit leads to a dramatic loss of observations, resulting in a biased logit analysis.

Chapter 10. Democracy, Status Quo, and Military Manpower Systems

1. Dolman (2004, 27), however, astutely points to a significant, positive effect of military participation as well; evidence from a wide range of states associates it with "the rise of democratic or participatory institutions," with the franchise as the prime example. While this

positive by-product of more extensive military service is acknowledged, the point of departure for the present study is the belief that, with time, the more negative aspects associated with continuous conscription are likely to outweigh the positive side effects, which are expected to decline by definition once political rights such as voting are achieved.

2. Exceptions are Oneal's (1992) analysis of budgetary savings from conscription among NATO members, Choi and James' (2003) analysis of the impact of conscription on interstate disputes, and Pickering's (2011) work on the impact of state military manpower systems on the initiation of both traditional, belligerent military missions and operations other than war.

3. Sociological analysis in recent years also probes a wide range of issues related to force structure, with considerable attention to conscription (Haltiner 1998; Barkawi 2002; Jehn and Selden 2002; Kestnbaum 2002; Møller 2002; Leander 2004). These studies, however, differ from the present investigation in method. The sociological studies take the form of theoretical essays or comparative case studies and provide guidance rather than a paradigm for a cross-national, time-series analysis of aggregate data on conscription vis-à-vis cause and effect.

4. It should be noted that cross-national analysis is often criticized for its static nature.

5. Counter-examples are the Afghanistan War (2001) and Iraq War (2003), where the United States did not use conscripted soldiers. Use of a volunteer military by the United States may be the result of political rather than military considerations; that is, it may be a by-product of the U.S. experience with the Vietnam War (Chambers 1987). Moreover, the extremely high level of U.S. defense spending designates it as a virtually singular actor in world politics with respect to its military preparedness or strength.

6. The hypothesis may not apply to navies in the modern interstate system.

7. This study is aware of Haltiner's (1998, 17) admonition that "it makes little sense to dichotomize conscript systems and all-volunteer systems" (see also Kestnbaum (2002, 128) and Møller (2002, 294–300) for nuances in modes of recruitment and personnel structure, respectively). Haltiner's compelling analysis of European states shows a continuum rather than a dichotomy in terms of force structures; for example, states with a conscription ratio below 50 percent, between 50 and 66 percent, and above 66 percent show important differences from each other that would be hidden by a simple "yes/no" coding (Haltiner 1998, 16–18). In the absence of cross-national, time-series data with this type of nuanced coding, this study proceeds with caution, but also with the hope that the eventual availability of more fine-grained data will produce stronger support for these hypotheses, which in the present study might, in some instances, be held back by significant measurement error for the dependent variable.

8. Zeev Maoz, Dyadic Militarized Interstate Disputes (DYMID1.1) Dataset, Version 1.1, Dyadic MID Codebook (1999): 1–9, downloaded from ftp://spirit.tau.ac.il/zeevmaoz/dyadmid .html. It should be noted that the level of hostility is originally based on Militarized Interstate Disputes (MIDs) data assembled from the Correlates of War Project (see Gochman and Maoz 1984).

9. Dixon (1993, 1994) has standardized this operationalization by calling it the "weak link" assumption. The likelihood of an international dispute within a dyad should be a function primarily of the degree of constraint experienced by the less constrained state (i.e., the smaller value) in each dyad; that is, the less democratic of the two. In the present context, the higher value of military expenditure by percentage in a dyad establishes the "lowest common denominator."

10. See http://liberalarts.oregonstate.edu/spp/polisci/research/inflation-conversion-factors -convert-dollars-1774-estimated-2024-dollars-recent-year for an explanation of this method.

Chapter 11. Selectorate Theory, Democracy, and Terrorism: Null Results

1. Some studies contend that because democracies with high levels of civil liberties promote ideas such as freedom of movement, opinion, expression, and association, they offer terrorist organizations more opportunity to plan and execute their schemes than do non-democracies (e.g., Eubank and Weinberg 2001; LaFree and Ackerman 2009). Other studies, however, assert that since democracies encourage political participation and rule of law, their chances of experiencing illegal terrorist incidents are small (e.g., Eyerman 1998; Li 2005; Choi 2010b).

2. In this study, terrorism is referred to as "the threatened or actual use of illegal force, directed against civilian targets, by non state actors, in order to attain a political goal, through fear, coercion or intimidation" (LaFree and Ackerman 2009, 348).

3. Zero-inflated negative binomial regression is introduced here because it appears to be a popular estimator in existing terrorism studies. Yet, readers should be informed of several estimation problems related to the estimator that are discussed in chapter 7.

4. Although there are other ways to measure a state's efforts to fight terrorism, this study focuses on a simple count of terrorist attacks due to the dearth of longitudinal data on, for example, counterterrorism spending and data mining (see Jonas and Harper 2006; Drakos 2009).

5. One might speculate that although democratic countries present a dramatic response to terror or the threat of terror, those efforts might not always be effective (for reasons such as the technical skill of the terrorists, the inherent difficulties of stopping terrorist attacks in a democracy, or the possibility of blowback); or one could argue that counterterrorism efforts in one place may generate an increase in activity in another area (recall the popular critique of Bush-era terrorism policy). Because no existing data can measure these factors, this study leaves their empirical applications for future research.

6. The availability of data on terrorism, which are compiled only after 1970, and W, the data point of which ends in 1999, limits the number of sample countries as well as the period of study.

7. In fact, the way this study treats terrorism as a combination of domestic and international terrorist events is consistent with that of Morrow et al. (2008, 397); for a more detailed discussion, see Bueno de Mesquita et al.'s (2003, 184–85) definition of war as a combination of civil and interstate wars.

8. It is worth noting that despite the fact that the GTD includes terrorist attacks committed by either individual terrorists or groups, about half of the attacks are unattributable to a specific individual or group due to insufficient information (Dugan 2010). This makes an analysis of terrorist groups extremely challenging.

9. The GTD website can be found at http://www.start.umd.edu/gtd/features/GTD-Data-Rivers.aspx.

10. Despite the comprehensiveness, data for 1993 is missing due to an office move (LaFree and Dugan 2007). For cross-sectional, time-series data analysis to be completed, the missing data are interpolated based on the average of the preceding and subsequent years. With respect to the significance of W and executive constraints, there is no substantive difference between estimations with or without the missing 1993 data. The results can be obtained from the author upon request. Because the GTD relies on newspaper accounts of terrorist activity and because autocratic regimes tend to suppress the freedom of the press, it may contain some inherent limitations and shortcomings (e.g., underreporting bias, see Drakos and Gofas 2006a). However, it should be noted that Drakos and Gofas do not analyze the GTD. Instead they examine the National Memorial Institute for the Prevention of Terrorism (MIPT)

Knowledge Base and conclude that it may represent an understatement of the true number of terrorist incidents. It should also be noted that the GTD does not distinguish between threats and actual incidents.

11. The data on W and executive constraints can be found at http://www.nyu.edu/gsas/dept/politics/data/bdm2s2/Logic.htm.

12. Morrow et al. (2008, 396) write that "we normalize XCONST to fall between 0 to 1 to make its range comparable to our measure of W."

13. Li (2005) presents evidence that freedom of the press is positively associated with international terrorism. However, the preliminary results of this study show that freedom of the press is negatively associated with terrorism. It is significant at the 0.01 level.

14. In addition, as pointed out by Achen (2000), a one-year lagged dependent variable can soak up variation in the dependent variable that attenuates the explanatory power of theoretically interesting independent variables.

15. Fixed-effects estimation is not new in studies of terrorism. Li's (2005) study, for instance, reports a connection between different features of democracy and international terrorism after taking into consideration regional differences. It also should be noted that Morrow et al.'s (2008) study includes the interaction of geographic region and year as a set of fixed-effect dummy variables.

16. Similar sentiment echoes in Kennedy's (2009) study, which casts doubt on the validity of the selectorate theory after examining the relationship between resource endowments and the political survival of authoritarian leaders.

Chapter 12. *The Political Economy of Foreign Direct Investment*

1. Since this study introduces domestic media as one of the key features of democracy, the potential effect of international media on FDI is left for future research. In addition, empirical analysis on international media is not currently plausible due to a lack of systemic data.

2. An implicit assumption of this argument is that leaders will intend to change policies affecting multinationals while the public will voice its disagreement. However, it is also possible that the population may desire a reversal of policy while the politicians resist it. An example is Indonesia under Suharto, who favored certain multinationals that then became the target of an angry public. Similar examples have occurred in democratic countries as well (e.g., Enron's experience in India and Mercedes' experience in the United States).

3. However, there is a possibility that even in democratic regimes, politicians are not simply making policy based on the preferences of voters—interest groups also matter. In addition, global production may temper populist (trade) policies (e.g., Milner and Judkins 2004). These possibilities go beyond the scope of this study and so are left for future research.

4. Multinational corporations may be capable of holding individual leaders politically accountable for policy reversal in the future. Since the focus here is on domestic audience benefits, international audience costs that may arise from multinationals are left for future research.

5. Tufte's (1993, 186) study finds that domestic economic conditions are one of the main determinants of electoral outcomes. It concludes that "the vote cast in midterm congressional elections, then, is a referendum on the performance of the president and his administration's management of the economy."

6. That Carlos Menem's Argentinean government bowed to the principles of the Washington consensus in 1989 is a notable exception. It tried to reinforce its ties to MNCs (multinational corporations) in order to deal with a down economy with hyperinflation.

7. To alleviate a concern that the hypothesized link between democracy and FDI may be driven by advanced industrialized democratic countries, this study uses a sample of seventy developing countries. When the sample is extended to include developed countries, the results are similar to those reported in the following section and may be obtained from the author upon request.

8. Another possible estimation method is fixed effects to control for country-level heterogeneity. However, according to the Hausman's specification test, we cannot reject the null hypothesis that the coefficients estimated by the efficient random-effects estimator are the same as the ones estimated by the consistent fixed-effects estimator. Thus, it is logical to use random effects.

9. It is worth noting that despite the coherent theoretical argument in the existing studies of international relations regarding audience costs, no empirical studies with longitudinal data have directly tested the core argument because no direct measure of audience costs is available.

10. The economic crisis countries that belong to the twenty-fifth percentile are also identified and tested. The results for the twenty-fifth percentile are similar to those for the tenth percentile.

11. Although a measure of debt divided by GNP is tested in Frankel and Rose's study, it fails to show significance in a consistent manner across models. One might argue that inequality is another indicator of economic crisis, assuming a close connection between inequality and economic crisis: a country's economic crisis entails disparities in the distribution of economic assets and income among individuals within a society, which may ignite public anger toward foreign firms. When the Gini-coefficient—the most commonly used measure of inequality in the literature—is incorporated to test this line of reasoning, no statistically meaningful results are produced (for the Gini data, both World Bank [2003 and UNU-WIDER [2008] are consulted). One possible reason for the insignificance is the fact that the Gini-coefficient is merely a measure of the income inequality caused by rapid economic development and is not a direct phenomenon of a nation's economic crisis. In any event, a more fine-grained empirical probe with a further refinement of conceptual reasoning and inequality data should be pursued in future research. Also left for future research is the issue of how different types of autocratic leaders will deal with multinational corporations in times of economic crisis.

12. One might argue for the inclusion of other control variables such as human rights, exchange rate, regional cluster, diffusion effects, and so on. However, as Achen (2002) aptly points out, as the number of independent variables in multivariate regression models increases, some variables may become redundant, making it more difficult to interpret the results. Furthermore, all of the FDI-related predictors may not be essential to the explanation of the variation of inflows of FDI in the first place. This study chooses the seven control variables above because scholars and policy makers alike consider them to be the most common predictors of FDI inflows.

13. This study has conducted three diagnostic tests for muliticollinearity: the R^2 statistic, variance inflation factor (VIF), and tolerance. No serious multicollinearity problem is found between independent variables. The test results may be obtained from the author upon request.

14. The "lincom" command in Stata is used to calculate those statistics.

15. The marginal effect is obtained with Brambor, Clark, and Golder's (2006, 75–76) method.

16. One might contend that a lagged dependent variable should be included as an additional control variable. The sensitivity test with the lagged dependent variable reveals that with respect to random effects, the joint coefficient estimating the effect of domestic audience bene-

fits is −0.891, and its standard error is 0.477, which is significant at the 0.05 level; in terms of GEEs, the joint coefficient is −0.911, and its standard error is 0.345, which is significant at the 0.01 level; in relation to PCSEs, the joint coefficient is −0.931, and its standard error is 0.396, which is also significant at the 0.01 level. The use of a lagged dependent variable, however, is criticized in Achen's (2000) study because it may take up too much variation in the dependent variable that could be explained by other substantive variables.

Chapter 13. The United States Use of Military Force and Terrorism

1. This definition appears to be among the most comprehensive (see Dugan 2010, 9).

2. See http://www.defense.gov/faq/pis/mil_strength.html.

3. Military interventions can be classified into nine different types as follows: a regime or policy change mission (to change or target a political regime or its core policies); a territorial mission (intervention for the acquisition or retention of territory, delineation of frontiers, or the specification of sovereign status); an economic mission (to protect economic or resource interests of self or others); a strategic mission (to maintain regional power balances, stability, or ideological missions stated by the intervener); a domestic political mission (intervention to take sides in a domestic dispute); a socioethnic minority protective mission (to protect a socioethnic faction or minority in the target country); a rebel pursuit mission (pursuing rebel or terrorist forces across borders); a humanitarian mission (to save lives, relieve suffering, or distribute foodstuffs to prevent starvation); and a diplomatic protective mission (an intervention to protect one's own military or diplomatic interests and property inside or outside the target country) (see Pearson and Baumann 1993).

4. Although it is possible to see certain types of interventions as being more regularly associated with increases in domestic terrorism than with increases in international terrorism (and vice versa), this possibility is not explored in this study due to the fact that there is no way to empirically compare the differing magnitudes. Estimated coefficients that are obtained from two different statistical equations for domestic and international terrorism cannot be compared because they are estimated separately.

5. One may ask why certain rebel groups would "forget" their rational/strategic goals of achieving regime or policy change in order to fight against Americans, who may, in fact, share those objectives. This question overlooks the possibility that when U.S. military intervention is perceived as an ultimate threat to the territorial integrity of a state, the United States becomes the common enemy for rebel groups and the government; a good example of this is the Second United Front, which was an alliance between the Kuomintang (KMT) and Communist Party of China (CPC) that was formed in order to fight against the Japanese; this alliance effectively suspended the Chinese Civil War from 1937 to 1946. In this historical case, the KMT and the CPC put aside their own political goals and differences in order to fight against a common enemy.

6. The warning of Deputy Prime Minister for Defense and Security Affairs Rashed Al-Aleemi of Yemen is also telling: "Any intervention or direct (military) action by the United States could strengthen the Al-Qaeda network and not weaken it" (qtd. in *NewsWala* 2010).

7. Of course, when conceptualizing the impact each type of military intervention has on terrorism, future research should also pay close attention to some more nuanced variations. For example, when the United States intervenes to support a government in a domestic dispute, that government may benefit from the intervention and have less reason to urge terrorist activity against U.S. interests. On the other hand, if the United States intervenes in support of an opposition group in a domestic dispute, the government will have more incentive to

turn their citizens against U.S. interests. Accordingly, when it comes to military intervention in domestic disputes, future research should distinguish which side (the government or an opposition group) the U.S. military intervention aims to support and how that choice influences a change in the frequency of terrorist activity. There is also a possibility that the pursuit of terrorists by U.S. soldiers may reduce the incidence of terrorism, as it usually results in the capture or killing of key terrorist members, thereby threatening the very existence of the organizations. However, this possibility may be questionable given the warning of Pakistani president Asif Ali Zardari, who addressed a Joint Session of Pakistan's Parliament regarding American military incursions in his homeland in September 2008, saying: "we will not tolerate the violation of our sovereignty and territorial integrity by any power in the name of combating terrorism" (quoted in Gall 2008).

8. See http://www.start.umd.edu/gtd/features/GTD-Data-Rivers.aspx.

9. Although the GTD provides comprehensive terrorism data since 1970, the data for 1993 are missing due to an office move (LaFree and Dugan 2007). In order to complete the cross-national, time-series data analysis, the missing data are interpolated based on the average between the previous and following years.

10. When diagnostic tests for multicollinearity are performed, none of the test statistics indicates severe multicollinearity among the predictors. For instance, when the VIFs test is used to determine if multicollinearity is a problem in the estimation, this study finds that none of the variables' VIFs exceeds the threshold of 10; therefore multicollinearity is of no concern.

11. The results of Model 2 also do not support the presumption that a strategic goal of a terrorist organization may be to draw their opponent into a direct counterterrorist response that, in its effort to eradicate terrorists, also results in significant collateral damage among the terrorists' "subgroup"—the population of nominal compatriots in which terrorists seek sanctuary from state retribution (see Marighella 1969; Crenshaw 1990). If successful, then, this may account for a short-term decrease in terrorist activity. It does, however, remain likely that terrorism will increase in the longer term, if the collateral damage results in increased terrorist recruitment from the previously "apathetic" subgroup. However, Model 2 actually shows no increasing long-term effects of U.S. military intervention on terrorist activity, as the lagged terms at t−6 to t−10 achieve no significance.

12. The main purpose of Azam and Thelen's (2010) work is to examine the relationship between the number of U.S. troops deployed and international terrorism in 132 countries during the period from 1990 to 2004.

13. The Granger causality test is a statistical hypothesis test for determining whether one time series is useful in forecasting another. Since this study employs cross-sectional, time-series data, the Granger causality test is less useful.

14. The data set is publicly available at http://www-management.wharton.upenn.edu/henisz/.

15. As indicated in note 3, the nine different missions are based on the typology of Pearson and Baumann's (1993) study.

Conclusion

1. It is interesting to note that despite the obvious flaws in the empirical analysis, Davies' (2002) work has been cited sixty-eight times as of April 2015 according to the Google Scholar. Because the total citations are not a small number, a critical question comes to mind. How can we progress the discipline when we continuously cites articles that lack scientific foundations?

REFERENCES

Abadie, Alberto. 2004. "Poverty, Political Freedom, and the Roots of Terrorism." NBER Working Paper no. W10859.

Abadie, Alberto, and Javier Gardeazabal. 2008. "Terrorism and the World Economy." *European Economic Review* 52, no. 1: 1–27.

Abowd, John M., Francis Kramarz, and David N. Margolis. 1999. "High Wage Workers and High Wage Firms." *Econometrica* 67, no. 2: 251–333.

Abu-Nimer, Mohammed. 2001. "Conflict Resolution, Culture, and Religion." *Journal of Peace Research* 38, no. 6: 685–704.

Acemoglu, Daron, Simon Johnson, James A. Robinson, and Pierre Yared. 2005. "From Education to Democracy?" *American Economic Review* 95, no. 2: 44–49.

————. 2008. "Income and Democracy." *American Economic Review* 98, no. 3: 808–42.

Achen, Christopher H. 2000. "Why Lagged Dependent Variables Can Suppress the Explanatory Power of Other Independent Variables." Working paper, Society for Political Methodology, Washington University in St. Louis.

————. 2002. "Toward a New Political Methodology." *Annual Review of Political Science* 5: 423–50.

Adame, Marshall. 2007. "Where There Is No Rule of Law, There Is No Law and Order." American chronicle.com, January 18. http://www.americanchronicle.com/articles/viewArticle.asp?articleID=19295.

Agresti, Alan, and Barbara Finlay. 1997. *Statistical Methods for the Social Sciences.* 3rd ed. Upper Saddle River, N.J.: Prentice Hall.

Ahlquist, John S. 2006. "Economic Policy, Institutions, and Capital Flows." *International Studies Quarterly* 50, no. 3: 681–704.

Alexander, Matthew (pseudonym). 2008. "I'm Still Tortured by What I Saw in Iraq." *Washington Post*, November 30. http://www.washingtonpost.com/wp-dyn/content/article/2008/11/28/AR2008112802242_pf.html.

Allison, Graham T. 1971. *Essence of Decision: Explaining the Cuban Missile Crisis.* Boston: Little, Brown.

Altman, Stuart H., and Alan E. Fechter. 1967. "The Supply of Military Personnel in the Absence of a Draft." *American Economic Review* 57, no. 2: 19–31.

Americas Watch. 1982. *Report on Human Rights in El Salvador.* New York: Vintage.

Anderson, Gary M., Dennis Halcoussis, and Robert D. Tollison. 1996. "Drafting the Competition." *Defence Economics* 7, no. 3: 189–202.

Anderson, Martin, ed. 1976. *Conscription: A Select and Annotated Bibliography.* Stanford: Hoover Institution Press.

Anderson, Martin, ed., with Barbara Honegger. 1982. *The Military Draft: Selected Readings on Conscription.* Stanford: Hoover Institution Press.

Anderson, Paul Russell. September 1945. "Universal Military Training and National Security" (Main Theme). *Annuals of the American Academy of Political and Social Science* 241.

Archer, Keith, Roger Gibbins, Rainer Knopff, Heather MacIvor, and Leslie Pal. 2002. *Parameters of Power.* Toronto: Nelson Thomson Learning.

Arellano, Manuel and Stephen Roy Bond. 1991. "Some Tests of Specification for Panel Data." *Review of Economic Studies* 58, no. 2: 277–97.

Atlas Narodov Mira. 1964. Moscow: Glavnoe Upravlenie Geodezii Ikartografii.

Aykut, Dilek, Himmat Kalsi, and Dilip Ratha. 2003. "Sustaining and Promoting Equity-Related Finance for Developing Countries." In *Global Development Finance 2003: Striving for Stability in Development Finance*, 85–106. Washington, D.C.: World Bank.

Azam, Jean-Paul, and Véronique Thelen. 2010. "Foreign Aid versus Military Intervention in the War on Terror." *Journal of Conflict Resolution* 54, no. 2: 237–61.

Bai, Jushan. 2009. "Panel Data Models with Interactive Fixed Effects." *Econometrica* 77, no. 4: 1229–79.

Banks, Arthur S. 2010. Cross-National Time-Series Data Archive. http://www.databanks international.com/71.html.

Barber, Benjamin R. 2003. *Fear's Empire: War, Terrorism, and Democracy*. New York: W.W. Norton.

Barkawi, Tarak. 2002. "Democratic States and Societies at War." In *The Comparative Study of Conscription in the Armed Forces*, edited by Lars Mjøset and Stephen Van Holde, 361–76. New York: Elsevier Science.

Barro, Robert J. 1999. *Determinants of Economic Growth: A Cross-Country Empirical Study*. Cambridge: MIT Press.

Beck, Nathaniel, and Jonathan N. Katz. 1995. "What to Do (and Not to Do) with Time-Series Cross-Sectional Data in Comparative Politics." *American Political Science Review* 89, no. 3: 634–47.

Beck, Nathaniel, Jonathan N. Katz, and Richard Tucker. 1998. "Taking Time Seriously in Binary Time-Series, Cross-Section Analysis." *American Journal of Political Science* 42, no. 4: 1260–88.

Beck, Thorsten, and Ian Webb. 2003. "Economic, Demographic, and Institutional Determinants of Life Insurance Consumption across Countries." *World Bank Economic Review* 17, no. 1: 51–88.

Belsley, David A., Edwin Kuh, and Roy E. Welsch. 1980. *Regression Diagnostics: Identifying Influential Data and Sources of Collinearity*. New York: John Wiley & Sons.

Bennett, D. Scott, and Allan Stam. 2000. "*EUGene*." *International Interactions* 26, no. 2: 179–204.

Bergholt, Drago, and Päivi Lujala. 2012. "Climate-Related Natural Disasters, Economic Growth, and Armed Civil Conflict." *Journal of Peace Research* 49, no. 1: 147–62.

Bernhard, William, J. Lawrence Broz, and William Roberts Clark. 2002. "The Political Economy of Monetary Institutions." *International Organization* 56, no. 4: 693–723.

Besley, Timothy, and Marta Reynal-Querol. 2011. "Do Democracies Select More Educated Leaders?" *American Political Science Review* 105, no. 3: 552–66.

Betts, Richard K. 1991. *Soldiers, Statesmen, and Cold War Crises*. New York: Columbia University Press.

———. 1998. "The New Threat of Mass Destruction." *Foreign Affairs* 77, no. 1: 26–41.

Beukema, Herman. 1982. "The Social and Political Aspects of Conscription." In *The Military Draft*, edited by Martin Anderson, 479–91. Stanford: Hoover Institution Press.

Biglaiser, Glen, and Karl DeRouen Jr. 2007. "Following the Flag." *International Studies Quarterly* 51, no. 4: 835–54.

Blanton, Shannon Lindsey, and Robert G. Blanton. 2006. "Human Rights and Foreign Direct Investment: A Two-Stage Analysis." *Business and Society* 45, no. 4: 464–85.

———. 2007. "What Attracts Foreign Investors?" *Journal of Politics* 69, no. 1: 143–55.

Blattman, Christopher, and Edward Miguel. 2009. "Civil War." Center for Global Development. Working paper no. 166.

Blinder, Alan S. 1996. *Hard Heads, Soft Hearts: Tough-Minded Economics for a Just Society.* Reading, Mass.: Addison-Wesley.

Bloom, Mia. 2005. *Dying to Kill: The Allure of Suicide Terror.* New York: Columbia University Press.

Blumenthal, Monica D., Letha Chadiha, Gerald Cole, and Toby Jayaratne. 1975. *More about Justifying Violence: Methodological Studies of Attitudes and Behavior.* Ann Arbor: Survey Research Center, Institute for Social Research, University of Michigan.

Bollen, Kenneth A. 1986. "Political Rights and Political Liberties in Nations." *Human Rights Quarterly* 8, no. 4: 567–91.

———. 1990. "Political Democracy." *Studies in Comparative International Development* 25, no. 1: 7–24.

Bollen, Kenneth A., and Robert W. Jackman. 1985. "Regression Diagnostics." *Sociological Methods & Research* 13, no. 4: 510–42.

Bowman, William, Roger Little, and G. Thomas Sicilia, eds. 1986. *The All-Volunteer Force after a Decade: Retrospect and Prospect.* Washington, D.C.: Pergamon-Brassey's.

Brambor, Thomas, William Roberts Clark, and Matt Golder. 2006. "Understanding Interactions Models." *Political Analysis* 14, no. 1: 63–82.

Braumoeller, Bear F. 2004. "Hypothesis Testing and Multiplicative Interaction Terms." *International Organization* 58, no. 4: 807–20.

Brautigam, Deborah. 1992. "Governance, Economy, and Foreign Aid." *Studies in Comparative International Development* 27, no. 3: 3–25.

Brecher, Michael. 1996. "Crisis Escalation." *International Political Science Review* 17, no. 2: 215–30.

Brigance, W. Norwood. 1945. "How to Produce a Third World War." In *Peacetime Military Training,* edited by Bower Aly, 193–202. Columbia, Mo.: Lucas Brothers.

Broad, William, and Nicholas Wade. 1983. *Betrayers of Truth.* New York: Simon and Schuster.

Broder, John M., and James Risen. 2007. "Armed Guards in Iraq Occupy a Legal Limbo." *New York Times,* September 20. http://www.nytimes.com/2007/09/20/world/middleeast/20blackwater.html?em&ex=1190433600&en=2101831599e1231f&ei=5087%0A.

Brown, Michale E., ed. 1996. *The International Dimensional of Internal Conflict.* Cambridge: MIT Press.

Broz, J. Lawrence. 2002. "Political System Transparency and Monetary Commitment Regimes." *International Organization* 56, no. 4: 861–87.

Bueno de Mesquita, Bruce, James D. Morrow, Randolph M. Siverson, and Alastair Smith. 2004. "Testing Novel Implications from the Selectorate Theory of War." *World Politics* 56, no. 3: 363–88.

Bueno de Mesquita, Bruce, Alastair Smith, Randolph M. Siverson, and James D. Morrow. 2003. *The Logic of Political Survival.* Cambridge: MIT Press.

Bueno de Mesquita, Ethan. 2005. "Review of Jonathan Fox's Religion, Civilization, and Civil War." *Studies in Conflict and Terrorism* 28, no. 4: 343–45.

Busse, Matthias. 2004. "Transnational Corporations and Repression of Political Rights and Civil Liberties." *Kyklos* 57, no. 1: 45–66.

Busse, Matthias, and Carsten Hefeker. 2007. "Political Risk, Institutions, and Foreign Direct Investment." *European Journal of Political Economy* 23, no. 2: 397–415.

Büthe, Tim, and Helen Milner. 2008. "The Politics of Foreign Direct Investment into Developing Countries." *American Journal of Political Science* 52, no. 4: 741–62.

Cameron, A. Colin, and Pravin K. Trivedi. 1998. *Regression Analysis of Count Data*. Cambridge: Cambridge University Press.

Caplan, Bryan. 2007. *The Myth of the Rational Voter: Why Democracies Choose Bad Policies*. Princeton: Princeton University Press.

Carsey, Thomas M. 2014. "Making DA-RT a Reality." *PS: Political Science & Politics* 47, no. 1: 72–77.

Carter, David B., and Curtis S. Signorino. 2010. "Back to the Future." *Political Analysis* 18, no. 3: 271–92.

Cederman, Lars-Erik, and Luc Girardin. 2009. "Beyond Fractionalization." *American Political Science Review* 101, no. 1: 173–85.

Central Intelligence Agency (CIA). 2008. The World Factbook. https://www.cia.gov/library/publications/the-world-factbook/.

Chalk, Peter. 1995. "The Liberal Democratic Response to Terrorism." *Terrorism and Political Violence* 7, no. 4: 10–44.

Chambers, John Whiteclay II. 1987. *To Raise an Army: The Draft Comes to Modern America*. New York: Free Press.

Chan, Steve. 1997. "In Search of Democratic Peace." *Mershon International Studies Review* 41, no. 1: 59–91.

Chan, Steve, and Melanie Mason. 1992. "Foreign Direct Investment and Host Country Conditions." *International Interactions* 17, no. 3: 215–32.

Cheibub, José Antonio, Jennifer Gandhi, and James Raymond Vreeland. 2010. "Democracy and Dictatorship Revisited." *Public Choice* 143, nos. 1–2: 67–101.

Chenoweth, Erica. 2010. "Democratic Competition and Terrorist Activity." *Journal of Politics* 72, no. 1: 16–30.

Choi, In. 2001. "Unit Root Tests for Panel Data." *Journal of International Money and Finance* 20, no. 2: 249–72.

Choi, Seung-Whan. 2002. "Civil-Military Dynamics, Democratic Peace, and International Conflict, 1886–1992." PhD diss., University of Missouri.

———. 2009. "The Effect of Outliers on Regression Analysis." *Quarterly Journal of Political Science* 4, no. 2: 153–65.

———. 2010a. "Beyond Kantian Liberalism." *Conflict Management and Peace Science* 27, no. 3: 272–95.

———. 2010b. "Fighting Terrorism through the Rule of Law?" *Journal of Conflict Resolution* 54, no. 6: 940–66.

———. 2010c. "Legislative Constraints." *Journal of Conflict Resolution* 54, no.): 438–70.

———. 2011. "Re-evaluating Capitalist and Democratic Peace Models." *International Studies Quarterly* 55, no. 3: 759–69.

———. 2013. "The Democratic Peace through an Interaction of Domestic Institutions and Norms." *Armed Forces & Society* 39, no. 2: 255–83.

Choi, Seung-Whan, and Patrick James. 2003. "No Professional Soldiers, No Militarized Interstate Disputes?" *Journal of Conflict Resolution* 47, no. 6: 796–816.

———. 2005. *Civil-Military Dynamics, Democracy, and International Conflict: A New Quest for International Peace*. New York: Palgrave Macmillan.

———. 2007. "Media Openness, Democracy, and Militarized Interstate Disputes." *British Journal of Political Science* 37, no. 1: 23–46.

Choi, Seung-Whan, and Shali Luo. 2013. "Economic Sanctions, Poverty, and International Terrorism." *International Interactions* 39, no. 2: 217–45.

Choi, Seung-Whan, and Yiagadeesen Samy. 2008. "Reexamining the Effect of Democratic Institutions on Inflows of Foreign Direct Investment in Developing Countries." *Foreign Policy Analysis* 4, no. 1: 83–103.

Chowdhury, Mahfuz R. 2010. "Can the United States Contain Islamic Terrorism?" http://rethinkingislam-sultanshahin.blogspot.com/2010/01/islamic-world-news-26-jan-2010.html.

Chung, Myung-Chang, ed. 2000. *The Bank of Korea.* Seoul: Bank of Korea.

Cingranelli, David L., and David L. Richards. 1999. "Measuring the Level, Pattern, and Sequence of Government Respect for Physical Integrity Rights." *International Studies Quarterly* 43, no. 2: 407–17.

———. 2010a. "The Cingranelli and Richards (CIRI) Human Rights Data Project." *Human Rights Quarterly* 32, no. 2: 401–24.

———. 2010b. The Cingranelli-Richards (CIRI) Human Rights Dataset. http://www.humanrightsdata.com.

Clarke, Kevin A., and Randall Stone. 2008. "Democracy and the Logic of Political Survival." *American Political Science Review* 102, no. 3: 387–92.

Clausewitz, Carl von. 1976. *On War.* Edited and translated by Michael Howard and Peter Paret. Princeton: Princeton University Press.

Cook, R. Dennis. 1977. "Detection of Influential Observations in Linear Regression." *Technometrics* 19, no. 1: 15–18.

Crain, Nicole V., and W. Mark Crain. 2006. "Terrorized Economies." *Public Choice* 128, nos. 1/2: 317–49.

Crenshaw, Martha. 1990. "The Logic of Terrorism." In *Origins of Terrorism: Psychologies, Ideologies, Theologies, States of Mind,* edited by Walter Reich, 7–24. Washington, D.C.: Woodrow Wilson Center Press.

———. 2002. "The Global Phenomenon of Terrorism." In *Responding to Terrorism: What Role for the United Nations?,* edited by Clara Lee, 27–31. International Peace Academy. New York: Chadbourne & Park.

Dafoe, Allan. 2011. "Statistical Critiques of the Democratic Peace." *American Journal of Political Science* 55, no. 2: 247–62.

———. 2014. "Science Deserves Better." *PS: Political Science & Politics* 47, no. 1: 60–66.

Dafoe, Allan, John R. Oneal, and Bruce Russett. 2013. "The Democratic Peace." *International Studies Quarterly* 57, no. 1: 201–14.

D'Agostino, Ralph B., Albert Belanger, and Ralph B. D'Agostino Jr. 1990. "A Suggestion for Using Powerful and Informative Tests of Normality." *American Statistician* 44, no. 4: 316–21.

Dahl, Robert A. 1971. *Polyarchy.* New Haven: Yale University Press.

Davenport, Christian. 1995. "Assessing the Military's Influence on Political Repression." *Journal of Political and Military Sociology* 23, no. 1: 119–44.

———. 2007. "State Repression and the Tyrannical Peace." *Journal of Peace Research* 44, no. 4: 485–504.

Davenport, Christian, David A. Armstrong II, and Mark I. Lichbach. 2008. "From Mountains to Movements: Dissent, Repression and Escalation to Civil War." Unpublished paper. http://www.researchgate.net/publication/228823796_From_Mountains_to_Movements_Dissent_Repression_and_Escalation_to_Civil_War.

Davies, Graeme A. M. 2002. "Domestic Strife and the Initiation of International Conflicts." *Journal of Conflict Resolution* 46, no. 5: 672–92.

Davies, Warnock. 1981. "Beyond the Earthquake Allegory." *Business Horizons* 24, no. 4: 39–43.

Defense Science Board. 1998. "The Defense Science Board 1997 Summer Study Task Force on Department of Defense Responses to Transnational Threats." Vol. 3: "Supporting Reports." Washington, D.C.: Office of the Under Secretary of Defense for Acquisition & Technology.

DeLuca, Tom. 1995. *The Two Faces of Political Apathy*. Philadelphia: Temple University Press.

Dent, M. J. 1970. "The Military and the Politicians." In *Nigerian Politics and Military Rule: Prelude to the Civil War*, edited by S. K. Panter-Brick, 78–93. London: Athlone Press for the University of London.

DeRouen, Karl R., Jr. 2000. "Presidents and the Diversionary Use of Force." *International Studies Quarterly* 44, no. 2: 317–28.

DeRouen, Karl R., Jr., and David Sobek. 2004. "The Dynamics of Civil War Duration and Outcome." *Journal of Peace Research* 41, no. 3: 303–20.

Desch, Michael C. 1998. "Soldiers, States, and Structures." *Armed Forces & Society* 24, no. 3: 389–405.

———— 2001. *Civilian Control of the Military*. Baltimore: Johns Hopkins University Press.

Dewald, William G., Jerry G. Thursby, and Richard G. Anderson. 1986. "Replication in Empirical Economics." *American Economic Review* 76, no. 4: 587–603.

Diamond, Larry. 1999. *Developing Democracy toward Consolidation*. Baltimore: Johns Hopkins University Press.

Dixon, William J. 1993. "Democracy and the Management of International Conflict." *Journal of Conflict Resolution* 37, no. 1: 42–68.

————. 1994. "Democracy and the Peaceful Settlement of International Conflict." *American Political Science Review* 88, no. 1: 14–32.

Dolman, Everett Carl. 2004. *The Warrior State: How Military Organization Structures Politics*. New York: Palgrave Macmillan.

Drakos, Konstantinos. 2009. "Security Economics." Economics of Security Working Paper 6. Berlin: Economics of Security.

Drakos, Konstatinos, and Andreas Gofas. 2006a. "The Devil You Know but Are Afraid to Face." *Journal of Conflict Resolution* 50, no. 5: 714–35.

————. 2006b. "In Search of the Average Transnational Terrorist Attack Venue." *Defence and Peace Economics* 17, no. 2: 73–93.

Drèze, Jean, and Amartya Sen. 1989. *Hunger and Public Action*. New York: Oxford University Press.

Drukker, David M. 2003. "Testing for Serial Correlation in Linear Panel-Data Models. *Stata Journal* 3, no. 2: 168–77.

Dugan, Laura. 2010. "The Making of the Global Terrorism Database and What We Have Learned about the Life Cycles of Terrorist Organizations." Unpublished paper.

Duindam, Simon. 1999. *Military Conscription: An Economic Analysis of the Labour Component in the Armed Forces*. Heidelberg: Physica-Verlag.

Dunne, Tim. 2009. "Liberalism, International Terrorism, and Democratic Wars." *International Relations* 23, no. 1: 107–14.

Easterly, William. 2003. "Can Foreign Aid Buy Growth?" *Journal of Economic Perspectives* 17, no. 3: 23–48.

Easterly, William, and Ross Levine. 1997. "Africa's Growth Tragedy." *Quarterly Journal of Economics* 112, no. 4: 1203–50.

Economist Intelligence Unit. 2008. "Economist Intelligence Unit's Index of Democracy 2008." *Economist*, 1–31. http://graphics.eiu.com/PDF/Democracy%20Index%202008.pdf.

Eland, Ivan. 1998. "Does U.S. Intervention Overseas Breed Terrorism?" *CATO Institute, Foreign Policy Briefing.*

———. 2007. "Excessive U.S. Military Action Overseas Breeds Anti-U.S. Terrorism." Unpublished paper.

Elbadawi, Ibrahim, and Nicholas Sambanis. 2002. "How Much War Will We See?" *Journal of Conflict Resolution* 46, no. 3: 307–34.

Enders, Walter, Adolfo Sachsida, and Todd Sandler. 2006. "The Impact of Transnational Terrorism on U.S. Foreign Direct Investment." *Political Research Quarterly* 59, no. 4: 517–31.

Enders, Walter, and Todd Sandler. 1999. "Transnational Terrorism in the Post-Cold War Era." *International Studies Quarterly* 43, no. 1: 145–67.

———. 2006. *The Political Economy of Terrorism.* Cambridge: Cambridge University Press.

Enders, Walter, Todd Sandler, and Khusrav Gaibulloev. 2011. "Domestic versus Transnational Terrorism." *Journal of Peace Research* 48, no. 3: 319–37.

Esposito, John L., and John O. Voll. 1996. *Islam and Democracy.* New York: Oxford University Press.

Eubank, William, and Leonard Weinberg. 1994. "Does Democracy Encourage Terrorism?" *Terrorism and Political Violence* 6, no. 4: 417–43.

———. 1998. "Terrorism and Democracy." *Terrorism and Political Violence* 10, no. 1: 108–18.

———. 2001. "Terrorism and Democracy." *Terrorism and Political Violence* 13, no. 1: 155–64.

Eyerman, Joe. 1998. "Terrorism and Democratic States." *International Interactions* 24, no. 2: 151–70.

Falkenrath, R. 2001. "Analytic Models and Policy Prescription." *Studies in Conflict and Terrorism* 24, no. 3: 159–81.

Fearon, James D. 2003. "Ethnic and Cultural Diversity by Country." *Journal of Economic Growth* 8, no. 2: 195–222.

———. 2006. "Ethnic Mobilization and Ethnic Violence." In *Oxford Handbook of Political Economy*, edited by Barry R. Weingast and Donald Wittman, 852–68. Oxford: Oxford University Press.

Fearon, James D., Kimuli Kasara, and David D. Laitin. 2007. "Ethnic Minority Rule and Civil War Onset." *American Political Science Review* 101, no. 1: 187–93.

Fearon, James D., and David D. Laitin. 2000. "Violence and the Social Construction of Ethnic Identity." *International Organization* 54, no. 4: 845–77.

———. 2003. "Ethnicity, Insurgency, and Civil War." *American Political Science Review* 97, no. 1: 75–90.

Feaver, Peter D. 1999. "Civil-Military Relations." *Annual Review of Political Science* 2: 211–41.

Feaver, Peter D. and Christopher Gelpi. 2004. *Choosing Your Battles: American Civil-Military Relations and the Use of Force.* Princeton: Princeton University Press.

Feng, Yi. 2001. "Political Freedom, Political Instability, and Policy Uncertainty." *International Studies Quarterly* 45, no. 2: 271–94.

Finer, Samuel E. 1975. *The Man on Horseback: The Role of the Military in Politics.* Hammondsworth, UK: Penguin.

Fish, Steven M. 2002. "Islam and Authoritarianism." *World Politics* 55, no. 1: 4–37.

Fisher, Anthony C. 1969. "The Cost of the Draft and the Cost of Ending the Draft." *American Economic Review* 59, no. 3: 239–54.

Fjelde, Hanne. 2010. "Generals, Dictators, and Kings." *Conflict Management and Peace Science* 27, no. 3: 195–218.

Fox, Jonathan. 2004. *Religion, Civilization, and Civil War: 1945 through the Millennium.* Lanham, Md.: Lexington Books.

Frankel, Jeffrey A., and Andrew K. Rose. 1996. "Currency Crashes in Emerging Market." *Journal of International Economics* 41, nos. 3–4: 351–66.

Freedom House. 2009. *Freedom in the World 2009*. Washington, D.C.: Freedom House.

Freeman, John R. 2002. "Competing Commitments." *International Organization* 56, no. 4: 889–910.

Frey, Bruno S., and Simon Luechinger. 2003. "How to Fight Terrorism." *Defence and Peace Economics* 14, no. 4: 237–49.

———. 2005. "Measuring Terrorism." In *Law and the State: A Political Economy Approach*, edited by Alain Marciano and Jean-Michel Josselin, 142–81. Cheltenham, UK: Edward Elgar.

Frey, Bruno S., Simon Luechinger, and Alois Stutzer. 2007. "Calculating Tragedy." *Journal of Economic Surveys* 21, no. 1: 1–24.

Friedman, Milton. 1968. "The Role of Monetary Policy." *American Economic Review* 58, no. 1: 1–17.

———. 1972. *An Economist's Protest: Columns in Political Economy*. Glen Ridge, N.J.: Thomas Horton.

Fuller, Lon L. 1969. *The Morality of Law*. New Haven: Yale University Press.

Gall, Carlotta. 2008. "Pakistan's President Calls for End to Terrorism and Criticizes Intervention by U.S." *New York Times*, September 21. http://www.nytimes.com/2008/09/21/world/asia/21pstan.html.

Gall, Carlotta, and David Rohde. 2008. "Militants Escape Control of Pakistan, Officials Say." *New York Times*, January 15. http://www.nytimes.com/2008/01/15/world/asia/15isi.html.

Garland, David. 1996. "The Limits of the Sovereign State." *British Journal of Criminology* 36, no. 4: 445–71.

Gartzke, Erik. 2007. "The Capitalist Peace." *American Journal of Political Science* 51, no. 1: 166–91.

Gause, F. Gregory, III. 2005. "Can Democracy Stop Terrorism?" *Foreign Affairs* 84, no. 5: 62–76.

Geddes, Barbara. 1999. "What Do We know about Democratization after Twenty Years?" *Annual Review of Political Science* 2: 115–44.

Gellner, Ernest. 1983. *Nations and Nationalism*. Ithaca: Cornell University Press.

Gibler, Douglas M. 2007. "Bordering on Peace." *International Studies Quarterly* 51, no. 3: 509–32.

——— 2008. "United States Economic Aid and Repression." *Journal of Politics* 70, no. 2: 513–26.

Gibney, Mark, Linda Cornett, and Reed M. Wood. 2011. "Political Terror Scale, 1976–2008." http://www.politicalterrorscale.org/.

Gilroy, Curtis L., Robert L. Phillips, and John D. Blair. 1990. "The All-Volunteer Army." *Armed Forces & Society* 16, no. 3: 329–50.

Glaeser, Edward L., Rafael La Porta, Florencio Lopez-de-Silanes, and Andrei Shleifer. 2004. "Do Institutions Cause Growth?" *Journal of Economic Growth* 9, no. 3: 271–303.

Glaser, Charles L. 1997. "The Security Dilemma Revisited." *World Politics* 50, no. 1: 171–201.

Gleditsch, Kristian. 2002. "Expanded Trade and GDP Data." *Journal of Conflict Resolution* 46, no. 5: 712–24.

Gleditsch, Nils, Peter Wallensteen, Mikael Eriksson, Margareta Sollenberg, and Harvard Strand. 2002. "Armed Conflict, 1946–2001." *Journal of Peace Research* 39, no. 5: 615–37.

Global Terrorism Database. 2009. Personal email exchange with Erin Miller, Global Terrorism Database staff, February 3.

Gochman, Charles S., and Zeev Maoz. 1984. "Military Interstate Disputes, 1816–1976." *Journal of Conflict Resolution* 28, no. 4: 585–615.

Goemans, H. E., Kristian Gleditsch, and Giacomo Chiozza. 2009. "Introducing Archigos." *Journal of Peace Research* 46, no. 2: 269–83.

Gopin, Marc. 2000. *Between Eden and Armageddon: The Future of World Religions, Violence, and Peacemaking.* New York: Oxford University Press.

Gowa, Joanne. 1999. *Ballots and Bullets: The Elusive Democratic Peace.* Princeton: Princeton University Press.

Grandin, Greg. 2000. *The Blood of Guatemala: A History of Race and Nation.* Durham, N.C.: Duke University Press.

———. 2004. *The Last Colonial Massacre: Latin America in the Cold War.* Chicago: University of Chicago Press.

Gray, Colin S. 1975. "Hawks and Doves." *Journal of Political and Military Sociology* 3, no. 1: 85–94.

Green, Donald P., Soo Yeon Kim, and David H. Yoon. 2001. "Dirty Pool." *International Organization* 55, no. 2: 441–68.

Greene, William H. 2003. *Econometric Analysis.* Upper Saddle River, N.J.: Prentice Hall.

Gujarati, Damodar N. 2003. *Basic Econometrics.* New York: McGraw-Hill.

Gurr, Ted Robert. 1970. *Why Men Rebel.* Princeton: Princeton University Press.

———. 1986. "Persisting Patterns of Repression and Rebellion." In *Persistent Patterns and Emergent Structures in a Waning Century,* edited by Margaret P. Karns, 149–168. New York: Praeger.

———. 2000. *Peoples versus States: Minorities at Risk in the New Century.* Washington, D.C.: U.S. Institute of Peace.

Gurr, Ted Robert, Keith Jaggers, and Will H. Moore. 1991. "The Transformation of the Western State." In *On Measuring Democracy: Its Consequences and Concomitants,* edited by Alex Inkeles, 69–104. New Brunswick, N.J.: Transaction.

Gurses, Mehmet, and T. David Mason. 2010. "Weak States, Regime Types, and Civil War." *Civil Wars* 12, nos. 1–2: 140–55.

Hall, Daniel B. 2000. "Zero-Inflated Poisson and Binomial Regression with Random Effects." *Biometrics* 56, no. 4: 1030–39.

Haltiner, Karl W. 1998. "The Definite End of the Mass Army in Western Europe?" *Armed Forces & Society* 25, no. 1: 7–36.

Hamilton, Lawrence C. 2004. *Statistics with Stata: Updated for Version 8.* Belmont, Calif.: Books/Cole-Thomson Learning.

———. 2009. *Statistics with Stata: Updated for Version 10.* Belmont, Calif.: Books/Cole-Thomson Learning.

Hansen, W. Lee, and Burton A. Weisbrod. 1967. "Economics of the Military Draft." *Quarterly Journal of Economics* 81, no. 3: 395–421.

Hardin, Russell. 2001. "Law and Social Order." *Philosophical Issues* 11: 61–85.

Harms, Philipp, and Heinrich W. Ursprung. 2002. "Do Civil and Political Repression Really Boost Foreign Direct Investments?" *Economic Inquiry* 40, no. 4: 651–63.

Hausman, Jerry. 1978. "Specification Tests in Econometrics." *Econometrica* 46, no. 6: 1251–71.

Hayes, Jarrod. 2012. "The Democratic Peace and the New Evolution of an Old Idea." *European Journal of International Relations* 18, no. 4: 767–791.

Hegre, Håvard. 2002. "Toward a Democratic Civil Peace?" *American Political Science Review* 95, no. 1: 33–48.

Hegre, Håvard, John R. Oneal, and Bruce Russett. 2010. "Trade Does Promote Peace." *Journal of Peace Research* 47, no. 6: 763–74.

Hegre, Håvard, and Nicholas Sambanis. 2006. "Sensitive Analysis of Empirical Results on Civil War Onset." *Journal of Conflict Resolution* 50, no. 4: 508–35.

Henisz, Witold J. 2000. "The Institutional Environment for Economic Growth." *Economics and Politics* 12, no. 1: 1–43.

———. 2002. *Politics and International Investment: Measuring Risks and Protecting Profits.* Cheltenham, UK: Edward Elgar.

Hibbs, Douglas A. 1973. *Mass Political Violence: A Cross-National Causal Analysis.* New York: John Wiley.

Hilbe, Joseph. 2007. *Negative Binomial Regression.* Cambridge: Cambridge University Press.

Hinnen, Todd. 2009. "Prepared Remarks to the Washington Institute for Near East Policy." Remarks presented to the Washington Institute for Near East Policy, Stein Program on Counterterrorism and Intelligence, April 28. http://www.washingtoninstitute.org/html/pdf/hinnen.pdf.

Hirshman, Albert O. 1970. *Exit, Voice, and Loyalty: Responses to Decline in Firms, Organizations, an States.* Cambridge: Harvard University Press.

Hoaglin, David C., and Roy E. Welsch. 1978. "The Hat Matrix in Regression and ANOVA." *American Statistician* 32, no. 1: 17–22.

Hobbes, Thomas. 1985. *Leviathan.* London: Penguin.

Hobsbawm, Eric. 2007. *Globalisation, Democracy, and Terrorism.* London: Little, Brown.

Hoffman, Aaron M., Crystal Shelton, and Erik Cleven. 2013. "Press Freedom, Publicity, and the Cross-National Incidence of Transnational Terrorism." *Political Research Quarterly* 66, no. 4: 896–909.

Hoffman, Bruce. 1998. *Recent Trends and Future Prospects of Terrorism in the United States.* Santa Monica: RAND.

Hoffmann, John P. 2004. *Generalized Linear Models: An Applied Approach.* Boston: Pearson A and B.

Hogg, Russell, and David Brown. 1998. *Rethinking Law and Order.* Annandale, N.S.W.: Pluto Press.

Horeman, Bart, and Marc Stolwijk, eds. 1998. *Refusing to Bear Arms: A World Survey of Conscription and Conscientious Objection to Military Service.* London: War Resister's International.

Horowitz, Michael C., and Allan C. Stam. 2012. "How Prior Military Experience Influences the Future Militarized Behavior of Leaders." Unpublished paper. http://papers.ssrn.com/sol3/papers.cfm?abstract_id=2012633.

Huntington, Samuel P. 1957. *The Soldier and the State: The Theory and Politics of Civil-Military Relations.* Cambridge: Belknap Press of Harvard University Press.

———. 1991. *The Third Wave: Democratization in the Late Twentieth Century.* Norman: University of Oklahoma Press.

———. 1996. *The Clash of Civilizations and the Remaking of World Order.* New York: Simon & Schuster.

Hurwitz, Agnès. 2008. "Civil War and the Rule of Law." In *Civil War and the Rule of Law: Security, Development, Human Rights,* edited by Agnès Hurwitz with Reyko Huang, 1–18. Boulder: Lynne Rienner.

International Institute for Strategic Studies. 1970–2000. *The Military Balance, 1970–1971* through *The Military Balance, 2000–2001.* London: Oxford University Press.

Isham, Jonathan, Daniel Kaufmann, and Lant H. Pritchett. 1997. "Civil Liberties, Democracy, and the Performance of Government Projects." *World Bank Economic Review* 11, no. 2: 219–42.

Ishiyama, John. 2014. "Replication, Research Transparency, and Journal Publications." *PS: Political Science & Politics* 47, no. 1: 78–83.

Israel Insider. 2007. "Palestinian PM Says He "Cannot Impose Law and Order in West Bank." August 6. http://web.israelinsider.com/Articles/Security/11820.htm.

Ivanova, Kate, and Todd Sandler. 2007. "CBRN Attack Perpetrators." *Foreign Policy Analysis* 3, no. 4: 273–94.

Jacobsen, Tor G., and Indra de Soysa. 2009. "Give Me Liberty, or Give Me Death!" *Civil Wars* 11, no. 2: 137–57.

Jakobsen, Jo, and Indra de Soysa. 2006. "Do Foreign Investors Punish Democracy?" *Kyklos* 59, no. 3: 383–410.

James, Patrick. 2003. "Replication Policies and Practices at International Studies Quarterly." *International Studies Perspectives* 4, no. 1: 85–88.

———, ed. 2010. *Religion, Identity and Global Governance: Ideas, Evidence and Practice.* Toronto: University of Toronto Press.

James, Patrick, and Athanasios Hristoulas. 1994. "Domestic Politics and Foreign Policy." *Journal of Politics* 56, no. 2: 327–48.

James, Patrick, and John R. Oneal. 1991. "The Influence of Domestic and International Politics on the President's Use of Force." *Journal of Conflict Resolution* 35, no. 2: 307–32.

James, Patrick, and Jean-Sébastien Rioux. 1998. "International Crises and Linkage Politics." *Political Research Quarterly* 51, no. 3: 781–812.

James, Patrick, Eric Solberg, and Murray Wolfson. 1999. "An Identified Systemic Model of the Democracy-Peace Nexus." *Defense and Peace Economics* 10, no. 1: 1–37.

Janowitz, Morris. 1971. *The Professional Soldier: A Social and Political Portrait.* New York: Macmillan.

———, ed. 1981. *Civil-Military Relations: Regional Perspectives.* Beverly Hills: Sage.

Jarque, Carlos M., and Anil K. Bera. 1987. "A Test for Normality of Observations and Regression Residuals." *International Statistical Review* 55, no. 2: 163–72.

Jehn, Christopher, and Zachary Selden. 2002. "The End of Conscription in Europe?" *Contemporary Economic Policy* 20, no. 2: 93–100.

Jensen, Nathan M. 2003. "Democratic Governance and Multinational Corporations." *International Organization* 57, no. 3: 587–616.

———. 2006. *Nation-States and the Multinational Corporation: A Political Economy of Foreign Direct Investment.* Princeton: Princeton University Press.

Jensen, Nathan, and Fiona McGillivray. 2005. "Federal Institutions and Multinational Investors." *International Interactions* 31, no. 4: 303–25.

Jervis, Robert. 1978. "Cooperation under the Security Dilemma." *World Politics* 30, no. 2: 167–214.

Johnson, Chalmers A. 2000. *Blowback: The Costs and Consequences of American Empire.* New York: Henry Holt.

———. 2004. *The Sorrows of Empire: Militarism, Secrecy, and the End of the Republic.* New York: Henry Holt.

Jonas, Jeff, and Jim Harper. 2006. "Effective Counterterrorism and the Limited Role of Predictive Data Mining." *Policy Analysis*, no. 584: 1–12.

Jonas, Susanne. 1991. *The Battle for Guatemala: Rebels, Death Squads, and U.S. Power.* Boulder: Westview Press.

Jones, Daniel M., Stuart A. Bremer, and J. David Singer. 1996. "Militarized Interstate Disputes, 1816–1992." *Conflict Management and Peace Science* 15, no. 2: 163–213.

Jones, Seth G., Jeremy M. Wilson, Andrew Rathmell, and K. Jack Riley. 2005. *Establishing Law and Order after Conflict.* Santa Monica: RAND.

Kahn, Joseph, and Tim Weiner. 2002. "World Leaders Rethinking Strategy on Aid to Poor." *New York Times*, March 18, A(1), 3.

Kahneman, Daniel, and Amos Tversky. 1979. "Prospect Theory." *Econometrica* 47, no. 2: 263–91.

Kalyvas, Stathis N. 2006. *The Logic of Violence in Civil War.* New York: Cambridge University Press.

———. 2007. "Civil Wars." In *The Oxford Handbook of Comparative Politics*, edited by Carles Boix and Susan C. Stokes, 416–34. New York: Oxford University Press.

——— 2008. "Ethnic Defection in Civil War." *Comparative Political Studies* 41, no. 8: 1043–68.

Kaufmann, Chaim. 1996. "Possible and Impossible Solutions to Ethnic Civil Wars." *International Security* 20, no. 4: 136–75.

Keech, William. 2009. "A Scientifically Superior Conception of Democracy." Paper presented at the Midwest Political Science Association Conference, Chicago, April 16–19.

Keegan, John. 1979. *World Armies.* New York: Facts on File.

———. 1983. *World Armies.* 2nd ed. Detroit: Gale Research.

Kennedy, Ryan. 2009. "Survival and Accountability." *International Studies Quarterly* 53, no. 3: 695–714.

Kerstens, K., and E. Meyermans. 1993. "The Draft versus an All-Volunteer Force." *Defence Economics* 4, no. 3: 271–84.

Keshk, Omar M. G. 2003. "CDSIMEQ." *Stata Journal* 3, no. 2: 157–67.

Keshk, Omar M. G., Brian M. Pollins, and Rafael Reuveny. 2004. "Trade Still follows the Flag." *Journal of Politics* 66, no. 4: 1155–79.

Keshk, Omar M.G., Rafael Reuveny, and Brian M. Pollins. 2010. "Trade and Conflict." *Conflict Management and Peace Science* 27, no. 1: 3–27.

Kestnbaum, Meyer. 2002. "Citizen-Soldiers, National Service and the Mass Army." In *The Comparative Study of Conscription in the Armed Forces*, edited by Lars Mjøset and Stephen Van Holde, 117–44. New York: Elsevier Science.

Kim, Dongsuk. 2010. "What Makes State Leaders Brutal?" *Civil Wars* 12, no. 3: 237–60.

King, Gary. 1995. "Replication, Replication." *PS: Political Science and Politics* 28, no. 3: 444–52.

King, Gary, Robert O. Keohane, and Sidney Verba. 1994. *Designing Social Inquiry: Scientific Interference in Qualitative Research.* Princeton: Princeton University Press.

King, Gary, Michael Tomz, and Jason Wittenberg. 2000. "Making the Most of Statistical Analyses." *American Journal of Political Science* 44, no. 2: 347–61.

King, Gary, and Langche Zeng. 2001. "Explaining Rare Events in International Relations." *International Organization* 55, no. 3: 693–715.

King, Stephen. 2013. "Era of Independent Central Banks Is Over." *Financial Times*, January 10. http://www.ft.com/cms/s/0/a4e41f16-5b1b-11e2-8ccc-00144feab49a.html#axzz2NB00zUS1.

Kleinbaum, David G., Lawrence L. Kupper, Keith E. Muller, and Azhar Nizam. 1998. *Applied Regression Analysis and Multivariable Methods.* 3rd ed. Pacific Grove, Calif.: Duxbury Press.

Kobrin, Stephen J. 1979. "Political Risk." *Journal of International Business Studies* 10, no. 1: 67–80.

———. 1980. "Foreign Enterprise and Forced Divestment in LDCs." *International Organization* 34, no. 1: 65–88.

Kohler, Ulrich, and Frauke Kreuter. 2005. *Data Analysis Using Stata*. College Station, Tex.: Stata Press.

Krueger, Alan B., and Jitka Maleckova. 2002. "Does Poverty Cause Terrorism?" *New Republic*, June 24. http://www.newrepublic.com/article/books-and-arts/91841/does-poverty-cause -terrorism.

————. 2003. "Education, Poverty, Political Violence and Terrorism." *Journal of Economic Perspectives* 17, no. 4: 119–44.

Kruglanski, Arie, and Shira Fishman. 2006. "The Psychology of Terrorism." *Terrorism and Political Violence* 18, no. 2: 193–215.

Krugman, Paul. 2013. "The Excel Depression." *New York Times*, April 18. http://www.nytimes .com/2013/04/19/opinion/krugman-the-excel-depression.html?_r=0.

Kutner, Michael H., Chris J. Nachtsheim, and John Neter. 2004. *Applied Linear Regression Models*. Boston: McGraw-Hill.

Kydland, Flynn E., and Edward C. Prescott. 1977. "Rules Rather Than Discretion." *Journal of Political Economy* 85, no. 3: 473–91.

LaFree, Gary, and Gary Ackerman. 2009. "The Empirical Study of Terrorism: Social and Legal Research." *Annual Review of Law and Social Science* 5: 347–74.

LaFree, Gary and Laura Dugan. 2007. "Introducing the Global Terrorism Database." *Terrorism and Political Violence* 19, no. 2: 181–204.

LaFree, Gary, Laura Dugan, and Susan Fahey. 2007. "Global Terrorism and Failed States." In *Peace and Conflict 2008*, edited by J. Joseph Hewitt, Jonathan Wilkenfeld, and Ted Robert Gurr, 39–54. Boulder: Paradigm Press.

LaFree, Gary, Sue-Ming Yang, and Martha Crenshaw. 2009. "Trajectories of Terrorism." *Criminology & Public Policy* 8, no. 3: 445–73.

Laitin, David D. 2013. "Fisheries Management." *Political Analysis* 21, no. 1: 42–47.

Lambert, Diane. 1992. "Zero-Inflated Poisson Regression, with an Application to Defects in Manufacturing." *Technometrics* 34, no. 1: 1–14.

Lasswell, Harold D. 1941. "The Garrison State." *American Journal of Sociology* 46, no. 4: 455–68.

————. 1997. *Essays on the Garrison State*. New Brunswick, N.J.: Transaction.

Leander, Anna. 2004. "Drafting Community." *Armed Forces & Society* 30, no. 4: 571–99.

Lee, Dwight R., and Richard B. McKenzie. 1992. "Reexamination of the Relative Efficiency of the Draft and the All-Volunteer Army." *Southern Economic Journal* 58, no. 3: 644–54.

Lee, Joonghoon. 2008. "Exploring Global Terrorism Data." *ACM Crossroads* 15, no.): 7–16.

Leeds, Brett Ashley. 1999. "Domestic Political Institutions, Credible Commitments, and International Cooperation." *American Journal of Political Science* 43, no. 4: 979–1002.

Lemke, Douglas, and William Reed. 2001. "The Relevance of Politically Relevant Dyads." *Journal of Conflict Resolution* 45, no. 1: 126–44.

Levy, Jack S. 1989. "The Diversionary Theory of War." In *Handbook of War Studies*, edited by Manus I. Midlarsky, 259–88. Boston: Unwin Hyman.

Lewis-Beck, Michael S. 1988. *Economics and Elections: The Major Western Democracies*. Ann Arbor: University of Michigan Press.

Lewis-Beck, Michael S., and Mary Stegmaier. 2000. "Economic Determinants of Electoral Outcomes." *Annual Review of Political Science* 3: 183–219.

Li, Quan. 2005. "Does Democracy Promote or Reduce Transnational Terrorist Incidents?" *Journal of Conflict Resolution* 49, no. 2: 278–97.

————. 2009. "Outlier, Measurement and the Democracy-FDI Controversy." *Quarterly Journal of Political Science* 4, no. 2: 167–81.

Li, Quan, and Adam Resnick. 2003. "Reversal of Fortunes: Democratic Institutions and Foreign Direct Investment Inflows to Developing Countries." *International Organization* 57, no. 1: 175–211.

Li, Quan, and Drew Schaub. 2004. "Economic Globalization and Transnational Terrorist Incidents." *Journal of Conflict Resolution* 48, no. 2: 230–58.

Little, Richard. 1987. "Revisiting Intervention." *Review of International Studies* 13, no. 1: 49–60.

Lizzeri, Alessandro, and Nicola Persico. 2001. "The Provision of Public Goods under Alternative Electoral Incentives." *American Economic Review* 91, no. 1: 225–39.

Londregan, John B., and Keith T. Poole. 1996. "Does High Income Promote Democracy?" *World Politics* 49, no. 1: 1–30.

Long, J. Scott, and Jeremy Freese. 2006. *Regression Models for Categorical Dependent Variables Using Stata.* College Station, Tex.: Stata Press.

Luckham, Robin. 1974. *The Nigerian Military: A Sociological Analysis of Authority and Revolt, 1960–67.* New York: Cambridge University Press.

Ludwig, Arnold M. 2002. *King of the Mountain: The Nature of Political Leadership.* Lexington: University Press of Kentucky.

Lumley, Thomas, Paula Diehr, Scott Emerson, and Lu Chen. 2002. "The Importance of the Normality Assumption in Large Public Health Data Sets." *Annual Review of Public Health* 23: 151–69.

Lupia, Arthur, and Colin Elman. 2014. "Openness in Political Science." *PS: Political Science & Politics* 47, no. 1: 19–42.

Lupton, Tom, and C. Shirley Wilson. 1959. "The Social Background and Connections of 'Top Decision Makers.'" *Manchester School* 27, no. 1: 30–51.

Maddala, G. S. 1983. *Limited-Dependent and Qualitative Variables in Econometrics.* Cambridge: Cambridge University Press.

Mancuso, Anthony J., Cassandra E. Dirienzo, and Jayoti Das. 2010. "Assessing Terrorist Risk and FDI using Relative Information Measures." *Applied Economics Letters* 17, no. 8: 787–90.

Maoz, Zeev, and Belgin San-Akca. 2012. "Rivalry and State Support of Non-State Armed Groups (NAGs), 1946–2001." *International Studies Quarterly* 56, no. 4: 720–34.

Marighella, Carlos. 1969. "Minimanual of the Urban Guerilla." http://files.meetup.com/1332202/Minimanual%20of%20the%20Urban%20Guerrilla.pdf.

Marshall, Monty G., and Keith Jaggers. 2007. "Polity IV Individual Country Regime Trends, 1946–2013." Polity IV Project: Political Regime Characteristics and Transitions, 1800–2013. http://www.systemicpeace.org/polity/polity4.htm.

Mason, T. David, and Dale A. Krane. 1989. "The Political Economy of Death Squads." *International Studies Quarterly* 33, no. 2: 175–98.

Masood, Salman. 2008. "12 Killed in Suicide Bombing at Shiite Mosque in Pakistan." *New York Times*, January 18. http://www.nytimes.com/2008/01/18/world/asia/18pakistan.html?partner=rssnyt&emc=rss.

Matthew, Richard, and George Shambaugh. 2005. "The Pendulum Effect." *Analyses of Social Issues and Public Policy* 5, no. 1: 223–33.

Matthews, David R. 1954. *The Social Background of Political Decision-Makers.* New York: Random House.

Mazzetti, Mark. 2006. "Spy Agencies Say Iraq Worsens Terrorist Threat." *New York Times*, September 24. http://www.nytimes.com/2006/09/24/world/middleeast/24terror.html?_r=1&oref=slogin.

McKinlay, R. D., and A. S. Cohan. 1976. "Performance and Instability in Military and Nonmilitary Regime Systems." *American Political Science Review* 70, no. 3: 850–64.

McLean, Elena V., and Taehee Whang. 2010. "Friends or Foes? Major Trading Partners and the Success of Economic Sanctions." *International Studies Quarterly* 54, no. 2: 427–47.

Meernik, James, Rosa Aloisi, Marsha Sowell, and Angela Nichols. 2012. "The Impact of Human Rights Organizations on Naming and Shaming Campaigns." *Journal of Conflict Resolution* 56, no. 2: 233–56.

Mersch, Yves. 2006. "Monetary Policy and Time Inconsistency in an Uncertain Environment." Speech delivered at the NOBELUX Seminar, Luxembourg, September 11. http://www.bis .org/review/r060915a.pdf.

Mickolus, Edward F. 1982. "International Terrorism: Attributes of Terrorist Events, 1968–1977 (ITERATE 2)." Ann Arbor: Inter-University Consortium for Political and Social Research. http://doi.org/10.3886/ICPSR07947.v1.

Mickolus, Edward F., Todd Sandler, Jean M. Murdock, and Peter Flemming. 2006. International Terrorism: Attributes of Terrorist Events (ITERATE), 1968-2005. Dunn Loring, Va.: Vinyard Software.

Midlarsky, Manus I. 1998. "Democracy and Islam." *International Studies Quarterly* 42, no. 3: 485–511.

Miguel, Edward, Shanker Satyanath, and Ernest Sergenti. 2004. "Economic Shocks and Civil Conflict." *Journal of Political Economy* 112, no. 4: 725–53.

Miller, James C., III, ed. 1968. *Why the Draft? The Case for a Volunteer Army.* Baltimore: Penguin Books.

Milner, Helen, and Benjamin Judkins. 2004. "Partisanship, Trade Policy and Globalization." *International Studies Quarterly* 48, no. 1: 95–119.

Møller, Bjørn. 2002. "Conscription and Its Alternatives." In *The Comparative Study of Conscription in the Armed Forces,* edited by Lars Mjøset and Stephen Van Holde, 207–305. New York: Elsevier Science.

Montalvo, José G., and Marta Reynal-Querol. 2005. "Ethnic Polarization, Potential Conflict, and Civil War." *American Economic Review* 95, no. 3: 796–816.

Moore, Will H., and Stephen M. Shellman. 2007. "Whither Will They Go? *International Studies Quarterly* 51, no. 4: 811–34.

Morgan, Patrick M. 1993. "Disarmament." In *The Oxford Companion to Politics of the World,* edited by Joel Krieger, 246–47. New York: Oxford University Press.

Morrow, James D., Bruce Bueno de Mesquita, Randolph M. Siverson, and Alastair Smith. 2008. "Retesting Selectorate Theory." *American Political Science Review* 102, no. 3: 393–400.

Mousseau, Demet Yalcin. 2001. "Democratizing with Ethnic Divisions" *Journal of Peace Research* 38, no. 5: 547–67.

Mousseau, Michael. 2002/3. "Market Civilization and Its Clash with Terror." *International Security* 27, no. 3: 5–29.

———. 2011. "Urban Poverty and Support for Islamist Terror." *Journal of Peace Research* 48, no. 1: 35–47.

———. 2012. "Capitalist Development and Civil War." *International Studies Quarterly* 56, no. 3: 470–83.

———. 2013a. "Contract Intensity of National Economies (CINE), version 2.0." http:// politicalscience.cos.ucf.edu/people/mousseau-michael/.

———. 2013b. "The Democratic Peace Unraveled." *International Studies Quarterly* 57, no. 1: 186–97.

Moynihan, Daniel P. 1993. *Pandaemonium: Ethnicity in International Politics.* New York: Oxford University Press.

Munck, Gerardo L. 2009. *Measuring Democracy: A Bridge between Scholarship and Politics*. Baltimore: Johns Hopkins University Press.

National Advisory Commission on Selective Service. 1967. *In Pursuit of Equity: Who Serves When Not All Serve? Report of the National Advisory Commission on Selective Service*. Washington, D.C.: U.S. Government Printing Office.

NewsWala. 2010. "US Military Intervention Could Strengthen Qaeda: Yemen." http://www .newswala.com/International-News/US-military-intervention-could-strengthen-Qaeda -Yemen-1227.html.

Nixon, Richard M. 1982. "The All-Volunteer Armed Force." In *The Military Draft: Selected Readings on Conscription*, edited by Martin Anderson with Barbara Honegger, 603–9. Stanford: Hoover Institution Press.

Nordlinger, Eric A. 1970. "Soldiers in Mufti." *American Political Science Review* 64, no. 4: 1131–48.

O'Donnell, Guillermo. 2004. "Why the Rule of Law Matters." *Journal of Democracy* 15, no. 4: 32–46.

Oi, Walter Y. 1967. "The Economic Cost of the Draft." *American Economic Review* 57, no. 2: 39–62.

Oneal, John R. 1992. "Budgetary Savings from Conscription and Burden Sharing in NATO." *Defence Economics* 3, no. 2: 113–25.

———. 1994. "The Affinity of Foreign Investors for Authoritarian Regimes." *Political Research Quarterly* 47, no. 3: 565–88.

Oneal, John R., and James Lee Ray. 1997. "New Tests of the Democratic Peace." *Political Research Quarterly* 50, no. 4: 751–75.

Oneal, John R., and Bruce Russett. 1997. "The Classical Liberals Were Right: Democracy, Interdependence, and Conflict, 1950–1985." *International Studies Quarterly* 41, no. 4: 267–93.

———. 1999a. "Assessing the Liberal Peace with Alternative Specifications." *Journal of Peace Research* 36, no. 4: 423–42.

———. 1999b. "The Kantian Peace." *World Politics* 52, no. 1: 1–37.

———. 2005. "Rule of Three, Let It Be?" *Conflict Management and Peace Science* 22, no. 4: 293–310.

Oneal, John R., Bruce Russett, and Michael Berbaum. 2003. "Causes of Peace: Democracy, Interdependence, and International Organizations, 1885–1992." *International Studies Quarterly* 47, no. 3: 371–93.

Oneal, John R., and Jaroslav Tir. 2006. "Does the Diversionary Use of Force Threaten the Democratic Peace?" *International Studies Quarterly* 50, no. 4: 755–79.

OnIslam and News Agencies. 2009. "Singapore Muslims Fight Extremism." OnIslam, May 16. http://www.onislam.net/english/news/asia-pacific/438348.html.

Oseghale, Braimoh. 1993. *Political Instability, Interstate Conflict, Adverse Changes in Host Government Policies and Foreign Direct Investment*. New York: Garland.

Panter-Brick, S. K., ed. 1970. *Nigerian Politics and Military Rule: Prelude to the Civil War*. London: Athlone Press for the Institute of Commonwealth Studies, University of London.

Pape, Robert A. 2003. "The Strategic Logic of Suicide Terrorism." *American Political Science Review* 97, no. 3: 343–61.

———. 2005. *Dying to Win: The Strategic Logic of Suicide Terrorism*. New York: Random House.

Park, Hun Myoung. 2008. "Univariate Analysis and Normality Test Using SAS, Stata, and SPSS." Working paper. University Information Technology Services (UITS) Center for Statistical and Mathematical Computing, Indiana University.

Parry, Geraint. 2005. *Political Elites*. Colchester, UK: ECPR Press.

Paul, Ron. 2003. "Conscription—The Terrible Price of War." *Congressional Record* 149, pt. 22 (November 20-23).

Pearl, Judea. 2000. *Causality: Models, Reasoning, and Inference*. Cambridge: Cambridge University Press.

Pearson, Frederic S., and Robert A. Baumann. 1993. *International Military Intervention, 1946-1988*. Ann Arbor, Mich.: Inter-University Consortium for Political and Social Research.

Penn World Table. Center for International Comparisons of Production, Income and Prices at the University of Pennsylvania. https://pwt.sas.upenn.edu/php_site/pwt_index.php.

Petersen, Roger D. 2002. *Understanding Ethnic Violence: Fear, Hatred, and Resentment in Twentieth-Century Eastern Europe*. New York: Cambridge University Press.

Piazza, James A. 2007. "Draining the Swamp." *Studies in Conflict and Terrorism* 30, no. 6: 521-39.

———. 2008. "Incubators of Terror." *International Studies Quarterly* 52, no. 3: 469-88.

———. 2011. "Poverty, Minority Economic Discrimination, and Domestic Terrorism." *Journal of Peace Research* 48, no. 3: 339-53.

Pickering, Jeffrey. 2011. "Dangerous Drafts? A Time-Series, Cross-National Analysis of Conscription and the Use of Military Force, 1946-2001." *Armed Forces & Society* 37, no. 1: 119-40.

Pickering, Jeffrey, and Emizet E. Kisangani. 2005. "Democracy and Diversionary Military Intervention." *International Studies Quarterly* 49, no. 1: 23-43.

———. 2009. "The International Military Intervention Data Set." *Journal of Peace Research* 46, no. 4: 589-600.

Political Instability Task Force. Internal Wars and Failures of Governance, 1955-2006. http://globalpolicy.gmu.edu/pitf/pitfpset.htm.

Pope, Barbara H. Pope, ed. 1987. *World Defense Forces*. Santa Barbara: ABC-CLIO.

Popper, Karl Raimund. 1963. *Conjectures and Refutations: The Growth of Scientific Knowledge*. London: Routledge.

Posner, Daniel N. 2004. "Measuring Ethnic Fractionalization in Africa." *American Journal of Political Science* 48, no. 4: 849-63.

Powell, G. Bingham. 1982. *Contemporary Democracies*. Cambridge: Harvard University Press.

Powers, Matthew, and Seung-Whan Choi. 2012. "Does Transnational Terrorism Reduce Foreign Direct Investment?" *Journal of Peace Research* 49, no. 3: 407-22.

Poynter, Thomas A. 1985. *Multinational Enterprises & Government Intervention*. New York: St. Martin's.

Prasad, Devi, and Tony Smythe, eds. 1968. *Conscription—A World Survey: Compulsory Military Service and Resistance to It*. London: War Resisters' International.

President's Commission on an All-Volunteer Armed Force. 1970. *The Report of the President's Commission on an All-Volunteer Armed Force*. New York: Macmillan.

Przeworski, Adam, Michael Alvarez, José Antonio Cheibub, and Fernando Limongi. 2000. *Democracy and Development: Political Institutions and Well-Being in the World, 1950-1990*. New York: Cambridge University Press.

Qassem, Naim. 2005. *Hizbullah: The Story from Within*. Translated from the Arabic by Dalia Khalil. London: Saqi Books.

Rasler, Karen. 1996. "Concession, Repression, and Political Protest in the Iranian Revolution." *American Sociological Review* 61, no. 1: 132-53.

Rawls, John. 1971/1999. *A Theory of Justice*. Cambridge: Harvard University Press.

Ray, James Lee. 2013. "War on Democratic Peace." *International Studies Quarterly* 57, no. 1: 198–200.

Raz, Joseph. 1977. "The Rule of Law and Its Virtue." *Law Quarterly Review* 93: 195–211.

Reiter, Dan, and Allan C. Stam. 2004. "Democracy, Peace, and War." Unpublished paper, December 7.

Remmer, Karen L. 1991. "Economic Crisis and Elections in Latin America, 1982–1990." *American Political Science Review* 85, no. 3: 777–800.

Reuters AlertNet. 2008. "Chechnya War." March 9. http://www.alertnet.org/db/crisisprofiles /RU_WAR.htm?v=in_detail.

Reynal-Querol, Marta. 2002. "Ethnicity, Political Systems, and Civil Wars." *Journal of Conflict Resolution* 46, no. 1: 29–54.

Rogowski, Ronald, and Mark Andreas Kayer. 2002. "Majoritarian Electoral Systems and Consumer Power." *American Journal of Political Science* 46, no. 3: 526–39.

Ross, Jeffrey Ian. 1993. "Structural Causes of Oppositional Political Terrorism." *Journal of Peace Research* 30, no. 3: 317–29.

Ross, Thomas W. 1994. "Raising an Army." *Journal of Law and Economics* 37, no. 1: 109–31.

Rotberg, Robert I. 2002. "Failed States in a World of Terror." *Foreign Affairs* 81, no. 4: 127–40.

Royston, J. P. 1982. "An Extension of Shapiro and Wilks's *W* Test for Normality to Large Samples." *Applied Statistics* 31, no. 2: 115–24.

———. 1983. "A Simple Method for Evaluating the Shapiro-Francia *W'* Test of Non-Normality." *Statistician* 32, no. 3: 297–300.

———. 1991a. "Comment on sg3.4 and an Improved D'Agostino Test." *Stata Technical Bulletin* 3: 13–24.

———. 1991b. "Estimating Departure from Normality." *Statistics in Medicine* 10, no. 8: 1283–93.

Russett, Bruce, and John R. Oneal. 2001. *Triangulating Peace: Democracy, Interdependence, and International Organizations.* New York: W.W. Norton.

Russett, Bruce, John R. Oneal, and David R. Davis. 1998. "The Third Leg of the Kantian Tripod for Peace: International Organizations and Militarized Disputes, 1950–85." *International Organization* 52, no. 3: 441–67.

Salehyan, Idean. 2009. *Rebels without Borders: Transnational Insurgencies in World Politics.* Ithaca: Cornell University Press.

Salehyan, Idean, and Kristian Skrede Gleditsch. 2006. "Refugees and the Spread of Civil War." *International Organization* 60, no. 2: 335–66.

Sambanis, Nicholas. 2001. "Do Ethnic and Nonethnic Civil Wars Have the Same Causes?" *Journal of Conflict Resolution* 45, no. 3: 259–82.

Sandler, Todd. 1995. "On the Relationship between Democracy and Terrorism." *Terrorism and Political Violence* 12, no. 2: 97–122.

Santifort-Jordan, Charlinda, and Todd Sandler. 2014. "An Empirical Study of Suicide Terrorism: A Global Analysis." *Southern Economic Journal* 80, no. 4: 981–1001.

Santos Silva, J. M. C., and Silvana Tenreyro. 2006. "The Log of Gravity." *Review of Economics and Statistics* 88, no. 4: 641–58.

Savun, Burcu, and Brian J. Phillips. 2009. "Democracy, Foreign Policy, and Terrorism." *Journal of Conflict Resolution* 53, no. 6: 878–904.

Schmid, Alex P. 2004. "Statistics on Terrorism." *Forum on Crime and Society* 4, nos. 1–2: 49–69.

Schneider, Friedrich, and Bruno S. Frey. 1985. "Economic and Political Determinants of Foreign Direct Investment." *World Development* 13, no. 2: 161–75.

Schneider, Gerald, Katherine Barbieri, and Nils Petter Gleditsch. 2003. "Does Globalization Contribute to Peace?" In *Globalization and Armed Conflict,* edited by Gerald Schneider, Katherine Barbieri, and Nils Petter Gleditsch, 3–29. Lanham, Md.: Rowman & Littlefield.

Schneider, Gerald, and Nina Wiesehomeier. 2010. "Ethnic Polarization, Potential Conflict, and Civil Wars: Comment." http://www.prio.no/files/file47696_schneider-wiesehomeier.pdf.

Schumacher, Rose, Gail K. Sevrens, Timothy S. O'Donnell, Lee Torrence, and Kate Carney, eds. 1989. *World Defense Forces*. Santa Barbara: ABC-CLIO.

Scraton, Phil. 2004. "Streets of Terror: Marginalization, Criminalization, and Authoritarian Renewal." *Social Justice* 31, nos. 1–2: 130–58.

Sechser, Todd S. 2004. "Are Soldiers Less War-Prone Than Statesmen?" *Journal of Conflict Resolution* 48, no. 5: 746–74.

Seier, Edith. 2002. "Comparison of Tests for Univariate Normality." *Interstat*, January, 1–17.

Senese, Paul. 2005. "Territory, Contiguity, and International Conflict." *American Journal of Political Science* 49, no. 4: 769–79.

Shanker, Thom, and Steven Lee Myers. 2008. "U.S. Asking Iraq for Wide Rights on War." *New York Times*, January 25. http://www.nytimes.com/2008/01/25/world/middleeast/25military .html?ex=1359003600&en=702b1e0e93bb57e3&ei=5088&partner=rssnyt&emc=rss.

Shapiro, S. S., and R. S. Francia. 1972. "An Approximate Analysis of Variance Test for Normality." *Journal of the American Statistical Association* 67, no. 337: 215–16.

Shapiro, S. S., and M. B. Wilk. 1965. "An Analysis of Variance Test for Normality (Complete Samples)." *Biometrika* 52, no. 3/4: 591–611.

Singer, J. David. 1987. "Reconstructing the Correlates of War Dataset on Material Capabilities of States, 1816–1985." *International Interactions* 14, no. 2: 115–32.

Singer, J. David, Stuart Bremer, and John Stuckey. 1972. "Capability Distribution, Uncertainty, and Major Power War, 1820–1965." In *Peace, War, and Numbers*, edited by Bruce Russett, 19–48. Beverly Hills: Sage.

Singer, Peter W. 2007. "Can't Win with 'Em, Can't Go to War without 'Em: Private Military Contractors and Counterinsurgency." Executive Summary, September. Brookings Institution. http://www.brookings.edu/papers/2007/0927militarycontractors.

Skanning, Svend-Erik. 2008. "The Civil Liberty Dataset." *Zeitschrift für Vergleichende Politikwissenschaft* 2, no. 1: 29–51.

Slantchev, Branislav L., 2005. "The Watchful Eye." Unpublished paper.

Slater, Dan. 2010. *Ordering Power: Contentious Politics and Authoritarian Leviathans in Southeast Asia*. Cambridge: Cambridge University Press.

Snyder, Jack. 1984. "Civil-Military Relations and the Cult of the Offensive, 1914 and 1984." *International Security* 9, no. 1: 108–46.

Sobek, David. 2010. "Masters of Their Domains: The Role of State Capacity in Civil Wars." *Journal of Peace Research* 47, 3: 267–71.

Staiger, Douglas, and James H. Stock. 1997. "Instrumental Variables Regression with Weak Instruments." *Econometrica* 65, no. 3: 557–86.

Stanley, William. 1996. *The Protection Racket State: Elite Politics, Military Extortion, and Civil War in El Salvador*. Philadelphia: Temple University Press.

Starr, Harvey. 1991. "Democratic Dominoes: Diffusion Approaches to the Spread of Democracy in the International System." *Journal of Conflict Resolution* 35, no. 2: 356–81.

Stata Press. 2007. *Stata Base Reference Manual Release 10*. College Station, Tex.: Stata Press.

Stock, James H. 2002. "Instrumental Variables in Economics and Statistics." In *International Encyclopedia for the Social and Behavioral Sciences*, edited by N. J. Smelser and P. B. Bates, 7577–82. Amsterdam: Elsevier.

Stockholm International Peace Research Institute. 1985. *World Armaments and Disarmament*. London: Taylor & Francis.

Svolik, Milan. 2008. "Authoritarian Reversals and Democratic Consolidation." *American Political Science Review* 102, no. 2: 153–68.

Tabuchi, Hiroko. 2014. "*Study Called an Advance in Stem Cells Had Faults.*" *New York Times*, March 14. http://mobile.nytimes.com/2014/03/15/health/study-called-an-advance-in-stem-cells-had-faults.html.

Taydas, Zeynep, Dursun Peksen, and Patrick James. 2010. "Why Do Civil Wars Occur?" *Civil Wars* 12, no. 3: 195–217.

Tessler, Mark, and Michael D. H. Robbins. 2007. "What Leads Some Ordinary Arab Men and Women to Approve of Terrorist Acts against the United States?" *Journal of Conflict Resolution* 51, no. 2: 305–28.

Thies, Cameron G. 2010. "Of Rulers, Rebels and Revenue: State Capacity, Civil War Onset, and Primary Commodities." *Journal of Peace Research* 47, no. 3: 321–32.

Thomas, Jonathan, and Tim Worrall. 1994. "Foreign Direct Investment and the Risk of Expropriation." *Review of Economic Studies* 61, no. 1: 81–108.

Thoms, Oskar N. T., and James Ron. 2007. "Do Human Rights Violations Cause Internal Conflict?" *Human Rights Quarterly* 29, no. 3: 674–705.

Thomson, R., T. Royed, E. Naurin, J. Artes, M. Ferguson, P. Kostadinova, and C. Moury. 2012. "The Program-to-Policy Linkage." Paper prepared for the 2012 Annual Meeting of the American Political Science Association, New Orleans, August 30–September 2.

Tomz, Michael. 2007. "Domestic Audience Costs in International Relations." *International Organization* 61, no. 4: 821–40.

Tomz, Michael, Gary King, and Langche Zeng. 1999. RELOGIT. Cambridge: Harvard University.

Tsebelis, George. 1999. "Veto Players and Law Production in Parliamentary Democracies." *American Political Science Review* 93, no. 3: 591–608.

———. 2002. *Veto Players: How Political Institutions Work*. Princeton: Princeton University Press.

Tsebelis, George, and Seung-Whan Choi. 2009. "The Democratic Peace Revisited." Paper presented at the American Political Science Association Conference, Toronto, Ontario, Canada, September 3–6.

Tufte, Edward R. 1993. "Economic and Political Determinants of Electoral Outcomes." In *Classics in Voting Behavior*, edited by Richard G. Niemi and Herberty F. Weisberg, 181–187. Washington, D.C.: CQ Press.

Tullock, Gordon. 1971. "The Paradox of Revolution." *Public Choice* 11, no. 1: 89–99.

Tzu, Sun. 1971. *The Art of War*. Translated by Samuel B. Griffith. New York: Oxford University Press.

Ullah, Aman. 1990. "Finite Sample Econometrics." In *Contributions to Econometric Theory and Application*, edited by R. A. L. Carter, J. Dutta, and A. Ullah, 242–92. New York: Springer-Verlag.

United Nations Conference on Trade and Development. 2008. *World Investment Report*. FDI Stat Interactive Database. http://stats.unctad.org.

United States Census Bureau, Population Division. 2008. International Database (IDB). http://www.census.gov/ipc/www/idb/summaries.html.

UNU-WIDER. May 2008. *World Income Inequality Database*. http://www.wider.unu.edu/research/Database/.

U.S. Agency for International Development (USAID). 2008. "Who We Are." http://www.usaid.gov/about_usaid/.

Van Belle, Douglas A. 1997. "Press Freedom and the Democratic Peace." *Journal of Peace Research* 34, no. 4: 405–14.

———. 2000a. *Press Freedom and Global Politics*. Westport, Conn.: Praeger.

Van Belle, Douglas A., with John Oneal. 2000b. "Press Freedom and Militarized Disputes." In Van Belle, *Press Freedom and Global Politics*, 47–75.

Van Evera, Stephen. 1984. "The Cult of the Offensive and the Origins of the First World War." *International Security* 9, no. 1: 58–107.

Vanhanen, Tatu. 2000. "A New Dataset for Measuring Democracy, 1810–1998." *Journal of Peace Research* 37, no. 2: 251–65.

Vasquez, John A. 1993. *The War Puzzle*. Cambridge: Cambridge University Press.

———. 1997. "The Realist Paradigm and Degenerative versus Progressive Research Programs." *American Political Science Review* 91, no. 4: 899–912.

———. 1998. *The Power of Power Politics: From Classical Realism to Neotraditionalism*. Cambridge: Cambridge University Press.

Vreeland, James Raymond. 2008. "The Effect of Political Regime on Civil War." *Journal of Conflict Resolution* 52, no. 3: 401–25.

Wade, Sara Jackson, and Dan Reiter. 2007. "Does Democracy Matter? Regime Type and Suicide Terrorism." *Journal of Conflict Resolution* 51, no. 2: 329–48.

Warner, John T., and Beth J. Asch. 1995. "The Economics of Military Manpower." In *Handbook of Defense Economics*, edited by Keith Hartley and Todd Sandler, 347–98. Amsterdam: Elsevier.

Wayman, Frank W. 1975. *Military Involvement in Politics: A Causal Model*. Beverly Hills: Sage.

Wayman, Frank W., and Atsushi Tago. 2010. "Explaining the Onset of Mass Killing, 1949–87." *Journal of Peace Research* 47, no. 3: 3–13.

Weede, Erich. 2003. "Globalization." In *Globalization and Armed Conflict*, edited by Gerald Schneider, Katherine Barbieri, and Nils Petter Gleditsch, 311–323. Lanham, Md.: Rowman & Littlefield.

———. 2005. *Balance of Power, Globalization, and the Capitalist Peace*. Potsdam, Germany: Liberal Institute.

Weigel, George. 1991. "Religion and Peace." *Washington Quarterly* 14, no. 2: 27–42.

Weinstein, Jeremy M. 2005. "Autonomous Recovery and International Intervention in Comparative Perspective." Center for Global Development. Working paper no. 57. 1–35.

Welsch, Roy E. 1982. "Influence Functions and Regression Diagnostics." In *Modern Data Analysis*, edited by Robert L. Launer and Andrew F. Siegel, 149–69. New York: Academic Press.

Welsch, Roy E., and Edwin Kuh. 1977. *Technical Report 923–77*. Cambridge: MIT.

Western, Bruce. 1995. "Concepts and Suggestions for Robust Regression Analysis." *American Journal of Political Science* 39, no. 3: 786–817.

Whang, Taehee. 2010. "Structural Estimation of Economic Sanctions." *Journal of Peace Research* 47, no. 5: 561–73.

White, Michael D. 1989. "Conscription and the Size of Armed Forces." *Social Science Quarterly* 70, no. 3: 772–81.

Whitten, Guy D., and Henry S. Bienen. 1996. "Political Violence and Time in Power." *Armed Forces & Society* 23, no. 2: 209–34.

Wicherts, Jelte M., Marjan Bakker, and Dylan Molenaar. 2011. "Willingness to Share Research Data Is Related to the Strength of the Evidence and the Quality of Reporting of Statistical Results." *PLoS ONE* 6, no. 11: e26828. doi:10.1371/journal.pone.0026828.

Wilson, Jeremy M. 2006. "Law and Order in an Emerging Democracy." *Annals of the American Academy of Political and Social Science* 605, no. 1: 152–77.

Wimmer, Andreas, Lars-Erik Cederman, and Brian Min. 2009. "Ethnic Politics and Armed Conflict." *American Sociological Review* 74, no. 2: 316–37.

Wimmer, Andreas, and Brian Min. 2006. "From Empire to Nation-State." *American Sociological Review* 71, no. 6: 867–97.

Wolpin, Miles D. 1983. "Comparative Perspectives on Militarization, Repression and Social Welfare." *Journal of Peace Research* 20, no. 2: 129–55.

Wood, Elisabeth Jean. 2003. *Insurgent Collective Action and Civil War in El Salvador.* New York: Cambridge University Press.

Wood, Reed M., and Mark Gibney. 2010. "The Political Terror Scale (PTS)." *Human Rights Quarterly* 32, no. 2: 367–400.

Woodard, James P. 2006. Review of *The Last Colonial Massacre: Latin America in the Cold War,* by Greg Grandin. *Democratiya* 5: 90–94.

Wooldridge, Jeffrey M. 2002. *Econometric Analysis of Cross Section and Panel Data.* Cambridge: MIT Press.

———. 2009. *Introductory Econometrics: A Modern Approach.* 4th ed. Mason, Ohio: South-Western, Cengage Learning.

World Bank. 1999. World Development Indicators, 1999. http://econ.worldbank.org/external /default/main?pagePK=64165259&theSitePK=469372&piPK=64165421&menuPK=641660 93&entityID=000094946_99042010290379.

———. 2003. World Development Indicators, 2003. http://econ.worldbank.org/external /default/main?pagePK=64165259&theSitePK=469372&piPK=64165421&menuPK=641660 93&entityID=000094946_03051504051563.

———. 2008. Worldwide Governance Indicators, 1996–2007. http://info.worldbank.org/gov ernance/wgi/index.aspx#home.

———. 2010. World Development Indicators, 2010. http://data.worldbank.org/data-catalog /world-development-indicators/wdi-2010.

Yang, Benhua. 2007. "Autocracy, Democracy, and FDI Inflows to the Developing Countries." *International Economic Journal* 21, no. 3: 419–39. http://www.tandfonline.com/toc/riej20 /21/3#.VQBv6UaodTY. 00a_Choi_FM.doc

Yazici, Berna, and Senay Yolacan. 2007. "A Comparison of Various Tests of Normality." *Journal of Statistical Computation and Simulation* 77, no. 2: 175–83.

Zaidise, Eran, Daphna Canetti-Nisim, and Ami Pedahzur. 2007. "Politics of God or Politics of Man?" *Political Studies* 55, no. 3: 499–521.

Zakaria, Fareed. 2004. "Islam, Democracy, and Constitutional Liberalism." *Political Science Quarterly* 119, no. 1: 1–20.

Zelner, Bennet A. 2009. "Using Simulation to Interpret Results from Logit, Probit, and Other Nonlinear Models." *Strategic Management Journal* 30, no. 12: 1335–48.

Ziegenhagen, Eduard A. 1986. *The Regulation of Political Conflict.* New York: Praeger.

Zorn, Christopher. 1998. "An Analytic and Empirical Examination of Zero-Inflated and Hurdle Poisson Specifications." *Sociological Methods & Research* 26, no. 3: 368–400.

———. 2001. "Generalized Estimating Equation Models for Correlated Data." *American Journal of Political Science* 45, no. 2: 470–90.

INDEX

"c" indicates chapter. "f" indicates material in figures. "n" indicates material in endnotes. "t" indicates material in tables.